The Catholic Connections Handbook

for Middle Schoolers

Second Edition

Janet Claussen

Pat Finan

Diana Macalintal

Jerry Shepherd

Brian Singer-Towns

Susan Stark

Chris Wardwell

Pray It! Study It! Live It!® resources offer a holistic approach to learning, living, and passing on the Catholic faith.

saint mary's press

The Subcommittee on the Catechism, United States Conference of Catholic Bishops, has found this catechetical text, copyright 2014, to be in conformity with the *Catechism of the Catholic Church*.

Nihil Obstat:	Rev. Timothy J. Hall, STL
	Censor Librorum
	December 19, 2013
Imprimatur:	† Most Reverend John M. Quinn, DD
	Bishop of Winona
	December 19, 2013

The nihil obstat and imprimatur are official declarations that a book or pamphlet is free of doctrinal or moral error. No implication is contained therein that those who have granted the nihil obstat or imprimatur agree with the contents, opinions, or statements expressed, nor do they assume any legal responsibility associated with publication.

The publishing team included Maura Thompson Hagarty and Brian Singer-Towns, editors; Jeanette Fast Redmond, contributing editor. Prepress and manufacturing coordinated by the production departments of Saint Mary's Press.

Cover images: www.Shutterstock.com

Printed in the United States of America

2152 (PO4523)

ISBN 978-1-59982-331-7

Library of Congress Cataloging-in-Publication Data

The Catholic connections handbook for middle schoolers / Brian Singer-Towns, Janet Claussen, Pat Finan, Diana Macalintal, Jerry Shepherd, Susan Stark, Chris Wardwell. — Second edition.
        pages cm
        Includes index.
ISBN 978-1-59982-331-7 (pbk.)
        1. Catholic Church—Doctrines—Juvenile literature. I. Singer-Towns, Brian.
BX1754.5.C38 2014
248.8'3088282—dc23

                                                                2013020419

CONTENTS

The Church

Part 2: Liturgy and Sacraments **275**

PART 3: CHRISTIAN MORALITY AND JUSTICE 405

PART 4: PRAYER 503

Appendices

List of People of Faith

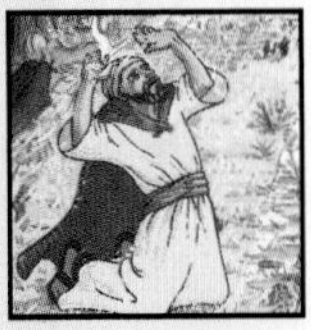

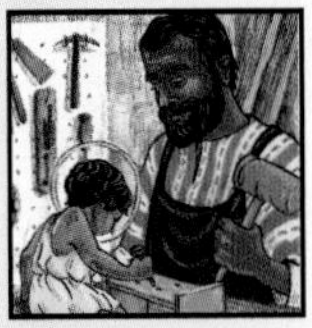

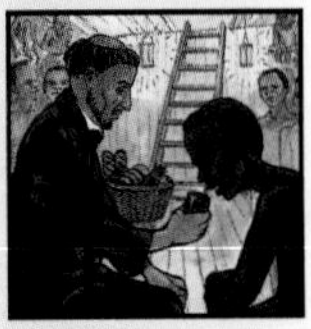

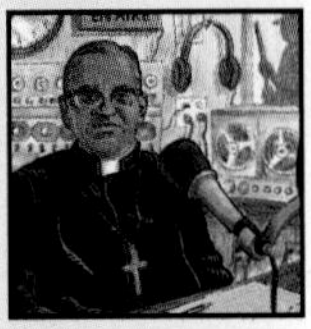

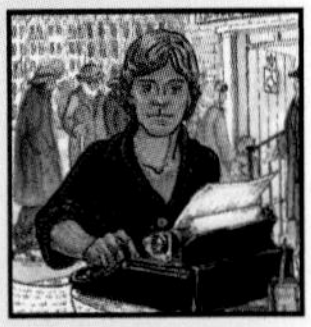

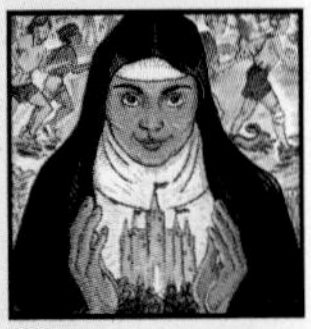

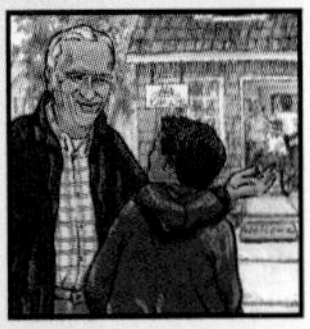

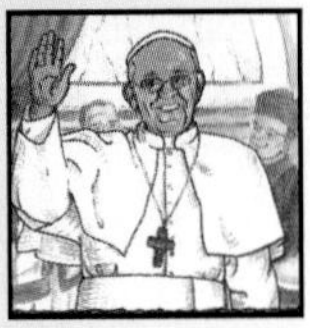

INTRODUCTION

Come with Me

"Come with me" (Matthew 4:19). Jesus said this to his first disciples, and it is his message to us today. Following Jesus is at the heart of being Catholic. Even though following Jesus isn't always easy, it's the most fulfilling and meaningful way to live life.

The Catholic Connections Handbook for Middle Schoolers is a guide for young teens on what it means to follow Jesus and to be Catholic today. This handbook offers a summary of what God has revealed to us through his Son, Jesus Christ, and what the Church has passed on from generation to generation through the working of the Holy Spirit. The handbook is a companion to the Bible and aims to help you learn about God—Father, Son, and Holy Spirit—the Sacraments, Christian morality and justice, and prayer.

Study It!

This handbook is divided into the following four sections, according to the four pillars, or parts, of the *Catechism of the Catholic Church*. Each a different color so you can more easily find the part you are looking for:

Part 1: The Creed
Part 2: Liturgy and Sacraments
Part 3: Christian Morality and Justice
Part 4: Prayer

The handbook is a great tool for study, but it is more than that. It includes many prayers and excellent guidance for living the Catholic faith.

Each of the handbook's fifty chapters has a number of special features. These are short articles set in special boxes. Along with the main text in the chapters, these articles are intended to help you further study, pray, and live the Catholic faith. Following are descriptions of the special articles you'll see throughout the handbook.

PRAY IT!

Faith becomes more alive through prayer. In each chapter you'll see a short prayer just right for times when you are by yourself or when you are with a group of peers.

Did You Know?

The many Did You Know? articles take topics from the chapter they appear in and explore them in more depth.

FUN FACT

The Fun Fact articles in every chapter are brief notes designed to provide instructive and entertaining information.

LITURGY CONNECTION

Faith is celebrated in the Church's liturgy and Sacraments. The Liturgy Connection articles will help you see the relationship between Catholic beliefs and worship.

CHURCH HISTORY

Sometimes a little history provides a better understanding of aspects of Catholic beliefs and practices. The Church History articles appear occasionally to provide you with this type of historical insight.

THink About It!

Every chapter has a Think About It! article with a topic or questions for you to ponder on your own or to discuss with your friends or family members.

Live It!

Being Catholic has to do with beliefs, but it also has to do with the way you live. The Live It! articles suggest ways you can put your faith into action.

PEOPLE OF FAiTH

© 2013 Saint Mary's Press/Illustrations by Vicki Shuck

This handbook introduces you to, or reacquaints you with, approximately twenty-five of the many people who have strengthened the Church and inspired others with their faith.

Catholic Prayers, Beliefs and Practices, and Key Words

Several handy sections at the end of the handbook provide the following easy-to-access information:

- a collection of Catholic prayers
- a brief summary of core Catholic beliefs and practices
- a glossary of the handbook's key words

The authors and everyone at Saint Mary's Press who had a hand in creating this book wish you many blessings as you use it to explore more deeply what it means to follow Jesus and to be a member of the Catholic Church.

PART I

The Creed

I believe in God,
the Father almighty,
Creator of heaven and earth.

Revelation, Sacred Scripture, and Sacred Tradition

Key Words

Revelation
Sacred Scripture
Gospels
Inspiration
Sacred Tradition

It's Saturday morning. You wake up, turn on the TV, and start flipping through the channels. On the way to your favorite show, you find a preacher on one channel. He explains that the Creation story in the Bible happened just as it is written in the Bible. He insists that the world was created in only six days and that this should be taught in schools. Later that day, in the grocery store checkout line, you see a magazine cover that tells why scientists support the idea that our universe began billions of years ago in a huge explosion. Inside, another article talks about how apes slowly changed over time to become human beings.

At school on Monday, you find out that your newest friend at school is an atheist—someone who doesn't believe in God. His mother has told him that people made up the idea of God so they wouldn't feel bad.

In the beginning God created the world. A powerful hand shows God's role in the creation of the universe.

© Mike Agliolo/Corbis

All these different ideas make you wonder about the things you have been taught about God. How can you know the truth?

Revelation

One place where you can begin to look for answers is under your own two feet. The earth itself is a sign of God's existence. In fact, you can find the evidence of God's handiwork everywhere: the trees that give you shade, the sun that warms your back, the dogs that bark in the distance, and, of course, all the people around you. Though we do not fully understand God and his ways, we can use our minds to see that God truly exists because of the wonder of creation itself.

In fact, throughout all history, God has made himself known to human beings in a number of ways. He continues to do so today through the signs of creation around us, through the voice of the Church, and through the voices of our consciences speaking from within us. You may already have had an experience where God became known to you. Maybe after going to confession, you have felt the relief of having God remove the burden of your guilty feelings and your sins. Maybe you have felt God's presence in the prayerful quiet of the church before Mass. If anything like this has ever happened to you, you know it comes as a gift. God makes himself

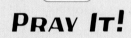

PRAY IT!

Lord God, I ask,
When I . . .
. . . am lost, make yourself known to me.
. . . am lonely, make yourself known to me.
. . . am confused, make yourself known to me.
. . . am sick, make yourself known to me.
. . . am joyful, make yourself known to me.
. . . doubt you, make yourself known to me.
. . . am in need, make yourself known to me.
. . . pray, make yourself known to me.
Amen.

Fun Fact

Did you know that the Catholic Bible contains seven books that are not part of the Protestant Bible? The Old Testament books of Tobit, Judith, 1 Maccabees, 2 Maccabees, Wisdom, Sirach, and Baruch are excluded from Protestant Bibles, but because these books are all inspired by the Holy Spirit, they are included in all Catholic Bibles.

known to us because he loves us. Even more amazing, he wants to give himself to us so we know that we are never alone.

What God has made known about himself and his plan for humanity is called **Revelation**. Throughout history God's Revelation has been made known through his creation, through events, and through other people; it is most especially and fully made known through Jesus Christ. Though it is certainly possible for one to have a personal experience of God, Revelation is communicated to the whole world in two main ways: Sacred Scripture and Sacred Tradition. Scripture and Tradition are distinct, yet very closely related. Both communicate or transmit the Word of God. Scripture and Tradition make up a single sacred deposit of the Word of God,

Did You Know?

The Case of the "Missing" Gospels

From time to time, in the newspaper or in other news media, you might hear about a newly discovered "gospel" that somehow mysteriously never made it into the Bible. Often, these reports suggest that these books were deliberately left out of the Bible as a way to hide a secret the Church doesn't want us to know. Actually the truth is far less dramatic: early in the Church's history, some writings (or books) were considered misleading or incomplete or just did not express the true faith of the Church, and were therefore not accepted by the Church Fathers as part of Sacred Scripture.

and have been given to the Church to be safe-guarded and passed on so that all generations will know God's Revelation. The Church, in her teachings, life, and worship, transmits to every generation what God has revealed through Scripture and Tradition.

God fully revealed himself by sending his only Son, Jesus Christ. There is nothing new that God needs to reveal until Christ comes again to establish a new Heaven and a new earth. But what the Father revealed through his Son needs to be explained and taught to all people. Teaching what God has revealed through Sacred Tradition and Sacred Scripture became the responsibility of the Apostles and their successors, the popes and bishops of the Church.

Sacred Scripture

Sacred Scripture is the seventy-three divinely inspired books we recognize as the Word of God. Another name for Sacred Scripture is the Bible. The seventy-three books of the Bible include the forty-six books of the Old Testament and the twenty-seven books of the New Testament. God is the ultimate author of the Bible. The Holy Spirit inspired the human authors to communicate what God wants us to know for our salvation.

Four special books in the New Testament are called the **Gospels**. The word *gospel* means "good news." The Gospels are special because they tell us

Think About It!

Sometimes people say God speaks to them. If you were to ask them, though, whether they hear voices in their heads, they would probably say, "Of course not! I'm not crazy!" How does God communicate with us without using an actual voice? What are some ways God might make his will known to us?

The Bible helps us discover who God is and how he relates to us. Do you make time to read the Bible?

© Saint Mary's Press

LITURGY CONNECTION

The Liturgy of the Word

We listen to God's Revelation every time we go to Mass. When we celebrate the Liturgy of the Word (the part of Mass when the Word of God is proclaimed), God is revealed to us in a special way. In the Scripture readings, we hear about what God has done for our salvation. We listen to how God led Moses and the Israelites out of slavery, how the prophets reminded the people of their promise to be faithful to God, about what Jesus taught and did, about the events of Jesus' Passion, death, Resurrection, and Ascension, and about how the early Christians carried on Christ's mission. In all the readings from Sacred Scripture, God is revealed to be all powerful, all loving, and all forgiving, always caring for his people, no matter what.

about the life, teachings, Passion (suffering), death, Resurrection, and Ascension of our Lord, Jesus Christ, in whom God's Revelation is complete.

Although the Bible often contains accurate scientific facts and history, we must be careful in looking for that kind of information. God did not give us the Bible as a source of information about scientific or historical events; rather, he gave us the words of Sacred Scripture to share with us the truths that will bring us our salvation. God is the author of Sacred Scripture because he inspired its human authors. The Holy Spirit guided the Bible's authors to record without error what God wants us to know for our salvation. This is called **Inspiration**.

Remember that even though the Holy Spirit guided these writers, they were still human beings. They wrote in ancient languages and lived in cultures different from ours. Just like us, they had an incomplete understanding of the world. Because of this, the meaning of the words of the Bible is not always readily apparent. The Pope and our bishops provide the Church with the authentic interpretation of the Bible. Guided by the Holy Spirit, they teach us about God's message of salvation as revealed through the inspired writers of the Bible. The Church is assisted in this work by biblical scholars, who study the Bible closely to find out exactly what its human authors intended to say. Biblical scholars must always follow the guidance of the Church and ensure that their work reflects the unity of all Church teachings.

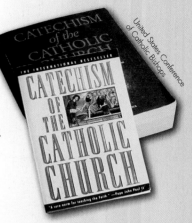

United States Conference of Catholic Bishops

Sacred Tradition

To fully learn the truths God wants to reveal to us for our salvation, we must look to Sacred Tradition and Sacred Scripture. **Sacred Tradition** is based on a word meaning "to hand on." So, Tradition means both the central beliefs of our faith and the way in which that content has been handed down through the centuries under the guidance of the Holy Spirit.

This handbook is based on the *Catechism of the Catholic Church*, a summary of the central teachings of our Tradition. Read the handbook along with your Bible to discover who God is.

Live It!

Be a Prophet

Prophets are people who speak God's Word. In the Bible, the prophets reveal God's will to the people. Jesus Christ is the Word Made flesh, the ultimate prophet who was sent by the Father and anointed by the Holy Spirit. In Baptism, we are anointed to share in Christ's prophetic ministry. We are all called to be prophets in some way. We are all called to speak God's Word.

That doesn't mean we have to preach on street corners, but it does mean our words and actions should reveal the faith we claim as our own. If someone were to follow you around for a day, would he or she be able to see God in the way you interact with your classmates? If it were illegal to be a Catholic, how many of us would be found guilty?

Tradition is not the same thing as tradition with a lowercase *t*. You probably take part in a number of traditions. They might include things like your family eating a certain kind of pie every year for your Thanksgiving meal, or everyone at school wearing the school colors to all the sporting events. The Church's Tradition has some things in common with these, but it is still different.

Sacred Tradition started with the preaching of the Apostles. Although some of this preaching was written down in the Bible, the Bible does not contain all of Sacred Tradition. Tradition includes our belief in the Trinity, the Incarnation of Jesus Christ, the Seven Sacraments, and many other matters revealed through the teachings of the Pope and bishops under the guidance of the Holy Spirit. Through Sacred Scripture and Sacred Tradition, God actively leads us to salvation.

?

Did You Know?

The Flat Earth Under the Dome

The Holy Spirit inspired the human authors of the Bible, but they still had the same mistaken ideas about the earth as everyone else during the times they lived. For example, when the Book of Genesis was written, people believed the world was flat and covered by a giant dome. They believed water surrounded the dome. When the Creation accounts were written, this incorrect scientific information was described. Whether the earth is as flat as a pancake or as round as a ball is not important when it comes to our salvation. What is important is that God created everything in the world out of love for us. That truth is part of God's Revelation.

God's Mystery

Although God does make himself known to us, we cannot expect to fully understand all of his ways. We can come to know a lot about God, but our human understanding cannot completely grasp him.

The Book of Job tells the story of a man named Job. Job was trying to understand why bad things were happening to him. At the end of the story, God asks him questions that no one but God could answer (see Job, chapter 38). Job then realizes something important. Even if we stand face-to-face with God, we will still never be able to understand some things about him (see 42:1–6).

CHURCH HISTORY

Scripture, Tradition, and the Ecumenical Councils

In the early 1500s, a German priest named Martin Luther began to teach that the Bible was the only necessary source of truth. Shortly afterward all the bishops in the world gathered at the Council of Trent (1543–1565), in Italy, to respond to Luther's ideas. At the Council of Trent, the Pope and the bishops affirmed that both Scripture and Tradition are necessary ways of passing on, or transmitting, God's Revelation.

Ecumenical Councils such as the Second Vatican Council are official meetings of all the world's Catholic bishops with the approval of the Pope. These councils are how the Church addresses important issues or questions that come up from time to time. The councils do not occur often. In fact, throughout the entire history of the Church, there have been only twenty-one Ecumenical Councils.

2 THE BIBLE: God's PLAN FOR SALVATION

Key Words

salvation history
covenant
Exodus
Exile
Gentiles

Are you looking forward to learning how to drive? Driving is a lot of fun, but it requires learning new physical and mental skills, such as following directions to get from one place to another. Most people use printed maps or get driving directions on a GPS unit or smartphone. However you do it, you need to know two things for sure: your starting address and the address of your destination. Without knowing both, you can spend hours driving in circles.

Have you ever gotten wrong directions from your phone or computer? God's directions never mislead us. Even when we choose to ignore God, he always guides us back to the right path.

© Kraska/Shutterstock.com

Through Sacred Scripture and Sacred Tradition, God has given us a roadmap with directions for our life. If we follow God's roadmap, at the end of our life we will reach the destination he has prepared for us since the beginning of time: eternal union with him in Heaven. We must study the Bible to learn how God has revealed himself and his plan for our salvation. By reading the Bible, we will learn about the people and events through which God reveals himself and his saving actions. We call this pattern of events **salvation history**.

To plan a trip across the entire United States, you would probably look at a big map of the whole country. In a similar way, this chapter looks at salvation history through the whole Bible so that you can understand the big picture of God's saving plan. And just like a long road trip can be broken into stages, we will break salvation history into stages: the six stages found in the Old Testament, followed by two stages found in the New Testament. Later chapters will explore these stages of salvation history in greater detail.

> In the past God spoke to our ancestors many times and in many ways through the prophets, but in these last days he has spoken to us through his Son.
> Hebrews 1:1–2

PRAY IT!

Jesus, you said, "I am with you always." Help me to keep my heart open today, Lord, so I can feel your love at work in me and understand my role in your saving plan. You are always present to me, Lord. Today let me be present to you. Amen.

FUN FACT

The Bible is the most translated book in the world. Parts of the Bible are available in more than two thousand languages, and the whole Bible has been translated into more than 450 languages!

Stage 1: Primeval History

The first stage of salvation history is sometimes called primeval history. *Primeval* means that the events happened before recorded history. Examples of primeval history in Scripture include the accounts of Adam and Eve, Cain and Abel, Noah and the Flood, and the Tower of Babel. You can read these accounts in the first eleven chapters of the Book of Genesis. From these Scripture accounts, we can learn some very important things:

- God created everything that exists, and everything he created is good.
- God intended that all creatures live together in peace and harmony.

Did You Know?

Jesus Christ Saves All

Salvation is possible for anyone, Catholic or not. Christ is the Savior of all people. The Church has stated that non-Christians who "sincerely seek God and moved by grace strive by their deeds to do his will" may achieve eternal salvation (*Dogmatic Constitution on the Church [Lumen Gentium]*, 16). In other words, no one is out of reach for God in his plan of salvation. But this does not mean every religion is equal. The full truth and grace needed for salvation can be found only in the Catholic Church.

- God created human beings to have a special relationship with him. He gave human beings the responsibility of caring for creation.
- The sin of our first parents, Adam and Eve, damaged their relationship with God, with each other, and with all creation.
- Without God's help, sin leads to death and destruction.

This period of salvation history starts with human beings' living in perfect harmony with God. But it ends with our separation from God and eternal happiness, all because of sin.

Stage 2: The Patriarchs

The second stage of salvation history is the period of the patriarchs, told in chapters 12–50 of the Book of Genesis. In this stage God begins the process of repairing our damaged relationship with him. He forms a special relationship with a Chosen People by making a special promise, called a **covenant**, with a man named Abraham and his wife, Sarah. God promises that their descendants will be numerous and that they will inherit a Promised Land.

> I will give you many descendants, and they will become a great nation. I will bless you and make your name famous, so that you will be a blessing.
>
> Genesis 12:2

Stage 3: Egypt and the Exodus

© Bill Wittman/www.wpwittman.com

God gave the Ten Commandments to provide the Israelites a moral structure for their society. How do the civil laws we live under today relate in some way to the Ten Commandments?

The third stage of salvation history is the account of the **Exodus** from slavery in Egypt. At the beginning of the Book of Exodus, we discover that the descendants of Jacob's children—called the Israelites—were enslaved in Egypt. God heard their cries and called Moses to lead them out of slavery. But Pharaoh, the Egyptian leader, had a hard heart. God had to send terrible plagues to make Pharaoh let the Israelites go. The Israelites' escape from Egypt and journey to the Holy Land is called the Exodus.

On the way to the Promised Land, the Israelites stopped at Mount Sinai. There God renewed the covenant he had made with Abraham, and he extended it to all the Israelites. He gave Moses the Ten Commandments, which the people must obey as part of the covenant. During the Exodus the people frequently complained and lost their faith in God. As a consequence they were forced to wander in the desert for forty years, and only their children were able to enter the Promised Land.

Stage 4: The Promised Land and the Judges

In the fourth stage of salvation history, the Israelites reach and settle the Promised Land. These accounts appear in the Books of Joshua and Judges in the Old Testament. Moses died before the Israelites could enter the Promised Land, called Canaan. So God chose a new leader, Joshua, to lead the people into Canaan. Much of Canaan was inhabited by other people. So the Israelites needed to fight to gain control of the land. Whenever they trusted God, they were successful in their battles; whenever they lost faith in God, they failed.

Eventually they gained control of the Promised Land, and each of the twelve tribes received its own section of the land. Then new invaders, the Philistines, tried to capture the land. During this stage of salvation history, the Israelites had no king; God was their ruler. But God called special prophets and warriors, called Judges, to help deliver justice and defend the land against the Philistine invasions.

THiNK ABouT IT!

The Bible tells us that when God made his covenant with Abraham, Abraham was overcome by terror (see Genesis 15:12). When the prophet Jonah heard God, he ran the other way (see Jonah 1:3). When Jesus' disciples heard God on the mountaintop, they too were terrified (see Matthew 17:6). God speaks to us because he wants us to know something new or to act differently. That can be scary. What do you think God wants you to do differently? Why might that be scary?

29

Stage 5: The Kings and the Prophets

The Old Testament also tells us about the fifth stage of salvation history: the kingdoms of Judah and Israel. First and Second Samuel, First and Second Kings, and several books of the prophets tell us about these kingdoms. At the end of the Book of Judges, the Israelites wanted their own king. God reluctantly answered their plea. He had Samuel—the last of the Judges—anoint Saul as the first king of Israel. David followed Saul as the next king. David, a mighty warrior, united all twelve tribes into one kingdom. When David's son, Solomon, became king, he followed God's instructions to build a Temple in Jerusalem, the capital city. However, after Solomon died, a disagreement arose between the tribes, and the kingdom split in two. Israel became the name of the northern kingdom alone, and Judah became the name of the southern kingdom.

Many of the kings of Israel and Judah worshipped foreign gods and allowed unjust practices in the kingdom. So God called prophets to encourage the people to obey their covenant with him. Prophets like Amos, Hosea, and Isaiah reminded God's Chosen People to stop worshipping idols, to practice justice, and to care for those in need.

> Let justice flow like a stream, and righteousness like a river that never goes dry.
>
> Amos 5:24

Stage 6: The Exile and the Return

The sixth stage of salvation history covers the **Exile** and the return from the Exile. You can learn about these events in the Books of Ezra, Nehemiah, First and Second Maccabees, and some of the later prophets. Despite the prophets' warnings, the people of Israel and Judah continued to turn away from God's covenant. So God let their kingdoms be conquered.

Live It!

You Are Part of God's Plan

There are no excuses when it comes to doing God's work. Some of the greatest figures in the Bible seem at first like they aren't well suited to what God asks of them. For example, Abraham and Sarah were too old to have children, yet God chose them to be the parents of a new nation. Moses was a poor speaker, but God still made him his spokesman. The prophet Jeremiah says he is too young, yet God knows he will become a great leader.

You are also a part of God's plan of salvation. You have a special task to do. Each morning think of one thing you can do to help another person. You could make sure the family car is always stocked with bottled water ready to give to someone in need. You could help a friend prepare for a test. Countless possibilities await your help, even if at first you do not think you are the right person for the job.

LITURGY CONNECTION

Easter Vigil

The Easter Vigil is celebrated on the Saturday evening before Easter Sunday. It begins the Church's remembrance of Jesus' Resurrection. The Easter Vigil is also special for two other reasons. First, we welcome new members into the Church on this night. Second, during the Easter Vigil, we recall God's saving actions throughout history. The liturgy for the Easter Vigil includes as many as seven readings from the Bible. They recall the seven days of Creation; the Israelites' crossing the Red Sea; the prophets' pointing the way toward the Messiah; and Christ's Passion, death, and Resurrection.

The Easter Vigil liturgy gives us an overview of God's plan of salvation. The Easter Vigil is a dramatic thanksgiving for all God has done for us. If you have never attended the Easter Vigil, plan with your family to attend next Easter.

Israel was conquered by the Assyrians in 721 BC. Judah was conquered by the Babylonians in 587 BC. We call this time the Exile because many of God's people were taken into captivity. During the Exile, prophets like Ezekiel comforted the Israelites with the promise that God was still with them. The prophets also foretold the coming of a savior, or messiah, who could lead the people to peace.

Fifty years passed in exile. Then a new Persian king conquered Babylon and allowed God's Chosen People—now called Judeans, or Jews—to return to rebuild Jerusalem and the Temple. After Alexander the Great conquered Babylon, the Greeks ruled Israel. But around 150 BC the Maccabees, a Jewish family, led a successful revolt against the Greeks to restore Jewish independence. During all of these troubled times, many of the Chosen People continued to hope for a messiah to make them great again.

Stage 7: The Life of Jesus Christ

As you have seen, the Old Testament tells us about the first six stages of salvation history. Now the history continues with two more stages described in the New Testament.

The life of Jesus Christ forms the seventh stage of salvation history. God never abandoned his Chosen People, even though they often did not keep their part of the covenant. When the time was right, God sent his only Son, Jesus Christ, into the world.

By the time Jesus was born, the Roman Empire had conquered Israel. Some of the Chosen People continued to hope for a messiah, but they envisioned a mighty warrior and king, like David, who could drive out the Romans. Instead, Jesus preached love, justice, and forgiveness. He healed and worked miracles as signs of God's power. He showed that true salvation comes through faith and a change of heart, not through violence and political power. When Jesus was killed by the Romans—with the approval of the Jewish leaders—his followers believed all was lost. Then, after three days, God raised Jesus from the dead. Jesus' followers then understood that he was truly the Messiah, the promised Savior who had come to fulfill God's plan.

Simon Peter answered him, "Lord, to whom would we go? You have the words that give eternal life. And now we believe and know that you are the Holy One who has come from God."

John 6:68–69

Stage 8: The Church

The final stage of salvation history began with the early Christian Church and continues today. You can read about the early Church in the Acts of the Apostles, the letters in the New Testament, and the Book of Revelation. After his Resurrection, Jesus instructed his closest followers, the Apostles, to go and spread the Good News of salvation to all people. Then after Jesus' Ascension, he sent the Holy Spirit to empower his followers to carry out his mission.

Jesus' followers began by preaching to other Jews. Sometimes they were persecuted by Jewish leaders who did not believe in Jesus. One of those persecutors, named Paul, had a vision of Jesus and became a Christian. God revealed to Paul that Christ came for all people. Paul began preaching to non-Jews, who were called **Gentiles**. Many other believers, women and men, helped him. Soon Christianity spread throughout the whole Roman Empire.

Today the Church continues Christ's mission by telling the whole world about God's saving love. The Church will continue to share the Gospel until the end of time, when Christ will come again to judge the living and the dead. As members of the Church, we take part in Christ's mission too.

PEOPLE OF FAITH
Saint Jerome

© 2013 Saint Mary's Press/Illustration by Vicki Shuck

The next time you pick up your Bible, think of Saint Jerome. He was a priest and scholar who lived in the fourth century.

The Pope commissioned Jerome to revise the Latin translation of the Bible. Catholics today have experienced some of the struggles Jerome faced when he revised the Bible, because the translation we use at Mass has also gone through revisions in recent years. Some people are resistant to the changes, but others have welcomed them, believing that the changes make the words more meaningful, perhaps more accurate and faithful to the original language.

Jerome had both fans and critics, and discussions weren't always pleasant. But this scholar loved the Word of God and wanted to make it understood. Although some focused on an exact, word-for-word translation of the Bible, Jerome focused on translating the overall meaning. The new translation he created came to be known as the Vulgate. Today the Vulgate is still the official Latin version of the Bible used by the Church.

Jerome raised a great question: How do you and I make the Word of God understood by the people we meet each day? As people who believe in God's Word, we are asked to live that Word in a way that makes God known to those we meet.

3 God the Father

When you picture God in your mind, what do you see? Many people see an old man with white hair and a beard sitting on a throne in a cloud up in the sky. Is this what God really looks like? Not really. It seems that many of us have adopted this image of God, which resembles that of the Greek god Zeus, whom the stories about the ancient Greek gods describe just like this.

Michelangelo painted God as an old man with a white beard. What image comes to your mind when you think of God? What are some other ways to think about God?

© Alinari Archives/CORBIS

You might be curious why you have the image of this Greek god in your head when you think about the one, true God. Centuries ago, artists needed some way to portray God in their works, but the Bible contained no physical descriptions of God the Father. Some painters used Zeus as the model because he was the most powerful of the Greek gods. The image of Zeus helped many people connect to some of the traits of God. That image has stuck with us. It is not wrong to picture God like this. However, remember that this is not an accurate representation of God. If God is not an old man with a white beard in the clouds, then who is he?

Who Is God?

If you were asked to describe a friend, you might answer in a few different ways. You could say something about her relationships to others (she is a daughter, a sister, and a friend). You might talk about what she does (she is a student and a softball player). Maybe you would say what kind of person she is (she is smart and kind). We get to know people through their relationships with others and by observing what they do and listening to what they say.

Everything we know about God, we know because he revealed it to us. God first revealed his name to Moses. It is pretty simple but very powerful: I AM. The Hebrew word for I AM is **Yahweh**. The name I AM, or Yahweh, reminds us how immense and beyond us God truly is. I AM may seem like an incomplete sentence ("I am . . . what?"), but that is what makes the name so powerful. Think about all the possibilities that could complete this sentence: the who, what, when,

PRAY IT!

God, our Father, you exist beyond the farthest star, but I also know you are here with me now. I do not know everywhere I will go in the future, but I do know I came from you. I do not always understand your ways, but I do know I can trust you. I cannot even guess how you came to be, but I do know you will always be with me. Amen.

Fun Fact

In the Bible, God often appears in the form of a cloud. When the Israelites escaped from Egypt, they followed a cloud (see Exodus 13:20–22). They camped in one place as long as the cloud covered the Tent of the Lord's presence (see Numbers 9:15–23). In the New Testament, a cloud came over Jesus, Peter, James, and John, and said, "This is my own dear Son!" (Matthew 17:5).

where, how, and why. There are an infinite number of ways for God to be. God sustains every person, place, time, and condition that exists. At the same time, God exists beyond all people, places, times, and conditions.

Many of our Jewish brothers and sisters do not even say the name of God. The ancient Israelites believed that naming someone or something gave one power over the person or thing. Out of respect for the name of God and for how beyond us he truly is, they substituted "LORD" for the name Yahweh.

Though God is so great and beyond us, he is still close to and intimate with us. He knows every hair on our heads and every passing thought that flows through our minds. The Book of Psalms says it best:

> LORD, you have examined me
> and you know me.
> You know everything I do . . .
> Where could I go to escape
> from you?
> Where could I get away
> from your presence?
> If I went up to heaven, you
> would be there;
> if I lay down in the world
> of the dead, you
> would be there . . .
> When my bones were
> being formed,

carefully put together in
my mother's womb,
when I was growing there
in secret,
you knew that I was there—
you saw me before I was born.
(139:1–2,7–8,15–16)

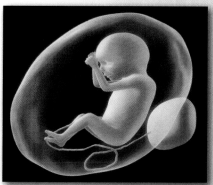

© Sebastian Kaulitzki/Shutterstock.com

God said, "I am who I am. You must tell them: 'The one who is called I AM has sent me to you.'"

Exodus 3:14

The author of Psalm 139 expresses how deeply God knows and loves each one of us—from the earliest days in our mother's womb.

The Trinity

Long after God told Moses his name was Yahweh, he revealed much more about himself. He revealed himself as the Holy Trinity—one God in three Divine

Live It!

Growing Our Relationships

In reading the Bible, you'll learn that God did not just create us and then run off. He continues to care for us with truth and love. Some of his care for us comes in the form of people in our lives with whom we have important relationships. These people include our parents and other family members, friends, and teachers. Take time to recognize God's work in your life through these people. In a similar way, be a source of God's care for others. Provide a helping hand, words of encouragement, and companionship to others, especially those who might be most in need. Be an instrument of God's love and care for others.

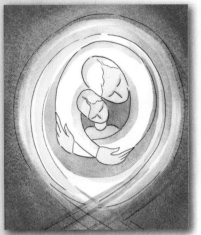

Illustration by Elizabeth Wang, "God the Father loves each one of us with a passionate love, and holds us in His tender embrace," copyright © Radiant Light 2008, www.radiantlight.org.uk

Imagine being held in the arms of God! God holds each one of us in his loving embrace, as a mother loves her child.

Persons: the Father, Son, and Holy Spirit, who is the Holy Trinity. This is the central belief of our Christian faith. God, in three Divine Persons, is all knowing, all-powerful, and present everywhere. Try to imagine that. Even when God reveals himself to us, he remains a **mystery**. As hard as we try, we can't fully understand this mystery. (See chapter 4, "The Holy Trinity," of this handbook for more about the Trinity.)

God the Father

Let's explore the First Divine Person of the Trinity—God the Father. He is far beyond any image we can conjure in our minds. The Bible portrays God as having both masculine and feminine qualities, but still God is

Did You Know?

"Abba": Jesus' Name for His Father

In the Gospels, Jesus addresses God as "**Abba**." The language Jesus spoke was Aramaic, and *abba* is the Aramaic word for "father." This gives us an idea of the special bond Jesus has with his Father. The Father loves Jesus, much as a human father loves his children by protecting, feeding, and teaching them. Yet the Bible also sometimes portrays God's motherly characteristics. "As a mother comforts her child, so will I comfort you," says the Lord (Isaiah 66:13, NRSV). Jesus teaches us to address God as "Father" and to share in his special close relationship with God, our loving Father.

neither male nor female. We praise God as a loving, powerful Father, at the same time recognizing that our picture of him is incomplete. Despite our limited understanding of God, we know and profess in faith through our Creed that God the Father is maker of "all things visible and invisible," the Creator of Heaven and earth.

> "My thoughts," says the LORD, "are not like yours, / and my ways are different from yours. / As high as the heavens are above the earth, / so high are my ways and thoughts above yours."
>
> Isaiah 55:8–9

Jesus called God "Father," and we do the same. In calling God "Father," Jesus expresses his unique relationship with him. "My Father has given me all things. No one knows the Son except the Father, and no one knows the Father except the Son and those to whom the Son chooses to reveal him" (Matthew 11:27).

God the Father is most certainly a distinct and special person, but unlike us, he is not a human being. Though this might seem obvious, it is important to note this difference between God and us. We should remind ourselves that God's ways are not human ways.

The universe has been around for billions of years. You might think that because—as we confess in the Creed—God is the Creator of the universe, he must be at least

THINK ABOUT IT!

Jesus called the Father "Abba" or "Father" (see the article "'Abba': Jesus' Name for His Father") and said we should also do this when we pray. Jesus tells us we should rely on God as children rely on their parents. How do you rely on your parents? How do they provide for you? What are some good things you have seen fathers do for their children? How is your relationship with God like a child's relationship with his or her parents?

LITURGY CONNECTION

Thanks to the Father

Have you ever noticed that most of our prayers at Mass are directed to God the Father? Although our prayers also address Jesus Christ, his Divine Son, they are mostly spoken to the Father. If you think about it, it makes sense. During Mass, we recall all the good things God the Father has done for us, including sending his Son. His Son, Jesus, is the greatest way for human beings to get to know the Father. We also thank God for doing this. But again, Jesus is a key part of our gratitude. We offer thanks to the Father in the same way we come to know the Father: "through Jesus Christ, our Lord."

several billion years old, right? (See chapter 6 for more about creation.) The only problem with this idea is that time itself is a part of God's creation. God lives outside time, and because he created it, he is not limited or confined by it. If this boggles your mind, do not worry. It can baffle the most intelligent minds on our planet.

Logically, one could say that God created everything in the universe, but the next step backward is the difficult one. Who made God? The answer is that no one made God. God is not a created being, but rather one who is, always was, and always will be.

If this somehow doesn't make sense, do not worry. This is why we call God a **mystery**. A religious mystery is not like a story the reader has just not figured out. Rather this kind of mystery refers to a truth so big that no human being can completely know or understand it.

God Is Truth and Love

Throughout time, God has revealed himself to us. He is Yahweh. God is Father, Son, and Holy Spirit, three Divine Persons in one being. He is Truth and Love.

God is Truth simply because what he tells us is true. We can trust God's Word.

We can count on God, more than even the most trusted human being we know. God always keeps his promises.

God is also Love. First and foremost, God created us out of love. God's love does not end at creation though. The Bible is filled with stories describing what God has done for us. Even though we human beings have failed to keep our part of the bargain, God forgives us and continues to be faithful to his people. Most important, God became one of us out of love for us. God the Father gave his only Son for our salvation and sent the Holy Spirit to be with us always. There is no greater sign of love than this.

Church History

Teaching about the One God of the Old and New Testaments

In the second century AD, a man named Marcion thought the God of the New Testament could not be the same as the one in violent stories of the Old Testament. He argued that the loving and forgiving God was revealed only by Jesus in the New Testament. Marcion did not consider what the human authors of the Old Testament thought about God. The Old Testament writers pictured God this way because they thought of him as a warrior who protected his people when they were good. Without considering the intentions of the human authors, people like Marcion can misunderstand Scripture. The Church Fathers (the leaders of the early Church) declared that Marcion was incorrect and emphasized that there is only one true God of both the Old and New Testaments.

4 THE HOLY TRINITY

Think of the many different ways you have reached out to God in the past. There may have been times when you wanted the comfort of the all-knowing Father, who could help you see that everything was going to be okay. Or maybe you reached out to God as one who could move mountains and change lives. Other times you may have reached out to God when you were confused. Maybe you wanted God

We share in the life and love of the Trinity. Pictures like this one help us to imagine our relationship with the Father, Son, and Holy Spirit, three Persons in one God.

Illustration by Elizabeth Wang, "Through faith, baptism, and loving obedience, we share in the life of the Holy Trinity," copyright © Radiant Light 2008, www.radiantlight.org.uk

to inspire you or reveal his will to you. Of course there were times when you just wanted God's presence, providing comfort during a hard time, like having a friend who is always there to listen to you—someone who has gone through the same pain and suffering as you. The good news is that God satisfies all of these needs.

> The grace of the Lord Jesus Christ, the love of God, and the fellowship of the Holy Spirit be with you all.
>
> 2 Corinthians 13:13

One God, Three Divine Persons

"In the name of the Father, and of the Son, and of the Holy Spirit." How many times have you said or heard these words? Have you ever really thought about what the phrase means? During Mass on Sundays, Catholics stand to say the Creed. Together we state, "I believe in one God . . ." But if someone thinks the Father, Son, and Holy Spirit are three separate individuals, he or she would be misunderstanding the central truth of our faith.

The earliest Christians were Jews who followed Jesus when they recognized that he was the Messiah sent from God to save Israel. Because they were Jewish, they knew there could be only one God. One of the

PRAY IT!

In the name of the Father, who created everyone I love and all I know; and of the Son, who became a human being like me, and showed me the right way to live; and of the Holy Spirit, who inspires me with courage and creativity. Father, Son, and Holy Spirit, in you I place my trust. Amen.

FUN FACT

The Bible often refers to God as the Father, the Son, and the Holy Spirit, but it never uses the word Trinity. Instead, this understanding of God as the Blessed Trinity comes from Sacred Tradition. All the major Christian traditions share a common belief in this central mystery of faith.

most basic prayers of the Jewish faith is taken from the Book of Deuteronomy, as follows: "Hear, O Israel: The LORD is our God, the LORD alone. You shall love the LORD your God with all your heart, and with all your soul, and with all your might" (6:4–5, NRSV). Yet these Jewish Christians knew that Jesus was the Son of God and was one with the Father. They were also aware that the Hebrew Scriptures—our Old Testament—spoke of the Spirit of God. Through these experiences, they realized that the one true God revealed himself as three Persons: the Trinity.

> In the beginning the Word already existed; the Word was with God, and the Word was God. From the very beginning the Word was with God. Through him God made all things.
>
> John 1:1–3

The Trinity is the central mystery of our Christian life and faith. God has made himself known to us in the three Divine Persons of the **Trinity**: the Father, the Son, and the Holy Spirit. Yet these three Divine Persons are one God and cannot be separated from one another.

The Trinity is not divided into three parts. For example, a baseball team is made up of a pitcher, catcher, first baseman, and so on. When all nine players are assembled, you have a complete baseball team. This is not so for the Trinity. Each Divine Person of the

Trinity does not make up one-third of the whole God. Instead, the complete presence of God can be found in each of them. The Father, Son, and Holy Spirit cannot be separated from one another.

If you have ever watched a pair of truly great dancers in action, it almost seems as if you are watching just one dancer. They move in complete harmony together. When one dancer lifts the other, it seems as if there is no effort. Each move flows naturally into the next. It seems as though the two blend into one single dancer.

In a similar, but far more real, way, the three Divine Persons of the Trinity live in complete harmony. They are distinct Persons, yet they are completely united. Unlike the dancers, they are not united just by their actions. They are also united by what and who they are: one Divine Being.

The Work of the Trinity

The Father, Son, and Holy Spirit are one God. Therefore all the works of God are done by all three Divine Persons. However, some of God's works are more strongly associated with either the Father, the Son, or the Holy Spirit.

God the Father is the First Person of the Blessed Trinity. When we speak of

THiNK AbouT IT!

When making the Sign of the Cross, we say, "In the name of the Father, and of the Son, and of the Holy Spirit." We also move our hands in the shape of a cross on our head, chest, and shoulders. Why do you think the Sign of the Cross connects the Trinity and Jesus' sacrifice on the cross? How are each of the three Divine Persons of the Trinity connected to Jesus' suffering, death, Resurrection, and Ascension?

God as the Creator, we tend to think of God the Father. However, even though the work of Creation is associated with God the Father, the Father, Son, and Holy Spirit together are one source of creation. Like a parent, the Father is the source from which life comes. It is natural to think of God the Father when we think of the Creator.

> Go, then, to all peoples everywhere and make them my disciples: baptize them in the name of the Father, the Son, and the Holy Spirit, and teach them to obey everything I have commanded you. And I will be with you always, to the end of the age.
>
> Matthew 28:19–20

God the Son is the Second Divine Person of the Blessed Trinity, Jesus Christ. The title **Son of God** points to Jesus' divine relationship with the Father as the only Son of God. We also call Jesus Christ the "Savior" to recognize his saving actions on our behalf. But we cannot forget that the Father and the Holy Spirit also save us.

The Trinity is a never-ending circle of love. Family members mirror the love of the Trinity when they share love with one another.

© Richard Hutchings/CORBIS

God the **Holy Spirit** is the Third Divine Person of the Blessed Trinity. He inspires, guides, and makes the lives of the believers holy. The Gifts of the Holy Spirit are truly given by the Father and the Son too. Yet it is proper to recognize the gifts as being from the Holy Spirit.

The Trinity Is a Communion

Because God is three Divine Persons in one, the Trinity is the communion of those three Persons. Another way of saying this is that the Father, Son, and Holy Spirit are completely in union with one another. They communicate perfectly and are in perfect harmony.

Did You Know?

The Sign of the Cross

Christians have been making the Sign of the Cross for almost two thousand years. In the early days of Christianity, Christians moved their thumbs across their foreheads in the shape of a cross. It was a reminder to carry the cross of Christ in their lives. In other words, we are called to sacrifice ourselves to help others. During the times and in the places Christianity was illegal, making the Sign of the Cross became a secret way for Christians to recognize one another. Today, Catholics often make the Sign of the Cross when we enter a church. We dip our fingers into the holy water to make the Sign of the Cross, as a reminder of our Baptisms.

© ABDESIGN/iStockphoto.com

Saint Patrick used
a shamrock to teach
people about the Trinity.
What does a shamrock
have in common with
the Trinity?

Because the Trinity is a perfect communion of the three Divine Persons, we can see how the Trinity is the perfect community. The love and unity that the Father, Son, and Holy Spirit share are so perfect that they flow out to us. Our families share in this love and community. The love of a mother and father extends past them to the children they share. That love can extend even past the family. The love in our families should flow out in service to the rest of the community and the entire world.

Live It!

Harmony at Home

The Trinity is a community that lives in complete harmony, unity, and love. Unlike the Trinity, human families are not perfect communities. But you can work toward creating a home of harmony, unity, and love by doing some simple things. For example, you might do your chores without being asked. This might seem like a typical corny thing an adult would tell you. But what would happen if you did it? Your parents would quit having to nag you about simple chores. You wouldn't have to listen to them complain. And they would be less frustrated too! Doesn't that sound like a more harmonious community to you? This is only one way of making a home of unity, harmony, and love. However you do it, it will take some work, but the payoff is worth it.

PEOPLE OF FAITH
Saint Patrick

© 2013 Saint Mary's Press/Illustration by Vicki Shuck

Saint Patrick was born in the fourth century AD in what later became Great Britain. As a youth Patrick was kidnapped and taken to Ireland, where he became the slave of a warlord for several years. At that time Ireland was a rough place to live. The Irish tribes were often at war, slavery was common, and human sacrifice was practiced. After several years Patrick either escaped or was released. He returned home, where he soon became a priest. Later Patrick returned to Ireland, the land of his former captors, to preach the Gospel. This was an extremely brave step. Ireland certainly had been a difficult place for him earlier, and at that time, few people had traveled to such a foreign place to convert others to Christianity. He bravely went and later was appointed the Bishop of Ireland.

Patrick planted the seeds of Christianity in Ireland. Over the next few decades, the practices of both slavery and human sacrifice ended in Ireland. Legend says that Patrick used a shamrock to explain the Trinity to the Irish people. Like the three Persons united in one God, the shamrock is made up of three leaves united to make this single, unique plant. Today, Patrick is remembered for his courage and his strong faith, and for his teaching about the one true God in three Divine Persons.

5 THE BIBLE: THE OLD TESTAMENT

As Christians we have Jewish roots. This is because we are followers of Jesus, and Jesus was a Jew. He obeyed the Jewish Covenant and Law. He worshipped in synagogues (a Jewish community center and place of prayer) and at the Temple in Jerusalem. And he knew the Jewish Scriptures very well. In the Gospels, Jesus frequently quotes the Jewish Scriptures—essentially the Old Testament of the Bible—in his teaching and preaching.

We owe the Jewish people a debt of gratitude for preserving God's Revelation in the books of the Old Testament so that we can read them today.

The Old Testament

Pentateuch (5 Books)	Historical Books (16 Books)	Wisdom and Poetry Books (7 Books)	Books of the Prophets (18 Books)
	Joshua		Isaiah
	Judges		Jeremiah
	Ruth		Lamentations
	1 Samuel		Baruch
	2 Samuel		Ezekiel
	1 Kings		Daniel
	2 Kings		Hosea
	1 Chronicles		Joel
	2 Chronicles		Amos
	Ezra	Job	Obadiah
	Nehemiah	Psalms	Jonah
Genesis	Tobit	Proverbs	Micah
Exodus	Judith	Ecclesiastes	Nahum
Leviticus	Esther	Song of Songs	Habakkuk
Numbers	1 Maccabees	Wisdom	Zephaniah
Deuteronomy	2 Maccabees	Sirach	Haggai
			Zechariah
			Malachi

© Saint Mary's Press

Our faith is built upon the Jewish faith practiced by Jesus. We are the spiritual descendants of the Jewish people—God's Chosen People. To understand our faith better, we can study and pray with the Old Testament to understand the Chosen People's relationship with God.

The Old Testament is divided into four major sections:

1. the Pentateuch
2. the historical books
3. the wisdom and poetry books
4. the prophets

This chapter looks at each of these sections and discusses some important stories and people you will find in them. Other chapters in this handbook cover some of these sections in greater detail. But the best way to learn about the Old Testament is to read it, so this chapter identifies many Bible passages for you to look up.

This chapter also introduces you to several different kinds of writing in the Bible. These different kinds of writing are called literary genres. The Bible includes symbolic writing, laws, songs for worship, historical accounts, proverbs, short stories, love poetry, speeches, and prophetic sayings. Knowing the literary genre of a Bible passage is one step toward interpreting the passage correctly.

PRAY IT!

Give thanks to the LORD,
  because he is good,
  and his love is eternal.
Let the people of Israel say:
  "His love is eternal."
Let the priests of God say,
  "His love is eternal."
Let all who worship him say,
  "His love is eternal."
This is the day of the
  LORD's victory;
  let us be happy, let us
  celebrate!
Save us, LORD, save us!
  Give us success, O LORD!
  (Psalm 118:1–4, 24–25)

The Pentateuch

The **Pentateuch** is the first five books of the Bible: Genesis, Exodus, Leviticus, Numbers, and Deuteronomy. *Pentateuch* is a Greek word that means "five containers of scrolls"—the books of the Bible were originally written on scrolls. You may also have heard Jewish people call these five books the Torah. Let's look at these five books more closely.

The first book, Genesis, tells about the creation of the world, Adam and Eve, Original Sin, Cain and Abel, Noah and the Flood, and the Tower of Babel. Genesis goes on to describe the beginning of the Chosen People through God's covenant with Abraham, his son Isaac, and Isaac's son Jacob.

Jacob's descendants, the Israelites, were forced to migrate to Egypt because of drought. Their population grew so large that the Egyptian rulers felt threatened and enslaved them all. That is where the Book of Exodus picks up the history. This book tells how the Jewish people escaped from slavery in Egypt with the help of God and the leadership of Moses. The Book of Exodus includes accounts of the ten plagues, the crossing of the Red Sea, Moses' receiving God's Law (summarized in the Ten Commandments), the Israelites' worship of the golden calf, and the Israelites' wandering in the desert in search of the Promised Land.

The remaining three books of the Pentateuch tell us more about God's Law and his covenant with the Israelites, as well as the Israelites' journey to the

Promised Land. The Book of Leviticus is a collection of laws followed by the Chosen People—laws about religious worship, ways to stay pure, and guidelines for the fair and just treatment of one another. The Book of Numbers takes its name from the census in which Moses counted all the people. This book also describes the Israelites' successes and their failures in their first attempts to enter the Promised Land. The Book of Deuteronomy is presented as Moses' final words to the Chosen People before they entered the Promised Land. The accounts in Deuteronomy repeat many of the stories and laws found in Exodus, Leviticus, and Numbers.

> Israel remember this! The LORD—and the LORD alone—is our God. Love the LORD your God with all your heart, with all your soul, and with all your strength. Never forget these commands that I am giving you today.
>
> Deuteronomy 6:4–6

These five books of the Pentateuch reveal important things about God and his original plan for Creation and humanity. We need this knowledge to understand what is happening in the rest of the Bible. Here is a list of some of these teachings and where you can read more about them:

- God made everything, and everything he made is good (see Genesis 1:1—2:4).
- God made human beings to be in a special relationship with him and to participate in his work of caring for creation (see Genesis 2:5–15).

- God made man and woman to complement each other and to join together in marriage (see Genesis 2:18–25).
- Sin damages our relationship with God and with each other (see Genesis 3:1–24, 4:1–16).
- God wishes to be in a loving and committed relationship—covenant relationship—with human beings (see Genesis 17:1–9, Exodus 24:1–8, Deuteronomy 7:7—8:19).
- God hears us when we call out to him, and he rescues us from sin and evil (see Exodus, chapters 1–15).
- God gives us his Law to teach us how to live in a good relationship with him and with one another (see Exodus, chapters 19–20; Deuteronomy, chapters 5–6).

The Historical Books

The second section of the Old Testament contains the historical books (from Joshua to Second Maccabees). This label can be misleading, because these are not books of pure history. Most describe historical people and events, but they are written to emphasize God's actions in history—something modern history books never do.

The historical books form the largest section of the Old Testament. For now let's focus on a few key people and events described in the Books of Joshua,

Judges, First and Second Samuel, and First and Second Kings. The history told in these books starts immediately after the Exodus, when the Chosen People entered the Promised Land. They were led by Joshua, whom God appointed to lead the people after Moses died. Joshua was a wise and faithful man and also a skilled warrior. You can read about him in the Book of Joshua. Under Joshua's leadership the Israelites conquered the Promised Land—called Canaan, or Israel—and divided it among the Israelite tribes. Joshua is famous for having said, "As for my family and me, we will serve the Lord" (Joshua 24:15).

After Joshua's death the Chosen People did not have a king or appointed leader. But whenever trouble came, God raised up a spirit-filled leader who helped them fight off the threat. These leaders were called **Judges**, and their stories are told in the Book of Judges. One of the Judges was a famous woman named Deborah (see Judges, chapter 4). She led the

© Stefano Bianchetti/Corbis

In 1 Kings 18:25–39, the Prophet Elijah challenged the prophets of Baal. In answer to Elijah's prayer, fire came down from Heaven to consume God's altar and its offerings. The people then believed in the one true God.

people to victory against a Canaanite general named Sisera. Another famous Judge was Samson. Samson was very strong, but he was also sinful and broke many commitments to God. After Samson was captured by his enemies, God gave him one last chance to destroy them, but doing so cost Samson his life (see Judges, chapters 13–16).

The last Judge of Israel was Samuel. He was also a priest and a prophet and has two books of the Bible named after him: First and Second Samuel. During the time of Samuel, the people wanted a king. They believed a king would offer the nation more protection and also more importance. God told Samuel to do as the people asked, so Samuel anointed Saul as the first king of Israel (see 1 Samuel, chapters 8–10). At first Saul seemed like a good king, but he turned out to lack a strong faith in God. So

Live It!

Journal about Your Relationship with God

When you read the Old Testament, you encounter a long history of God's saving words and actions in the world. Today God is present to you through the people and events in your own life. As a spiritual exercise, consider starting a journal to observe God's presence in your life. Begin by thinking back on your childhood, and tell your story in terms of people or events that brought you closer to God. Continue writing in your journal every day or once a week to reflect on how God is present to you today.

God had Samuel anoint a young man named David to succeed Saul as king. David turned out to be a very good king—the best-known king of Israel (see 1 Samuel, chapters 16–19; 2 Samuel, chapters 2–8). But not even David was perfect. He committed several serious sins during his years as king. Still, he was also a model of servant leadership in repenting for his sins and serving his people (see 2 Samuel, chapters 11–12).

After David's death, Solomon, his son, became king. Solomon asked God for wisdom to rule the Chosen People justly. God granted Solomon not only wisdom but also wealth and a long life (see 1 Kings, chapter 3). Solomon built a beautiful Temple for God in the capital city of Jerusalem (see 1 Kings, chapters 5–8). But like his father, Solomon also committed some serious sins, especially the sin of idolatry. After Solomon's death, civil war split the kingdom of Israel into two separate kingdoms. The northern kingdom was now called Israel, and the southern kingdom was called Judah (see 1 Kings, chapters 11–12).

The stories of many less famous kings are told in First and Second Kings: nineteen kings in the kingdom of Israel and nineteen more in the kingdom of Judah. Most of these kings were sinful in the eyes of God. They worshipped false gods and goddesses and were not fair in their dealings with people. But we also

THiNk AbouT IT!

Look back at the four sections of the Old Testament that are introduced in this chapter. Which section most interests you after reading this overview? If you could pick one Old Testament book to begin reading today, which would it be and why?

FUN FACT

When Moses asked God what his name is, God told Moses that his name is Yahweh, which means something like "I Am." The Jewish people believe that God's name is too holy to speak out loud, so they say or write *Lord* instead. This is why many English-language Bibles use the word LORD (in all caps or small caps) instead of the name Yahweh.

read about some good kings, such as Hezekiah (see 2 Kings, chapters 18–20) and Josiah (see 2 Kings, chapters 22–23). Nonetheless, because the kings and the people had broken their covenant with God so many times, God allowed both kingdoms to be conquered, Israel by the Assyrians and Judah by the Babylonians.

> I am in trouble, God—listen to my prayer!
> I am afraid of my enemies—save my life!
> Psalm 64:1

After Judah was conquered, the Babylonians took many of the Israelites back to Babylon to live in slavery. This was called the Babylonian Exile, or just the Exile, and it was a very sad time for the Chosen People. God allowed this Exile so his people could learn the importance of trusting in him and staying true to their covenant with him. After about fifty years, the Babylonians were conquered by the Persians, whose king allowed the Israelite slaves to return to the Promised Land and rebuild Jerusalem and their Temple. The story of their return and rebuilding is told in the Books of Ezra and Nehemiah.

As you can see, the Books of Joshua, Judges, First and Second Samuel, and First and Second Kings tell us much about the history of God's Chosen People after the Exodus. The historical writings of the Old Testament include other books that help flesh out the history of God's People. First and Second Chronicles provide different accounts of the history of the kings of Israel and Judah. The Book of Tobit is a short story about the angel Raphael, a faithful Jew named Tobit, and Tobit's son Tobias's search for a wife. The Books of Ruth, Judith, and Esther tell us about brave women who helped the Jewish people. And First and Second Maccabees—the last of the historical books in the Old Testament—tell us about five brothers and their father who led a revolt against an evil Greek ruler after the Israelites returned from the Exile.

Did You Know?

The Relationship between the Old and New Testaments

Another word for *testament* is *covenant*. So the Old Testament is about the covenant God made with his Chosen People at Mount Sinai, and the New Testament is about the covenant God made with all people through the saving work of Christ. But even the words Old and New can be misleading. For Jesus said, "Do not think that I have come to do away with the Law of Moses and the teachings of the prophets. I have not come to do away with them but to make their teachings come true" (Matthew 5:17). So when you hear "Old Testament," you might think of "original covenant," and when you hear "New Testament," you might think of "fulfilled covenant." The *Catechism of the Catholic Church* quotes an old saying: "The New Testament lies hidden in the Old and the Old Testament is unveiled in the New"[1] (129).

The Wisdom and Poetry Books

The third section in the Old Testament contains the wisdom and poetry books: namely, Job, Psalms, Proverbs, Ecclesiastes, Song of Songs, Wisdom, and Sirach. These books contain many different kinds of writing: a long debate, hymns used for worship, teachings about wisdom, short proverbs, and even love poetry. Two things connect these books. First, most of them provide us with teachings about how to be a wise person—that is, how to live a good and holy life. The Chosen People knew that wise people pleased God by living good and holy lives and foolish people displeased God by living selfish and sinful lives.

The second element that connects the books in this section is that they all contain passages of poetry. But the poetry in the Old Testament is different from most poetry you might know. It doesn't rhyme or have a specific rhythm. Hebrew poetry is written in groups of two (sometimes three) alternating lines. In most Bibles today, the second line is indented. The second line usually repeats the main idea from the first line using different words and images, but sometimes the second line expands the idea in the first line.

Let's take a brief look at each of the wisdom and poetry books. The section begins with the Book of Job. Job was a man who lost everything. Most of the book describes a long debate between Job and his friends about why his bad fortune happened. Today people study the Book of Job to understand an age-old question: Why does God allow bad things to happen to good people?

You are probably most familiar with the Book of Psalms, the hymns and prayers for God's Chosen People. This book contains 150 prayers that were meant to be sung as part of Jewish worship. They cover nearly every human situation and emotion. Today you encounter the Psalms in the Responsorial Psalm at Mass. They are also an important part of the Liturgy of the Hours, the official prayer of the Church that clergy, religious men and women, and many laypeople pray each day.

The Psalms are followed by the Book of Proverbs, a collection of sayings that gives advice on how to be a good and wise person. Most of these are short, one-line sayings. Next, the Book of Ecclesiastes describes the unfairness of life and the things that

© Bill Wittman/www.wpwittman.com

We look to leaders in our Church and civic communities to share their wisdom with us. Who shares their wisdom and advice with you? Why is it important to listen to them and to follow their advice?

LiTURGy CONNECTION

Jewish Roots in the Mass

Much of our worship follows the Jewish forms of worship that Jesus and the Apostles knew. At Mass, the Liturgy of the Word echoes the Jewish custom of reading aloud from the Hebrew Scriptures in the synagogue. Jesus himself read from the Book of Isaiah at a synagogue service (see Luke 4:19–21). The Liturgy of the Word also includes a psalm, and the singing of psalms was part of Jewish worship.

The Liturgy of the Eucharist has roots in the Jewish Passover, which Jesus celebrated at the Last Supper. The Prayer over the Offerings, in which we thank God, is based on a Jewish form of prayer called the *berakah*. In this prayer, we thank God for the gifts of bread and wine that will soon become the Body and Blood of Christ.

Of course, the very fact that we have a day set apart for worship and rest has its roots in the Jewish Sabbath.

do not bring true happiness. The writer advises us to accept both the good and the bad parts of life.

The Song of Solomon (sometimes called the Song of Songs) is a unique book. At first it appears to be a collection of love poetry that celebrates the relationship between a man and a woman. Why does a book of love poetry appear in the Old Testament? For Jews the poems symbolize the love between God and his Chosen People. For Christians this book also symbolizes the love between Christ and the Church.

This section concludes with the Book of Wisdom and the Wisdom of Ben Sira. The Book of Wisdom teaches us that God will reward good people after death and punish evil people. For God's Chosen People, the Book of Wisdom was also a reminder of their wise ancestors. Ben Sira contains the teachings of a man who lived about 150 years before Jesus was born. He gave very practical advice for living a good and holy life.

The Prophets

The fourth and final section of the Old Testament contains the writings of important Jewish prophets. A **prophet** is a person whom God calls to speak on his behalf. Many prophets appear in the Old Testament, but less than half have their own books. In the prophets section, we find sixteen Israelite prophets whose words were written in books named after them. Two other books in this section are not the words of prophets: Lamentations and Baruch. And as you have already seen, the accounts of other prophets like Moses, Nathan, Elijah, and Elisha are told in other books of the Bible.

The prophets of Israel had two basic messages. The first and most common message reminded the Chosen People that they had failed to live out their promises to God by keeping their part of the covenant. The prophets usually addressed failures such as idolatry, injustice, and false worship of God:

- **Idolatry.** Idolatry is the worship of false gods and goddesses. The Israelites kept turning to gods like **Baal and Asherah** instead of worshipping the true God (see Jeremiah 2:11).
- **Injustice.** God's Law called his Chosen People to treat one another fairly and justly, but wealthy and powerful people took advantage of others, creating an unjust society (see Isaiah 1:16–17).
- **False worship.** God was especially hurt when his people pretended to worship him with

pure hearts while they were also worshipping false gods and practicing injustice (see Amos 5:21–24).

But the prophets did not only condemn the Chosen People; at times they also delivered messages of hope. The Israelites went through many dark periods during their history, especially when they were attacked by foreign invaders, when the northern and southern kingdoms were conquered, and when the people were taken into Exile. During these times God's people needed to hear words of encouragement. God provided those words through the prophets too. Sometimes a prophet spoke a message of condemnation and then later spoke messages of hope on important themes about faithfulness, survival, and salvation.

- **God is faithful.** Even though the Chosen People were suffering because of their disobedience to God, God would be faithful to his covenant promises (see Jeremiah 46:27–28).
- **The faithful will survive.** God always promised that the faithful people would survive to continue his covenant. They might be a small group, but God would protect them (see Micah 2:12).
- **God will send a messiah.** God also promised to send a messiah—a word that means "anointed one"—to lead the people back to him. The prophet Isaiah described the Messiah as a servant who would suffer for the people. Isaiah's

prophecies were fulfilled in Jesus Christ (see Isaiah 53:11).

You can read more about the prophets in chapter 10, "The Bible: The Prophets," of this handbook. There you will also learn how Jesus Christ is the Messiah promised by God in the Old Testament.

> Make it your aim to do what is right, not what is evil, so that you may live. Then the LORD God Almighty really will be with you, as you claim he is.
>
> Amos 5:14

Church History

Biblical Studies

In 1943, during the darkest days of World War II, Pope Pius XII issued the encyclical *Divino Afflante Spiritu*. The Latin title is taken from the first words of the document, "Inspired by the Holy Spirit." This encyclical is a landmark for Catholic biblical scholars because it encouraged historical research into the books of the Bible. It also encouraged Scripture scholars to study biblical texts as they would ancient literature, in their original languages, with the aim of uncovering the truth God reveals to us in Sacred Scripture. This encyclical gave guidelines for the study of biblical texts, advocating the importance of the literal meaning of the words and the intention of the sacred writer.

All writing reflects the culture in which it was written. This encyclical urged Scripture scholars, also called *exegetes [EX-uh-jeets]*, to seek the original intention of the inspired human author, so that the truth God wished to reveal can be made clear. In order to do this, exegetes were encouraged to investigate the life and times of the Scripture writers, their written or oral sources, and their particular forms of expression.

6 CREATION

KEY WORDS

**Heaven and earth
creation
angels**

Think about the following: A falling star in the night sky away from city lights. A beaver building a dam. People doing good things for others. Friends having fun together. A family gathering to celebrate a special occasion. Have these or similar events from everyday life ever made you recognize God's goodness? Have you ever wondered where everything that exists has come from? Have you wondered why you exist or where you came from? Do

Beautiful scenes of nature are like billboards from God: See how much I love you! I created a world this awesome for you!

© podfoto/iStockphoto.com

you sometimes question where the world is headed or where life is taking you?

The first line of the Bible is a good place to begin looking for some answers. Genesis 1:1 proclaims that God created the heavens and the earth. **"Heaven and earth"** is a way of referring to the entire universe. This passage from Genesis tells us that God is the creator of all that exists. Everything depends on God. He created out of nothing and without help.

> In the beginning, when God created the heavens and the earth, the earth was a formless void and darkness covered the face of the deep, while a wind from God swept over the face of the waters. Then God said, "Let there be light"; and there was light.
>
> Genesis 1:1–3, NRSV

Scientists work on figuring out the physical nature of the universe. This includes trying to determine how big it is, how old it is, and what chemicals make it up. Why did God create the universe, the earth, and all living things? Why did God create us? Science can't answer these questions. The good news is that God can answer them. He has revealed to us that he created everything because of love.

God didn't have to create the world. It was a free choice motivated by love. He wanted to share his love with his creatures. **Creation** is a gift, and all creation is good. God wants all people

PRAY IT!

Lord, God of all creation, thank you for everything you have created and everything you have given me. Help me recognize my own goodness. Continue to bless all your people as we strive to understand your will for our lives and as we care for all creation. Amen.

to share in his wisdom, beauty, and goodness and to live in union with him. He desires a personal, loving relationship with each of us. He created the world and all of us so that we might share in his glory.

Why Does Evil Exist?

The things that help us recognize the goodness of God's creation are only part of the reality we know. Our world includes evil too. We see signs of this in such things as war and violence, people doing selfish and hateful things, nature spoiled by pollution, and people in many parts of the world suffering because they lack food, shelter, and other necessities. Why does evil exist when God created everything to be good? If you have ever wondered about this, you are not alone.

Part of the mystery of creation is that God makes good things happen, even in evil situations. This doesn't turn evil into goodness. It does, however, give us confidence that God would not allow an evil to happen if it were not possible for something good to come of it. Even though we can expect to continue to struggle to understand why evil exists, we trust that we will fully understand God's plan after we die. We will see God face-to-face and come to understand his ways of guiding the world.

Think About It!

We are called to be "coworkers" with God in the work of creation. What does this mean? Identify some examples of things people your age can do that help make the world around us what God wants it to be.

Our trust and hope are rooted in Jesus Christ. His suffering and death on the cross—his execution—were great evils, but that was not the end of the story. An amazing good followed. Jesus was raised from the dead and calls us to share in his new life.

We know that the final end to evil has not yet happened, but we live with the faith that it will. At that time God's plan for the world and for us will be fully realized.

Sin

One reason helps explain why some evil exists, and that reason is human sin. God created all people, "making them to be like himself" (Genesis 1:26). Another way to say this is that we are created in God's image. This means that we were created for love. For our love to be genuine, it must be something we freely choose to do. Think about it. If loving behavior is simply programmed into us, it isn't really love, is it? Because we have the freedom to choose to love, we also have the freedom to choose the opposite. We can choose to do things that are unloving. These choices separate us from God and from one another. Another word for this type of action is *sin*.

Any sin is like polluting the delicate balance in the environment of love God created. Even a small sin has a ripple effect. Can you think of an example?

© narvikk/iStockphoto.com

71

LiTURGY CONNECTioN

Gifts of Bread and Wine

At the next Sunday Mass, notice the bread and wine as they are carried to the altar during the Presentation and Preparation of the Gifts. These are God's gifts to us more than our gifts to God. We are simply giving back to God the things he has already given us. The gifts are from the earth (the grain for the bread) and the vine (the grapes for the wine). They are also the work of human hands, because we work to make bread from grain and wine from grapes. These gifts are signs of the goodness of God and of our cooperation with God. They are signs of our dependence on God's creation for our physical lives—just as we depend on God for our spiritual lives.

Sins also include things we should do but choose not to. Our sins can lead to results that harm other people and God's creation. Unfortunately, sin is a reality that affects us all because of Original Sin.

Adam and Eve, our first parents, whom we hear about in the Book of Genesis, rejected God's love in the Garden of Eden. By committing this sin, which we call Original Sin, they disrupted God's plan for creation. They wounded themselves and all of us by passing on to us a tendency to sin. The good news, however, is that God did not abandon us as a result of Adam and Eve's sin. His plan for creation continues to unfold in history. God's creation is not finished yet. He continues to work to bring about the loving relationships he desires.

The high point of God's plan for creation is Jesus Christ. In him God became man to save us. Christ is sometimes called the New Creation, because he came to give us new life. He came to restore and deepen our union with God.

The Journey of Creation

It is helpful to keep in mind that creation is not simply one event that happened a long time ago. God's love and presence are never-ending, and his work of creation keeps going. One way to imagine this is to think of the universe as a journey. God has a map for the journey and is guiding creation to a final end. Can you imagine all things being perfect and everyone being completely happy? This is the destiny of the human race. Everything has been created for us. This means that among all creatures, human beings are most valuable in God's eyes. This special place in creation comes with a responsibility.

> I am putting you in charge of the fish, the birds, and all the wild animals.
>
> Genesis 1:28

We trust in God's plan, but that doesn't mean we go about our lives just waiting for it to unfold. We have a part to play. We have a special role on this journey. We must keep our eyes open so we recognize God's presence in our lives and the world around us. What's more, we are called to cooperate with God and be his coworkers. This means we share in the responsibility of helping the world around us be what God wants it to be—a place where love rules. Our challenge is to think about God's desires for the world and all his creatures. We must make choices about our relationships and our care of the earth that

FUN FACT

Science confirms that creation isn't finished. Every second the universe grows larger, and the rate of growth keeps getting faster.

are in line with God's will. We don't do this on our own, however, apart from God. Through the Holy Spirit, God is always at work in our actions.

The Role of the Trinity in Creation

When Catholics talk about God as Creator, we are referring to all three Persons of the Trinity—Father, Son, and Holy Spirit. We associate Creation most closely with God the Father, but it is important to remember that the Father, Son, and Holy Spirit together are one God. If we think of the Father creating alone, we can make the mistake of thinking

God created the world, and it was good. How do we help one another restore the world to a place of peace and harmony where love rules? Why is care of the earth so important to peace among all God's people?

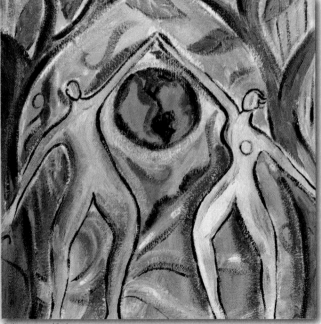

© Ikon Images/Corbis

Jesus Christ and the Holy Spirit came into being after the Father and are not one with him, even today. Saint Irenaeus offers a helpful image. He emphasizes that creation is the work of all three Persons of the Trinity by referring to the Son and the Spirit as the hands of the Father. God the Father keeps the universe going through his Word, Jesus Christ, and through the creative power of the Holy Spirit, the Giver of Life.

One symbol for the Trinity is an equilateral triangle—with three sides of equal length. This signifies that all three Persons—Father, Son, and Holy Spirit—are equal. The one triangle emphasizes that the Persons are unified and that they are one God.

Did You Know?

Creation and Creationism

Perhaps you have heard the word *creationism* in news stories about how the creation of the world is covered in public school classrooms. Creationists read the Bible like a science textbook and believe that the accounts of the Creation in Genesis are scientifically accurate. Creationists believe God created everything in a matter of days. This leads them to completely discount evolution, the scientific theory that life has changed over time from earlier forms of life. Catholic teaching about Creation differs. Catholics don't read Genesis like a science textbook, recognizing that biblical writers didn't write scientific reports. If we read the accounts of Creation as science, we would miss the main points and set up unintended conflicts between faith and science.

The Visible and the Invisible

When we pray the Nicene Creed, we describe God as the maker of both what is visible and what is invisible. We recognize that there is more to creation than the material things we can see and touch. Knowing of an invisible part of reality opens us up to the miraculous. It helps us understand that God is present and at work, even if we do not see any signs. Although we must be careful about making too many assumptions about the invisible aspects of creation, we know about one thing for certain: the existence of **angels**.

Angels are as real as you and me, but they are beings of spirit, not matter. They have intelligence, will, and individuality, and they are immortal. The word *angel* comes from a Greek word that means "messenger." Angels are God's servants and messengers. They glorify God without ceasing and watch over each of us every moment of our lives.

Live It!

Capture God's Creation

Keep a camera with you for a few days and snap photos of things that offer glimpses of the goodness of creation. Create a slide show or photo collage and share it with friends or family. Remember to thank God for all the goodness he has given us in creation.

People of Faith
Saint Francis of Assisi

© 2013 Saint Mary's Press/Illustration by Vicki Shuck

Can you imagine giving away all of your possessions and choosing to live in poverty? That's just what Saint Francis of Assisi did. He was born into a wealthy family in Italy in the twelfth century AD. Early in his life, Francis wanted to be popular and wealthy. In his twenties he spent time as a prisoner of war and then had a serious illness. While he was recovering, he had a dream that urged him to follow Jesus.

Francis felt called to live more as Jesus had lived. He started to live in a simpler way. He began to spend more of his time praying, preaching, and giving to the poor. Francis's father, a successful cloth merchant, wasn't happy with his son's new way of life. After Francis sold some expensive cloth from the family business to raise funds to rebuild a chapel, his father took him to court. Francis repaid the money, gave back his fine clothes, and gave up his share of his family's wealth. Many people were attracted to Francis's preaching and simple manner of living and began to follow him. This community became the Franciscan order of religious.

Francis is known also for his love of creation, including animals. He is the patron saint of environmentalists. We celebrate his feast day on October 4.

1 THE HUMAN PERSON

KEY WORDS

human person
soul
Original Sin
temptation

Steven was a seven-year-old boy much like most other kids his age. There was one big difference though. Most days after school, when his friends went home to play, Steven went to the hospital for regular medical treatments. Steven had leukemia, a type of blood cancer.

When Steven and his family first found out about his illness, they were angry. They wondered why God would let this happen to him. He did not do anything to deserve it. But as time moved along, Steven and his family began to focus on the

Have you ever considered why bad things, like the serious illness of a child, often bring out the best in families and communities?

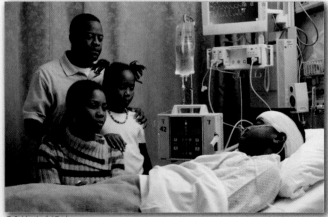

© Rubberball/Corbis

goodness of the many people who offered them help. Family members, friends, classmates, teachers, church members, doctors, nurses, and many other people helped Steven and his family. Even people whom Steven had never met played a big role in helping him regain his health.

After a while Steven and his family were no longer angry with God. They no longer spent their time wondering why this had happened to Steven. They were just grateful to God for the help that came from so many good people.

Being Human

For all of us, life can be a joyful, exciting, confusing, and painful experience. There is so much to experience in a single lifetime that we often forget to stop and look at the meaning of the events that occur.

We also do not always understand why things happen the way they do, especially the difficult or painful experiences. Being human also means we are not perfect, and therefore sometimes we all make bad decisions.

Being human is not all dark and dreary though. It also means we are not alone and have many people in our lives—family, friends, and the people in communities to which we belong. Being human also means we are made in God's

PRAY IT!

God, everything you have created is good. Every human being is your child, including me. Like all human beings, I am good because I am made to be like you. Even when I do something wrong, you love me. Please give me the courage to do what you have created me to do. Help me see others as you see them. Help me forgive others as you forgive them. Help me love others as you love me. Amen.

Fun Fact

In the Book of Genesis, the name that God gives the first human being is Adam. This is an appropriate name because *Adam* comes from the Hebrew word for "man." Eve's name is just as appropriate, because it comes from a Hebrew word that means "life."

image. We all have the ability to love and care for one another. For the most part, that is what we do. But the effects of sin often keep us from loving in the way God calls us to love—especially when it comes to loving the poor and vulnerable, as well as those with whom we don't get along. We must continually develop our ability to love as God wants us to love. His grace and mercy help us in our efforts.

Body and Soul

The **human person** is a living being made up of both a physical body and an immortal, spiritual soul. A **soul** is the spiritual element that gives humans life and survives after death.

Having fun with friends gives us a sign of how God made us—to be in relationship with one another.

© mandygodbehear/iStockphoto.com

Our soul is created by God at the moment of conception. After our death our soul will be reunited with our resurrected body at the final resurrection. It is important to remember that humans are not just physical bodies. God created us to be both body and soul, existing together in perfect unity.

You may notice that many young people look like their parents in some way. They might have similar-sounding voices or similar facial features. Sometimes they have the same color eyes or hair. That is because physical bodies are determined to a great extent by the parents' genes. When God made Adam, he formed the soil into his body and then breathed life into him (see Genesis 2:7). Like Adam, we also have God's breath or spirit within us. Each of us has a soul

?

Did You Know?

Not Just Our Souls

Because human beings are both physical and spiritual, the Church cares about all aspects of human life, not only our souls. For example, in 1891, Pope Leo XIII advocated that working people be paid appropriately and treated with dignity by their employers. During his papacy, Saint John XXIII wrote a letter that addressed human rights, freedom, and world peace. As Pope, in 1995 Saint John Paul II addressed a number of human life issues, such as abortion and the death penalty. In 2007 Pope Benedict even issued ten suggestions for driving to encourage us to be safe and responsible when we are on the road.

that comes from God and that is united with our bodies when we are conceived in our mothers' womb. Although our bodies will one day get old and die, our soul never will.

> **So God created human beings, making them to be like himself. . . . God looked at everything he had made, and he was very pleased.**
>
> Genesis 1:27,31

When God created Adam, he did not want him to be alone, so God created a companion for him. God does not want us to be alone, either. Just as the Trinity is a communion of Persons in loving relationship with one another, we are created to be in loving relationships with other people. The biggest evidence of this is that God created human beings to be male and female. Men and women are created to be equal but still different. Men are particularly good at some things. Women are especially good at others. God created us so that men and women would need each other and bond together in close relationship. This is why the union of one man and one woman in marriage is directly imprinted on the human family by God's Law. The Creation accounts in the Bible explain why human beings need communities, especially families.

Think About It!

God is not male or female. God is not a human being. God does not even have the same kind of physical presence humans have. But you are made in the image of God. There is something special about you that is like God. What makes you like God? What can you do that is similar to what God does?

Original Sin

The Scripture account of Adam and Eve explains how human beings were meant to live and how we fell away from God's plan. Adam and Eve represent the first human beings. At first, Adam and Eve were at peace with God. Because of this, they were also at peace with every living thing on the earth. They were happy and free, and experienced no pain or suffering.

God had given Adam and Eve just one rule to follow: "You may eat the fruit of any tree in the garden, except the tree that gives knowledge of what is good and what is bad" (Genesis 2:16–17). However, tempted by the serpent, they thought that by eating from the tree, they could know what God knows. Adam and Eve chose to disobey God. The first parents of the human race wrongly decided they could be happy without God and his guidance.

As a result, human beings were banished from the Garden of Eden. We separated ourselves from God. Because of Adam and Eve's choice, they and every human being since then—except Jesus and Mary—no longer had that same perfect relationship with God. We lost the freedom and the holiness we were meant to have.

This condition is called **Original Sin**. Original Sin means two things. First of all, it is the sin that Adam and Eve committed. Second, it is the sinful condition that all human beings have from birth. The first human beings' wrongdoing wounded them. Their wound, or the condition of Original Sin, was passed on to every human being. The grace we receive in Baptism washes us clean of Original Sin and makes us adopted children of God the Father, but we still struggle with the temptation to sin.

A **temptation** is something that makes sinful things seem fun, exciting, or even good to do. Original Sin makes it hard for us to resist temptation and makes us prone to sin. For example, have you ever seen someone drop money from a pocket without realizing it? If no one was nearby, you might have felt the temptation to pick up the money and keep it. Original Sin is what makes us want to be selfish rather than do what is good. It makes us think of our own pleasure instead of doing what is right.

You might think that Original Sin is not fair. Original Sin is much like the sick boy in the introduction to this chapter. He did not do anything to deserve the disease he had. He also didn't have a choice about being sick. Similarly, how Original Sin is transmitted is a mystery we do not fully understand. But we do

"Everybody does it." The temptation to cheat is an example of how Original Sin affects all of us. But the truth is we were born to be good. As Jesus said, "The truth will set you free."

© Lise Gagne/iStockphoto.com

know that it is passed on from one generation to the next. Except for Jesus and his mother, Mary, Original Sin affects every person.

Even though we all have the wound of Original Sin, we are not born evil. We are still created in God's image and have the desire to be united with God and to be good. Even though Original Sin affects us all, it does not stop us from returning to God.

Coming from God, Heading toward God

Have you have ever been away from home for a long time? If so, then you might know what it feels like to be homesick and want to return to the place where you are loved and things are familiar. This is also true in people's spiritual lives. Being with God is our true home. Returning to God is what will make us happy. Our worries and spiritual restlessness are kinds of spiritual homesickness.

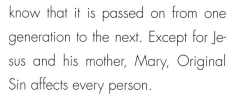

LITURGY CONNECTION

Sharing in the Divinity of Christ

During Mass there comes a moment when the priest pours a little bit of water into the wine. As he does this, he whispers something that the assembly usually cannot hear. He says, "By the mystery of this water and wine, may we come to share in the divinity of Christ, who humbled himself to share in our humanity." This mixing of the water and wine is a gesture that reminds us that the Son of God, the Second Divine Person of the Trinity, became one of us. The priest is also saying that humans are supposed to share in the divinity of Christ. We do that by receiving the Eucharist and also by living our faith so one day we will once again be in union with God.

© Anna Peisl/Corbis

An act of kindness is one way of being Christ's Body here on earth. When we help others, we are being the people God created us to be.

Human beings are all religious in the sense that we are all trying to find our spiritual homes. It is our job to help ourselves and others realize that being with God is our true home. This does not mean that God has left us. Even though we cannot physically see him, God is still with us.

There is one God and Father of all people, who is Lord of all, works through all, and is in all.

Ephesians 4:6

Christ is the model of the perfect human being. It is our destiny to live as he did. By doing God's will, we can become like Christ—his image for others to

LiVE IT!

Respect for God's Image

Every human being is made in the image of God. Remembering this when dealing with other people, especially people you do not like, can make a big difference in your relationships. It is easy to see the good in your friends and in those who do nice things for you. But God asks us to be good even to those whom we do not like. For example, when people insult you, you might want to strike back in the same way and hurt them like they hurt you. But when you do this, you sink to their level. On the other hand, if you respond with understanding and kindness, you acknowledge that these people are worthy of the same respect you deserve. When you do this, you allow them to see the image of God within you.

see. The following prayer, thought to be written by Saint Teresa of Ávila, says it best:

> Christ has no body now but yours,
>> no hands but yours,
>> no feet but yours.
> Yours are the eyes through which
>> Christ's compassion must look
>>> out on the world;
> Yours are the feet with which
>> He is to go about doing good.
> Yours are the hands with which
>> He is to bless us now.

Church History

Defending Humanity During War

During World War II (1939–1945), the world confronted a major threat to human life and dignity. Germany's Nazi Party did terrible things intended to wipe out the Jewish people, as well as people with disabilities and anyone they thought was homosexual. Germany and its allies also mistreated captured soldiers.

Pope Pius XII and the Vatican worked to save as many people as they could. Some were saved through diplomacy. Officials hid others in monasteries and convents in Rome. The Vatican even issued false baptismal certificates to protect Jews who might be discovered. All of this was dangerous work, because Italy fought on Germany's side. Historians believe the Vatican helped nearly 900,000 Jews and countless others escape capture.

8 THE BIBLE: COVENANTS

Trust is an extremely important part of life. We trust people so routinely that we often do not even think about it. We trust that our parents will have food for us to eat. We trust that our teachers will tell us the correct information. We trust that other drivers will obey the traffic laws. We trust that our friends will keep our private talks a secret. To ensure this trust, we sometimes make promises to each other.

Trust cannot be given all at once. Trust takes time, and it must be earned. How can you earn a friend's trust? How can someone earn your trust?

© Ocean/Corbis

Imagine what life would be like if you could trust no one. What would be different about getting in a car? How would your friendships change if you could not trust anyone with your secrets? What would it be like if you could not count on your parents to provide for you? Sooner or later you would probably become isolated and lonely. You would travel less, talk less, and rely on others less.

Fortunately, God is not like that. God is someone we can trust. Trusting God brings us closer to him. Throughout history he has made promises that he keeps. Yet we human beings have not always kept our part of the bargains. When we don't keep our promise, things fall apart. Despite our sins and weaknesses, God is always faithful in his promise to save us from sin and death. We can trust God because he has always been faithful to his promises.

God Gives Second Chances

We can read about many promises in the Bible that are part of salvation history. Some promises are between people or groups of people. But the most important promises are the ones between God and people. These are sacred

PRAY IT!

God, people are not perfect. My parents make mistakes. My friends do not always do what they promise. Teachers tell us to act one way, but even they sometimes act differently. We human beings are not perfect. We are easily tempted to sin. Guide me in choosing the path of goodness. Help me to trust in your righteousness. Even though I do not always understand your ways, I know you keep your promises. Amen.

A leap of faith is like jumping into the arms of God. We trust that he will always be there for us.

© urosr/Shutterstock.com

agreements between God and human beings, called covenants, where everyone vows to keep a promise forever. Even in the account of Adam and Eve in the Book of Genesis we see a hint of the covenants that God will make and keep later on.

God created Adam and Eve to live in happiness with him forever. The only condition was that they were to obey him. God told Adam: "You may eat the fruit of any tree of the garden, except the tree that gives knowledge of what is good and what is bad. You must not eat the fruit of that tree; if you do, you will die the same day" (Genesis 2:16–17). Sadly Adam and Eve disobeyed God by eating from the forbidden tree. As one consequence of their disobedience, they had to leave the Garden of Eden (see 3:23–24). Humans had separated themselves from God.

This does not mean God abandoned Adam and Eve to the power of sin and death. To the snake, God said: "I will make you and the woman hate each other; her offspring and yours will always be enemies. Her offspring will crush your head, and you will bite her offspring's heel" (Genesis 3:15). Sacred Tradition teaches us that the snake represents **Satan**, the fallen angel who is always looking for ways to tempt us to disobey God. God predicted that Eve's offspring would crush the snake's head, destroying his power forever. Tradition teaches us that the offspring of the woman is Jesus Christ. So as early as the story of Adam and Eve, God promised to deliver us from the power of sin and death.

Live It!

Keeping the Covenant with God

In a covenant all sides make commitments and promises to one another. As one of God's children, what are your responsibilities to him? On a sheet of paper, list everything that comes to mind when you think about your commitment to God. Be as specific as possible. Then look back at your list. What responsibilities are you meeting well? Which commitments need more of your attention? What promises can you add to make your faith more real and present in your daily life? For example, maybe you can set aside five minutes in the morning to pray for God's guidance throughout the day. Or you might add an examination of conscience to your routine before bed. Everything you do to become more aware of God's call each day will help you to grow in a loving relationship with him.

FUN FACT

In Scripture when God makes a covenant with someone, the person's name is often changed. For example, Abram became Abraham and his wife, Sarai, became Sarah. Jacob took on the name Israel. The name change symbolizes the new relationship with God.

Unfortunately, as time passed, people continued to sin. God saw the violence and corruption that filled the earth. He told Noah that he would destroy the whole earth and all its people because of their sinfulness (see Genesis 6:9–12). Chapters 7 and 8 in the Book of Genesis tell how God wiped out all the human wickedness from the earth with a flood. Noah, who had "found favor with the LORD" because of his righteousness (Genesis 6:8), was spared. After the Flood, only he and his family remained.

God then made a covenant with Noah, the first covenant described in the Bible (see Genesis 9:1–17). God promised Noah that he would never again destroy the human race with a flood. The Bible identifies the rainbow as the symbol of that covenant.

> "When the rainbow appears in the clouds, I will see it and remember the everlasting covenant between me and all living beings on earth."
>
> **Genesis 9:16**

Despite his people's sins, God still promised salvation. Like a good parent, God cared for his children. He gave them a second chance. Today we know that even when we do something wrong, God still loves us. He continues to give all of us second chances.

God's Covenants with Abraham, Moses, and David

Throughout salvation history God has called certain individuals to lead his people back to him. The first was Abraham, the father of our faith, through whom God established his people. When God called Abraham, he and his wife, Sarah, were childless. They were also already old and had given up hope of having children (see Genesis 11:29–12:5).

God made a covenant with Abraham. He promised to give him land and many descendants, who would be a blessing to all people (see Genesis 15:1–6 and 17:1–9). In return Abraham promised

Did You Know?

Other Promises in the Bible

We can read about many promises in the Bible and can learn from them. Here are a few:

- Ruth's promise to follow her mother-in-law (see Ruth 1:6–17)
- God's promise that he knows us completely (see Psalm 139)
- Isaiah's promise to be God's messenger (see Isaiah 6:1–8)
- Peter's promise never to deny Jesus (see Mark 14:27–31,66–72)

to be faithful to God. Amazingly Abraham and Sarah had a son in their old age. The son's name was Isaac. Abraham's many descendants became God's **Chosen People**, the Israelites.

At the end of the Book of Genesis, we find that the Israelites had to migrate to Egypt because of a food shortage. Eventually Egypt's ruler, the Pharaoh, forced the Israelites to become slaves. When the Israelites cried out to God to deliver them, God called a man named Moses to lead them to freedom. Moses confronted Pharaoh and through God's power led the Israelites out of slavery (see Exodus, chapters 1–14).

While the Israelites traveled through the desert, they stopped at a holy mountain, Mount Sinai. Through Moses, God appeared to them there and made a new covenant—called the Mosaic Covenant or the Sinai Covenant—with his Chosen People. He promised to be their God and protect them if they would be his people and obey his Law. Moses received the Law from God and brought it to the Israelites. The **Ten Commandments** summarize the Law Moses received. Through the Law, God told the Israelites how he wanted them to live. The Law guided all parts of the Israelites' daily lives. Following the

Think About It!

A covenant spells out the relationship we have with someone. When we are in a good, healthy relationship, each person in the relationship fulfills his or her commitments to the other person. What are the most important relationships in your life? What are your commitments in those relationships? How well are you keeping them? A sign of your covenant with God can be found in how well you are keeping your important commitments to other people.

Law was the Israelites' responsibility under their covenant with God (see Exodus, chapters 19–20).

We find one other important covenant in the Old Testament: a promise that God made to King David. David wanted to build a temple to honor God. But through Nathan the prophet, God told David not to build him a temple. Rather, God said, David's son would be the one to build him a temple (see 2 Samuel 7:1–16). Then God promised something more. He told David: "You will always have descendants, and I will make your kingdom last forever. Your dynasty will never end" (2 Samuel 7:16).

If you know salvation history, you might spot a problem with this covenant that God made with David. After nineteen of David's descendants ruled as kings of Israel, the kingdom was conquered by the Babylonians. A descendant of David would never again sit on the throne in Jerusalem, the capital city of Israel. But Scripture and Tradition teach us that God's covenant with David was not about an earthly kingdom. God's promise was about the eternal Kingdom of God. Jesus Christ was a descendant of David (see Matthew 1:1). He established the Kingdom of God and then ascended into Heaven to rule there as the Prince of Peace forever. When we turn to the New Testament, we can see that all of God's covenants in the Old Testament are fulfilled, and all his promises have come true.

LITURGY CONNECTION

Eucharistic Prayer IV

The Eucharistic Prayer begins with a short dialogue between the priest and the people. The priest urges us to lift up our hearts in prayer and to give thanks to God. After we agree to join with him in prayer, the priest prays a long prayer that explains exactly why we are praising and thanking God in this Eucharist. This long prayer, which includes the consecration of the bread and wine, making them the Body and Blood of Christ, is called the Eucharistic Prayer.

There are four Eucharistic Prayers. Eucharistic Prayer IV retells the story of salvation. It recounts the disobedience that lost God's friendship, but also affirms that God never gave up on his people. Over and over again, God offered them covenants—promises that he would be with them and that in him they would find salvation.

The New Covenant

All through history God has been faithful to his promise of salvation. When we human beings have gone astray, he has sent his prophets to guide us. In his greatest act of salvation, God became one of us. In the New Testament, we can read how he fully revealed himself by sending his only Son. Through his Son, Jesus Christ, he established the covenant forever (see Luke 22:19–20). This is sometimes called the **New Covenant**, but it is really the fulfillment of the covenants God made with Noah, Abraham, Moses, and David. You will read much more about Jesus in later chapters.

The Good News that God's promise of salvation was now fulfilled in Jesus Christ was preached to everyone. Jesus gave his Apostles the power to carry on his mission. They passed their work on to others. They passed it down too. This continued through the centuries to us today. The Holy Spirit continues to guide the Church and will do so until Christ returns. When Christ returns, God's promise of salvation will be complete.

> And the LORD said to himself, "I will not hide from Abraham what I am going to do. His descendants will become a great and mighty nation, and through him I will bless all the nations."
>
> Genesis 18:17–18

Church History

Mary, Mother of the Church

Mary was named Mother of the Church by Pope Paul VI in 1964. This was a new title for Mary, but it acknowledged something the Church, the Body of Christ, has always known: Mary is our Mother. Mary is Mother of the Church because she is the Mother of Christ. At Baptism we are made part of Christ's Body, the Church.

Even before Mary was officially given this title, many popes had spoken of Mary as Mother of the Church, beginning with Pope Leo XIII. Later, both Pope Saint John XXIII and Pope Paul VI spoke of Mary in this way.

For example, in his teachings on Mary, Pope Paul VI often refers to the *Dogmatic Constitution on the Church* from Vatican Council II, which called her "a most beloved mother" (53). In a speech at the end of the third session of the Council, he proclaimed her "Mary, Mother of the Church."

This title for Mary was adopted enthusiastically by the Church. Many new parishes established after Vatican Council II have taken the name "Mary, Mother of the Church."

9 Faith: Responding to God

Some of life's most difficult questions are matters of faith. God does not expect us to have all the answers.

Often people say you need to have faith. They might say, "Keep the faith" or "Have faith in God." Has anyone ever asked if you have faith in God? Have you ever considered what your response would be? Maybe your first thought was, "Yes, of course I do!" If so, that is a fine answer. Maybe this is the first time you have ever thought about it, and you do not have a quick answer. That is okay too. Just considering the question is one of the first steps of faith. This chapter will look into what having faith means. Afterward, you may realize you have more faith than you thought you did.

© Junial Enterprises/Shutterstock.com

What Is Faith?

Throughout history God has called upon people to follow his will. **Faith** is the way people respond to God's call. On a simple level, faith means a belief in God. For Christians it means more than that. Faith is believing and accepting that God made himself known to us through his words and actions, especially through Jesus Christ. It is accepting God's truth with our minds. Faith is something that guides our entire lives.

In a way it would be simple to say, "I believe that Jesus Christ is the Son of God, who is our Savior." It would be easy if that was all that was required for salvation. But having faith also requires us to live our lives based on this belief. The following short story illustrates this point.

A two-year-old boy is playing on a wooden playground structure that has all sorts of slides, swings, and ropes to climb. He runs toward a ledge near where his father is standing. As he gets closer to the ledge, his father smiles and moves closer, because he knows exactly what is going to happen. The little boy stops at the edge of the five-foot drop and starts to laugh. Then he throws his arms up over his head and flings his body into the air toward his father. As the dad has done a hundred times before, he reaches out and catches the boy. The boy is not even finished with his laughing before he runs back around to make the jump again.

To leap into his father's arms, the boy has to have faith in his father. He has to trust that his father will catch him.

PRAY IT!

Jesus, I am like the man who cried out to you: "I do have faith, but not enough. Help me have more!" (Mark 9:24). Sometimes it seems like my faith is as small as a mustard seed. But with even that much faith, you said I could do anything. With you nothing is impossible. I place my trust in you, knowing you will not disappoint me. Amen.

FUN FACT

When God promised Abraham and Sarah that they would be the parents of many descendants, they were so old that Sarah laughed at the thought. But Abraham and Sarah kept their faith in God. When their son was born, they named him Isaac, a Hebrew name that means "laughter."

Leaping is just the final step in his act of faith. Because he believes and trusts his father, it is the natural thing to do. A person with faith in God is like the child who leaps into the hands of his father.

Faith Is a Gift Freely Chosen

Faith is necessary for salvation and is a gift from God. Someone cannot have faith without the Holy Spirit, who helps us see our need for God. Before a person can have this gift of faith, he or she must first have the freedom to choose it. Being faithful can be achieved only by someone who understands and freely chooses to believe in God and his Church.

You might think, "My parents force me to go to Mass and practice my faith, so how can I ever freely choose it?" Think of it this way. What would you do

A leap of faith is like jumping into the arms of God. We trust that he will always be there for us.

© JulieVMac/iStockphoto.com

if someone offered you a box and said that if you accepted it, you would carry it around for the rest of your life? You would want to know what was in the box before you made a decision, right? Without looking inside it, you cannot really make a choice. The box is like the faith God wants to give you. It often comes to you through the words and examples of your parents. If you are ever going to choose to accept the faith God offers, you must look into it. You have to learn about it before you accept it. Only then can you really make a free and informed decision.

Faith Is Believing

Having faith means you believe, or accept something to be true. Christians believe in the life, death, and Resurrection of Jesus Christ. At Mass, we declare our core beliefs when we pray the Nicene Creed. A

Did You Know?

The "Heart" of Our Beliefs

The word *belief* can be traced back to Old English and Old High German words that mean "to hold dear and to love." The word *creed* can be traced back to two Latin words, *cor* and *do*. *Cor* means "heart" and *do* means "I give." So when we say our creed, or our beliefs, we are doing more than just saying the things that we think. We are stating what is in our hearts. A creed is the set of beliefs to which our hearts are devoted.

creed is an official statement of one's faith, or what one believes.

Believing is also an act of the entire Church. Don't confuse Church—with a capital *C*—with a building. The Church is the community of faithful people who put their faith in Jesus Christ. In a way your first Church is your family. It is the Church that teaches you. It is the Church that is a role model for you. It is the Church that supports and nourishes your own faith. Without your family and the Church, there is no one to pass on the faith.

Belief is not the end of the road when it comes to having faith. In fact, believing is only the beginning. Belief is the foundation on which the rest of our faith is built.

Faith Is Trusting

Having faith also means you trust. Trust is when you confidently turn control of your life (or part of your life)

The words from the beginning of the Nicene Creed are probably familiar to you. Check out the rest of the Creed in appendix A, Catholic Prayers.

Nicene Creed

I believe in one God, the Father almighty,

maker of heaven and earth,

of all things visible and invisible,

I believe in one Lord Jesus Christ,

© Saint Mary's Press

over to someone or something else with hope. If you have ever worked on a school project with others, you know what it is like to trust. Working hard on your part of the project, you trust that your partners will complete their parts. You have given some of the control over your grade to your partners with hope that they will do their jobs.

When we trust God, we acknowledge that we cannot ever be truly happy without him. We can do our part, but without God, our "project," which is our lives, will never be complete. So having faith means we trust God—we put God in control of our lives.

Trusting God is a required ingredient of faith. Trusting him does not mean things will always go the way we want them to go. Human beings are not perfect. We often bring much misery and pain upon ourselves. By trusting God and allowing him to lead our lives, we will give and receive more joy and happiness in this world and in the next.

> I assure you that if you have faith as big as a mustard seed, you can say to this hill, "Go from here to there!" and it will go. You could do anything!
>
> Matthew 17:20

THINK About It!

Being a faith-filled person does not mean all your questions will be answered. It also does not mean you will never have another doubt. God is mysterious, and it is part of your human nature to ask questions about who he is and about our faith in him. But your questions can bring you closer to God. How could bringing your doubts and questions to God in prayer be helpful in your spiritual life? What questions do you have for God?

Faith Is Doing

Finally, having faith means you do something about it. Doing means you act upon what you believe. In fact, without the doing, someone could argue that you don't have faith at all. You may have heard the saying "The proof is in the pudding." This means we see the true significance of ideas or beliefs when they are put into action. This applies to faith too. Your actions make real your belief and trust in God. The Letter of James says it best, as follows:

> My friends, what good is it for one of you to say that you have faith if your actions do not prove it? Can that faith save you? Suppose there are brothers or sisters who need clothes and don't have enough to eat. What good is there in your saying to them, "God bless you! Keep warm and eat well!"—if you don't give them the necessities of life? So it is with faith: if it is alone and includes no actions, then it is dead. (2:14–17)

Mother Teresa used the words "Jesus in disguise" to describe those who are most in need of our help. Like Mother Teresa, when we reach out to others, we are putting our faith into action.

© Gideon Mendel/Corbis

Faith in God Alone

Christianity is **monotheistic**, meaning we believe in only one God. Yet even we who call ourselves Christians do not always completely place our trust in God alone. Instead we sometimes look to money or worldly power for our protection. We can also spend too much time and attention trying to get lots of stuff. We begin to think we can be happy only when we have the best sports equipment, the newest video games, or whatever new thing catches our eye. Those things become like false gods when we forget that our true happiness can be found only in God. None of us is perfect, but as our faith in God grows, we will not allow anyone or anything to substitute for him. God is our true home, and we will be truly satisfied only by doing his will and being with him.

> Israel, remember this! The Lord— and the Lord alone—is our God.
>
> Deuteronomy 6:4

Liturgy Connection

Prayer of the Faithful

Every time we celebrate Mass, we offer our petitions, or requests, in what is called the Prayer of the Faithful. Here we ask God to fulfill our needs. In doing so we trustfully place our needs in God's hands. It does not mean that we expect God to give us all that we ask for.

God does not grant our every wish. We do not always understand why. Nonetheless, we trust that he will provide what is best for us. Next time during the Prayer of the Faithful, offer your own needs to God and trust that he will provide what is best for you.

Some Christians have chosen to give up all they have to place their faith in God alone. Some missionaries, for example, leave their homes to work in the poorest areas of the world. They choose to abandon the comfort and security of their homes. Led by their belief in the Good News of Jesus Christ, they trust God's call and act upon it.

Even Jesus was tempted to rely on something other than God. When he was in the desert, the devil tried to convince Jesus to look for material things and worldly power to save himself. Jesus replied "Go away, Satan! The scripture says, 'Worship the Lord your God and serve only him!'" (Matthew 4:10).

Small Things, Great Love

Mother Teresa is a wonderful inspiration for those who want to be faithful to God. But the stories about saintly people like her overwhelm many people. Many might think, "I could never be as great as she was," and then decide to do nothing. Mother Teresa did not see herself as someone great. She saw her work as simple—not easy, just simple. She read the Gospels. She believed in Jesus' call to serve those who are the neediest in our world. She trusted that God would help her. Then she went out and did it. When asked about her work, she emphasized that faithful people did not have to help the entire world. They just needed to help one person. She said, "We do no great things, only small things with great love." What is a small thing you can do with great love?

People of Faith
Blessed Mother Teresa

© 2013 Saint Mary's Press/Illustration by Vicki Shuck

Blessed Mother Teresa was a woman of great faith. She was born Gonxha Agnes Bojaxhiu in 1910 in Skopje, Macedonia. At age eighteen, she joined the Sisters of Loreto and took the name Teresa after Saint Thérèse of Lisieux. Teresa served as a school teacher in Calcutta, India, for almost twenty years.

Following an encounter with Christ in which she heard him tell her, "Come, be my light," Teresa was inspired to help those who suffered from the most extreme poverty. In 1948, after a few years of prayer and determination, Mother Teresa received permission to leave her convent to work with the poor in the streets of Calcutta. She soon formed the Missionaries of Charity, who set up hospitals and homes for the dying. In 1979 this "saint of the gutters" was awarded the Nobel Peace Prize for her work. By the 1990s the Missionaries of Charity could be found all over the world, helping homeless people, abused women, and orphans, as well as those suffering from AIDS, drug addiction, and other illnesses.

Mother Teresa died in 1997. She left behind a thriving order of priests, nuns, and laypersons devoted to the service of the neediest people in our world. Pope John Paul II beatified Mother Teresa in 2002. After she died, her private letters revealed that she had overcome many years of spiritual doubt and anguish. Despite these feelings, she trusted God and kept hard at work at her mission.

10 THE BIBLE: THE PROPHETS

KEY WORD

Messiah

Good friends encourage us to be our best selves. Friends who encourage us to take the wrong path are not true friends at all.

© Helder Almeida/Shutterstock.com

We all get on the wrong path of life sometimes. For some people the wrong path means holding on to anger and resentment. For other people the wrong path could mean telling little lies that turn into bigger and bigger lies. And for others the wrong path could be as serious as developing an addiction to alcohol, drugs, or pornography.

What kind of friend would you want to have if you start going down a wrong path of life? A friend who is brave and honest enough to tell you that what you are doing is wrong and that you need to change? Or a friend who pretends that everything is okay? The friend who is honest enough to tell you that you need to change is a true friend indeed. That friend loves you so much that he or she is willing to risk your friendship by telling you a truth that you need to hear, even if you do not want to hear it.

The prophets were the true friends of the Chosen People. When God called the prophets to tell the Israelites to change their lives, they bravely spoke the truth. Many times this caused trouble for the prophets because the kings and the people did not want to change. The prophets were ridiculed and imprisoned. Some even had their lives threatened. Yet they were faithful in speaking God's Word because of their great love for God and his people.

> "Then I heard the Lord say, 'Whom shall I send? Who will be our messenger?'
>
> I answered, 'I will go! Send me!'"
>
> Isaiah 6:8

The Non-Writing Prophets

A prophet is someone who speaks for God. In the earliest parts of salvation history, there was no need for prophets, because God spoke directly to people like Adam and Eve, Noah, and Abraham. But as salvation history progressed, God spoke directly to special individuals only—the prophets, who then carried his message to his

PRAY IT!

Lord, help me to go into the world to care for those who are oppressed and needy, to speak out against injustice, and to proclaim the Good News. Grant me the gifts of the prophets who have gone before me.

Grant me courage.

Moses, pray for me.

Grant me humility.

Jeremiah, pray for me.

Grant me trust.

Isaiah, pray for me.

All you holy people, pray for me! Amen.

FUN FACT

The most reluctant prophet in the Bible is Jonah. When God called him to go to Nineveh with his message, Jonah ran in the opposite direction!

people. Moses was the first of these special people. Joshua was another, followed by the judges. All these people can be considered prophets. You can read more about them in chapter 5, "The Bible: The Old Testament," of this handbook.

When Israel was ruled by kings, the prophets were a very important part of salvation history. It seemed that the more the kings focused on the things that kings do—fighting wars, building forts and cities, making laws—the more they forgot their covenant with God. So God kept sending prophets to remind the kings to keep their covenant with him. Today we can read the words of some of these prophets in their books, found in the fourth section of the Old Testament. But some prophets who preached during the time of the kings do not have their own books. We learn about them in the historical books of the Old Testament. Those prophets are called the non-writing prophets. Let's take a closer look at the most famous non-writing prophets, Elijah and Elisha.

We read about Elijah in the First Book of Kings. God sent Elijah to speak to King Ahab. Ahab was a king of Israel, the northern kingdom. He was one of the worst kings we learn about in the Bible. Ahab married a foreign woman, Jezebel, who became queen. Ahab and Jezebel worshipped Baal and Asherah, a false god and goddess (see 1 Kings 16:29–33). This is what the Bible says about Ahab:

"He did more to arouse the anger of the LORD, the God of Israel, than all the kings of Israel before him" (1 Kings 16:33). So God sent Elijah to confront this evil king and queen.

To prove to Ahab, Jezebel, and the people that the Lord is the true God, Elijah challenged the prophets of Baal to a contest (see 1 Kings, chapter 18). In the contest, Elijah and the prophets of Baal each made altars and piled them with wood and a sacrifice. Then they each prayed to their god to light the fire. The prophets of Baal prayed and prayed, but nothing happened. Then Elijah prayed, and the Lord incinerated the sacrifice, the wood, and the stones

Live It!

Live the Prophetic Mission

Whom does God call to be a prophet today? You! By virtue of your Baptism, you are called to participate in the priestly, prophetic, and kingly ministry of Christ. That means you don't need to be an ordained priest to share the Good News with the world. You can witness to Christ through every word and action, in every circumstance in which you find yourself.

How can you be a prophet to your community today? What messages about faithfulness to God's Law do your friends, family, or school need to hear? What social causes need you to speak out? Whom can you reassure about God's love in the midst of suffering? Take some time today to pray for the courage to live your faith publicly and to share your faith with others.

Liturgy Connection

The Prophets Today

In our liturgy the prophets still speak the Word of God to us today.

During Advent we often read the beautiful messianic prophecies of the prophet Isaiah. Other prophets we hear during Advent include Jeremiah, Baruch, and Micah.

During the Sundays of Lent, we hear the words of the prophets Jeremiah and Ezekiel, and, during the Easter Vigil, the six readings include the words of three prophets: Isaiah, Baruch, and Ezekiel.

During Ordinary Time we read many different sections of the Old Testament, including the prophets.

The only time we do not read from the Old Testament at Mass is during the Easter season. At that time the first reading is from the Acts of the Apostles, which recounts how the Apostles spread the Good News of Christ's Resurrection, which was the fulfillment of the hopes of all the prophets.

of the altar! No one could doubt whose god was real. Elijah also performed several miracles, including bringing a boy back to life. You can read about Elijah in 1 Kings, chapters 17–19, and 2 Kings, chapters 1–2.

Elijah recruited Elisha to be his helper (see 1 Kings 19:19–21). At the end of his life, Elijah was taken into Heaven in a chariot of fire. Then Elisha took Elijah's cloak to wear (see 2 Kings 2:1–18), symbolizing that Elijah's role as prophet passed to Elisha. So Elisha became a mighty prophet who performed many miracles. Through the power of God, Elisha multiplied olive oil for a poor widow, multiplied loaves of bread to feed hungry prophets, and brought a dead boy back to life. (Elisha's miracles may remind you of Jesus' miracles.) You can read about Elisha in 2 Kings, chapters 2–8. Through the words and actions of Elijah and Elisha, we learn that God punishes evil people and takes care of those who are suffering and poor.

The Classical Prophets

In the Old Testament, the words and actions of sixteen prophets are recorded in sixteen books named after them. These prophets are sometimes called the classical prophets or the writing prophets. Let's look at one minor prophet, Amos, and one major prophet, Ezekiel. (See the Did You Know? sidebar below for an explanation of these terms.)

Amos was the first of the classical prophets. He prophesied in Israel almost eight hundred years before the birth of Christ. We know little about the life of Amos. He was not a full-time prophet; rather, he was a shepherd and tree pruner (see Amos 7:14–15). God called him from his simple life to challenge the injustice in Israelite society. During this time some very wealthy people lived in Israel, but so did some very poor people. This injustice went against God's covenant with his Chosen People.

Did You Know?

Major Prophets and Minor Prophets

The Books of Isaiah, Jeremiah, and Ezekiel are quite long, so these three prophets are called the major prophets. The other prophets, whose books are shorter, are called the minor prophets. These labels do not mean that the major prophets are more important than the minor prophets. They only describe the length of the books of the prophets.

Amos was a clever preacher. In chapter 1 of the Book of Amos, we read how he condemned the sinfulness of foreign nations. So his listeners might have been thinking, "Oh good, he's not talking about us." But by chapter 2, we can see that Amos began to condemn the sins of the people of Israel. He did not hold back at all:

> The LORD says, "The people of Israel have sinned again and again, and for this I will certainly punish them. They sell into slavery honest people who cannot pay their debts, the poor who cannot repay even the price of a pair of sandals. They trample down the weak and helpless and push the poor out of the way." (Verses 6–7)

As terrible as the sins of the other nations were, God considered the sins of Israel even worse because they had the advantage of their covenant relationship with him. Amos continued his prophecies, predicting the destruction of Israel (see Amos, chapter 6). His words were mostly words of condemnation and doom. But his book concludes with hope-filled words, saying that God would rebuild the nation after its destruction (see Amos 9:11–15).

Ezekiel lived about two hundred years after Amos. He was a priest in the very first group of people taken to Babylon during the Exile. He did all of his prophesying from this foreign country. Jerusalem and the Temple had not yet been destroyed, so Ezekiel's early preaching was a warning that the final end of the kingdom was coming. To get his point across, God had Ezekiel perform symbolic acts. Ezekiel had to lay on his side for 430 days to symbolize the number of years the people of Israel and Judah would be punished. He had to bake his food on cow dung to symbolize that the Israelites would eat unclean food during the Exile (see Ezekiel 4:4–15). He even had to cut off all the hair on his head and then burn a third of it, chop up a third of it, and scatter a third in the wind. This symbolized how the Chosen People would be killed and scattered by the Babylonians (see 5:1–12).

© Fridmar Damm/Corbis

The Book of Ezekiel isn't all doom and gloom though. The last third of the book contains many hopeful prophecies that God would rescue his people after their punishment. Ezekiel described God as the Good Shepherd who would rescue his sheep after the destruction (see Ezekiel 34:11–31). In another famous prophecy, Ezekiel saw dry bones coming back to life:

The Prophet Ezekiel assured the people that God is not a God of death but of life and hope. Jesus, the Son of God, fulfilled these promises.

> God said to me, "Mortal man, the people of Israel are like these bones. They say that they are dried up, without any hope and with no future.
>
> When I open the graves where my people are buried and bring them out, they will know that I am the LORD. I will put my breath in them,

bring them back to life, and let them live in their own land. Then they will know that I am the Lord." (37:11,13–14)

As a priest, Ezekiel was very interested in the Temple in Jerusalem. The last chapters of his book describe a vision that the Temple will be rebuilt. Because the Temple is a symbol of God's presence with his Chosen People, this vision is a promise that God has not abandoned his people.

THiNk AbouT IT!

The biblical prophets called the people to return to God when they began to worship false gods and disobey God's Law. Then during the Exile, the prophets also reassured the people that God had not abandoned them. If the prophets were alive today, what societal situations do you think God would call them to address? What false idols would God tell them to warn us against?

The Hope for a Messiah

Through their words and actions, the prophets prepared the Chosen People for the coming of the Son of God, Jesus Christ. They reminded the people to show their faith in God by following the Law and the covenant. They told the people about God's love and forgiveness. They urged the people to take responsibility for their actions and to ask God to forgive their sins. These are teachings that Jesus Christ emphasized and fulfilled. But the most important way the prophets prepared people for the coming of Christ was by telling them that God would send a savior, who would also be called the **Messiah**. *Messiah* is a Hebrew word that means "anointed one" (the Greek word *Christ* means the same thing).

Let's look at one prophet, the prophet Isaiah, to see what he revealed about the Messiah. Isaiah was a very famous writing prophet whose book contains not only the words of the original Isaiah but also the words of some of his later followers. The original Isaiah lived during the period when the Assyrians were invading Israel and Judah. His words are recorded in the first thirty-nine chapters of the Book of Isaiah. Then during the Babylonian Exile, a follower of Isaiah (sometimes called Second Isaiah) comforted the Chosen People with a hopeful message. His words are recorded in Isaiah, chapters 40–55. Finally, after the Israelites returned from Exile and resettled in the Promised Land, another follower of Isaiah (sometimes called Third Isaiah) challenged them to be faithful to their covenant with God. His words are recorded in Isaiah, chapters 56–66.

All three Isaiahs offered prophecies that were fulfilled in the life, death, and Resurrection of Jesus Christ, the Messiah. For example, the Book of Isaiah foretold that a virgin would give birth to a child named Emmanuel, meaning "God is with us" (see Isaiah 7:14). Isaiah also explained that the Messiah would be filled with the Lord's Spirit for his public ministry: "To bring good news to the poor, / To heal the broken-hearted, / To announce release to captives, / . . . to comfort all who mourn" (Isaiah 61:1–2). And several passages in Isaiah describe a servant who would be beaten, insulted, and finally put to death for the forgiveness of our sins (see 50:4–9, 52:13—53:12).

As we know, all of these prophecies were fulfilled in Jesus Christ. He was the Son of God who became man and was born of a virgin, Mary. The angel Gabriel told Mary that Jesus would be called Emmanuel (the Son of God) (see Luke 1:34–38). The Holy Spirit descended on Jesus at his Baptism (see Mark 1:10). In fact, Jesus began his public ministry by reading that same passage of Isaiah 61:1–2 in the synagogue, concluding, "This passage of scripture has come true today, as you heard it being read" (Luke 4:21). And we now understand that Jesus was the Suffering Servant described in Isaiah— the servant who was beaten, insulted, and crucified for the forgiveness of our sins (see Mark 15:16–20, Matthew 26:26–28, Luke 24:44–47).

It is amazing to see how prophets like the three Isaiahs clearly described Jesus and his mission. Through them, God prepared the Chosen People for the completion of his plan of salvation, through the life, death, Resurrection, and Ascension of Jesus Christ.

> "The LORD has told us what is good. What he requires of us is this: to do what is just, to show constant love, and to live in humble fellowship with our God."
>
> Micah 6:8

CHURCH HISTORY

Prophetic Missionaries and Saints in Latin America

Beginning in the 1500s, Europeans sailed to Latin America to colonize the lands and conquer the native peoples. They were accompanied by missionaries who sought to share the Gospel of Christ with the Indians. Many missionaries cared for the poor and sick, and they worked to defend and protect the native peoples as well as the African slaves the Europeans were transporting to the New World.

Saint Martin de Porres, the illegitimate son of a freed slave and a Spanish noble, personally experienced the cruel treatment of the lower classes in his native Peru. He dedicated his life to caring for the poor and mistreated in Peru. Saint Peter Claver, a Spanish missionary working in Colombia, was horrified by the plight of African slaves who were brought to Cartagena in unspeakable conditions. He tended to their physical needs, but he also actively and publicly defended their rights. And Bartolomé de las Casas, another Dominican friar and Spanish missionary, was an outspoken defender of the Indians who were suffering at the hands of European colonizers. His message was simple: You will win over many more converts to Christ if you treat them with respect and dignity.

Can you think of other saints and holy people who, like the prophets, called for justice in their societies?

11 JESUS CHRIST, TRUE GOD AND TRUE MAN

KEY WORDS

Incarnation
Messiah
mediator

Imagine getting some really unbelievable good news. Imagine you've tried out for the basketball team but figured you had no chance of starting, or that you tried out for the school play but didn't expect to get the part. Or imagine you'd love to have another child in the family, but your parents have said it wasn't possible. Then suddenly you learn your dream has come true. You're named a starter. You're chosen to play the part. You're going to have a little brother or sister.

Can you think of some great news you have received? Think about all the people you wanted to tell. For the past two thousand years, the Church has been telling the best news ever.

© forestpath/Shutterstock.com

As good as news like this is, the Church has even better news for all people. The Gospel of John tells it as follows: "The Word became a human being, and full of grace and truth, lived among us. We saw his glory, the glory which he received as the Father's only Son" (1:14). This incredible Good News of the Gospels is called the mystery of the **Incarnation**, the truth that Jesus Christ, the Son of God and the Second Person of the Trinity, is both fully God and fully man. He took on our human nature, which means that the Son of God became one with us. By doing this, Jesus makes it possible for us to get to know him, trust him, love him, follow him, and show him to others.

> He always had the nature of God, but . . . of his own free will he gave up all he had, and took the nature of a servant. He became like a human being and appeared in human likeness.
>
> Philippians 2:6–7

Who Is Jesus Christ?

How do we get to know who Jesus Christ is? We might start by thinking about how we get to know and understand people in general. We spend time working, playing, and relaxing with them. We think about what they say and do. We get to know them as persons. We get to know their talents and abilities.

Pray It!

Jesus, help me to honor and love you as my Savior, Lord, and God in all my thoughts, words, and actions. Teach me through your holy life to live a holy life too. Through the Holy Spirit, give me the grace to know and follow your teachings with humility, generosity, and persistence. Amen.

© Brooklyn Museum/Corbis

Jesus wept when his friend died. He must have laughed sometimes too, because he was one of us. He was like us in all things except sin and experienced the same emotions we do.

We get to know Jesus Christ in a similar way, but because his earthly life is long in the past, we have to rely on the reports of others who were with him at the time. Those reports are part of God's Revelation, which is passed on to us through Scripture and Tradition. What do Scripture and Tradition tell us about Jesus?

They show us that Jesus is a Divine Person with two natures. He keeps the divine nature that he has had for eternity. He also took on our human nature. He is not just God or just man or some sort of half-and-half mix of the two. He is truly and fully divine and truly and fully human, but without sin.

Jesus Christ is truly human, like us. He grew, walked, talked, worked, had friends, and joked around. He enjoyed meeting and talking with all kinds of people. When Jesus' friend Lazarus died and when Jesus thought about how his own people would reject him, he cried. He enjoyed a good meal, good talk, the beauty of flowers, and the innocence of children. He got hungry, tired, and angry. When people ignored him or were ungrateful, his feelings were hurt.

The Son of God . . . worked with human hands; he thought with a human mind. He acted with a human will, and with a human heart he loved. Born of the Virgin Mary, he has truly been made one of us, like to us in all things except sin.[1] (CCC, 470)

Jesus Christ is truly God. We see in the Gospels that he did things only God can do. He performs miracles of healing and raises the dead. He forgives sins and foretells the future. He dares to explain and add to God's teachings from the Old Testament. Simon Peter calls Jesus "the Son of the living God," and Jesus agrees, saying, "For this truth did not come to you

Live It!

Getting to Know Jesus

How can we get to know Jesus better?

To learn more about Jesus and grow in your relationship with him, begin by paying special attention to the Good News of his life and lessons. We can read Sacred Scripture on our own and listen to the Word of God at Mass.

We can speak with Jesus. We can pray to him in a group or on our own. The Holy Spirit will use our openness to Jesus to help us grasp his life and message.

We can be touched by Christ in the Sacraments, especially the Eucharist. Jesus works through them to help us know and follow him better.

We can see Christ shine through the witness of faithful people. We can study the lives of saints and learn to see goodness in people we know. Jesus gives us many ways to build our relationship with him.

© Brooklyn Museum/Corbis

Miracles, like Jesus'
walking on water, are
signs of Jesus' divinity.
He truly is God.

from any human being, but it was given to you directly by my Father in heaven" (Matthew 16:16–17).

Jesus has existed from the beginning of time, before God established his covenant with Abraham and promised him many descendants: "Before Abraham was born, 'I AM'" (John 8:58). "I AM" is the name God gave himself when he spoke to Moses on Mount Sinai (see Exodus 3:14). Jesus is the only Son of God and is God himself. He says, "The Father and I are one" (John 10:30). Jesus' accusers charged that he

?

Did You Know?

Jesus Talks about His Divinity

Jesus was slow to reveal that he is God. In the Gospels he sometimes refused to answer questions about his godhood (see, for example, Matthew 16:20, Mark 8:11–12, and Luke 20:1–8). Why? If you look closely, you will see that it depends on when and to whom he was talking.

God had taught the Jewish people that he was the only God. Rather than claiming to be God right from the beginning of his public ministry, Jesus showed by words and deeds that he shared in God's divinity. Thus his followers could accept his word that he was one with God. Jesus often would not answer questions about his divine nature from those who ignored the proof of his words and deeds, recognizing that they wished only to entrap him, not know him.

broke Jewish Law "because he claimed to be the Son of God" (19:7). He did not deny this charge.

Jesus also allowed others to call him "Lord." We might think this is just an older way of showing respect for people. It might be like saying "sir" or "ma'am." But in the Greek translation of the Bible, *Lord* is the word used in place of the Hebrew word *Yahweh*, which is a special name for God. So to call Jesus Lord is like calling him God. It expresses the belief in his divinity. That is especially clear in the reaction of Thomas to the Risen Jesus: "My Lord and my God" (John 20:28).

> "This is my own dear Son—listen to him!"
>
> Mark 9:7

What the Incarnation Means for Us

The *Catechism of the Catholic Church* gives the following summary of who Jesus is. "At the time appointed by God, the only Son of the Father, the eternal Word, that is, the Word and substantial Image of the Father, became incarnate; without losing his divine nature he has assumed human nature" (479).

LITURGY CONNECTION

To the Father through the Son

Jesus is at the center of every liturgy and especially the Eucharist. It is only through him, with him, and in him that we can approach the Father.

Because he experienced our human longings and needs, Jesus will understand us in our weaknesses. He can and will present our needs to the Father and will respond to them.

There are many reasons why it is important for us to understand that Jesus is really both God and man. First, Jesus is called the *Christ*. This is the Greek word for the Hebrew word **Messiah**, or "anointed one." In the Old Testament, priests, kings, and sometimes prophets were anointed. That is, they had precious olive oil poured over them to show that God had chosen them for a special purpose. The Messiah promised by God was expected to be a priest, prophet, and king who would save the people of Israel. In fact, the name Jesus means "God saves." That is the prime goal of his mission to us. He comes to save us from the Original Sin that we all inherit and that taints human nature. He also can save us from our personal sins that hurt us and our relationships with God and others. Christ comes to give us the grace—that is, a share in God's own divine life and love—to save us from sin and death.

> For God loved the world so much that he gave his only Son, so that everyone who believes in him may not die but have eternal life.
>
> John 3:16

Second, because Jesus is both true God and true man, he is the one and perfect **mediator** between us and God. A mediator helps restore broken relationships.

THiNK ABouT IT!

As a fully human person, Jesus is an example for us. But we need to think about his life and teachings. For example, Christ tells us we will be happy if we work for peace (see Matthew 5:9). How can you work for more peace in your family? for more peace among your friends? What other teachings of Jesus do you remember, and how can they guide your life?

As our mediator, Christ offers himself in sacrifice on the cross and in Mass to restore our relationships with his loving Father. He goes to the Father on our behalf and comes to us on behalf of the Father to reveal the love of the Father for us.

Third, by becoming truly man, Jesus shows he wants to and can be our friend. Good friends understand us well and stick by us. They are there for us, stubbornly loyal, sometimes brutally honest.

As God, Jesus knows us better than we know ourselves and has the highest hopes for the saints we can become. He loves us and is patient with us beyond all human measure. As man, Jesus understands us, our strengths and weaknesses, joys and sorrows, emotional highs and lows. He sympathizes, encourages, advises, and corrects, all with great affection.

"Lean on me." Imagine Jesus saying that to you, especially in tough times when you need a friend the most.

Illustration by Elizabeth Wang, "Jesus's love is personal, tender, and unchanging; he is present with us always, especially in the Blessed Sacrament, and consoles us with His Presence," copyright © Radiant Light 2008, www.radiantlight.org.uk

FUN FACT

Ordinary people in Jesus' time did not have last (or family) names. They were identified by their first names and by their hometowns or their fathers. Our Lord is called Jesus of Nazareth and Jesus, son of Joseph. Christ or Messiah is not Jesus' last name but rather his title and role. It is like saying George Washington, President.

Fourth, Jesus offers himself as a teacher and a model for us to imitate. You probably have heroes already whom you imitate. You may admire and try to become like a certain athlete or performer. Christ is our model for a holy life: "I am the way, the truth, and the life; no one goes to the Father except by me" (John 14:6). Jesus presents the Beatitudes as ideals that we should strive for, but he also lives them. If we want to follow him, he tells us that we must love one another as he loves us (see 15:12).

But how can we possibly become like Christ? Saint Thomas Aquinas wrote, "The only-begotten Son of God, wanting to make us sharers in his divinity, assumed our nature, so that he, made man, might make men

Jesus became one of us in order to meet us where we are. He understands us "from the inside out." Which of these titles of Jesus means the most to you today?

SAVIOR • MEDIATOR • FRIEND • TEACHER • MODEL

© Saint Mary's Press

gods.² " Through the grace Christ gains for us, we become children of God. Especially in Baptism and the other Sacraments, the Holy Spirit helps us think, feel, and act as Jesus would. "God's divine power has given us everything we need to live a truly religious life through the knowledge of one who called us to share in his own glory and goodness" (2 Peter 1:3).

Church History

Early Church Councils Teach about Jesus' Divinity

The Church has always upheld Jesus Christ's divinity and humanity in response to heresies. A heresy is a deliberate rejection of Church dogma.

Some early heresies focused on Jesus' divinity. Arianism claimed that Jesus was more than human but less than divine. Nestorianism argued that Jesus was actually two Persons: one divine and one human. Other heresies denied Jesus' humanity. Docetism claimed Jesus was God in a human disguise. Monophysitism argued that Jesus' divinity wiped out his humanity.

Early Ecumenical Councils responded to these heresies. The Council of Nicaea (325) affirmed Jesus' full divinity. The Council of Chalcedon (451) declared that Jesus' human and divine natures cannot be separated. Today we still say the Nicene Creed, which was drafted at the Council of Nicaea and approved at the Council of Constantinople (381).

12 THE BIRTH OF JESUS

Every baby is a miracle. A baby is the result of the love between a man and a woman. A baby is the result of God's love. God has created the physical laws that form the baby's body. God has directly given the baby a spiritual soul.

We would expect Jesus' birth to be even more miraculous. As the eternal Son of God, the Second Divine Person of the Trinity, he has always existed. But he wants to be like us, which means having a human birth.

An angel appeared to Mary to announce that she would be Jesus' mother. Her yes has made all the difference in the world.

© Brooklyn Museum/Corbis

In the Bible, we read of God sending the angel Gabriel to ask Mary to become Jesus' mother. Gabriel explains the wonderful way it will happen: "The Holy Spirit will come on you, and God's power will rest upon you. . . . For there is nothing that God cannot do" (Luke 1:35,37). According to the Apostles' Creed, Jesus is "conceived by the Holy Spirit, born of the Virgin Mary" (see appendix A, "Catholic Prayers," of this handbook). We call Gabriel's message to Mary the **Annunciation**.

© Glayan/Shutterstock.com

Can you see signs of God's love in the faces of babies?

Every Christmas we remember the story of Jesus' birth. It is good to look at the Gospels closely and think about them prayerfully. The Gospels of Matthew and Luke have stories about Jesus' birth. (John starts with a hymn about the Son of God.) Only the Son of God has ever been able to choose how he will be born as a human. He seems to make his birth as humble and difficult as possible.

Expectant mothers usually try to prepare everything perfectly for the babies. But in Luke's Gospel, Mary and Joseph have to be away from home among strangers as they await the birth of Jesus. They cannot even find a place to stay or a proper bed. So the Son of God is born in some kind of stable. His cradle is a manger, a box that holds food for animals. "She gave birth to her first son, wrapped him

PRAY IT!

Hail Mary, full of grace, the Lord is with you. Blessed are you among woman, and blessed is the fruit of your womb, Jesus. Holy Mary, Mother of God, pray for us sinners now and at the hour of our death. Amen.

Fun Fact

Over the centuries people have developed many ways to prepare for the coming of Christ during Advent and to celebrate his birth at Christmas. Saint Francis of Assisi built the first Nativity scene, or crèche, in AD 1223. He wanted people to see how poor the baby Jesus was. The first Christmas carols come from the fourteenth century. Carols show our joy and unity at Christ's birth. What traditions does your family have to celebrate the birth of Christ?

in cloths and laid him in a manger—there was no room for them to stay in the inn" (Luke 2:7). The Gospel of Luke shows us that God is one with even those who seem to be the poorest of people. Luke warns us from the start not to judge the true worth of others by what they have or how they appear.

> This very day in David's town your Savior was born—Christ the Lord!
>
> Luke 2:11

God does reveal Jesus' true nature to some people. Angels suddenly appear in the sky where shepherds are tending their flocks. An angel announces: "Don't be afraid! I am here with good news for you, which will bring great joy to all the people" (Luke 2:10). In the Gospel of Matthew, a strange star guides **Magi**, wise men who studied the skies, over a long trip to greet the King of the Jews. We hear the Magi say: "Where is the baby born to be the king of the

Kings and shepherds come to worship Jesus. How do you worship Jesus?

© Pascal Deloche/Godong/Corbis

Jews? We saw his star when it came up in the east, and we have come to worship him" (Matthew 2:2).

Both the simple Jewish shepherds and the educated foreigners respond with faith to these heavenly signs. They adore the child who appears poor and helpless, without any important friends. Through the shepherds and the Magi, God reminds us that Christ has come to all people.

In the Gospel of Matthew, King Herod is not happy to get the news of Jesus' birth (see 2:1–3). Herod fears the baby will take over as king. Like the pharaoh in the Book of Exodus, Herod doesn't care what it takes to destroy the threat to his kingdom. The Gospel of Matthew tells us, "He gave orders to kill all the boys in Bethlehem and its neighborhood who were two years old and younger" (2:16). But Jesus was protected from Herod just as the infant Moses was saved from Pharaoh. In this way Matthew shows us that Jesus is like the great leaders of the Old Testament. He is the Savior promised by God.

Mary, the Mother of Jesus

God chose Mary to be the mother of the Savior. She is a human being like us. She is also truly the Mother of God. She gave birth

THiNK ABOUT IT!

Sometimes we lose the true spirit of the Christmas season. How can we keep Christ's spirit of self-giving? Maybe we can help with cleaning or cooking without being asked. We might visit a shelter or nursing home, where people might feel lonely, especially at Christmas. Most of all, we can observe the season with prayerfulness, by participating in the Sacraments, and by reading and reflecting on Sacred Scripture.

to the Second Person of the Trinity when he became man. In this way Mary is the Mother of God, because Jesus is God. She also becomes the Mother of the Church, which is the Body of Christ. She is our spiritual mother, and she leads us to her son, Jesus.

> But when the right time finally came, God sent his own Son. He came as the son of a human mother and lived under the Jewish Law, to redeem those who were under the Law, so that we might become God's children.
>
> Galatians 4:4–5

When we pray the Hail Mary, we echo the words of the angel Gabriel by describing Mary as "full of grace." She is the first and best fruit of Jesus' coming to redeem us. God keeps her from the stain of Original Sin. We call this fact the **Immaculate Conception**. From the moment Mary came into being (her conception), she was immaculate, without a spot of sin. God also gave her the strength to remain pure from all personal sin throughout her life. In becoming the mother of Jesus and throughout her life, Mary remained a virgin. Saint Augustine says she remained a virgin in conceiving her Son, a virgin in giving birth to him, a virgin in carrying him, a virgin in nursing him at her breast, always a virgin."

Liturgy Connection

The Liturgical Year

The Church's liturgy has a yearly rotation of seasons. Each season stresses a different stage in the history of salvation. The Liturgical Year starts with Advent. For four weeks we prepare for the Lord's coming into the world and into our hearts. The Christmas season begins with celebrating the Lord's birth on Christmas Day. It ends with the feast of the Baptism of Jesus on the second Sunday in January. It includes the Feasts of the Holy Family, Mary's Motherhood, and the Epiphany. In this season we relive the early history of the Holy Family. We rejoice in Christ's coming.

Mary made it clear to the angel Gabriel that she is wholly the servant, or handmaid, of the Lord (see Luke 1:38). Jesus needed a human mother to become fully human himself. Mary cooperated by giving herself completely to God's plan, body and soul.

Mary's Example

Because Mary is both a married person and a virgin, she is an example for all the ways God calls people to follow him. She inspires those whose calling is to marriage and those whose calling is to follow God along other paths. She is a model for the Church. She is especially an example to us of faith and charity.

Did You Know?

Jesus' Birth and the Old Testament

The Old Testament foretells some details of the Messiah's birth. Matthew's Gospel refers to some of them. For example, the Gospel begins with the list of the ancestors of Jesus Christ to show that he is "a descendant of David, as Isaiah had said (see Matthew 1:1, Isaiah 11:1). Matthew says the Incarnation was foretold by the prophet Isaiah. "A virgin will become pregnant and have a son, and he will be called 'God is with us'" (Matthew 1:22–23, Isaiah 7:14). The priests quote the prophet Micah to Herod to prove that the Messiah will be born in "Bethlehem in the land of Judah" (Matthew 2:4–6, Micah 5:2).

© Francis G. Mayer/Corbis

Mary was just a young teenager when she became the Mother of God. Now one of the most famous women in history, she is recognized for her holiness and her inner beauty.

Mary is the one most closely united with her son's redeeming act. She freely obeys God's desire. "May it happen to me as you have said" (Luke 1:38). We do not hear her complain about the difficulties she must face. Following God's plan, she helps reverse the effects of the first sin and disobedience to God. As Jesus is the new Adam, Mary is the new Eve. She teaches us to freely and faithfully obey God's will.

Mary teaches us humility and reliance on God. She insists that she is great and will be called blessed only because of God's love and gifts (see Luke 1:46–49). She serves others humbly. She hurries to help her older cousin Elizabeth, who is also expecting (see Luke 1:36–40). She encourages us both to pray and to act in faithfulness to God.

Live It!

Listen for God's Voice

In Luke's Gospel we read: "Mary remembered all these things and thought deeply about them" (2:19). Mary prayed about the events in her life. She tried to see God's will and hand in all of them.

We may tend to drift from day to day without thinking about what we are doing or why. We need some regular quiet time to think in God's presence, to be attentive to his voice, and to be open to his will in all the circumstances of our lives.

People of Faith
Saint Nicholas of Myra

© 2013 Saint Mary's Press/Illustration by Vicki Shuck

Sometimes Santa Claus is called Saint Nick. Why? Saint Nicholas, sometimes known as Saint Nick, was a fourth-century bishop of Myra, in Asia Minor. He was holy and lived simply. He used his family's wealth for the needs of others. When invaders captured Myra in the eleventh century, his remains were moved to Bari, which today is located in southern Italy.

Many stories of Saint Nicholas's generosity have come down to us. One story tells of the daughters of a poor family who needed money to get married. Saint Nick left a purse of gold for each of them. He provided food for children and families who were poor and hungry.

Such stories about the life of Saint Nicholas led to the custom of giving gifts in his name. In some traditions the gift giving takes place on Christmas. In other traditions, it is done on December 6, Nicholas's feast day, or on the Feast of the Epiphany, when the Magi brought gifts to Jesus. Saint Nicholas reminds us to use our talents and wealth to help those in need.

13 JESUS TEACHES

Some fairy tales tell how bad rulers take over a good king's rightful realm. The king comes back in disguise and throws out the evildoers. He loves his people and shows them how to be good and happy.

Jesus Christ is that good king. He is the Son of God who came into the world to reclaim God's Kingdom and free his people from sin and death.

Jesus was not the kind of king Israel was expecting. How was Jesus different from their expectations?

Illustration by Elizabeth Wang, "Jesus urges us to draw closer to the Father and to direct our prayers to Him," copyright © Radiant Light 2008, www.radiantlight.org.uk

The Kingdom of God

Some travelers tell stories about distant places. They show maps and slides. They inspire you to want to go there also.

Jesus tells us about the **Kingdom of God**. The Kingdom of God is not a specific place. Rather, it is a state of living in harmony with God and with one another. John the Baptist declares: "The right time has come and the Kingdom of God is near! Turn away from your sins and believe the Good News!" (Mark 1:15). John makes it clear that the Kingdom is made real when we live God's rule of love and goodness. It's what Heaven is like. It's what the earth could become if we all live as Jesus taught us. The Kingdom of God is present wherever the children of God are.

Good teachers show us how to do things. They lead us through math problems. They talk us through writing assignments. Jesus does not just tell us about the Kingdom of God. He shows us how we should live to be a seed of the Kingdom. He promises the power of the Holy Spirit to help us live in the Kingdom.

All of Jesus' life teaches us. He teaches by what he says and by his silence. He teaches by his big miracles, his smaller acts, and his prayers. He teaches by his love for people, especially people who are poor or in need. He teaches by his willing sacrifice on the cross and his rising from the dead.

PRAY IT!

Jesus, thank you for revealing your Kingdom to us and for inviting me to be part of it. Through the Holy Spirit, lead me to learn your Kingdom's Law of Love. Teach me to live your Kingdom's Law of Love with faith and hope. Help me bring others to be part of your Kingdom through my example and words. Amen.

Jesus Teaches in His Hidden Life

When he was about thirty years old, Jesus began his public life as a teacher. Before that he lived quietly in a small village. This early period of his life is sometimes referred to as his "hidden life." The Gospels record only a few of his words during this time. How does he teach us even in this time?

Jesus shows us that an ordinary life, lived well with love of God and others, has great worth. After all, Jesus, who is God, lived as you might have lived back then. Enjoying and helping family and friends

Did You Know?

John the Baptist's Mission

As the last prophet before the coming of Jesus Christ, John the Baptist had a mission to "prepare a road for the Lord" (Matthew 3:3). John called people to repent and reform. For their own good, he corrected those who had done wrong. He practiced the self-control he preached by living in the desert, surviving on locusts and wild honey (see 3:4).

John also put the Messiah's role above his own ego. He said to his followers, "I am not good enough even to carry his sandals" (Matthew 3:11). He sent his own disciples to follow Jesus (see John 1:35–36). And of his role in relationship to Jesus, he says, "He must become more important while I become less important" (3:30).

Jesus praised John's firmness and humility, saying, "John is greater than anyone who has ever lived" (Luke 7:28).

© Historical Picture Archive/CORBIS

Jesus grew up in a small town. He must have been like most boys and young men of his time. What do you think it would have been like to grow up with Jesus?

were part of his life. So were studying, working, playing, praying, and worshipping with his community.

Jesus made all these acts holy by doing them humbly and lovingly. We can unite ourselves to Christ in doing the same things well and with love.

Events in Jesus' life before his public ministry also teach us how to live in the Kingdom. His birth shows us how to be truly humble and poor. The Holy Family's flight into Egypt to escape Herod's massacre of the innocents warns us that not everyone will welcome the Kingdom. We too may suffer for its sake.

> In the past God spoke to our ancestors many
> times and in many ways through the prophets,
> but in these last days he has spoken to us through
> his Son.
>
> Hebrews 1:1–2

When Jesus was twelve, his family traveled to Jerusalem for the Passover feast. When his parents started for home, he stayed behind without telling them. When they found him in the Temple in Jerusalem, he

FUN FACT

Some Jewish customs may seem strange to us. "Look at the straps with scripture verses on them which they wear on their foreheads and arms, and notice how large they are!" (Matthew 23:5). This custom of strapping Scripture verses to their heads and arms—which many Jews still follow today when they pray—reminds Jewish people to keep God's Law in their minds and hearts (see Deuteronomy 6:6–8). Jesus criticizes those who do it just to look holy.

explained: "Didn't you know that I had to be in my Father's house?" (Luke 2:49). But Jesus returned home in obedience to Mary and Joseph. He teaches us also to respect those who care for us and have authority over us.

As he grew older, Jesus became known as "the carpenter, the son of Mary" (Mark 6:3). He shows us that using our talents of mind and body to do honest work is a noble way of praising God and serving others.

Jesus Teaches in His Public Life

Jesus started his public life by having John the Baptist baptize him. Jesus' humility and respect in doing so teaches us how we should act in the Kingdom. During his public life, Jesus talked about and ushered in the Kingdom. He gathered followers who,

Imagine having Jesus as a teacher. He taught small groups and large crowds without white boards, technology, or microphones. How did he keep their attention?

© Brooklyn Museum/Corbis

after him, would help the Kingdom on earth grow. He looks forward to the Kingdom's coming through his death and rising. He teaches that all people are welcome in the family of God. "When I am lifted up from the earth, I will draw everyone to me" (John 12:32).

To enter the Kingdom, Jesus tells us, we need the faith and humility to accept his words. We need to try to admit our sins and become better. "The gate to life is narrow and the way that leads to it is hard" (Matthew 7:14). But we can rely on God's great mercy and help. "Happy are those who know they are spiritually poor; the Kingdom of heaven belongs to them!" (5:3).

Good teachers often use something we know about to explain something new to us. For example,

Live It!

Sharing in Christ's Mission

In the Bible, prophets sometimes foretell the future. Their main mission, though, is to speak for God. Jesus acts as a prophet when he teaches about the Kingdom in his Father's name.

Everyone who is baptized shares in Christ's prophetic mission. We do so in many different ways. But whenever we reveal God's Kingdom in word or action, we help pass on Jesus' teachings.

For instance, you may teach younger kids a prayer or correct their behavior. You might answer a friend's questions about your faith or give good moral advice to the friend. You may pray with friends in hard times. If you try to follow Christ daily, you will teach others by example. Sometimes you may have to stand up to others and argue for what is right. What else might you do?

they might compare radio waves to the waves we have seen in water. Jesus did the same. Often he told **parables**, or stories about situations known to his listeners that also teach surprising lessons about the Kingdom of God.

Jesus said the Kingdom is like a small seed that will produce a huge tree of faith and love. But it needs to grow in the rich soil of good hearts (see Matthew 13:3–23, Mark 4:30–32). Jesus also told a story of how the Kingdom is like a great feast or party that everyone enjoys but must be prepared for. Through his parables Jesus teaches us that we don't have to be perfect. But we must truly try to change bad attitudes and habits so we can grow in love for God and for one another. We must discover and use the talents God has given us to serve others. We show our love through our deeds, helping others because we see Christ in them (see Matthew 22:1–14, 25:1–40).

During Jesus' public ministry, the three Apostles closest to him—Peter, James, and John—witness a special view of the Kingdom of God and Jesus' divinity. This event is called the Transfiguration (see Matthew 17:1–9). At the **Transfiguration** Jesus is transformed in appearance. The Gospel of Matthew tells us, "His face was shining like the sun, and his clothes were dazzling white" (17:2). A voice spoke from a cloud: "This is my own dear Son, with whom I am pleased—listen

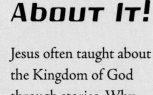

THiNk ABouT IT!

Jesus often taught about the Kingdom of God through stories. Why can stories be a good way to teach? How can they help you understand and recall something more easily? Do you know other stories about the Kingdom? Can you make up a story that explains to people your age something about the Kingdom of God?

Parables of Jesus

Barren Fig Tree, Luke 13:6–9
Canceled Debts, Luke 7:41–43
Cost of Discipleship, Luke 14:25–33
Dishonest Manager, Luke 16:1–8
Faithful or Unfaithful Slave, Matthew 24:45–51, Luke 12:42–48
Fig Tree, Matthew 24:32–35, Mark 13:28–31, Luke 21:29–33
Good Samaritan, Luke 10:30–37
Great Dinner, Luke 14:16–24
Growing Seed, Mark 4:26–29
Hidden Treasure and Pearl, Matthew 13:44–46
Honor at a Banquet, Luke 14:7–14
Laborers in the Vineyard, Matthew 20:1–16
Light of the World, Matthew 5:14–16
Lost Coin, Luke 15:8–10
Lost Sheep, Matthew 18:12–14, Luke 15:3–7
Mustard Seed, Matthew 13:31–32, Mark 4:30–32, Luke 13:18–19
Net, Matthew 13:47–50
New Wine in Old Wineskins, Matthew 9:16–17, Mark 2:21–22, Luke 5:36–39
Persistent Friend, Luke 11:5–8
Persistent Widow, Luke 18:2–8
Pharisee and the Tax Collector, Luke 18:10–14
Prodigal Son, Luke 15:11–32
Rich Fool, Luke 12:16–21
Rich Man and Lazarus, Luke 16:19–31
Salt, Matthew 5:13, Mark 9:50, Luke 14:34–35
Sheep and the Goats, Matthew 25:31–46
Sower, Matthew 13:3–8,18–23; Mark 4:3–9,14–20; Luke 8:5–8,11–15
Talents, Matthew 25:14–30
Ten Bridesmaids, Matthew 25:1–13
Ten Pounds, Luke 19:11–27
Two Sons, Matthew 21:28–31
Unforgiving Servant, Matthew 18:23–35
Watchful Servants, Luke 12:35–40
Wedding Banquet, Matthew 22:1–14
Weeds among the Wheat, Matthew 13:24–30,36–43
Wicked Tenants, Matthew 21:33–44; Mark 12:1–12, Luke 20:9–18
Wise and Foolish Builders, Matthew 7:24–27, Luke 6:47–49
Worthless Slaves, Luke 17:7–10
Yeast, Matthew 13:33, Luke 13:20–21

to him!" (Matthew 17:5). The vision of the transformed Christ deepened the faith of these three leaders of the early Church.

Jesus and the Law

God first taught the Jewish people through the Law of Moses and the prophets. But only through Jesus, the Son of God become man, did God fully reveal all that we need to know for our salvation. First, Jesus affirmed all the true teachings that were passed down in the past. He did not do away with the Law of Moses and the teachings of the prophets. Instead, Jesus came into the world to fulfill their teaching and reveal its true meaning.

At the Transfiguration, Jesus hears his Father say, "This is my own dear son—listen to him!" (Mark 9:7). What do you think God was saying to and about his Son?

© Brooklyn Museum/Corbis

Second, Jesus made clear the bigger picture of living the Law in the Kingdom. He said: "You have heard that people were told in the past, 'Do not commit murder. . . .' But now I tell you: if you are angry with your brother you will be brought to trial" (Matthew 5:21–22). Jesus tells us that we should not just avoid doing what a Commandment forbids. We should seek to be pure of heart and to act with love. Jesus sums up all the laws into two. We must love God with our whole hearts and love our neighbors as ourselves (see Matthew 22:36–40).

> Simon Peter answered him, "Lord, to whom would we go? You have the words that give eternal life."
>
> John 6:68

Third, Jesus rejected some ways the Jewish teachers lived and explained the Law. For instance, they attacked Jesus because he heals on the Lord's Day. They believed the command to keep the Sabbath holy by avoiding extra work was more important than doing good deeds (see Luke 13:10–17). They were so

LITURGY CONNECTION

The Lenten Season

The liturgical season of Lent lasts from Ash Wednesday up to Holy Thursday. The Holy Triduum begins that evening with the Mass of the Lord's Supper. Lent prepares us for Easter. It reminds us that to live in the Kingdom, we need to change bad habits and express sorrow for our faults.

The Gospel readings of the first Sunday in Lent tell how Jesus prepared to announce the Kingdom. The Spirit led Jesus into the desert, where he fasted for forty days. Then the devil came and tempted Jesus to set up an earthly kingdom over which he could rule. Jesus rejected the devil's offer and refused to go against his Father's plan. The season of Lent reminds us that we need to sacrifice for the Kingdom. The Holy Spirit will give us the grace to be faithful and to use our gifts to serve God and others.

caught up in rules about eating and washing that they forgot that a clean heart is more important (see Mark 7:18–22).

Jesus does not just preach the true Law. His whole life shows how to live these teachings perfectly. He carries out the promises made about the Messiah. He freely offers himself on the cross to redeem us from sin. He sends the Holy Spirit to enable us to freely live as God's children in his Kingdom.

> As long as heaven and earth last, not the least point nor the smallest detail of the Law will be done away with.
>
> Matthew 5:18

Did You Know?

The Prodigal Son

Read and think about Jesus' Parable of the Prodigal Son in Luke 15:11–32. What key truths does this parable teach about our relationship to God and others?

Here are some lessons the parable teaches us. The younger son's behavior is wrong. Egotism and disregard for others, like his, are the core of every sin. But the son comes to his senses and repents. The father, who has every right to be upset, doesn't reject him. Instead, he welcomes his son and throws a big party to celebrate his return. Like the father in the parable, God is merciful and loving, and he will always welcome us, even after we sin. We only need to repent, ask for forgiveness, and resolve not to sin again.

Church History

The Church's Teaching Mission

The Church's mission of education has taken many forms throughout the centuries, because the Church has taken seriously this Work of Mercy: "Instruct the ignorant."

Under the Roman Empire, most of the common people were uneducated. Charlemagne, who became emperor in the eighth century, himself did not learn to write until he was an adult. But he valued education and expanded educational opportunities by supporting libraries and monastic schools. These schools offered skills in basic literacy but were limited to boys. When a cathedral was built, a cathedral school for boys and young men was often attached to it.

Over the centuries, changes in society meant that many families were forced to leave rural areas to find work in cities, and a new educational need surfaced: the need to educate the growing numbers of poor urban children. It was at this time, in 1679, that Saint John Baptist de La Salle founded the Brothers of the Christian Schools to teach poor boys. Women's communities, such as the Ursuline Sisters, founded in 1535, were dedicated to the education of girls. The Ursulines arrived in the United States in 1727. The Ursuline Academy in New Orleans is the oldest continually operating Catholic school for girls and the oldest Catholic school in the United States. For many years, religious brothers and sisters were responsible for staffing most Catholic grade and high schools in the United States. Today, laypeople have followed in their footsteps, carrying the teaching mission of Jesus into the present.

14 JESUS HEALS

KEY WORDS

miracle

reconciles

Works of Mercy

We trust people who can actually do what they say they can do. They show us some signs of their ability. People who say they are good baseball players should be able to hit. People who say they can star in a musical should be able to sing.

Jesus said he was God. One way he showed this was through his **miracles**, special signs of the presence and power of God active in human

Jesus calmed the storm when his Apostles thought all was lost. Miracles like this helped them realize who Jesus is. Jesus can calm the storms of your life when you feel afraid or lost.

© Brooklyn Museum/Corbis

150

history. These actions went beyond our understanding of the normal laws of human or physical behavior. For example, Jesus walked on water. He ordered the wind and waves to become calm in a storm (see Matthew 14:22–33, Mark 4:35–41).

Jesus' miracles help people have faith in him. Most of his miracles also relieve people's suffering. The Gospels point to these as signs that Jesus is the Messiah the prophets predicted. Jesus' healing of people in body and soul is done out of the love and compassion that mark the Kingdom of God.

> All the people tried to touch him, for power was going out from him and healing them all.
>
> Luke 6:19

Jesus Heals the Body

Good doctors don't make people better to show how smart they are. Instead, they are motivated by a spirit of caring and compassion. They want their patients to be well and happy.

Jesus cured people's illnesses and diseases out of concern for the people. The Gospels tell us that Jesus healed many people. The Gospels focus on a few healing miracles that present

PRAY IT!

Jesus, Divine Doctor, heal our bodies and soul. Bring relief to those who suffer from sickness or disease. Clean the minds of those who suffer from bitterness or loneliness. Cure the hard hearts of those who suffer from sin of any kind. Work through us to bring your healing to others. Help us sow joy and love among our friends. Inspire in us deeds of reconciliation. Give us words of comfort for those who are suffering in any way. Amen.

FUN FACT

The evangelist, or Gospel writer, Luke may have been a doctor (see Colossians 4:14). Maybe that's one reason the Gospel of Luke and the Acts of the Apostles recall so many cures. Luke's Gospel tells of about fifteen of Jesus' healing miracles, more than any of the other Gospels. A doctor would know how truly miraculous some of the cures were and would be especially amazed.

common points. First, Jesus helps people of all kinds. They can be important people like Jairus, an official whose daughter was very ill. Or they can be unimportant people in society, like the widow who suffered in poverty because her only son and support has died. Out of compassion Jesus raised Jairus's daughter and the widow's son from the dead (Mark 5:21–43 and Luke 7:13–15).

Second, Jesus often linked the cures to belief in him. For example, a woman with a bleeding disease touched Jesus in a crowd. Even though others were also reaching out for Jesus, she alone was cured of her illness. Jesus said that her faith made her well (see Luke 8:43–48). When messengers tell Jairus that his daughter had died, Jesus encouraged him not to be afraid and to just keep believing (see Mark 5:35–36). In Nazareth, where Jesus is rejected, he does not work many miracles. The people there have too little faith (see Matthew 13:53–58).

Third, Jesus often cured the body to benefit a person's soul. The father of the boy with an evil spirit saw this need in himself. "I do have faith, but not enough. Help me have more!" (Mark 9:24). Jesus cured a man who was born blind and had not even been his follower before (see John 9:35–38). The man came to believe in Jesus. He said to him, "I believe, Lord!" and knelt down before him (see 9:38).

Fourth, Jesus' main work is to cure spiritual evils. Sometimes he makes this clear even when healing the body. For instance, while Jesus is in a crowded house teaching those gathered, some friends of a paralyzed man decided to bring the man to Jesus. Because of the crowd, they could only reach Jesus by making a hole in the roof and lowering the man down. Jesus said to the paralyzed man, "My son, your sins are forgiven" (Mark 2:5). Some of the people who saw this complained that only God can forgive sins. Then Jesus proved that he has the power to forgive sins by also healing the man's paralysis. The man picked up his mat and walked home (see 2:1–12).

Jesus Heals the Soul

When we're physically sick, perhaps weak with no strength to do anything, we can feel terrible. In a similar way, we can also become sick in our inner thoughts and desires, that spiritual part of human beings we call the soul. When our soul is sick, we are stuck in sinful actions and desires. The Gospels say this sickness of the soul is even worse than physical sickness.

THiNK AbouT It!

Jesus sometimes used physical miracles to teach important lessons for salvation. For instance, when he fed a large crowd with five loaves of bread and two fish, he told the crowd to work instead for "the food that lasts for eternal life" (John 6:27).

Read about two of Jesus' miracles in Matthew 8:5–13 and Luke 5:1–11. What spiritual lessons can you learn from them?

Miracles of Jesus

These miracles are listed in the order in which they first appear in the Gospels.

Leper, Matthew 8:1–4, Mark 1:40–45, Luke 5:12–16

Centurion's Servant, Matthew 8:5–13, Luke 7:1–10

Many at Peter's House, Matthew 8:14–17, Mark 1:29–34, Luke 4:38–41

Gadarene (Gerasene) Demoniacs, Matthew 8:28–34, Mark 5:1–20, Luke 8:26–39

Paralytic, Matthew 9:1–8, Mark 2:1–12, Luke 5:17–26

Woman with Bleeding, Matthew 9:20–22, Mark 5:25–34, Luke 8:43–48

Two Blind Men, Matthew 9:27–31

Mute Man, Matthew 9:32–34

Man with a Withered Hand, Matthew 12:9–13, Mark 3:1–5, Luke 6:6–11

Blind, Mute, and Possessed Man, Matthew 12:22

Canaanite Woman's Daughter, Matthew 15:21–28, Mark 7:24–30

Boy with a Demon, Matthew 17:14–21, Mark 9:14–29, Luke 9:37–43

Blind Bartimaeus, Matthew 20:29–34, Mark 10:46–52, Luke 18:35–43

Man with an Unclean Spirit, Mark 1:21–28, Luke 4:31–37

Deaf Man, Mark 7:31–37

Blind Man at Bethsaida, Mark 8:22–26

Crippled Woman, Luke 13:11–13

Man with Dropsy, Luke 14:1–4

Ten Lepers, Luke 17:11–19

High Priest's Servant, Luke 22:50–51

Official's Son, John 4:46–54

Man at the Pool of Bethzatha, John 5:1–9

Jesus can cure these ills of the soul. He can heal our pride, laziness, self-seeking, and bad desires. He wants to help heal our worries, doubts, and anxiety. This healing can require some work on our part, especially the effort to turn away from sin and bad habits. But we will feel more peaceful because of it.

> Peace is what I leave with you; it is my own peace that I give you. I do not give it as the world does. Do not be worried and upset; do not be afraid.
>
> John 14:27

In the Gospels, we see that Jesus always seeks out people whose soul needs healing. One Gospel story is about Zacchaeus, a tax collector living in Jericho. He has become rich by working for the

© Look and Learn/The Bridgeman Art Library

Zacchaeus was up a tree without Jesus. But Jesus turned around the tax collector's life, healing his soul just as he had cured the physical ailments of others.

occupying Romans. When he collects the taxes, he also takes extra money for himself. But Jesus' words and kindness move Zacchaeus to change his ways. He says to Jesus: "Listen, sir! I will give half my belongings to the poor, and if I have cheated anyone, I will pay back four times as much" (Luke 19:8). Jesus rejoices that Zacchaeus has been saved (see Luke 19:1–10).

Jesus' healing of the soul **reconciles** sinners. It restores our relationship with God and other people. Zacchaeus's change of heart set him right with God and his fellow Jews. He could also be at peace with himself.

Live It!

Everyday Healing

How can we, in simple ways, bring Jesus' healing love to others?

Do we look down on certain people? Could we be more open and understanding and change our attitude toward these people? Could we help our friends do the same?

In what ways can you reach out to people whom you think are different, in your school or in other groups to which you belong? How can you bring healing to those who feel rejected or alone? In simple ways, through friendliness and simple acts of kindness, you can bring Jesus' healing and love to others. Think of one way you can do this each day, and commit to doing it.

Jesus also continues to heal the souls of those who are already close to him. For example, when the guards came to arrest Jesus, the Apostles fled, breaking their promises to stay with him. Peter, who had boasted the most of his loyalty, was afraid even to admit he knew Jesus. Later Peter expressed sorrow for his sin. Jesus forgave him and asked Peter to take care of the others now that he had reconciled himself with the Lord (see John 21:15–19).

We all need this healing of the soul. Jesus is always ready and willing to heal us. He just needs us to desire to be sorry for our sins and to be reconciled with God, the Church, others, and ourselves. We express our repentance and are healed by Jesus through prayer, the Eucharist, and acts that show our sorrow. We are healed in a special way through the two Sacraments of Healing: the Sacrament of Penance and Reconciliation and the Sacrament of Anointing of the Sick (see chapter 35, "The Sacraments of Healing," of this handbook).

LITURGY CONNECTION

Healing Power

The Rite of the Mass often refers to the healing power of God. For example, just before Communion the priest says of the Eucharist: "Behold the Lamb of God, behold him who takes away the sins of the world. Blessed are those called to the supper of the Lamb" (*Roman Missal*). We respond, "Lord, I am not worthy that you should enter under my roof, but only say the word and my soul shall be healed" (*Roman Missal*). Our words echo those of a Roman officer in the Gospels who is confident that Jesus can heal his sick servant even from a distance (see Matthew 8:5–10). Like him, we ask God's mercy. We humbly admit we are not worthy. We have faith that Jesus can and will heal us spiritually. The Eucharist can strengthen us to follow our good impulses and cure us of giving in to our bad ones.

Jesus Sends Us to Heal

Jesus passed on to the Apostles his mission to heal the body and soul. He gave them the power to expel demons and cure sickness. The Twelve, another name for the Apostles, went throughout the region, teaching and healing (see Luke 9:1,6). Through the Holy Spirit, Jesus keeps this power to heal always alive and active in his Church.

Playing bingo may not seem like a work of mercy, but anytime we lift the spirits of others, we help heal their soul. Works of mercy are good for our soul too.

God calls all Christians to help in this healing mission. The **Works of Mercy** sum up some of the ways we can help heal others. They are acts of charity by which we help others meet their basic needs. By the Corporal Works of Mercy, we help others in their physical needs. We can live out our concern for the

© Gabe Palmer/CORBIS

needs of the body, for example, by providing money, food, housing, and clothes for people who are poor. We can visit the sick, the aged, and those in prison.

We should be just as concerned with the needs of the soul. Those who are sick, for example, need our encouragement to keep their spirits up. We can help them unite their sufferings with those of Christ.

Corporal and Spiritual Works of Mercy

Corporal Works of Mercy

Feed the hungry.

Give drink to the thirsty.

Shelter the homeless.

Clothe the naked.

Care for the sick.

Help the imprisoned.

Bury the dead.

Spiritual Works of Mercy

Share knowledge.

Give advice to those who need it.

Comfort those who suffer.

Be patient with others.

Forgive those who hurt you.

Give correction to those who need it.

Pray for the living and the dead.

The Spiritual Works of Mercy include generously sharing our knowledge, advice, and sympathy with those who need it. We do works of mercy when out of love we correct, forgive, and are patient with others' mistakes. We live these works whenever we model and explain the faith to others or give them good Christian guidance. We live them whenever we comfort those who are sad or discouraged and when we are patient and forgiving toward those who annoy or hurt us. (See appendix B, "Catholic Beliefs and Practices," of this handbook.)

Did You Know?

The Early Christians Heal

The Acts of the Apostles provides accounts of the first Christians healing people physically just as Jesus did. They do it in Jesus Christ's name, so it is clear that it is his power doing the healing, not theirs. Peter orders a lame man to walk "in the name of Jesus Christ of Nazareth" (Acts 3:6). Later, he tells a paralyzed man that "Jesus Christ makes you well" (Acts 9:34). When the people see the man walk, they become Christians.

Paul's cures make the people of Lystra think he is a Greek god. Paul has to explain: "We ourselves are only human beings like you! We are here to announce the Good News, to turn you to the living God" (14:15). Paul identifies the power to heal as one way the Holy Spirit might be present in a person for the good of all (1 Corinthians 12:7,9).

Church History

A History of Healing

Since the early days of Christianity, the Church has been faithful to Christ's concern to heal both body and spirit. In the Early Middle Ages, monks and nuns in monasteries established the first hospitals, and the tradition of Catholic hospitals has continued since, throughout the world.

Today, the Catholic Hospital Association runs more than 600 hospitals and 1,400 long-term care and other health facilities in all fifty states. It is the largest group of nonprofit care providers in the United States. Like Catholic schools, many Catholic hospitals were begun by religious communities and are now staffed by laypeople. Catholic hospitals combine the best of medical care with the Gospel values of love and compassion.

15 THE DEATH OF JESUS

Key Words

Passion

Passover

Paschal Mystery

People often give of their time and talents to make others happy. They could be doing something just for themselves, but instead they work hard to please someone else. Perhaps you've shared a talent or helped a young child learn how to do something or volunteered at your parish food pantry. Or maybe you went with your parents to visit a sick relative, even though it meant missing going out with your friends.

> The greatest love you can have for your friends is to give your life for them.
>
> John 15:13

God is the origin of such selfless acts. As the first letter of John tells us: "This is what love is: it is not that we have loved God, but that he loved us and sent his Son to be the means by which our sins are forgiven" (4:10). In previous chapters we learned that Jesus freely came into this world to save us from our sins, heal us, and make us friends of God and one another. But it is in Christ's Passion and his suffering and death on the cross that his saving work for us is completed. The **Passion** is the extreme sufferings of Jesus' last hours—the whipping, the crown of thorns, the carrying of the cross, and his agony while nailed on the cross—and his death. Through his suffering and death, Jesus freed us from death, which came with sin. Through Christ we can live with God after death and forever.

Throughout his whole public life, Jesus was aware of this future final act of love for us. Several times he foretold that he would undergo suffering and death in Jerusalem but also that he would rise again after three days (see, for example, Matthew 16:21). He freely gave himself up for each of us. His whole life was given to doing the will of the Father, to bring about our salvation.

Jesus' Passion

At Mass throughout the year, but most especially during Holy Week and the Easter season, we hear the account of Christ's final sacrifice. We can meditate and pray about Christ's Passion and death at any time to recall how much God loves us. This prayer and reflection encourage us to love Christ

PRAY IT!

Jesus, thank you for your generous love in sacrificing yourself for me and all people. Help me forget about myself and give my life for others. Show me how I can take up your cross by serving people in little ways. Remind me to offer everything I do in union with you in joy and hope. Teach me to bear pains well and to comfort others who are in pain. Amen.

well and to avoid sin. It also teaches us to bear our own sufferings with patience and to have compassion for others who suffer.

In chapters 22 and 23 of the Gospel of Luke, we read about the events leading to Jesus' Crucifixion as follows: Some of the Jewish leaders decided that Jesus must die because his teachings were challenging their authority and because he claimed to be the Messiah. Judas, one of Jesus' Apostles, betrays him for money. Judas led Jesus' enemies to a garden where Jesus was praying on the Passover evening. Peter and the other disciples deserted Jesus. The Jewish council's guards mocked and beat him. Unfairly, the council judged him a liar because he claimed to be the Messiah.

They brought Jesus before Pilate, the Roman governor, who has Jesus whipped and then permitted his crucifixion. Jesus carried his cross through the streets like a common criminal to a place outside the city. There the Roman soldiers stripped him of his clothes, nailed his hands and feet to the wood, and raised up the cross. Jesus felt lonely and deserted even by the Father. He breathed his last breath and died on the cross.

Even while experiencing this suffering, Jesus forgave his torturers, saying: "Forgive them, Father! They don't know what they are doing" (Luke 23:34).

THiNk AbouT IT!

Taking up Christ's cross means growing in habits of love. It means accepting the suffering in our lives without becoming bitter. It means giving up some of our comforts and leisure time to help others. What are some ways young people can take up the cross? What people in your family, parish, and community seem to be taking up Christ's cross?

Images of Jesus' Suffering and Death

The New Testament compares Christ in his suffering and death to several images that Jewish readers would recognize. For instance, John the Baptist calls Jesus "the Lamb of God, who takes away the sin of the world!" (John 1:29). The name recalls the time when God had to force the stubborn Egyptian pharaoh to free the Jewish people from slavery. The angel of death took the oldest male child and animal in each home. But the angel passed over the Jewish homes that had the blood of a lamb sprinkled on the door (see Exodus 12:1–14). The Jews remember this event during the **Passover** festival each year.

The Stations of the Cross

Christians have always made pilgrimages to Jerusalem to pray at holy sites along the path Jesus walked to his Crucifixion. But not everyone could make the trip. As early as the fifth century, some churches began to set up local images of these holy places so those unable to travel could still participate in this devotion. Today, nearly all churches have depictions of the Stations of the Cross. You too can participate in this ancient devotion. The next time you are at a church, pause at each of the Stations, imagine the scene, and pray about it.

1. Jesus is condemned to death.
2. Jesus takes up his cross.
3. Jesus falls the first time.
4. Jesus meets his mother.
5. Simon helps Jesus carry the cross.
6. Veronica wipes the face of Jesus.
7. Jesus falls the second time.
8. Jesus meets the women of Jerusalem.
9. Jesus falls the third time.
10. Jesus is stripped of his garments.
11. Jesus is nailed to the cross.
12. Jesus dies on the cross.
13. Jesus is taken down from the cross.
14. Jesus is laid in the tomb.

FUN FACT

It is interesting to try to imagine the stories of people who appear only briefly in the Bible. Remember Simon of Cyrene, who was forced to help Jesus carry the cross (see Mark 15:21)? Simon must have been upset. He was just walking by. This criminal, Jesus, was none of his business. Ever wonder how this meeting with Jesus affected Simon and his family? Our tradition tells us that Simon's sons, Alexander and Rufus, were faithful Christians later.

Jesus celebrated the Passover with his disciples at the Last Supper, which we recall on Holy Thursday. He himself became the Passover Lamb who sacrificed himself so his people might escape their slavery to sin and death. In Luke's Gospel we read:

> Then he took a piece of bread, gave thanks to God, broke it, and gave it to them, saying, "This is my body, which is given for you. Do this in memory of me." In the same way, he gave them the cup after the supper, saying, "This cup is God's new covenant sealed with my blood, which is poured out for you." (22:19–20)

The Last Supper was the first Eucharist. The bread that was broken became Jesus' Body broken for us, and the wine poured out became Jesus' Blood shed for us.

In the Gospel of John, Jesus is both shepherd and sacrificed lamb. Jesus calls himself the Good Shepherd, who cares for

"Lamb of God, you take away the sins of the world." We pray these words at Mass to remember that Jesus is the Passover Lamb who is sacrificed to free the people from the slavery of sin.

© Randall Stevens/Shutterstock.com

his sheep and is willing to die to save them when wolves attack (see 10:11–13). Jesus gives up his life for us. Because *paschal* is another word that means "Passover," Jesus is sometimes called the Paschal Lamb. The mystery of how his Passion, death, Resurrection, and Ascension save us from sin and death is called the

Illustration by Elizabeth Wang, "On the night before He died, Jesus instituted the Holy Eucharist, at the Last Supper. Every Mass, makes present the sacrifice of Calvary," copyright © Radiant Light 2008, www.radiantlight.org.uk

Paschal Mystery.

The Gospel of Matthew quotes from chapter 53 of the Book of Isaiah, which describes the Messiah as the Suffering Servant (see Matthew 8:17). In one verse from Isaiah, we read, "My devoted servant, with whom I am pleased, will bear the punishment of many and for his sake I will forgive them" (53:11). Many of Isaiah's details of the Messiah's suffering actually happen to Christ.

Sometimes we wonder why innocent people suffer. Why does God allow children to die from hunger or disease? Why do terrible wars that take the lives of innocent people happen? We cannnot understand the mysterious ways in which God is at work in the world, but we know that sometimes good results come from suffering. We also know that God leaves us free to love, and that sometimes people can misuse freedom to hurt others. Even from this evil God can bring about good. Still, innocent suffering is hard to accept.

When Jesus told the Apostles that he would give them his Body and Blood, they must have been very puzzled. When you participate in Mass, what connection do you see between the Last Supper and Jesus' death on the cross?

167

LITURGY CONNECTION

The Presentation and Preparation of the Gifts

The Liturgy of the Eucharist begins with the Presentation and Preparation of the Gifts. The bread and wine, which will become Christ's Body and Blood, are presented for the sacrifice. We are also invited to add our own offerings.

Usually a few people attending the Mass bring the bread and wine to the altar. They might also bring money or other goods that have been collected. The priest blesses God, through whose goodness we have the bread and wine. God has also willed that human hands have helped to make them. We respond by praying that God accept our sacrifice "for the praise and glory of his name, for our good, and the good of all his holy Church" (*Roman Missal*).

Jesus shows us through his totally undeserved suffering that God understands and feels our pain. He teaches us that our pain can be offered to God as a pleasing sacrifice and prayer. We can unite our sufferings and all our efforts to do good with the sufferings and good deeds of Christ. In a way we cannot fully understand, they will help Christ's saving and healing action in the world.

Jesus Frees Us from Death

Jesus was without sin. Unlike other human beings, he did not have to experience human suffering and death. He accepted these things to save us from spiritual death.

Still, Jesus did not want to suffer or die. In the garden at Gethsemane, he prayed that he might avoid suffering and death. But he wanted to do the Father's will (see Matthew 26:39). Jesus teaches us to overcome our fear of sacrificing ourselves for God and others. He masters his fear of death so we will no longer fear it as our final state.

Jesus Christ has tasted death so we can live forever with God after our earthly lives have ended. He can accomplish this because he is the Son of God made man, who died and was buried. Of course, as the Second Divine Person of the Trinity, Christ is eternal and cannot cease to exist. But for a human being, death means the body is so damaged that it can no longer support earthly life. The soul and body separate. Earthly life ends. Jesus freely accepted death in this sense for our sake.

From Good Friday until Easter Sunday, Jesus' body was in the tomb. It did not decay, because his

© Brooklyn Museum/Corbis

Jesus suffered torture, humiliation, and severe pain on the cross, but he spoke words of forgiveness and love to those around him. He even forgave his executioners!

Did You Know?

Jesus' Death and the Old Testament

The Old Testament foretells many details of Christ's Passion. For example, Isaiah, chapter 53, says that Jesus will be looked down on, rejected, wounded, beaten, arrested, and sentenced. "He took the place of many sinners and prayed that they might be forgiven" (53:12).

In Matthew and Mark's Gospels, while on the cross Jesus began praying Psalm 22: "My God, my God, why have you abandoned me?" (verse 1). Other parts of that psalm fit Christ's death. "I am no longer a human being; I am a worm, despised and scorned by everyone! All who see me make fun of me; they stick out their tongues and shake their heads" (verses 6–7).

Amazingly, Psalm 22 also refers to Christ's weakness, stretched bones, thirst, and torn hands and feet. People even gamble for his clothes in the psalm. All these things happen at the Crucifixion.

© State Russian Museum, St. Petersburg, Russia/The Bridgeman Art Library

This icon shows Jesus descending into Hell to free the souls of those who had died before him.

physical body was still united to the Divine Person of Christ.

The Apostles' Creed tells us that after death, and before his Resurrection, Jesus "descended into hell." Hell here means the place where the souls of all the people who had died before Christ's coming, good and bad, had gone after death. None of them could go to Heaven until Christ reconciled them with God. Now Jesus opened Heaven's gate for the just who had gone before him. Christ led their way to Heaven when he was raised from the dead on Easter Sunday.

Live It!

Do Everything for the Glory of God

All baptized Christians can unite their efforts to be holy with Christ's sacrifice on the cross. We all can offer sacrifices to God through Christ. But what exactly can we offer?

A good, basic rule of thumb comes from Paul's First Letter to the Corinthians: "Whatever you do . . . do it all for God's glory" (10:31). You can offer family time, classes, fun things, and chores. You can offer your efforts to be friendly, patient, and kind. You can offer all your joys and pains. You can offer your attempts to bring others to Christ and to be Christ to them.

Trying to follow the guidance of the Holy Spirit, we can offer everything, big or small, that happens in our daily lives. At Mass we can unite our offerings with Jesus' sacrifice. Through them we can praise and thank God. We can ask for help and show our sorrow for our sins.

PEOPLE OF FAITH
Saint Dismas

© 2013 Saint Mary's Press/Illustration by Vicki Shuck

Do you know the story of Saint Dismas, the Good Thief? You can read it in Luke 23:32–43. One of the two criminals crucified with Christ insults him. The other, known to us as Dismas, defends Jesus as an innocent man. "And he said to Jesus, 'Remember me, Jesus, when you come as King!' Jesus said to him, 'I promise you that today you will be in Paradise with me'" (42–43). Jesus sees that Dismas has a good heart and is sorry for his sins. Jesus promises him a place in Heaven.

Dismas is the patron saint of criminals and condemned prisoners. We might see him as the saint of so-called hopeless cases. His story reminds us not to give up on anyone. Even very bad people can turn to God's mercy while they live. Many great sinners have become great saints. We celebrate the Feast of Saint Dismas on March 25.

16 THE RESURRECTION OF JESUS

In any class or activity, some basic facts are especially important. In math you need to grasp what the different math signs mean. In soccer you need to learn what you're expected to do in playing your position. In chess you need to know how the different pieces can move.

When Jesus rose from the dead, it was great news for his followers. Why does the Resurrection continue to be Good News for Christians today?

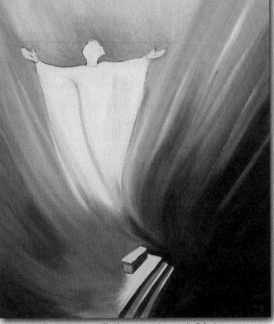

Illustration by Elizabeth Wang, "The Resurrection," copyright © Radiant Light 2008, www.radiantlight.org.uk

Jesus said to her, "I am the resurrection and the life. Those who believe in me will live, even though they die."

John 11:25

Jesus' **Resurrection**, the fact that on the Sunday after Good Friday he rose from the dead, is a key fact of our faith that enables us to understand and live our faith. It is God's greatest miracle. It proves beyond doubt the truth of Jesus' claims, teachings, and mission. It completes our reunion with God. It promises our own resurrection and eternal life with God.

Christ's first followers clearly saw the importance of the Resurrection. They either saw the Risen Jesus with their own eyes or knew honest people who had seen him. What if Jesus hadn't risen, asked Paul? "Then we have nothing to preach and you have nothing to believe" (1 Corinthians 15:14). Some people made fun of Paul for preaching that Christ was raised from the dead, but others were curious and wanted to know more (see Acts 17:32). Let's take a closer look at why it is so important for us to believe in Jesus' Resurrection.

The Risen Christ

Jesus had told the disciples he would rise again. Still, most of them were not expecting that Jesus would actually die, especially

PRAY IT!

Jesus, help us recall your Resurrection often. May its hope be with us always. May we desire, pray, and work to hasten your Kingdom's coming on earth. May we enjoy its glory with you forever. Amen.

FUN FACT

After the Resurrection, Jesus could have just shown himself to the disciples on the road to Emmaus. Instead, he hid his true identity from them when they first met. Finally he revealed himself and gave them great hope (see Luke 24:13–35).

in such a horrible way. Why? The disciples had often seen Jesus brush aside his enemies. They saw the people of Jerusalem hail him as a hero a few days before his arrest. He was their superstar who would triumph against the opposing team—who in this case was the Jewish and Roman leaders.

Then suddenly something completely unexpected happened. Their hero, who seemed so strong and in control, now seemed weak and powerless. After his arrest Jesus seemed totally defeated. Within one day he was put to a horrible death. The disciples were in shock.

Imagine the great joy Mary Magdalene felt when she recognized Jesus in the garden! She was the first witness to the Resurrection. How would you have reacted if you had seen Jesus alive after he was crucified? Whom would you have told? Whom will you tell about Jesus?

© Alinari Archives/CORBIS

They didn't believe it when the women reported the empty tomb and the angel's message. They thought it was nonsense (see Luke 24:1–12). They believed only after Jesus had appeared several times to a variety of people. Even after he appeared to Simon and the others, John's Gospel says that the absent Thomas refused to believe (see 20:24–28). Jesus even scolded the disciples because they did not have faith and for being too stubborn to believe those who had seen him alive (16:14).

> May you always be joyful in your union with the Lord. I say it again: rejoice!
>
> Philippians 4:4

God gives us faith to believe in the Resurrection. "How happy are those who believe without seeing me!" (John 20:29), Jesus says. But for the first disciples it was an unexpected and wonderful reality that they believed, because they saw the Risen Jesus with their own eyes. They really saw and spoke with the Risen Christ.

Jesus raised others from the dead. His own return is different. His body and soul are reunited through God's power. His body is still human. It has the scars of his suffering and death. But his body is now glorified.

Think About It!

After the Resurrection, people recognize the Risen Christ in different ways. Mary Magdalene knew him by his voice. The disciples of Emmaus knew him by the way he broke the bread at the table. Thomas said he actually had to touch Jesus' wounds to believe it was truly him.

Do people see Jesus in you? Can they see him in the way you behave toward others? How else can others see Jesus in you?

LITURGY CONNECTION

A Time for Hope

Funerals are sad events. We will miss our friend or relative who has died. Especially when he or she is someone close to us, our loss can be painful. We know we will not be able to see him or her again in this life.

But the funeral liturgies remind us of our hope in the Resurrection. For example, in Masses for the dead, we pray that the dead person may share in the final resurrection. We also pray that "Christ will raise up in the flesh those who have died, and transform our lowly body after the pattern of his own glorious body" (*Roman Missal*). We ask Jesus to welcome his friends into his Kingdom. "There . . . you will wipe away every tear from our eyes. For seeing you, our God, as you are, we shall be like you for all the ages and praise you without end" (*Roman Missal*).

Jesus' humanity has entered a new realm beyond earthly time and space. He can pass through walls, appear and disappear at will, and change how he looks. His humanity has entered the divine life of God's Kingdom.

Jesus' death and Resurrection free us from sin. We begin to share in his death and Resurrection when we are baptized. We become reconciled with God, his children, and brothers and sisters of Christ. Jesus is the "first-born Son, who was raised from death" (Colossians 1:18). In and through him, we too will be resurrected. Our soul and body will be reunited. We die because we are descendants of Adam. But because of Christ's Resurrection, we too will be raised to new life. He will make our mortal bodies become like his glorious body (see Philippians 3:21).

The Ascension

In the Acts of the Apostles we read: "For forty days after his death he appeared to them many times in ways that proved beyond doubt that he was alive. They saw him, and he talked with them about the Kingdom of God" (1:3–4). During the forty days after his Resurrection, Jesus completes his teaching. He explains what is "said about himself in all the Scriptures, beginning with the books of Moses and the writings of all the prophets" (Luke 24:27). He again says Peter must follow him as the chief shepherd of the Church (see John 21:15–19). He again

Illustration by Elizabeth Wang, "Christ's Ascension to Glory," copyright © Radiant Light 2008, www.radiantlight.org.uk

gives all the Apostles the mission to teach and baptize in his name throughout the entire world (see Matthew 28:18–20).

At the Last Supper, the Gospel of John recalls, Jesus has already told them he must return to the Father. He must prepare a place for them. He must leave them for the Spirit to come (see John 14:2, 16:7). And so Jesus returns to the Father. By his **Ascension** Jesus' humanity enters God's heavenly realm completely. The glory of his resurrected body, veiled on earth so it would not overwhelm his disciples, shines forth fully. Jesus opens the way for us. He gives us the power to enter into God's life and eternal joy.

After the Resurrection and before Jesus ascended into Heaven, he gave his friends some final instructions. Read these pages to find out what Jesus wanted them to know.

The Creed says Jesus "is seated at the right hand of the Father." This shows the honor given Jesus' humanity. It also means he is the true ruler of the world. Now that he has ascended into Heaven, we his followers continue Jesus' mission of announcing his endless Kingdom of love and hastening its coming on earth.

Enemies attack the Kingdom often. The Church and God's people must suffer many trials. Scripture even refers to the antichrist, a wicked person or persons who put themselves in the place of God. They

Live It!

Let God's Kingdom Reign

All baptized people share in Christ's kingly mission. God calls us to help his Kingdom grow in the world.

First, we have to let God's Kingdom reign more in us. We need to overcome the reign of sin within us and let the Holy Spirit guide our minds, hearts, and wills. For example, we may need to control our temper, unkind talk, or impatience more.

We also need to make Christ's Kingdom more present around us. Our good example can help others live in the Kingdom more. If they see we treat people well, they are more likely to do the same. Our good leadership can also help others. As team captains or class officers, for instance, we might help the rest understand and respect one another better.

How can you help God's Kingdom reign in your family and among people you know?

will try to make people think that the world's problems can be solved without God's truth and help.

Jesus tells us to watch but not to worry. He is always with us, and he gives us the Holy Spirit to guide and strengthen us. He urges us to remain loyal, no matter what happens. At the end of time, he will come again in glory to reveal himself to the entire world.

Then he will judge the living and the dead. In this **Last Judgment**, he will reveal our inner thoughts and desires, good and bad. He will know

Illustration by Elizabeth "When we pray at Mass we are united with Christ in Glory and with the gathering of His saints and the souls of Purgatory," copyright © Radiant Light 2008, www.radiantlight.org.uk

All who follow Christ, both the living and the dead, share community. We live and pray with hope for the day when we will all be united in love with God in Heaven.

if we have accepted or refused the spiritual helps he gives us. He will judge whether we have known how to see and serve him in the needs of other people. He will give to each of us fairly according to our deeds.

In fact, Jesus' primary mission is not to judge us; rather his primary purpose is to save us so we can enjoy eternal life with God. In a sense, we really judge ourselves when we reject Jesus and the salvation he offers us. But God wants everyone to be saved (see 1 Timothy 2:3–4). We have to keep trying to grow in the Spirit, whom Jesus sends to us. Then we will live in the kingdom of love forever.

> My dear friends, we are now God's children, but it is not yet clear what we shall become. But we know that when Christ appears, we shall be like him.
>
> 1 John 3:2

Did You Know?

Views on Resurrection

Some Jews in Jesus' time had strong views about the rising of the dead. The Pharisees taught that the soul would join its body when the Messiah's reign ended. On the other hand, the Sadducees believed there was no life after death, that not even the soul lived after death.

Once, Paul was arrested but was not getting a fair trial. He delayed it by getting the two groups to argue over whether there was a resurrection (see Acts 23:6–11).

PEOPLE OF FAITH
Saint Mary Magdalene

© 2013 Saint Mary's Press/Illustration by Vicki Shuck

Mary Magdalene is among the first and greatest saints who lived in the company of Jesus. Yet she came from a very troubled past. We are told that Jesus cast out seven demons from her (see Mark 16:9 and Luke 8:2). This suggests that she suffered from severe physical and emotional illnesses. After her healing she became a devoted disciple of Jesus.

Mary Magdalene had courage. She was present at the cross when most of the men who followed Jesus had run away. In the Resurrection accounts, she is the first to see the empty tomb. Jesus chose to appear to her first, and sent her to tell the Good News to the others (see Matthew 28:1–10, Mark 16:1–10, Luke 24:1–12, and John 20:1–18). We see in the Bible how she rose from the shadows of society to great stature in the early Christian community.

The Church celebrates Mary Magdalene's feast day on July 22.

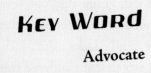 The Holy Spirit

Key Word

Advocate

"Let's see who can hold their breath the longest!" You and your friends have probably challenged each other to this contest at some time. You know how it goes. You watch each other take a deep breath and hold it until you both begin to turn red (or blue!). Your eyes start to bulge. Then one of you gasps for air. Have you gone under water to see if you can reach the other side of a pool without taking a breath? Have you run a 100-meter dash and thought, "I could have done better if I hadn't run out of breath"?

Actually, most of us don't think about our breathing often, maybe not at all (that is, until we're out of breath and gasping for air). At their children's birth, parents wait to hear the cry that tells them their babies are breathing. Why? A newborn who breathes is alive. The phrase "breath of life" definitely has meaning in human biology, even if we do take breathing for granted.

This is how one artist pictures the Holy Spirit's power to transform us. Take a deep breath and imagine this transforming power within you and around you.

Illustration by Elizabeth Wang, "If we surrender ourselves to God's will in prayer and in our daily lives, the Holy Spirit will transform us and make us holy," copyright © Radiant Light 2008, www.radiantlight.org.uk

What if we let our experiences of breathing lead us to a deeper reflection? What (or who) is the breath of life for the universe? What is the life force that makes it all hang together? Who brings us together, energizes us, gives us life, and helps us live fully—not just as a human who breathes, but also in a spiritual, holy way? These questions lead us straight to the Holy Spirit, the Third Divine Person of the Trinity.

PRAY IT!

Holy God, we praise and thank you for the gift of love that the Holy Spirit poured out on us. Help us recognize that the Holy Spirit is bringing us closer to your Son. Open our hearts and minds to the gifts the Holy Spirit gives us, so that we may live as your children. Amen.

FUN FACT

Since the day when the Holy Spirit descended upon the small group of Apostles and empowered them to make disciples of all nations, the number of people who believe in Jesus Christ has grown to more than two billion, or about 33 percent of the world's population. More than one billion of them are Catholic. In the United States, 23 percent of the population, more than 69 million people, are Catholic (Bunson, 2012 *Catholic Almanac*, page 438).

The Breath of God

The Holy Spirit might not be as familiar to you as God the Father and God the Son, the two other Divine Persons of the Holy Trinity. People don't talk about the Holy Spirit as much as they do the Father and the Son. He's more often behind the scenes rather than on center stage. We might not be aware of his activity, much as we don't notice our own breathing. Yet a truth of our faith is that the Father, Son, and Holy Spirit are one God, and together they are responsible for creation. Jesus Christ and the Holy Spirit, the Word and Breath of God, are inseparable from each other and from the Father. Whenever the Father sends his Son, he always sends his Spirit. Their mission is connected and inseparable.

One way to understand the Holy Spirit is with the image of breath. Think of it in the following way: God's Spirit breathes God's life into us. Much as our own breath, which keeps our bodies alive, the breath of the Holy Spirit gives us God's life. Through the Holy Spirit, we experience God's gift of love. We might not always be aware of the Holy Spirit's presence, but through him we come to know who God is. Through him we can know Jesus.

The Holy Spirit Prepares the Way

Let's take a minute to look at the movement of the Holy Spirit throughout time. The Holy Spirit first appears in the Book of Genesis as the wind that moves over the water: "In the beginning when God created the heavens and the earth, the earth was a formless void and darkness covered the face of the deep, while a wind from God swept over the face of the waters" (Genesis 1:1–2, NRSV). Here we focus on the word *wind.* In Hebrew, wind is *ruah,* which can also mean "breath" or "spirit." Substitute those words for *wind,* and we can read the verse the following way: "a Spirit of God, or Breath of God, swept over the face of the waters." We see that the Spirit of God was present in the beginning, bringing life out of nothingness.

Throughout the Old Testament, the Holy Spirit works quietly behind the scenes, preparing God's people for the coming of the Messiah. The Holy Spirit does amazing work to prepare a people for the Lord. God speaks through the prophets about what the Messiah will be like. "The spirit of the LORD will give him wisdom, and the knowledge and skill to rule his people" (Isaiah 11:2). Isaiah also announces that the Messiah to come is filled with God's Spirit and that

THINK ABOUT IT!

We describe the Holy Spirit as the breath of God. What does this image tell you about the Holy Spirit? What does this image tell you about the Holy Spirit's role in your life?

"he will bring justice to every nation" (Isaiah 42:1). Through the Holy Spirit, people will come to know Jesus Christ.

> The spirit of the LORD will give him wisdom,
> and the knowledge and skill to rule his people.
>
> Isaiah 11:2

In the Fullness of Time

The Holy Spirit's work of preparation for Christ's coming is completed in Mary. The Holy Spirit prepared Mary to give birth to Emmanuel, which means "God with us." Through her, God's plan of bringing Jesus into the world would be fulfilled. The *Catechism of the Catholic Church* calls Mary "the masterwork of the mission of the Son and the Spirit in the fullness of time" (721). Imagine being God's masterwork. This is what the Holy Spirit can do.

Read the Liturgy Connection article to find out what the priest is doing when he makes the Sign of the Cross over the bread and wine at Mass.

© Design Pics/Corbis

How did the Holy Spirit prepare Mary to welcome Jesus? By his power and love, Mary was "full of grace," full of God's life and love. Filled with the Holy Spirit, she conceived and gave birth to the Son of God. Watch what happened next. Thanks to Mary's cooperation, the Holy Spirit brought people together into relationship with her Son, Jesus Christ. The first of these people were the poor and humble like the shepherds, Simeon, and Anna.

Jesus and the Holy Spirit

Nearly two thousand years ago, Jesus began his earthly ministry with the following words:

> The Spirit of the Lord is upon me, because he has chosen me to bring good news to the poor. He has sent me to proclaim liberty to the captives and recovery of sight to the blind, to set free the oppressed and announce that the time has come when the Lord will save his people (Luke 4:18–19).

LITURGY CONNECTION

The Eucharistic Prayer

The next time you are at Mass, notice how, during Eucharistic Prayer II, the priest joins his hands and then holds them outstretched over the altar and makes the Sign of the Cross. He prays as follows:

> Make holy, therefore, these gifts, we pray, by sending down your Spirit upon them like the dewfall, so that they may become for us the Body and Blood of our Lord, Jesus Christ. (*Roman Missal*)

At this moment the priest asks the Holy Spirit to make holy the bread and wine so Christ will be truly present. The gift of Holy Communion, made possible by the Holy Spirit, is the food that nourishes us to bear fruit in the Church as disciples of Jesus.

By reading this Scripture passage to those gathered in the synagogue, Jesus tells them that his mission and the Holy Spirit's mission are the same. In fact, Jesus' whole work is a joint mission with the Holy Spirit. Jesus reveals this close connection with the Holy Spirit before his death when he makes the following promise to the disciples: "I will ask the Father, and he will give you another Helper, who will stay with you forever. He is the Spirit, who reveals the truth about God" (John 14:16–17).

Did You Know?

Symbols of the Holy Spirit

The Catholic Church uses visual symbols to help us understand the Holy Spirit. Water, fire, and a cloud and light are three symbols the Church uses to represent the Holy Spirit.

- **Water** symbolizes the Holy Spirit's actions in Baptism. Jesus tells us that the Holy Spirit is the living water that quenches our thirst for God (see John 7:37–39).
- **Fire** transforms. It is vibrant and full of energy. The Holy Spirit appears to the Apostles as tongues of fire at Pentecost (see Acts 2:1–4). The Holy Spirit energizes and transforms us.
- **A cloud and light** hide and reveal. In the Old Testament, God often appears as a fire or light within a cloud (see Exodus 40:38, Ezekiel 1:4). The Holy Spirit hides and reveals God's glory. Clouds play a role in Jesus' Baptism (see Matthew 3:13–17), Transfiguration (see Matthew 17:1–8), and Ascension (see Acts 1:6–11).

On a Mission

After Jesus was crucified and raised from the dead, he visited the Apostles. Remember that he had promised to send the Holy Spirit. But the disciples were afraid. They had just watched Jesus die on the cross. They were huddled behind locked doors when, suddenly, Jesus appeared in the middle of the room. He said to them: "'Peace be with you. As the Father sent me, so I send you.' Then he breathed on

© Naypong/Shutterstock.com

them and said, 'Receive the Holy Spirit. If you forgive people's sins, they are forgiven; if you do not forgive them, they are not forgiven'" (John 20:21–22).

On the Feast of Pentecost, fifty days after Jesus rises from the dead, the Holy Spirit descended on the disciples. The breath of God filled them in a new way. It gave them the courage to go out and preach the message of Jesus Christ. Think of it in the following way: through Christ and the Holy Spirit, God the Father gives the Church her mission: go to the ends of the earth. Spread the Good News of salvation. "The mission of Christ and the Spirit becomes the mission of the Church" (CCC, 730). At Pentecost the Church's mission began in a new way. Strengthened by the Holy Spirit and under his guidance, the Church continues the mission of Christ in the world.

Simple acts of kindness may not seem like a big deal. But they are actually signs of the Holy Spirit's life within us.

How does the Holy Spirit act in the Church? He prepares God's people and goes out to them with his love, to bring them to Christ. The Holy Spirit shows us who Christ is. He opens our minds to understand the mystery of Jesus' death and Resurrection. He makes present today the mystery of Christ through the Sacraments of the Church—especially the Eucharist, so that we will be one with God—in communion with him. The Holy Spirit, the Breath of God, works in the Church to build her up, to bring her life, and to make her holy.

Live It!

Filled with the Holy Spirit

God's gift of love is his first gift to us. He wants us to share in his life: "This hope does not disappoint us, for God has poured out his love into our hearts by means of the Holy Spirit, who is God's gift to us" (Romans 5:5). People who are filled with God's Spirit show their love for God through their attitudes and actions. They are loving, joyful, peaceful, and patient. The Holy Spirit helps people be kind and faithful, full of goodness, gentleness, and self-control (see Galatians 5:22). Whom do you know who shows God's love by doing kind things for others? For example, do you know someone who expresses love by his patience with others or her faithfulness to friends and family? Write that person a thank-you note for being a witness of God's gift of love.

PEOPLE OF FAITH
Saint John the Evangelist

© 2013 Saint Mary's Press/Illustration by Vicki Shuck

Saint John, a fisherman, was one of the first Apostles. Jesus chose him and his brother, James. Jesus "saw two other brothers . . . in their boat with their father Zebedee, getting their nets ready. Jesus called them, and at once they left the boat and their father, and went with him" (Matthew 4:21–22). John witnessed and participated in Jesus' ministry. He may also have been the beloved disciple in Saint John's Gospel, but this is unclear. If so, he was also at the foot of the cross with Mary, when Jesus told his mother that John would take care of her from now on: "Jesus saw his mother and the disciple he loved standing there; so he said to his mother, 'He is your son'" (John 19:26).

John is called the Evangelist because to evangelize means to "spread the Good News." An important part of John's message is Jesus' promise to send the Holy Spirit. John calls the Holy Spirit an **Advocate**, a helper and supporter who "will teach you everything and make you remember all that I have told you" (John 14:26, NRSV). John's Gospel spends more time reflecting on the meaning of Jesus' words and actions rather than describing them. You may recognize this Scripture passage: "For God loved the world so much that he gave his only Son, so that everyone who believes in him may not die but have eternal life" (3:16). John the Evangelist's message is that we love God and love one another. We celebrate his feast day on December 27.

191

18 Grace and the Gifts of the Holy Spirit

Key Words

grace
sanctifying grace
Gifts of the
Holy Spirit

Have you ever received a gift that was really amazing and unexpected? Maybe it wasn't a material thing that cost a lot of money. Maybe instead it was a kind gesture, help with a difficult task, or a thoughtful compliment from a friend. When you received this gift, maybe you thought to yourself: "Wow! That's really cool. I don't deserve it."

Compassion is evidence that grace, God's love, is at work. Can you think of times, both happy and sad, when you were aware of grace in your life?

© Andy Dean Photography/Shutterstock.com

We actually could say the same thing about the gift of God's grace. We can't do anything by ourselves to deserve or earn this amazing gift. What is grace? **Grace** is the gift of God's loving presence in our lives. It is the help he gives us through the Holy Spirit to participate in his life. God wants us to be with him. In the Sacrament of Baptism, we receive the life of the Holy Spirit. The gift of grace the Holy Spirit gives us draws us into close relationship with the Holy Trinity and gives us the help we need to become God's adopted sons and daughters.

God Takes the First Step

God made us to be with him. Every human heart longs for truth and goodness. This longing comes from God, and only he can satisfy it. God's gift of grace responds to the deepest yearnings of our hearts. One way to think about this is to imagine that there is a God-shaped vacuum or hole in every heart. Only God can fill it. We are made to be with God. God takes the first step with grace, his life. God does not force his gift of love on us. How we respond to it is up to us. God has created us in his image and given us the freedom and ability

PRAY IT!

God of all grace, I praise you and thank you for sharing your life with me. Through Jesus, your Son, I see how your grace can change the world. Help me accept your invitation to participate in your life. May the grace you offer me through the Holy Spirit put things right between you and me. Heal me and make me holy in your sight. Amen.

FUN FACT

One of the most common forms of prayer is meal prayers, or grace. Prayers of thanksgiving for food are found in religious texts and cultures all over the world. Praying grace is a way of acknowledging God's goodness to us in the gift of the food we eat. When we say grace at mealtimes, we acknowledge God's presence among us.

THINK ABOUT IT!

We are sharers in God's life. This means God can be part of our lives every minute of every day. How is your life different because God is a part of it?

to know him and love him. God will always love us. Nothing forces us to love him in return.

Let God's Grace In

What happens when we let God's grace in? Grace achieves real change in us. When a person is filled with God's life, it shows. In the Gospels Jesus used the metaphor of good fruit to explain what happens when a person says yes to God: "You will know them by what they do. Thorn bushes do not bear grapes, and briers do not bear figs. A healthy tree bears good fruit" (Matthew 7:16–17).

> Those who love me will obey my teaching. My Father will love them, and my Father and I will come to them and live with them.
>
> John 14:23

When we say yes to God's invitation to participate in his life, we act in a way that reflects Jesus' teachings and example. We don't do this to get something in return. We do good works out of love for God. It's not only what we do on the outside that matters. What is on the inside matters too. Look for the following indicators that God's grace is working in you and others: friendliness, willingness to forgive, respect for others, peacefulness, compassion, humility, thankfulness, and a helping spirit, just to name a few. All our actions that point others and ourselves to God are because of God's grace working in us.

Give Love Away

When we participate in God's life, we give love away. We have to. Why? Because God made us in his image and likeness, and that is what God does. He gives his love away. All the good we do and all the love we have belongs to God. It is for God. Grace is never something we earn. But something amazing

Did You Know?

Sanctifying Grace

God loves us. He wants to be part of our lives. He wants to be involved. God freely offers us the gift of his life, infused into our soul to heal us of sin and make us holy. We call this gift **sanctifying grace**. We need God's help to be holy, to be right with God. The sin of turning away from God, as Adam and Eve chose to do, damages the relationship God wants to have with us, his creatures. The gift of his sanctifying grace repairs the damage of sin and enables us to experience God's love. Through the Holy Spirit, we are united to Christ's dying and rising. We die to sin and are given new life.

happens when we choose to love. We open ourselves more and more to the gifts God constantly offers us. The love and the grace just keep coming. We keep giving it away to others because God's love has transformed us from the inside out.

Jesus was filled with God's love and gave it away to others. Jesus made God's life real for us; he was incarnate grace—that is, in-the-flesh grace. We can be in-the-flesh grace too. We can bring God to others.

Reference: 443-MW

JOB DESCRIPTION

Job Title: Being Christian

Reports To: God and the community

Job Summary: Living as disciples of Jesus Christ

Responsibilities: Loving God, loving others, loving ourselves

Job Requirements: Willingness to let God's grace work in you!

Everything Is Possible with God's Grace

Grace definitely has an eternal effect on our relationship with God. Exactly what the effect is depends on how well we accept the gift. Think about what you do when you receive a gift. You don't leave it wrapped and put it high on the shelf in your closet, do you? You open it. This is what we need to do with the gift of God's grace in our lives.

Did You Know?

Everything Is Possible

There are times when you might think, "Obeying God's will and doing what is right is hard." The fact is, we cannot, by ourselves, keep the Commandments. We cannot, on our own power, love as God calls us to love. The good news is, everything is possible with God in our lives. Jesus tells us: "I am the vine, and you are the branches. Those who remain in me, and I in them, will bear much fruit; for you can do nothing without me" (John 15:5). Even the very beginnings of our relationship with God are a result of his initial love for us. Through the grace of the Holy Spirit, we can earn for ourselves and for others all that we need for this life and eternal life. God makes all this possible because of his great love for us.

LiTURGY CONNECTION

The Confirmation Liturgy

During the liturgy for the Sacrament of Confirmation, the bishop recalls the grace of the Holy Spirit given to us at our Baptism. He extends his hands over the candidates and prays the following words:

> All-powerful God, Father of our Lord Jesus Christ, by water and the Holy Spirit you freed your sons and daughters from sin and gave them new life. Send your Holy Spirit upon them to be their Helper and Guide. Give them the spirit of wisdom and understanding, the spirit of right judgment and courage, the spirit of knowledge and reverence. Fill them with the spirit of wonder and awe in your presence. (*Rite of Confirmation*, 25)

Accepting the gift of God's grace means opening the gift and using it. This then allows us to fulfill our job descriptions as Catholics. We can reach out to the new person at school and offer our friendship. We can forgive the person who hurt us, even when it is difficult. We can clean out our closet and give our extra clothes to someone who needs them. We can pitch in at home to help with the chores and resist the urge to fight with our brothers or sisters. We can thank God, every day, for his blessings. We can love God and love our neighbors as ourselves.

> "As I have loved you, so you must love one another. If you have love for one another, then everyone will know you are my disciples."
> John 13:34–35

The Gifts of the Holy Spirit

God gives us the **Gifts of the Holy Spirit** to help us love him. These are special graces that help us respond to God's call to live holy lives. The seven Gifts of the Holy Spirit are Wisdom,

Understanding, Right Judgment (or Counsel), Courage (or Fortitude), Knowledge, Reverence (or Piety), and Wonder and Awe (or Fear of the Lord). These gifts help us follow Jesus Christ and live as his disciples. Let's take a closer look:

© Bill Wittman/www.wpwittman.com

In the Sacrament of Confirmation, the bishop anoints the candidate and says, "Be sealed with the Gift of the Holy Spirit."

- **Wisdom.** Wisdom is to see as God sees. Imagine that. A person with the gift of Wisdom looks at life through God's eyes, assessing the things going on in his or her life and in the world from God's point of view. A wise person recognizes where the Holy Spirit is at work in the world.

- **Understanding.** Understanding is an important gift for finding the meaning of God's truths and their significance for our lives. Understanding helps us recognize how God wants us to live.

- **Right Judgment (Counsel).** This gift helps us make choices that will lead us closer to God rather than away from God. The gift of Right Judgment, also called Counsel, helps us figure out what God wants. It helps us know the difference between right and wrong when we make decisions.

- **Courage (Fortitude).** Life can bring many challenges. The gift of Courage, also called Fortitude, is the special help we need when we face challenges or struggles. Those who have the gift of Courage don't let life's obstacles pull them away from God.

- **Knowledge.** This gift helps us understand the meaning of what God has revealed, particularly the Good News of Jesus Christ. A person with the gift of Knowledge keeps striving to learn more about God through Scripture and the Church's Tradition. This gift is closely related to the gifts of Understanding and Wisdom.

- **Reverence (Piety).** This gift, sometimes called Piety, gives us a deep sense of respect for God and the Church. A reverent person honors God and approaches him with humility, trust, and love.

Live It!

Possible through God's Grace

Every day this week, look at your life in a new way. Look around you to see what God makes possible in your life. Perhaps God's grace makes possible the random acts of kindness you witness and the loving forgiveness family members offer one another. Maybe you will find God's grace in the gesture of a consoling hug or the words of a grateful friend. Do you see that God's life in you gives you the courage to say no to choices that will hurt you or others? Do you recognize that through God's presence, you can say words like "I am sorry" and "I forgive you" and really mean them? God's grace makes it possible for us to live healthy and holy lives. Choose to be with God every day.

- **Wonder and Awe (Fear of the Lord).** The gift of Wonder and Awe makes us aware of God's greatness and power. This gift is also called Fear of the Lord, because the wonder of God's love and unlimited power can overwhelm us. It may fill us with tears of joy or bring us to our knees when we recognize that God is present in our midst.

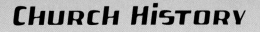

Church History

The Church and Other Religions

Declaration on the Relation of the Church to Non-Christian Religions is one of the final documents the Second Vatican Council approved in the 1960s. The document marks a special moment in the Church's history with other religions, including Judaism. It rejects attitudes of contempt for Judaism and the Jewish people, and it rejects anti-Semitic (anti-Jewish) teachings. The Jewish faith, unlike other non-Christian religions, is a response to God's Revelation in the Old Testament. The Church has a profound love and respect for the Jews.

Though the Church deeply respects other religions, it emphasizes that we can know the fullness of God's Revelation only through the Catholic Church. This does not mean that those who follow other religions are barred from eternal life with God. Many people are not Christian but seek God with sincere hearts. People who try to do God's will, even if they do not know Jesus Christ, may also achieve eternal friendship with God, or salvation.

19 THE BIBLE: THE GOSPELS

KEY WORDS

Gospels

synoptic

Almost everyone likes stories. Stories can encourage, motivate, and inspire us. They can help us have bigger dreams for our lives and become better people.

The Gospels contain sacred stories through which we meet Jesus Christ, our Lord and Savior, the Son of God. Written by the sacred authors, the Gospels are the inspired Word of God. They faithfully communicate what Jesus, the Son of God, did and taught for our salvation. The *Catechism of the Catholic Church* declares that the Gospels are "the heart of

Where would you be in this picture—close to Jesus, wanting to know and follow him, or standing outside the circle, afraid to change your life?

© Brooklyn Museum/Corbis

all the Scriptures" (125). In the Gospels we find stories that force us to stop and think about what we are doing and why. Jesus shows us that our lives have meaning and purpose. He assures us that we are loved and are able to love God and others in return.

Jesus invites us to get to know him. We sometimes hold back. We think we know him already. We think we are too busy or too young. Deep down we may fear—and it might be true—that we will need to change some things in our lives if we get to know Jesus well. But we cannot be afraid to let into our lives the person who best knows and loves us. Jesus will show us how we can become truly great.

> This is the Good News about Jesus
> Christ, the Son of God.
>
> Mark 1:1

Jesus and the New Testament

How can we get to know Jesus Christ and the fullness of truth he brings? To answer this, think about how we get to know people in our families who lived before us. Sometimes our older relatives tell all kinds of stories about family members who have died. Maybe the people who have died—or the people who lived with them—left written records like diaries or memoirs.

PRAY IT!

Dear God, thank you for telling me about yourself in Scripture. Thank you for showing me yourself most fully in the Gospels. May the Holy Spirit help me understand Jesus' life and teachings. Let them inspire me to grow in friendship with you. Help me serve you and others as the Gospels teach us to do. May I become more and more like Christ, so that others can see him in me. Amen.

FUN FACT

Have you ever had to copy some writing by hand? Now we have machines that can copy anything written or printed. But before the 1400s, even printing presses didn't exist. Trained people had to copy by hand writings like the Gospels.

This is the way it happened with Jesus. The men he was closest to, the Apostles, were the chief witnesses of his public life. After Jesus rose from the dead and ascended into Heaven, the Apostles told others about his life and teachings. They did this through their preaching and by their examples under the guidance of the Holy Spirit.

The Holy Spirit also led some of the Apostles or their helpers to write down their teachings about Jesus' life and message. These writings became the four **Gospels** of Matthew, Mark, Luke, and John. The word *gospel* means "good news."

For we did not follow cleverly devised myths when we made known to you the power and coming of our Lord Jesus Christ, but we were eyewitnesses of his majesty.

2 Peter 1:16

We learn about Jesus' life and teachings chiefly from the four Gospels, the Acts of the Apostles, and many letters in the New Testament. They are at the heart of the whole Bible because Jesus is their center. The Old Testament prepares the way for Christ, the promised Savior. The New Testament centers on him and on following him with the help of the Holy Spirit.

Other written reports of Christ's life appeared in early Christianity. But the Gospels of Matthew, Mark, Luke, and John are the only reports of Jesus' life the Church accepts among the inspired books of the Bible.

Writing the Gospels

Have you ever done one of those oral history reports that are popular assignments at some schools? They can be fun. You talk to people who lived through some big historical event. You may look at written records they have. Then you write a summary.

Other students may do a report on the same historical event. They may talk to different eyewitnesses. They may include other facts or order them differently. Their reports will end up slightly different from yours.

The Gospel writers did something similar. Each one chose facts about Christ's life and teachings that had been passed on by word of mouth. They may have used earlier writings about Jesus' life and teachings. For example, Luke's Gospel explains his approach and purpose clearly:

Many people have done their best to write a report of the things that have taken place among us. They wrote what we have been told by those who saw these things from the beginning and who proclaimed the message. And so, Your Excellency, because I have carefully studied all these matters from their beginning, I thought

THINK ABOUT IT!

"Go throughout the whole world and preach the gospel to all people" (Mark 16:15). Imagine that Christ has just given this mission to you and your friends. Even though you don't have a lot of money, or friends in important places, or much experience in speaking to other people, you know you want to accept the mission.

How would you go about spreading Jesus' teachings? What first steps would you take? How far would you try to spread the message? Through what means would you do so?

© Brooklyn Museum/Corbis

Mark's Gospel is the earliest of the four Gospels. It is also the shortest. Find out more about this Gospel and the other Gospels written by Matthew, Luke, and John.

it would be good to write an orderly account for you. I do this so that you will know the full truth about everything which you have been taught. (1:1–4)

The four Gospels all portray Jesus Christ, and so they do share many of the same stories about his life and teachings. In particular, the Gospels of Matthew, Mark, and Luke often record the same events in about the same order. They are called the **synoptic** Gospels. The Greek word from which *synoptic* comes means "seen together."

Did You Know?

Reading Sacred Scripture

Many people living during Jesus' earthly lifetime could not read. So the Jewish Scriptures were read out loud in the Jewish places of worship, called synagogues. Luke's Gospel, for example, shows Jesus returning to Nazareth, his hometown. In the synagogue he reads out loud a passage from the Book of Isaiah. In the passage is a promise of a savior coming to bring Good News to the poor. Jesus says that promise has come true in him (see Luke 4:14–21).

Christians have kept the practice of reading and explaining Scripture during worship. Especially in Catholic worship, we read from both the Old and New Testaments. This helps us see how they relate to each other.

But each of these Gospels is slightly different, because the sources and readers of each were different. Matthew, for example, writes mostly for Jewish people. He often shows how Jesus' life fulfills the promises and prophecies of the Old Testament. Mark writes more for Gentiles, that is, people who are not Jewish. So he explains Jewish customs and words. Early Christian writers say Mark gives us Peter's teachings.

The Gospel of Luke often reminds us that Jesus came to save all people. It records some unique stories and teachings that stress this point. For example, the Parable of the Prodigal Son shows that God's mercy can forgive the worst sinners (see Luke 15:11–32). The Parable of Lazarus and the Rich Man teaches that we should love people who are poor as God does (see Luke 16:19–31). Luke also tells more about Jesus' childhood. Even when Jesus is a child, some people see that he fulfills God's promise to send a savior (see Luke 2:22–50).

John wrote his Gospel some years after the others were finished. His organization and focus are different from those of the synoptic Gospels.

LITURGY CONNECTION

The Sunday Gospels

The Liturgy of the Word is the first major part of the Mass. A reading from the Gospels is always included. The order of readings for Sunday Masses follows a three-year rotation. Each year in the cycle is referred to by letter: A, B, or C.

Many of the Sunday Gospels during the seasons of Advent, Christmas, Lent, and Easter come from John's Gospel. A reading from the other three Gospels is usually read on the remaining Sundays. (We call these weeks outside special liturgical seasons Ordinary Time.) Readings from Matthew are proclaimed in Year A, readings from Mark in Year B, and readings from Luke in Year C. The Church helps us think about the whole Gospel message over time.

© asiseeit/iStockphoto.com

Have you ever participated in a Bible study group? Reading and discussing the Bible with others can be a great way to grow in faith and knowledge of God's Word and how it applies to your life.

He also reflects more deeply on Jesus' teachings. John's readers were mostly Greek-speaking and not Jewish. He wanted to make clear right from the beginning of the Gospel that Christ is truly divine, the Son of God. John's Gospel doesn't start with the earthly life of Jesus as the others do. Instead, John shows that the Second Person of the Trinity existed always with God and is God. Christ is the Word by which God expresses himself in creation and the Old Testament. God shows himself fully by having the Word become someone like us.

> I passed on to you what I received, which is of the greatest importance: that Christ died for our sins, as written in the Scriptures.
>
> 1 Corinthians 15:3

Getting to Know Christ

A few key ideas can help us get the most out of reading or hearing Scripture.

First, the writers' different audiences and purposes help explain what each author includes and stresses. Matthew, for example, is not trying to bore us with his lists of Jesus' ancestors. He's showing his Jewish readers that Jesus really is from the line of the Messiah (see Matthew 1:1–17).

© Jim Hollander/epa/Corbis

In 1947 herders discovered old manuscripts in a cave near where Jesus lived. These manuscripts are called the Dead Sea Scrolls. They include some of the oldest biblical writings ever found.

Second, we do not have to understand every word to get the basic idea. But knowing the literal meanings of words can deepen our appreciation. At the same time, the Gospels often use physical things to stand for spiritual things. For example, Jesus says his disciples will fish for men. By this Jesus means that his disciples will work to bring others to his Kingdom.

Third, events in the Gospels often complete or make perfect events that happened earlier in the Old Testament. In chapter 6 of John's Gospel, for instance, Jesus recalls how God provided a kind of bread for his people in the desert so they wouldn't die (see Exodus, chapter 16). Then Jesus reveals that he is the perfect Bread from Heaven that gives eternal life to everyone who believes in him.

Fourth, we do not have to figure out everything ourselves. Many Bibles have helpful notes and comments. Thoughtful Christians have written many commentaries on the Gospels.

Finally, we are not alone. The Holy Spirit especially guides the bishops who have succeeded, or followed, the Apostles. They have the full power and responsibility to explain Sacred Scripture and Sacred Tradition. But the Church also urges us to study and think about Jesus. If we ask in prayer, the Holy Spirit will guide us in our reading.

Reading the Gospels has changed lives. Missionaries have risked their own safety to bring the Good News to those who have not heard. Others have made the lives of those around their homes much better by their Gospel-inspired words and deeds.

Live It!

How to Read Scripture

God speaks to us personally in Sacred Scripture. We read Scripture to understand God's will for our lives. So, how can we get the most out of reading from Scripture, especially the Gospels?

First, we can ask the Holy Spirit to help us understand and live the Gospel message.

Second, we can read intentionally and carefully. We can imagine the people and events and even "make a movie" of them in our minds.

Third, we can pause to think about what we have read and how we can apply it to our own lives. How does the Holy Spirit encourage, teach, correct, challenge, comfort, or inspire us in this passage?

This way of reading and reflecting on Scripture can yield big insights. Of course, that will not always be the case, but if you keep trying with faith, the fruits will surely be great.

If you want to make a difference in the world, try reading the Gospels. You will meet unforgettable, real people like Mary, the Mother of God; Joseph; Peter; James; and John. Above all, you will get to know Jesus. He will enlighten, challenge, encourage, comfort, and amaze you. He will become your hero and ideal. He will make you truly happy in this life and the next.

Church History

The Language of the Gospels

All four of the Gospels were originally written in Greek, because that was the language that most educated people spoke at the time the Gospels were written.

Later, when Rome became the center of the known world, Latin became the universal language of the people. Saint Jerome, who was a scholar of languages, a hermit, and a priest, began translating the New Testament from Greek into Latin. He then went on to translate much of the Old Testament from its original Hebrew into Latin. His translation became known as the Vulgate edition of the Bible. The word *vulgate* means "the speech of the common people."

For centuries the Vulgate edition of the Bible was the only translation of Sacred Scripture that people read and heard. Gradually, translations into other languages began to be made. With the invention of the printing press in the sixteenth century, Bibles no longer needed to be copied by hand, and translations into German and English became available to the people, especially during the Protestant Reformation. In modern times, various parts of the Bible have been translated into over two thousand languages.

20 THE BIBLE: THE ACTS OF THE APOSTLES

KEY WORDS

evangelize
Pentecost
synagogues

In the early years of the Church, there were no twenty-four-hour news networks, cell phones, Internet, e-mail, texting, or blogs. There was no overnight mail or package delivery. Yet twenty years after Jesus' death, Christianity had spread across a large geographical area. How could Christianity have spread so quickly without the modern means of communication we take for granted?

Hop in a time machine. Take yourself back to the first century AD. Imagine that your friend next door is acting a bit differently. You can't quite pinpoint what it is. His family regularly gathers with other families in their homes. You're not sure what they do when they meet. His parents still go about their daily business, working and doing ordinary household tasks. Even your parents comment that something seems different about the neighbors, something that wasn't there before, a kind of peacefulness or joy. You notice this in your friend too. There's something different about how he is treating his sister (whom he's never gotten along with well), and he actually helps out around the neighborhood now.

Finally, you ask your friend what has changed. Your friend replies: "You are right. I have changed. My family is Christian now. We follow the teachings of Jesus Christ."

You're curious, so you say, "Tell me more." But remember, this is the first century. Your friend does not pull a Bible from his pocket or take a catechism off the shelf. Neither existed in the early Church. Instead, he relies on the spoken Word and his modeling of a new way of life. With the help of the Holy Spirit, he can share this new faith with you.

Pentecost

The Acts of the Apostles is a written account of the early Church—the Church that took shape right after Jesus' Resurrection and Ascension into Heaven. Acts describes what we call the Apostolic Church—the Church of the Apostles and their first followers. It focuses on the work of Saints Peter and Paul in spreading the Word of God to the far reaches of the Roman Empire. A main theme in Acts is how the Holy Spirit guided the Apostles so the Word of God could spread.

In the first chapter of Acts, we read about how Jesus stayed on earth for forty days after the Resurrection. He appeared to the Apostles and instructed them by the power of the Holy Spirit. He told them to stay in Jerusalem, saying, "In a few days you will be baptized with

PRAY IT!

Holy God, send the Holy Spirit to fill my heart with your love. Help me live in harmony with others as the first Christians did. Help me resolve differences and forgive. May the power of the Holy Spirit help me to teach others about your Son by the way I live. Come, Holy Spirit! Fill my heart and kindle in me the fire of your love. I pray this in the name of Jesus, your Son. Amen.

Illustration by Elizabeth Wang, "The Descent of the Holy Spirit at Pentecost," copyright © Radiant Light 2008, www.radiantlight.org.uk

Tongues of fire—this is what the disciples saw on the great feast of Pentecost. Filled with the power of the Holy Spirit, they went out to transform the world. When we are on fire with the Spirit, we can do the same.

the Holy Spirit" (Acts 1:5). He even gave them a hint about what the Spirit would help them do: "When the Holy Spirit comes upon you, you will be filled with power, and you will be witnesses for me in Jerusalem, in all of Judea and Samaria, and to the ends of the earth" (Acts 1:8). Jesus told the Apostles what they were to do: **evangelize**. This means continuing the mission of Jesus Christ by spreading the Good News to the ends of the earth.

Jesus' promise about the coming of the Holy Spirit was fulfilled a short while later. We call this event **Pentecost**. The Acts of the Apostles describes this day:

> When the day of Pentecost came, all the believers were gathered together in one place. Suddenly there was a noise from the sky which sounded like a strong wind blowing, and it filled the whole house where they were sitting. Then they saw what looked like tongues of fire which spread out and touched each person there. They were all filled with the Holy Spirit and began to talk in other languages, as the Spirit enabled them to speak. (2:1–4)

Imagine the scene after the Holy Spirit came. The Apostles were speaking in different languages. There was noise and confusion. People wondered, "What does this mean?" (Acts 2:12). Things were so wild and crazy that people laughed at Christ's followers: "These people are drunk!" (2:13).

What did Peter do? He stood in front of the crowd with the other Apostles gathered around him, and he spoke. He made a stunning announcement: "Jesus, whom you crucified, is the one that God has made Lord and Messiah!" (Acts 2:36). The people asked the Apostles, "What shall we do, brothers?" (2:37). Peter answered, "Each one of you must turn away from your sins and be baptized in the name of Jesus Christ, so that your sins will be forgiven; and you will receive God's gift, the Holy Spirit" (2:38).

From this moment forward, the job of Christ's followers was clear: spread the Good News. Baptize in the name of the Father, Son, and Holy Spirit. From this moment forward, the Holy Spirit took charge. Believers gathered in close community where they shared possessions, ate together, and prayed together. More and more people kept joining them (see Acts 2:43–47). The followers of Jesus Christ, on fire with the Holy Spirit, would take his message to the ends of the earth.

> [Paul said] "What I say is the very same thing which the prophets and Moses said was going to happen: that the Messiah must suffer and be the first one to rise from death, to announce the light of salvation to the Jews and to the Gentiles."
>
> Acts 26:22–23

Think About It!

Making the Good News of Jesus Christ known in the world today is the responsibility of every follower of Jesus. How do you participate in the call to make disciples of all nations? How does knowing that the Holy Spirit is alive in you affect how you see the world and your place in it?

LiTURGY CONNECTION

Pentecost

Every year the Church celebrates the Feast of Pentecost during the Easter season. When you go to Church on Pentecost Sunday, you will see red decorations and red vestments (the special religious clothing worn by priests). On Pentecost the color red symbolizes the Holy Spirit, who descended on the Apostles at Pentecost as red tongues of fire.

If you go to the vigil Mass on the Saturday evening before Pentecost, you will hear John 7:37–39 proclaimed. In this passage Jesus refers to the Holy Spirit as living water. What does this tell you about how the Holy Spirit works in your life?

The Work of Saint Peter

In the Acts of the Apostles, we see Peter emerge as the leader of the early Christian community struggling to find its way. He guided the Apostles in choosing a successor to Judas (see Acts 1:12–26) after Jesus ascended to Heaven. On Pentecost he bravely spoke to the gathered crowds (see 2:14–42). In chapters 3 through 12, we read how Peter continued Jesus' mission through his words and actions. He healed the lame and the sick (see Acts 3:1–10, 5:12–16) and continued to preach that Jesus is the Messiah promised in the Old Testament.

Peter's actions caught the attention of some Jewish leaders. They were jealous of Peter and the other Apostles and feared that Peter was turning the Jewish people against them. Twice they put Peter in prison (see Acts 5:17–21, 12:1–19). Both times Peter was miraculously set free by angels. He continued to evangelize bravely, despite the persecutions and threats to his life.

Peter and other early Christian leaders also started to travel outside Jerusalem to preach about Christ. This preaching attracted some non-Jewish people, called

Gentiles, to believe in Christ and to be baptized. The Apostle Philip taught an Ethiopian (African) official about Jesus. The official immediately confessed his faith in Jesus, and Philip baptized him right on the spot (see Acts 8:26–40). A Roman soldier named Cornelius had a vision of an angel, who told him to send for Saint Peter. At the same time, Peter had a vision that said people of all races can become followers of Christ. So when Peter went to Cornelius's house, he baptized Cornelius's whole family after the Holy Spirit descended on them. Events like this convinced Peter and the Apostles that they must preach about Jesus to all people, not just Jewish people.

On This Rock

Jesus knew that his disciples would need a leader after he returned to his Father in Heaven. He prepared the Apostle Peter for this role. Jesus asked Peter, "Who do you say I am?" (Matthew 16:15). Peter replied, "You are the Messiah, the Son of the living God" (16:16). Peter understood who Jesus is. Jesus said to him: "And so I tell you, Peter: you are a rock, and on this rock foundation I will build my church, and not even death will ever be able to overcome it. I will give you the keys of the Kingdom of heaven" (16:18–19). Peter would be the visible head of the Church on earth after Jesus' Ascension.

FUN FACT

Rome was the most important city in the Roman Empire at the time of Jesus' earthly ministry. Thanks to people like Saints Peter and Paul, Rome became the most important city in the Church, and the bishop of Rome became the most important Church leader, known as the Pope. Francis is the current Bishop of Rome and Pope.

The Travels of Saint Paul

The second half of the Acts of the Apostles focuses on another early Church leader, Saint Paul (who was called Saul before his conversion). When we meet Paul in chapters 7 and 8, he was not yet a Christian; rather, he was persecuting Christians (see 7:57—8:3)! He was a faithful Jew who believed that the followers of Jesus Christ were hurting the Jewish faith. But Jesus had important plans for Paul. Jesus appeared to him in a bright light and said: "Saul, Saul! Why do you persecute me?" (9:4). Jesus sent Paul into a city, where a Christian named Ananias received Paul and baptized him. From that moment, Paul became an Apostle and started teaching and preaching about Jesus to everyone who listened (see Acts, chapter 9).

The good news about Jesus spread far and wide. Check out this map of Saint Paul's travels. Trace his journey to Rome, where he was martyred.

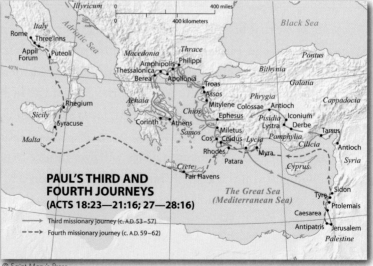

PAUL'S THIRD AND FOURTH JOURNEYS
(ACTS 18:23—21:16; 27—28:16)

→ Third missionary journey (c. A.D. 53–57)
---→ Fourth missionary journey (c. A.D. 59–62)

At first some Christians did not trust Paul. But Paul had supporters like Barnabas who spoke up for him. Paul was so sincere, so eager to preach about Jesus, that the Christian leaders in Jerusalem sent him on missionary journeys to cities that had not yet heard about Christ. He and his companions traveled to major cit-

© Bill Wittman/www.wpwittman.com

ies like Antioch, Corinth, and Thessalonica. When they arrived, Paul preached about Jesus in the Jewish meeting places, called **synagogues**. Those who believed in Jesus were baptized. Under Paul's leadership these converts formed communities—the first churches. They met together to learn more about Jesus, to pray, and to celebrate the Eucharist. When Paul decided that these churches were ready to survive without his presence, he and his companions moved on to the next city to start another church. Paul went on three long missionary journeys, each of which took several years and spanned thousands of miles of travel on foot or by boat.

Like Peter, Paul attracted the attention of Jewish leaders who did not agree with what he was doing. These people persecuted Paul by challenging his authority and even physically attacking him. Paul described his troubles in his Second Letter to the Corinthians:

> Five times I was given the thirty-nine lashes by the Jews; three times I was whipped by the Romans; and once I was stoned. I have been in

Saints Peter and Paul (center, in front of tapestry) took seriously the mission Jesus gave us to go out and make disciples. How do young people contribute to this mission?

219

three ship wrecks, and once I spent twenty-four hours in the water. In my many travels I have been in danger from floods and from robbers, in danger from my own people and from Gentiles. . . . There has been work and toil; often I have gone without sleep; I have been hungry and thirsty. (11:24–27)

Saint Paul endured all these things because he was so committed to telling others the Good News about Jesus Christ. Because of people like him, the early Church quickly spread and flourished. After his third missionary journey, Paul was arrested by the Romans. As a Roman citizen, he was sent to Rome so he could defend himself

Live It!

Share the Good News

After they received the Holy Spirit, the Apostles could speak to total strangers. They could spread the Good News to people with whom they shared nothing in common, not even language. You might experience a world of difference between you and another person—such as culture, interests, friends, race, age, and religion. Sometimes it is difficult to overcome those differences.

Get to know someone who is different from you. Take the time to find out about your shared beliefs and differing beliefs. Discover why people who are different from you can be a gift. They can help you to be more accepting and respectful. They can help you to become a better person. Maybe you will even have a chance to share why Jesus is important to you, as the early Christians did.

before the Roman emperor. While in Rome he continued his ministry. Acts tells us, "He preached about the Kingdom of God and taught about the Lord Jesus Christ, speaking with all boldness and freedom" (28:31). After two years Paul lost his case and was beheaded, becoming one of the Church's early martyrs.

> Peter and the other apostles answered, "We must obey God, not men. . . . We are witnesses to these things—we and the Holy Spirit, who is God's gift to those who obey him."
>
> Acts 5:29,32

Church History

The First Bishops

The Apostles formed new Christian communities when they traveled to preach the Good News. Before leaving these communities, the Apostles designated local Church leaders by laying hands on them. These leaders were the first bishops, called *episkopos* in Greek. Christianity spread quickly, and soon the Church communities were too large to be cared for by one bishop. Each bishop ordained priests to help him in his ministry. The Apostles also chose respected men to be the first deacons, who were responsible for distributing food to widows and others in need. By the end of the first century, the Church had defined the roles of bishops, priests, and deacons. You can read more about the ordained ministry of bishops, priests, and deacons in chapter 36, "The Sacraments of Matrimony and Holy Orders," of this handbook.

Peter was the first bishop of Rome and the first Pope. To this day the Bishop of the Church of Rome is the Pope. He is the successor of Peter and is the head of the universal Church on earth.

21 THE BIBLE: THE LETTERS

KEY WORD

resurrection
Gentiles

Today we have some pretty amazing ways to communicate with people, especially those who do not live close to us. We can post messages to online social networks, send texts or e-mails, or set up a video chat if we want to talk to someone face-to-face. But not too long ago— probably when your parents or grandparents were

Can you remember the last time you received a card or letter in the mail? Do you remember the last time you sent a card or letter? Because they take thought and time, cards and letters are special.

© jarenwicklund/iStockphoto.com

your age—the only ways to communicate over long distances were to make a phone call, send a telegram, or write a letter and mail it at the post office. And two thousand years ago, when the Church was just beginning, you could send a letter only with a messenger.

So imagine for a moment that you are Saint Paul, traveling from city to city to start new Christian communities. A messenger comes and gives you a letter from one of the communities. The letter says they are having some kind of trouble. What do you do? You cannot just leave the new community you are helping to develop right now. So you write a letter, giving advice to your old friends about how to deal with their problem. Then you send them the letter, maybe even using the same messenger who brought their letter to you.

The nice thing about letters written on paper is that you can keep them and treasure them. This is exactly what happened with the letters of Saint Paul and other early Church leaders. The communities who received these letters kept them and even shared them with other communities. Over time many of these letters were collected and added to the growing body of early Christian writings. Together with the four Gospels, the Acts of the Apostles, and the Book of Revelation, they formed the New Testament of the Bible.

PRAY IT!

God our Father, you sent
    your Holy Spirit
    upon the apostles,
and through them and
    their successors you
    give the Holy Spirit
    to your people.
May his work begun at
    Pentecost continue to
    grow in the hearts of
    all who believe.
We ask this through
    Christ our Lord.
Amen.
(*Rite of Confirmation,* 30)

FUN FACT

The four Gospels are not the oldest books in the New Testament. The oldest book is the First Letter to the Thessalonians. Saint Paul wrote this letter around AD 50, about twenty years after Jesus' death and Resurrection.

Understanding the New Testament Letters

The New Testament contains twenty-one letters, also called epistles (a Greek word meaning "letter"). Thirteen of the letters were written by Paul or his followers. Seven more were written by James, Peter, John, and Jude (or by their followers). The Letter to the Hebrews is by an unknown author, and it reads more like a sermon than a letter. Most of these letters follow this format:

- The letter begins with a greeting saying who wrote the letter and to whom it is written.

- The letter continues with the body, or message, addressing the writer's main concerns.

- The letter ends with personal messages to people in the community, followed by a blessing.

As you read these New Testament letters, you can see that understanding them is challenging, because we have only one side of the story. We do not have the original messages that prompted Paul or Peter or John to write their letters. So we have to make an educated guess about the concerns they were responding to. Sometimes the concern is obvious, but other times it is not. Many Bibles have introductions to each book. Reading these introductions can help you to understand the concerns a letter is responding to. But even if we do not know the exact details, the values in these New Testament letters can help us to live as Christians today.

> This is how it will be when the dead are raised to life. When the body is buried, it is mortal; when raised, it will be immortal. When buried, it is ugly and weak; when raised, it will be beautiful and strong.
>
> 1 Corinthians 15:42–43

© Bill Wittman/www.wpwittman.com

We hear the New Testament letters at the Sunday Eucharist, at the second reading. On weekdays, when there are only two readings, the first reading is from the New Testament letters and the second reading is the Gospel.

Themes in the Letters of Saint Paul

Saint Paul, whom we meet in the Acts of the Apostles, has more letters in the New Testament than any other author. Saint Paul was an early Church leader and missionary. He traveled from city to city to begin new communities and preach about the saving work of Jesus Christ. When one of his communities had problems, he would write a letter to its people, giving them advice and encouragement. Here are some themes you will find in Paul's letters.

Paul emphasized the importance of Jesus' death on the cross. Death by crucifixion was a terrible death, reserved for the worst criminals. So some Christians were embarrassed by the fact that Jesus had died on a cross. Paul assured them that Jesus' death was part of God's plan (see 1 Corinthians 1:18–25, Philippians 2:6–11). He told the Corinthians, "For the message about Christ's death on the cross is nonsense to those who are being lost; but for us who are being saved it is God's power" (1 Corinthians 1:18). He

Live It!

Make a Lasting Connection

Throughout his letters Paul made sure his recipients understood his love and care for them. At the beginning or end of his letters (or both), we find heartfelt greetings of love and concern. And Paul always mentions Jesus Christ, and his love, grace, or peace. How welcome these greetings must have been to those who knew Paul personally!

Today letter-writing is almost a lost art, but a real letter, not just a text message or an e-mail, is still meaningful. When you write a letter, you give a gift of yourself, and your letter becomes a tangible keepsake. Is there someone in your life who would love to receive a letter from you? Maybe a sibling, a friend, or a grandparent? Today write a real letter or note telling that person what is going on in your life and what he or she means to you—just a few words, in your own handwriting, to show you care.

encouraged them to be thankful for Jesus' death on the cross because through it our sins were forgiven, and we now have eternal life with God.

Paul also taught about the **resurrection** of the body. Some people in Paul's time did not believe in life after death. Instead, some believed that only the soul is immortal and that only our soul lives on after we die. In response Paul emphasized that everyone who believes in Christ will be raised to new life (see 1 Corinthians 15:12–34, 1 Thessalonians 4:13–18). He taught that not just our souls but our bodies will be resurrected, and our resurrected bodies will be perfect and immortal (see 1 Corinthians 15:35–50).

Another important theme in Paul's letters is that Jesus Christ came to save all people—not just God's Chosen People, the Jews. The first Christians were Jewish, just as Jesus was. Many of them believed that the Messiah came only to save Jewish people. They believed that **Gentiles**— those who were not Jewish—had to become Jewish in order to be Christians. Converting to Judaism meant following all the Jewish laws and customs. But God revealed to Paul that his saving plan is for all people and that no one has to become Jewish to be saved. Paul told the Galatians, "We know that a person is

THiNk AbouT IT!

Imagine that you live in one of the early Christian communities founded by Paul or one of the other early followers of Christ. What spiritual question or concern today would prompt you to ask your community's founder for advice? Who would write your letter? Who would you trust to carry it? Do you think your community would trust the response and follow its advice? Why or why not?

put right with God only through faith in Jesus Christ, never by doing what the Law requires" (Galatians 2:16). Paul constantly reminded people of this teaching (see Romans 3:9–31; Ephesians 2:11–22). He even had to correct Peter (see Galatians 2:11–14).

> Dear friends, let us love one another, because love comes from God. Whoever loves is a child of God and knows God.
>
> 1 John 4:7

Did You Know?

The Body of Christ

Have you ever heard the song "We Are the Body of Christ"? The image of the Church as the Body of Christ comes from the letters of Saint Paul. He wanted a way to tell early Christians that every person is needed by the Church. So he used the image of a human body. He said that each of us is like an eye, ear, foot, or hand. The eyes, ears, feet, and hands have unique roles and must work together. In the same way, every Christian has unique gifts to share with the Church. Paul told the Romans, "Though we are many, we are one body in union with Christ, and we are all joined to each other as different parts of one body" (Romans 12:5).

Paul also said that no person in the Body of Christ is more important than any other person. Some roles and some gifts may seem more important, but every person and every gift is needed. You can read more about the Body of Christ in 1 Corinthians, chapter 12.

Themes in the Other Letters

The first followers of Jesus had many challenges. Because Christianity was a new religion, people distrusted Christ's followers and even blamed them for things they didn't do or say (see the martyrdom of Stephen in Acts 6:8—7:60). Whole groups of people were learning about Jesus for the first time, so they naturally had misunderstandings and different opinions about how to live as a Christian. Under the inspiration of the Holy Spirit, the letter writers of the New Testament helped the early Christians to respond to these challenges.

The First Letter of Peter addressed the suffering the first Christians experienced for living their faith. Peter told them to remember how Christ suffered and to imitate him: "Do not pay back evil with evil or cursing with cursing; instead, pay back with a blessing" (1 Peter 3:9). The letter reassured them, "If you endure suffering even when you have done right, God will bless you for it" (2:20).

LiTURGY CONNECTION

The Second Reading

If the New Testament letters sound familiar, you may be used to hearing them at Mass. On most Sundays and special feasts, the second reading during the Liturgy of the Word comes from the New Testament— usually one of the Epistles. The New Testament letters are read somewhat continuously from Sunday to Sunday, which means that the second reading each Sunday begins near where it left off the previous Sunday. Some passages from the letters are never read, but this arrangement allows the Church to hear most of these New Testament letters on a regular cycle. At Sunday Mass pay close attention to the second reading. If it is from one of the New Testament Epistles, who wrote it? What do you know about this letter after reading this chapter?

The Letter of James addressed the concern of living our faith with integrity. It seems that some early Christians were saying one thing and doing another. The letter says: "Suppose there are brothers or sisters who need clothes and don't have enough to eat. What good is there in your saying to them, 'God bless you! Keep warm and eat well!'" (James 2:15–16). The letter warns against judging other people, against boasting, and against ignoring the poor and hungry.

The First Letter of John warns us not to believe people who deny that Jesus is the Messiah, even though they might sound convincing. It tells us to live in the light of God's revealed truth. How do you know if you are living in the light? The letter says: "If we love others, we live in the light, and so there is nothing in us that will cause someone else to sin. But if we hate others, we are in the darkness" (1 John 2:10–11). The letter could be called the "love letter" of the New Testament because the whole letter talks about the importance of love.

The letters of the New Testament are not just for Christians in the first century. Their message is for people of every time and culture. They tell us how to live as Christians. Read them and let them guide your life with Christ.

Church History

Enculturation

How many different peoples have embraced the Word of God over the centuries? Enculturation is the process of introducing the Gospel of Christ into diverse human cultures. Catechists (or religious educators) transform the beliefs and customs of different groups of people so they reflect God's Kingdom more clearly. They do this through the power of the Holy Spirit.

Let's look at the example of Matteo Ricci, an Italian Jesuit who introduced the Gospel to China between 1582 and 1610. Did he arrive in China and try to force everyone to convert? Not at all! Instead, Ricci worked hard to learn the Chinese language, and he began to wear Chinese clothing. He shared his knowledge of astronomy and other sciences by translating European books into Chinese. He demonstrated his respect for Chinese culture and tradition. As he became known and trusted in the court of the Chinese emperor, he began to teach about his Christian faith. He tried to show how the Christian faith could get along with Chinese traditions, and he wrote books on Christianity in a way that appealed to Chinese scholars. Nearly 150 years after Ricci's death, about 150,000 Chinese people had been baptized into Christianity.

Ricci's respect for Chinese culture taught the Church a lot about how to introduce Christianity to people who have never heard the Good News—including new generations of children in our own culture. Even today, catechists celebrate cultural practices that are compatible with the Catholic faith. In this way enculturation promotes a unity of faith among Christians throughout the world.

22 THE MISSION OF THE CHURCH

KEY WORDS

People of God

Marks of the Church

Catholic

Apostolic

Think about a group to which you belong, such as an orchestra or a school band. What is the purpose of the group? One of the main purposes of such groups is to produce good music. For the group to succeed, it takes the gifts and the commitment of each individual musician and the ability to work together as a team.

One artist imagines the Church. What is the image saying about our relationship with one another and with God?

Illustration by Elizabeth Wang, "We have an astonishing power when we pray with Jesus, in the Holy Sacrifice of the Mass. The whole Church is united in offering praise and thanks, to the delight of God the Father," copyright © Radiant Light 2008, www.radiantlight.org.uk

232

Groups of people joining to contribute their gifts to a larger goal can give us some idea about what the Church is like. The Church, however, is a type of community with characteristics that make it different from other groups. The word *church* means "convocation." To *convoke* means to "call together." A convocation is a community of people who gather in response to a call. What makes the Church unique is that it is an assembly of people who come together in response to God's call. God calls everyone, everywhere. The people who respond to God's call are one family through faith and Baptism. They are united in love by the Holy Spirit. They are the Body of Christ in the world.

God has a plan for the world, and the goal of the plan is the Church. Jesus founded the Church during his earthly ministry more than two thousand years ago. Since then the Church has been on a journey toward the full unity that God intends. Since the Paschal Mystery—the Passion, death, Resurrection, and Ascension of Jesus—was accomplished, the Church has been working to fulfill her mission to bring the Good News of salvation to all people.

How does the Church do this? With the help of the Holy Spirit, her members, the Body of Christ, strive to live like Jesus and love others without requiring anything in return. They pray and worship. They serve those in need. They act with justice.

PRAY IT!

Holy God, I praise and thank you for your goodness. Thank you for the new life you have given me in the waters of Baptism. I share in your life, through Christ, your Son, who died and rose for me. Help me be a good disciple of Jesus. Help me spread the Good News in my family and my community. Amen.

Images of Church

From the beginning of Christianity, leaders in the Church looked for ways to describe the who, what, and why about the Church. To help people understand the mystery of the Church, Peter and Paul used the images of the People of God, the Body of Christ, and the Temple of the Holy Spirit. These images help us understand that unity in the Church is rooted in the unity of the Father, Son, and Holy Spirit.

Did You Know?

The Church Is a Sacrament

Sacraments are encounters with Jesus Christ that help us see that God is with us. The first, or primary, sacrament is Jesus Christ. He, more than anyone or anything else, helps us see God's presence in the world. The Church is also a sacrament. She makes visible the communion we share with God—Father, Son, and Holy Spirit. The Church is sometimes referred to as a "sacrament of salvation." This phrase emphasizes that through the Church, we can come to know God and be saved. The Church shows us God's love for all people, everywhere. That is why we can add universal to our description and call the Church the "universal sacrament of salvation." God wants all people to be saved and to know he loves them. Jesus Christ gave to the Apostles the mission to preach the Gospel message to the whole world (see Matthew 28:18–20), and the Church continues to carry out this mission today. Through the Church the message of God's truth and love can be brought to all people.

The People of God

Long before Jesus' birth, the people of Israel under-stood themselves to be the **People of God,** the chosen ones through whom God would save the world (see Exodus 6:7). The first Christians, who were Jews, came to see that they were God's chosen ones through Christ and the Spirit. Peter wrote the fol-lowing in a letter to first-century Christians:

> You are . . . God's own people, chosen to proclaim the wonderful acts of God, who called you out of darkness into his own marvelous light. (1 Peter 2:9)

The people are "of God," because they do not belong to any one nationality, race, or region. Every-one is welcome. They don't inherit or earn member-ship. People become members of the Church through the Sacrament of Baptism and faith in Jesus Christ.

The Body of Christ

The Church is also the Body of Christ. Paul de-scribes the Church as follows:

> Christ is like a single body, which has many parts; it is still one body, even though it is made up of different parts. . . . All of us . . . have been baptized into the one body by the same Spirit. . . . All of you are Christ's body, and each one is a part of it. (1 Corinthians 12:12,13,27)

THiNK ABOUT IT!

Choose one of the images of the Church this chapter describes. How does the image help you understand the Church more fully? Which image most inspires you? Why?

235

In the Church there are many members and functions. Every person's gifts are important for the Church to carry out her mission. The Church is the whole body, the members united to the head, Jesus Christ. Our salvation comes through the Church, because salvation comes first through Christ. Christ lives with and in the Church. The Church gets its life from Christ. Nourished by him in the Eucharist, the Church becomes the Body of Christ for the world.

The Church is also called the Bride of Christ. This is an image of the Church presented in Scripture: "Husbands, love your wives, just as Christ loved the church and gave himself up for her" (Ephesians 5:25). Christ's relationship with the Church is compared with the relationship between husbands and wives.

Temple of the Holy Spirit

Saint Paul also explains the mystery of the Church as follows: "Surely you know that you are God's temple and that God's Spirit lives in you!" (1 Corinthians 3:16). In the Old Testament, the Temple in Jerusalem was the place where God dwelled. Paul tells us that God dwells in us, in the Church. Jesus Christ has poured out his

LITURGY CONNECTION

One, Holy, Catholic, and Apostolic

All baptized believers participate in the Church's mission of fulfilling the commission of Jesus to "go, and make disciples of all nations" (Matthew 28:19). Next time you pray the Nicene Creed at Mass, think about how believers have been witnesses of the Gospel over the centuries. Think about what it means to be a part of a Church that is One, Holy, Catholic, and Apostolic. Think about the gifts you have to offer the Church. Pray about what it means to be a part of the Body of Christ and a Temple of the Holy Spirit. Then go, be a believer.

Spirit onto all the members of the Church. The Holy Spirit is the center or soul of the Church's life. He gives the Church unity, even amidst the diversity of all her members. The Holy Spirit is the source of the Church's gifts.

> Surely you know that you are God's temple and that God's Spirit lives in you!
>
> 1 Corinthians 3:16

The Marks of the Church

In the Nicene Creed, we express belief in "One, Holy, Catholic, and Apostolic Church." These four characteristics, or **Marks of the Church**, are essential features of the Church. As we look at what

Live It!

Called to Serve

Find out more about how your parish accomplishes the mission of the Church. What gifts do members of the parish bring to help spread the Good News of Jesus Christ? How do members of your parish help one another know, love, and serve God more completely? What things are going on that bring people closer to God and support and nurture their faith? Think about how you are a part of the Body of Christ in your parish. Join several of your peers to discuss a way you can contribute your gifts to the parish. Then follow through.

FUN FACT

There are more than three million Catholic catechists in the world, sharing their gift of teaching the faith. (Bunson, *2012 Catholic Almanac*, page 335)

these marks tell us about the Church, it is important to keep in mind that the fullness of Jesus Christ's Church is found only in the Catholic Church. This means the Catholic Church, led by the Pope and the bishops in communion with him, is the only Church with the fullness of salvation. However, when we express our belief that the Church is One, Holy, Catholic, and Apostolic, we do so with humble hearts. We pray knowing the members of the Church struggle with sin.

We also recognize that many elements of holiness and truth can be found outside the visible organization of the Catholic Church.

> I pray that they may all be one, Father! May they be in us, just as you are in me and I am in you. May they be one, so that the world will believe that you sent me . . . and that you love them as you love me.
>
> John 17:21,23

One

When we say the Church is One, we profess one Lord, one faith, one Baptism, one Body, and one Spirit who gives us life and unites all the members of the Church. The Church, whose foundation is the Holy Trinity, reflects the unity of the Trinity—the loving communion of God the Father, Jesus Christ, and the

Holy Spirit. We believe we are children of God the Father, saved by Jesus Christ, and made one by the Holy Spirit. Unfortunately, divisions have developed among Christians. The many different ecclesial, or church, communities that people belong to today reflect this lack of unity. We share in the hope that one day, through the power of the Holy Spirit, unity among all Christians will be restored.

Holy

The Church is also Holy. This means she is blessed with the presence and love of God and is united with him. The Church's holiness is real but not yet perfect. We fall short of the holiness God wants for us, but the Holy Spirit is constantly guiding the Church in her efforts to overcome sin and grow in holiness.

The Church has been global for a very long time. Catholics live on every continent in the world. We number more than one billion.

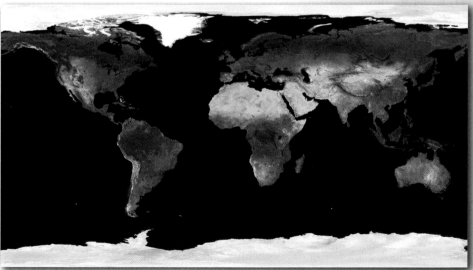

© Stasys Eidiejus/Shutterstock.com

A Nigerian woman receives Communion. Using a map, locate the countries represented by the Eucharistic celebrations pictured on pages 240–242.

© Barbara Davidson/Dallas Morning News/Corbis

Catholic

To say that the Church is **Catholic** is to say that she is comprehensive and universal. The Church is comprehensive because she proclaims the fullness of faith to us. The Catholic Church contains everything we need to be saved: God's complete Revelation, the Seven Sacraments, and the ministry of ordained men whose authority comes directly from the Apostles. The Catholic Church is universal, because she is out in the world, spreading the Word of God to all people, everywhere.

People of all ages in Mexico celebrate their First Communion.

© Jack Kurtz/ZUMA/Corbis

240

Apostolic

The Church is **Apostolic**, because she was founded on Jesus' Twelve Apostles. The Holy Spirit empowered them to spread Christ's message to the world. Christ leads the Church through the Apostles even today. They are present through their successors, the Pope

© ASIM TANVEER/X01009/Reuters/Corbis

A young woman attends Christmas Mass in Pakistan.

and the College of Bishops. Authority is passed from generation to generation, from bishop to bishop, through the laying on of hands in the Sacrament of Holy Orders (see chapter 36, "The Sacraments of Matrimony and Holy Orders," of this handbook). This is called Apostolic Succession. This process assures that future generations can know the truth of God's Revelation in Christ.

© Jeffrey L. Rotman/CORBIS

Midnight Mass is celebrated on Christmas in Israel two thousand years after the birth of Christ.

The Church Is Human and Divine

The Church is visible and spiritual. She is one, but is made up of two components, human and divine. We see the visible reality of the Church in such things as people gathered for the Eucharist; the church buildings; the Pope, bishops, and priests; young people praying on retreats and serving others; the Bible; and so on. But the Church is more than what we can see. The Church is also a spiritual reality. This is a mystery that we see only with the eyes of faith. It builds on the visible reality. Through the action of the Holy Spirit, the aspects of the Church that we can see communicate and put us in touch with the divine component of the Church. The Holy Spirit assures us that the Church is carrying out Christ's mission, despite the occasional sins and failures of her members. Through us God is doing what we could never do on our own. Our work is a participation in the real, but unseen, divine life of the Trinity.

Catholics in the communist country of Vietnam celebrate Christmas Mass.

© Nevada Wier/CORBIS

PEOPLE OF FAITH
Saint Josephine Bakhita

© 2013 Saint Mary's Press/Illustration by Vicki Shuck

In 1869, in a small village in the Sudan, in Africa, Bakhita (the "fortunate one" in a Sudanese language) was born. At the age of nine, she was kidnapped and sold into slavery. During her teenage years, she experienced unspeakable brutalities. In 1883 she was sold to an Italian family living in Africa and became the caretaker for a young girl. Bakhita traveled with the child to boarding school in Italy. The Catholic sisters at the school introduced her to the Gospel.

Although Bakhita knew in her heart that God wanted her to be free, the owners wanted her, their "property," to return to the Sudan. Bakhita prayed to the Lord for strength. She heard God's call, and she knew he wanted her for the Church's work and nothing else. She was going to stay in Italy, no matter what. Soon after, she discovered that slavery was illegal in Italy. This meant that she could not be forced to return to the Sudan. On January 9, 1890, she was baptized and took the name Josephine Bakhita. She then began to hear God's voice calling her to dedicate her life to him more fully. She responded by joining the community of sisters, serving God, whom she called the Master. Her holiness was known all around her town. She died in 1947 and was canonized a saint in 2000. She was the first native Sudanese to become a saint. We celebrate her feast day on May 17.

23 THE STRUCTURE OF THE CHURCH

Have you ever been entrusted with an important job? a job for which you needed to come through? a job where other people were counting on you? Maybe it was completing a task for a group assignment at school. Perhaps it was babysitting your younger sister and helping her with her homework. Maybe it was relaying an important telephone message to your mom or dad. At one time or another, we all have people counting on us to come through for them.

Spreading the Gospel is the work of everyone in the Church, including young people like you. You are part of the laity, aka (also known as) lay faithful.

© juanestey/iStockphoto.com

To the Ends of the Earth

Before Jesus returned to his Father in Heaven, he gathered his Apostles together. He told them he was entrusting them with an important job: to carry to the ends of the earth the message of God's love and salvation through Christ. At the end of the Gospel of Matthew, we read the Great Commissioning, when Jesus entrusted the Apostles with his mission, as follows:

> I have been given all authority in heaven and on earth. Go, then, to all peoples everywhere and make them my disciples: baptize them in the name of the Father, the Son, and the Holy Spirit, and teach them to obey everything I have commanded you. (Matthew 28:18–20)

Jesus asked his Apostles to share in the job of telling everyone about God's Kingdom. He wanted his followers to share in his mission. As Jesus' follower, we are called to share in his kingly role. He gives his Apostles and their successors the power to baptize in his name and act in his person.

Caretaker of Souls

Think about a community or group to which you belong. Most groups want to accomplish something. They are more successful if

PRAY IT!

Holy God, you invite me to share in the mission of your Son, Jesus, who wants all people to be one with you, his Father. May the way I live—the things I do and the things I say— point people to Jesus. May I be a signpost for others on their journeys to find you. Amen.

Fun Fact

Ever wonder how many Catholics serve in various roles? Following are some approximate worldwide figures:

- 411,000 priests
- 38,000 deacons
- 54,000 religious brothers
- 729,000 religious sisters
- 3,800 bishops
- 3,200,000 catechists

(Bunson, 2012 *Catholic Almanac*, page 335)

they have a leader to guide them. The conductor guides the orchestra. The coach guides the team. Your elected peer guides your class council. The principal guides the school. Jesus knew that his community of disciples needed a leader.

The Pope

Jesus made Simon Peter the foundation of the Church. He called Peter "the rock." He even entrusted the keys of the Church to him. Jesus said to Peter: "I will give you the keys to the Kingdom of heaven" (Matthew 16:19). When someone gives you a set of keys, that person is saying: "I trust you. You are in charge." Jesus didn't literally give Peter keys, but he entrusted him with leading the Church. Peter is the first bishop of the Church of Rome. Each bishop who succeeds Peter as the leader of the Church is called the **Pope**. The Pope is the head of the College of Bishops, which is made up of bishops from all around the world. The Pope is also called the Vicar of Christ. This means he is the chief minister for Christ. Just as many of our local parishes have a pastor, the Pope is the pastor for the whole world. Jesus entrusted Peter, and all the Popes who have followed, with the job of being the caretaker of the souls of all of the members of his Body, the Church.

Be holy in all that you do, just as God who called you is holy.

1 Peter 1:15

Bishops, Priests, and Deacons

The Holy Spirit is always working in the Church. He established bishops to succeed, or follow after, the Apostles. A **bishop** takes care of the Church in a particular geographical area called a diocese. He teaches the faith, celebrates the Sacraments, especially the Eucharist, and guides his diocese as its pastor. The bishops help all the parishes in their dioceses work together as a united whole. Each bishop is a sign of unity in his diocese and a member of the College of Bishops. Of course bishops can't do all this on their own. The priests and the deacons of the local Church are their ordained coworkers. They assist the bishop in leading the Church as it carries out its mission in the world. You

© Bill Wittman/www.wpwittman.com

Saint Peter had a starring role in the story of the new Church. Jesus called him "the rock" and gave him the keys to the Kingdom. The Church has been headed by a Pope ever since Saint Peter.

At the Chrism Mass on Holy Thursday, the bishop and priests celebrate Mass together. They bless the holy oils that parishes in the diocese will use for the celebration of the Sacraments.

© Bill Wittman/www.wpwittman.com

can read more about the ordained ministry of bishops, priests, and deacons in chapter 36, "The Sacraments of Matrimony and Holy Orders," of this handbook. Consecrated religious and laypeople also share in the responsibility for carrying out the Church's mission. Let's explore their roles.

Consecrated Religious

Some men and women dedicate their lives to Jesus by living a religious vocation in the Church. They are called consecrated religious. We also call them sisters and brothers. They make public vows or promises called evangelical counsels. The word *evangelical* pertains to living the Good News, or the Gospel. The three evangelical counsels—poverty, chastity, and obedience—help consecrated religious live as Jesus lived.

Think About It!

Reflect back on your week. Which of your attitudes and actions helped others praise God? Which taught others about what God is like? Which challenged others to act more justly or with more kindness? What acts of love and service might you do in the coming week?

The vow of poverty is a promise to live simply. This means they own nothing of their own. The vow of chastity is a promise to remain unmarried and celibate. This keeps them free to dedicate all their efforts to bringing Christ to the world. The vow of obedience means to listen attentively to God's will. They obey the Laws of God and the Church. They also follow the rules of their religious order or community.

We Share in Christ's Ministry

People in the Church who are not ordained are called laity, or lay faithful. These include men, women, children and young adults, married people, and single people. Even people who have taken religious vows who have not been ordained (meaning they are not bishops, priests, or deacons) are considered laity. The lay faithful have the special job of making Christ's presence known in the world. They do this by sharing in the priestly, prophetic, and kingly work of Christ. Let's take a look at these three aspects of Christ's ministry that we share in.

Liturgy Connection

A Prayer for the Church

When we gather to celebrate the Eucharist, we pray for one another and for the Church. During Eucharistic Prayer II, we pray with the celebrant as he says:

> Remember, Lord, your Church, spread throughout the world, and bring her to the fullness of charity, together with Francis our Pope and [Name], our Bishop and all the clergy. (*Roman Missal*)

We pray for all those whom Christ has called to be ordained leaders of the Church. We also pray for growth in love and unity for the whole Church.

Priest

To be priestly means to worship God by the way we live. It means striving to make our lives holy by being open to the Holy Spirit in all we do. This includes how we relate to our families and friends, our approach to schoolwork, and how we take care of ourselves and others. We also share in Christ's priestly work when we pray. This includes our prayers to God during ordinary moments of ordinary days. It also includes participation in the Church's prayers and worship, particularly going to Mass.

is a symbol for Christ. By Baptism, every role is connected to Christ's ministry. As the circles get smaller, the roles are more specific.

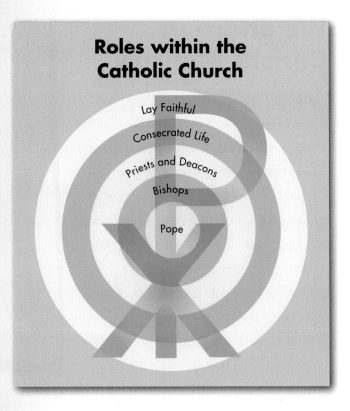

Roles within the Catholic Church

Lay Faithful

Consecrated Life

Priests and Deacons

Bishops

Pope

Prophet

To be a prophet is to announce the Good News of Jesus Christ. Christ wants all people everywhere to know about God. We can help contribute to this goal through our words and actions. When we point others to God, we are like signposts in the world. An effective signpost gives good directions. It helps people get where they want to go. A prophet is like a signpost that directs people to God. For us this means always learning more about our faith and being willing to share it. It means being Christ's witnesses through what we do and what we say.

Did You Know?

Not Catholic?

The image of a family can help us understand the Catholic Church's relationship with other Christians. Christians of other denominations are our brothers and sisters. We all believe in God the Father, Jesus Christ, and the Holy Spirit. Like members of the same family, all who are baptized share a certain communion or unity with one another. We also have some points of major and minor differences that keep us from being fully unified with our Christian brothers and sisters who are not Catholic. Catholics and Christians from many other denominations engage in dialogue and prayer in an effort to restore unity. This work, carried out with the help of the Holy Spirit, is called **ecumenism**.

King

To understand kingship, we need to clear our minds of images of rich, powerful kings and leaders who seek their positions for their own gain. Our model for kingship is Jesus, a servant king. Jesus leads by serving others. His power is the love he shares. Through his death and Resurrection, he gives of himself to bring us close to God the Father. He invites everyone into the Kingdom of God, not just the rich and famous. During his earthly ministry, Jesus always reached out to people who were poor or outcast. He befriended people who were lonely and forgotten. As Jesus' followers we are called to share in his kingly role. We do this whenever we lead in a genuine spirit of love and service. We take the gifts God has given us, and we follow Jesus' lead by using them to reach out to those in need.

Live It!

Week of Christian Unity

God calls all Christians to pray for and work toward full unity. Talk to some of your friends who belong to other Christian communities. What kinds of activities, such as service projects, could you do together as Christian disciples? Every year, a Week of Prayer for Christian Unity is celebrated January 18–25. Watch for news about how it will be celebrated in your community. Check out the website of the United States Conference of Catholic Bishops (USCCB) for ideas and plan a celebration. Pray for the unity of believers every day.

PEOPLE OF FAITH
Saint Catherine of Siena

© 2013 Saint Mary's Press/Illustration by Vicki Shuck

Catherine was born in 1347, in Siena, Italy, the twenty-fourth child born to her parents. Having experienced visions of Christ as a young child, she wanted to dedicate her life to Christ. Her family wanted her to marry instead. They responded to her desire by treating her as if she were a slave. She would retreat to her "secret cell." This was a place inside herself. She would pray and be with the Lord. In a vision, Christ told her that he was in her heart.

Catherine loved the Church deeply, and she became known for her teaching and writing. She served people who were poor and sick. She ministered to people in prison and those suffering during the plague of 1374. During the papacy of Urban VI, the Church was in chaos and disarray. Urban was power hungry. The cardinals, recognizing their mistake in electing him, elected another Pope. However, Urban refused to give up the papacy, so the Church had two rival popes. Catherine suffered, seeing the Church suffer. She prayed that her sufferings might heal this serious rift in the Church.

In 1380 Catherine collapsed from exhaustion and a practice of extreme fasting. Within months she was dead. At her death the marks of stigmata (the wounds of Jesus) were on her body. Catherine is also known for her writings on the spiritual life. She was canonized and was the first layperson named a Doctor of the Church. Saint Catherine's feast day is celebrated on April 29.

24 End Things: Heaven and Hell

The second-grade religion teacher had worked hard to prepare the youngsters for First Communion. While reviewing with the class one afternoon, she asked, "What do you have to be to get to Heaven?" Many of the children eagerly waved their raised hands. The teacher called

One artist depicts Heaven and Hell. How would you draw or describe these two concepts?

Illustration by Elizabeth Wang, "True prayer should lead us to love God and to serve our neighbor in our daily duties and in ordinary acts of kindness," copyright © Radiant Light 2008, www.radiantlight.org.uk

on little Susie. The teacher told the class to quiet down: "Susie is going to tell us what we have to be to get to Heaven." Without so much as a second's hesitation, Susie proudly responded, "Dead!"

Susie's answer was not what her teacher was looking for. It was the matter-of-fact answer of a child who knew that before we go to Heaven, we die—or at least our bodies do. What else, besides dead, do we have to be to get to Heaven? Perhaps you wonder about this and related questions such as, What happens when we die? What is Heaven? How do we get there? What is Hell? How do people end up there? What do Catholics believe about eternal matters like Heaven and Hell?

The title of this chapter, "End Things: Heaven and Hell," is a paradox of the Christian life. In the Nicene Creed, we profess belief in "the resurrection of the dead and the life of the world to come." For those who believe in Christ, the "end things" are not really the end at all. They are the end of things as we know them but the beginning of our eternal life with God.

> I am the resurrection and the life. Those who believe in me will live, even though they die; and those who live and believe in me will never die.
>
> John 11:25–26

PRAY IT!

Holy God, you invite me to spend eternity with you. You sent your Son, Jesus, to restore my relationship with you. Help me follow the way of Jesus and be his disciple. Help me live a life worthy of the Kingdom of Heaven you have prepared for me. Amen.

I Am the Resurrection

Do you know the story of Jesus' raising Lazarus from the dead? (see John, chapter 11). Amazing though this miracle is—that Jesus would bring a dead person to life—Lazarus will eventually die again, and that will be the end. Or will it? By raising Lazarus from the dead, Jesus gives us a preview of coming attractions. He lets us know what is in store for his disciples: resurrection to eternal life. Jesus says to Martha, the distraught sister of the dead Lazarus: "I am the resurrection and the life. Those who believe in me will live, even though they die; and those who live and believe in me will never die" (John 11:25–26). At death our soul is separated from our body. But in the resurrection, God will make our body rise again, be transformed, and be reunited with our soul. Like Christ, who rose from the dead and lives forever, we will rise on the last day.

God never intended for us to be apart from him. After the first man and first woman chose to turn away from him (see Genesis), God has continually been working on restoring our relationship with him. Jesus' life, Passion, death, Resurrection, and Ascension are all the proof we need. God's desire is for us to be with him. But he doesn't force us. We have free will to choose to be close to him or not. How we live our lives here on earth will determine whether we are headed for Heaven or for Hell.

THiNk AbouT IT!

What will Heaven be like? What is your image of Heaven? If someone asked you what to do or what kind of person to be to get to Heaven, how would you explain the Church's teaching?

Heaven

Imagine the perfect life, in which your deepest longings are satisfied and you are completely happy. That's a glimpse of Heaven. **Heaven** is not a place. It is the state of being in perfect friendship and union with God. It lasts for eternity. If Heaven is friendship with God, being close to God, and being with God, then certainly Heaven begins here on earth. It begins in the loving attitudes and actions we

© Brooklyn Museum/Corbis

choose and in how we let Jesus be the guide for all we do and say. It begins in the kindness we offer one another, our parents, our siblings, our friends—and to strangers and enemies.

Jesus raises his friend Lazarus from the dead. Lazarus's sisters and friends must have been overjoyed. Jesus promises us eternal life. That is joyful news for us too.

Hell

The opposite, of course, would be to turn away from God, to refuse to love, to refuse to care or forgive, to think only about ourselves. The choice is ours, but if we make this choice, then we risk the reality of Hell, or eternal death. **Hell** is separation from God forever. Like Heaven, Hell is not a place. It is a permanent state of separation from God. It is for God that we were created and in him alone that we can have true

FUN FACT

In Dante Alighieri's *Inferno*, a famous poem written in the 1200s, Dante gives a tour of Hell from his perspective. He describes Hell using nine concentric circles, like a target, with Satan at the center. Each circle represents a different level of seriousness of the sins committed, with the sins increasingly more serious as the circles come closer to Satan.

happiness. Eternal separation from God and from true happiness with him is the chief punishment of Hell.

Thoughts of Hell can be scary, and it might be easy at times to think about how hard it is to deserve Heaven. But we need to remember that we are sons and daughters of a God who is all loving and all forgiving. God's greatest desire is for us to be with him forever. God doesn't condemn anyone to Hell. He gives us the choice either to respond to his love or not. We respond to God's love and accept his invitation to be a part of his life by the way we live.

Art can have a big influence on how we picture difficult concepts like Heaven and Hell. This portion of a fifteenth-century painting by Fra Angelico shows Hell as a place of great agony and suffering.

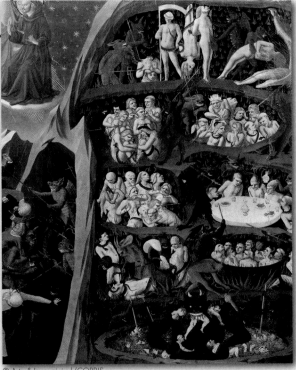

© Arte & Immagini srl/CORBIS

Judgment

What is your image of being judged after you die? However you imagine that judgment to be carried out, it is important to not confuse the word *judgment* with the word *condemnation*. The judgment that awaits us when we die is not condemnation. Christ, who is the judge of the living and the dead, will judge us at the time of our death by comparing our lives to the Gospel message. This is called the **particular judgment**. Saint Paul summed it up this way: "For all of us must appear before Christ, to be judged by him. We will each receive what we deserve, according to everything we have done, good or bad, in our bodily life" (2 Corinthians 5:10).

We will all experience a second judgment. This judgment will come at the end of time when God's plan for creation will be fully realized. At this Last Judgment, the King on his throne—who is Jesus Christ—will separate people into two groups, the

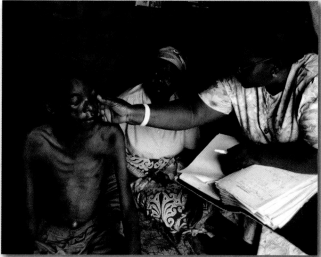

© Gideon Mendel/Corbis

"When, Lord, did we ever see you hungry?" (Matthew 25:37). Jesus tells us that those who help the poor and needy are actually helping him. He promises that those who respond in love will one day see the face of God in Heaven.

righteous people on his right and the others on his left. Which group a person is in will depend on the deeds that person did during his or her life. Those on the right will have a place in Heaven because they fed the hungry, gave drink to the thirsty, welcomed the stranger, clothed the naked, cared for the sick, and visited the imprisoned (see Matthew 25:31–40). Those who saw the face of Jesus in the people who were the most poor and vulnerable and reached out to them with love will see the face of God in Heaven. Those who turned their backs on those in need will not.

Let's go back to the question the teacher posed to her second-grade class: "What do you have to be to get to Heaven?" Think about all the times when you have loved well the people you are close to. Think

Live It!

Practice the Works of Mercy

Read Matthew 25:31–46. Notice that what Jesus says isn't simply a suggestion along the lines of "You might want to do these things." Jesus demands that we do these things if we are to be counted among the righteous. God will judge us on how well we care for others, particularly people who are poor. Take a piece of paper and label three columns: "My Family," "My Parish," and "My Community." Write down some ways the people listed in each column can follow Jesus' call to be righteous. Be specific. If you get the chance, discuss with a friend or family member what you discover. Choose one new thing you can do to help others. Then do it.

about the times when those who really needed your love received it from you. Think about the times when you and your family helped someone who didn't have a meal or when the toys you donated helped put a smile on a child's face. Think about all the times you helped a person in need or stood up for what is right. These are the times you will tell Christ about on the Day of Judgment, when he will ask you how you have lived your life. You will be able to say: "I was a loving person. I cared for people who needed my help. I respected life, and I stood up for what is right." On the Day of Judgment, each of us will be accountable for our actions.

> For all of us must appear before Christ, to be judged by him. We will each receive what we deserve, according to everything we have done, good or bad, in our bodily life.
>
> 2 Corinthians 5:10

At the end of time, the world will be the way God wants it. The Kingdom of God will be fully realized. The people who lived faithful, loving lives will be with Christ. Their bodies and soul will be glorified. All of creation will be transformed by God's presence.

LITURGY CONNECTION

Prayers for the Dead

Next time you are at Mass, listen for the times when we pray for those who have died. Generally, one intercession in the Prayer of the Faithful is for people who have died recently. Also during Eucharistic Prayer II, we pray in the following or similar words:

> Remember also our brothers and sisters who have fallen asleep in the hope of the resurrection and all who have died in your mercy: welcome them into the light of your face.

Purgatory

Many people die in God's grace and friendship, but their lives were not quite on target with the Gospel. Although these people have a place in Heaven, they will spend time becoming more holy before entering into eternity with God. This period is commonly called **Purgatory** because during it people's souls are purged from sin. United with Christ, the Church offers ways for people still living to reduce the purification needed in Purgatory. These are called indulgences. They make up for the harm caused by our sins. There are many things we can do to receive indulgences for ourselves and for all the souls in Purgatory. Some examples include certain ways of reading and praying with Scripture, reciting the Rosary with loved ones, or participating in the adoration of the Blessed Sacrament.

Did You Know?

Prayers for the Dead

The Church has always honored the memory of the dead. Prayers for the dying entrust the person to God and call him or her home to be with God, Mary, Joseph, and all the saints and angels. Catholics, in fact the whole "communion of saints" (that is, the living faithful along with all those in Heaven already), pray on behalf of the dead most especially at the celebration of the Eucharist. These prayers hand over the person to God's mercy and reflect the hope that the dead will see God face-to-face.

PEOPLE OF FAITH
Thomas à Kempis

The early Christian communities turned to the Apostles and other early Church leaders for guidance. Do you have someone you can always turn to for solid advice?

Thomas à Kempis (1380–1471) has provided sound moral guidance for hundreds of thousands of people for the last six hundred years. À Kempis was a German priest who lived in a monastery. He was in charge of the novice monks and other junior members of the monastery. He enjoyed reading, writing, and discussing questions about spirituality and Church teaching. In his duties he must have had many opportunities to provide advice and guidance. At some point À Kempis wrote down his advice in a book called *The Imitation of Christ*. This well-loved book contains his words of wisdom for walking the Christian moral path. It offers practical and detailed advice on how to be more like Christ by trying to become humble and prudent.

In Christian literature *The Imitation of Christ* is the most widely translated book, second only to the Bible. Many great saints over the centuries, including Thomas More, Ignatius of Loyola, and Thérèse of Lisieux, consulted this bestseller for moral guidance. Even today, you may be familiar with some of the book's sayings, such as "an old habit is hard to break" (book 1, chapter 14). If you would like to read more of Thomas's guidance, find out if your school library has a copy of *The Imitation of Christ*. Several translations can be found online as well.

25 Mary and the Saints

Imagine the scene: an invitation is about to be delivered to a girl, about the age you are now. This girl has no idea this invitation is coming. She is simply going about her daily chores. She is also a bit distracted because she has been thinking about her cousin, who is believed to be too old to be pregnant, but is pregnant anyhow (see Luke 1:5–25). Her mind is also wandering to thoughts of the man she is engaged to, a man named Joseph. (Yes, this girl lives in a time and culture where girls are engaged very young.)

In this chapter you will read about Mary and the saints, close friends of God. Asking saints to pray for you is like asking a friend for prayers.

© Alinari Archives/Corbis

Suddenly, an angel appears from nowhere and says: "Peace be with you! The Lord is with you and has greatly blessed you!" (Luke 1:28). These are powerful words. The angel is telling this girl, whose name is Mary, that she is full of God's grace. She is full of God's life. Scripture gives us insight into what Mary must have been thinking and feeling after being told that God has greatly blessed her: "Mary was deeply troubled by the angel's message, and she wondered what his words meant" (Luke 1:29).

The Gospel of Luke describes what happens next:

> The angel said to her, "Don't be afraid, Mary; God has been gracious to you. You will become pregnant and give birth to a son, and you will name him Jesus. He will be great and will be called the Son of the Most High God. . . . His kingdom will never end." (1:30–33)

This event is called the Annunciation.

Mary's Yes

How did Mary react to the announcement that she would give birth to the "Son of the Most High"? Remember that Mary was not yet married, and she had never been with a man. She was a virgin. Because of this, she asked the angel, "How can this be?" He told her she would conceive by the power of the Holy Spirit. God would take care of everything.

PRAY IT!

Holy Mary, you are my spiritual mother. Be with me today. Protect me and guide me with your love. Show me how to follow your Son, Jesus, in everything I do and say. Amen.

265

© Philadelphia Museum of Art/CORBIS

Look carefully at this picture of Mary at the Annunciation. Where is the angel? What is Mary thinking and feeling as she listens to God's invitation?

At this point, Mary could have chosen not to believe anything the angel was telling her. Or she could have run off in fear of what might lie ahead for her. But Mary had a deep love for God, and knew nothing was impossible for him. Therefore, she proclaimed her yes to God. She said to the angel, "I am the Lord's servant, . . . may it happen to me as you have said" (Luke 1:38). Mary consented to God's becoming man through her. By saying yes to the Incarnation, Mary cooperated in all the work that her Son, Jesus, was to accomplish.

THiNK ABouT IT!

The Church celebrates the feasts of Mary and the saints throughout the Liturgical Year. What feast days do you celebrate in special ways in your parish or with your family? How do you celebrate them?

Mary, Mother of God

Sometimes mothers are identified through their children. For example, people might say, "She's the mother of Tom" or "She's Ashley's mom." We read in the Gospels that Mary was the "mother of Jesus." Yet, early in the Gospel of Luke, Mary's cousin, Elizabeth, knew something no one else did about Mary's identity as a mother. Soon after the angel appeared to Mary, Mary went to visit Elizabeth, who was pregnant with John the

Baptist. Elizabeth greeted Mary with the following words: "You are the most blessed of all women, and blessed is the child you will bear! Why should this great thing happen to me, that my Lord's mother comes to visit me!" (Luke 1:42–43). Elizabeth exclaimed, at the prompting of the Spirit, that Mary was the mother of the Lord. Mary is truly the Mother of God, because she is the mother of the eternal Son of God made man, Jesus, who is God himself. We call Mary **Theotokos**, which means "God-bearer," or the one who gives birth to God.

> When Elizabeth heard Mary's greeting, the baby moved within her.
> Luke 1:41

© Brooklyn Museum/Corbis

Mary, Mother of the Church

With a mother's love, Mary supported Jesus throughout his life. The Gospels do not tell us much about Jesus' childhood. We can imagine that Mary provided all the guidance and nurturing of the most loving of mothers. Her support and love for Jesus continued throughout his ministry and to his cross, where she stood as he died. In the final moments of Jesus' earthly life, he gave the Church the gift of his mother. The

"Sorrow, like a sharp sword, will break your own heart" (Luke 2:35). When Jesus was a baby, Simeon said these words to Mary. As she stood at the Crucifixion and watched her son suffer and die, Simeon's prophecy was all too true. Can you think of other times when Mary was worried or sad about Jesus?

LITURGY CONNECTION

The Feast of the Assumption

Because of Mary's holiness and faithfulness, God took her into Heaven, both body and soul, at the end of her life on earth. This event is called the **Assumption**. Mary shared in Jesus' Resurrection from the dead as soon as her life on earth ended. She is in Heaven waiting for us and for all the faithful to join her. The Church celebrates the Feast of the Assumption on August 15.

Gospel of John recounts how Jesus spoke to his mother, and to John, the beloved disciple: "Jesus saw his mother and the disciple he loved standing there; so he said to his mother, 'He is your son'" (19:26). This simple statement shows us that the beloved disciple and all believers are Mary's children. "Then he said to the disciple, 'She is your mother'" (19:27). This means Mary is the mother of all Christians; she is our mother. Mary is the Church's model of faithfulness and love. Mary points us straight to Jesus. For this reason, the Church's devotion to the Blessed Mother is an important part of Christian worship. She is our model of holiness.

The Communion of Saints

When we recite the Nicene Creed at Mass, we profess our belief in the **Communion of Saints**. This refers to the Church. The Church is a communion of holy people, living and dead (but alive with God). There is a second, closely related, meaning of Communion of Saints. In English *saint* can translate the Latin *sancti* ("holy people") and the Latin *sancta* ("holy things"). The holy things are primarily the Sacraments, especially the Eucharist. When we profess belief in the Communion of Saints, we say something about our relationships with all faithful people living now and in the past, but that is not all. We are also saying that "holy things"—especially the Eucharist—bind us to one another and unite us to God. When we participate in the Sacraments, particularly the Eucharist, we are nourished with the Body and Blood of Christ, and we become the Body of Christ for the world.

Our Friends in Heaven

We've all had the experience of leaning on our friends in time of need. Not only that, but we count on our friends to help us celebrate life's moments. We

Live It!

Do as Jesus Tells You

At the Wedding Feast of Cana, where people had gathered for a wedding celebration, the wine had run out (see John 2:1–12). The servants were scrambling about, trying to decide how to solve this embarrassing dilemma. Imagine Mary, the mother of Jesus, who is at the wedding, nudging Jesus and whispering in his ear, "They are out of wine" (John 2:3). She wanted Jesus to do something about the problem. He replied, "You must not tell me what to do. . . . My time has not yet come" (John 2:4). What happens next is the only time in the Gospels that Mary gives directions. "Jesus' mother then tells the servants, 'Do whatever he tells you'" (John 2:5).

The Blessed Mother points us straight to Jesus. She tells us, "Do whatever he tells you." Spend some quiet time reflecting on Mary's words. What is Jesus telling you to do today?

FUN FACT

Have you ever wondered how many official saints there are? It is difficult to arrive at a definitive number. We do know that the names of more than ten thousand saints have been recorded in various historical records during the Church's history.

have a whole other group of friends too, our friends in Heaven. Mary is one of these—she is our spiritual mother, and she is joined by the saints, all those who have died and are with God in Heaven.

As Catholics we have a special connection to those who have died. The Holy Spirit unites all believers, those who have died and are being purified before entering Heaven, and the saints already in Heaven. All of these people are our heavenly friends. Our heavenly friends help us grow close to Jesus and be his faithful followers. And just as we ask our friends here on earth to help us or pray for us, we can ask our heavenly friends to put in a good word for us with God. We can ask them to bring our needs to God. We can also ask them to pray for us when we have difficult decisions to make. We believe that they hear our prayers and are with God in Heaven. It is an especially meaningful prayer to ask our own loved ones who have died to bring our needs before God.

The Saints

What do you think being a saint means? Saints embody what it is to be holy. To be holy is to seek God and to be filled with God. Mary is the first saint, the queen of all the saints. She was totally filled with God's life. The many saints who have come after her are also examples of what it means to live Christian lives, trying to do what God wants. You'll notice that a number of saints are highlighted in People of Faith articles in this handbook. This is because by reading about and studying the lives of the saints, their examples can inspire us.

We witness the Holy Spirit's activity in the Church through her saints. They are our companions in prayer. They, with Mary in Heaven, contemplate God, they praise him, and perhaps best of all, they

Liturgical Calendar

December 26: Saint Stephen
December 12: Our Lady of Guadalupe
December 8: Immaculate Conception
December 6: Saint Nicholas
November 5: Saint Elizabeth
November 1: All Saints
October 15: Saint Teresa of Ávila
October 11: Saint John XXIII
October 4: Saint Francis of Assisi
September 27: Saint Vincent de Paul
September 9: Saint Peter Claver
September 5: Mother Teresa
August 28: Saint Augustine
August 27: Saint Monica
August 15: Assumption of Mary
August 11: Saint Clare
August 8: Saint Dominic
July 29: Saint Martha

January 4: Saint Elizabeth Ann Seton
January 24: Saint Francis de Sales
February 3: Saint Blaise
February 8: Saint Josephine Bakhita
February 11: Our Lady of Lourdes
March 7: Saints Perpetua and Felicity
March 17: Saint Patrick
March 19: Saint Joseph
March 25: Feast of the Annunciation
April 7: Saint John Baptist de La Salle
April 29: Saint Catherine of Siena
May 14: Saint Matthias
June 3: Saint Charles Lwanga and Companions
June 13: Saint Anthony of Padua
June 29: Saints Peter and Paul
July 14: Blessed Kateri Tekakwitha
July 22: Saint Mary Magdalene

December · January · February · March · April · May · June · July · August · September · October · November

Advent · Christmas · Ordinary Time · Lent · Easter Triduum · Easter · Pentecost · Ordinary Time

care for people like us who are still living on earth. That's good news for us. The saints are our holy friends, looking out for us always. When we celebrate their feasts and memorials at liturgies throughout the year, we show that as Church, we are united with the liturgy of Heaven. All the official saints of the Church are a part of our Catholic family. These are the saints whom the Church has canonized. We can also use the term *unofficial* with *saint* to refer to all the people in the Church who are living and dead. This is the whole Communion of Saints.

? Did You Know?

Birthdays of the Saints

Have you ever wondered how the Church determines on what day a saint's feast will be celebrated? The vast majority of saints are remembered on the anniversary of the day they died. This is a sort of birthday because it is the first day of their new life in Heaven with God. The saints participate in Christ's passage from life on earth, through death, to a new life. Christ's passage is called the Paschal Mystery, and it includes his Ascension into Heaven after his Resurrection. When we celebrate the life of a saint, we affirm our belief in this mystery. Though the births of the saints are significant, by making a special point of remembering them on the anniversaries of their deaths, we commemorate all that Jesus Christ accomplished through them during their lives on earth. This practice also reminds us that they remain alive and offer us their friendship. Death was not the end for them, and it isn't for us either.

PEOPLE OF FAITH
Saint Juan Diego

© 2013 Saint Mary's Press/Illustration by Vicki Shuck

On December 9, 1531, a fifty-seven-year-old peasant named Juan Diego, who lived near Mexico City, was on his way to Mass. Suddenly he heard beautiful music and a woman's voice calling to him from Tepeyac Hill. At the top of the hill, he saw a beautiful woman, who revealed that she was the Virgin Mary. She told Juan to tell the bishop that a church should be built in her honor at the bottom of the hill.

Juan went to the bishop and told him about his vision, but the bishop wasn't ready to believe Juan's story. He said he needed a sign to prove the story true. Several days later Juan's uncle was sick. As Juan rushed to find a doctor, the Virgin appeared again. Juan told her about his uncle. She assured Juan that all would be well. That morning she appeared to his uncle and cured him. Then she told Juan to go to the top of the hill and in his cloak, gather the roses he would find there and take them to the bishop as the sign the bishop had requested. When Juan opened his cloak, the roses fell out, but the greatest sign of all was the beautiful portrait of the Virgin that suddenly appeared on Juan's cloak. Soon after, a church was built in Mary's honor. The Feast of Our Lady of Guadalupe is celebrated on December 12. She is the Patroness of the Americas.

274

PART 2

LITURGY AND SACRAMENTS

The Seven Sacraments of the Catholic Church

- *Baptism*
- *Confirmation*
- *The Eucharist*
- *Penance and Reconciliation*
- *Anointing of the Sick*
- *Matrimony*
- *Holy Orders*

26 THE BIBLE: WORSHIPPING God

KEY WORDS

worship
liturgy
Eucharist

We worship together as God's people. Our full participation in the liturgy helps create a bond of unity and love among us.

© CEFutcher/iStockphoto.com

What are the essential elements of any religion? Take a minute to think about your answer. What comes to mind? Did you think about a group of people who have common spiritual beliefs? A religion cannot exist with just one believer, nor can a religion exist in which everyone has completely different beliefs about God. Did you think about moral laws or guidelines? Most religions have moral laws guiding believers' moral choices. Did you think about public prayer or **worship**? Most religions have some kind of public, communal prayer so believers can worship God together.

The communal, public, official prayer or worship of the Catholic Church is called the **liturgy**. You will read more about liturgy in the next chapters. This chapter looks at how liturgy developed in the Bible. Our liturgy did not appear out of nowhere. Through all of salvation history, God has been preparing us for the liturgy we celebrate today. When we look in the Bible to learn about the different ways the Chosen People have worshipped God, we can better understand the meaning of the Mass and the other liturgies we celebrate today.

Sacrifices in the Old Testament

God's Chosen People were originally nomadic herders. That means they kept flocks of sheep and goats, and they kept moving from place to place to find new places for their herds to eat and drink. Here's a passage about Abraham doing just that:

> Abram went north out of Egypt to the southern part of Canaan with his wife and everything he owned, and Lot went with him. Abram was a very rich man, with sheep, goats, and cattle, as well as silver and gold. Then he left there and moved from place to place, going toward Bethel. He reached the place between Bethel and Ai where he had camped before and had built an altar. There he worshiped the LORD.
>
> (Genesis 13:1–4)

PRAY IT!

Receive, Lord, my entire freedom. Accept the whole of my memory, my intellect and my will. Whatever I have or possess, it was you who gave it to me; I restore it to you in full, and I surrender it completely to the guidance of your will. Give me only love of you together with your grace, and I am rich enough and ask for nothing more. Amen.

(Saint Ignatius of Loyola)

Fun Fact

In the Bible, *booth* is another name for *tent*. Each year, during the Festival of Booths, each family made a tent and lived in it for seven days to remind them of the time the Israelites spent in the desert during the Exodus. Some even built their tents on the roofs of their houses!

Abram (later Abraham), his children, and his grandchildren worshipped God by building altars in special places and sacrificing animals on the altars. They would take one of the best animals from their flock, kill it, and burn its meat in a fire on the altar. Because they believed that Heaven was above the sky, they believed the rising smoke of the fire carried their offering to God.

Sacrificing animals probably seems strange and cruel to you. But our ancestors in faith did this for good reasons. First, killing animals to cook and eat was a normal part of their life. This sacrifice did not seem unusually cruel to them. Second, by offering God an animal's life, they recognized that all life comes from God and returns to God. Third, offering one of their best animals back to God was a way to thank God for giving them everything they needed to live. Fourth, offering a valuable animal to God was seen as a way to seek his forgiveness for sins.

When the Chosen People settled in the Promised Land after the Exodus, they became farmers as well as herders. So they began to also offer God the first and best fruit and grain from their harvests. These offerings included bread and wine. The Covenant Law includes directions for making these offerings at planting and harvest times. Take a minute to read Leviticus, chapter 23. This chapter describes the festivals, also called feasts, that the Law commanded the Chosen

People to celebrate. Leviticus mentions six festivals, three of which required sacrificial offerings:

- **Festival of Unleavened Bread.** This festival lasted a whole week during the harvest of barley, a type of grain. During the festival the people offered a bundle of barley as well as a lamb, flour, olive oil, and wine.

- **The Harvest Festival.** This is also called the Festival of Weeks or Pentecost. It occurred fifty days after the Festival of Unleavened Bread, during the start of the wheat harvest. During this festival each family offered two loaves of bread, and the community sacrificed several animals.

- **Feast of Shelters (or Feast of Booths).** This festival was like our Thanksgiving, held at the end of the harvest season. During this festival each family offered God the best of their harvest.

In most cases the people did not burn the entire offering on the altar. Part of the offering was kept to support the priests and their ministry with the people.

So what do all these sacrifices have to do with our liturgy today? Our most important liturgy, the Mass, is also a sacrifice. In it we participate in the greatest sacrifice of all: the sacrifice of Jesus Christ on the cross for the forgiveness of our sins. Jesus' suffering and death fulfilled the Old Testament sacrifices, so we no longer sacrifice animals in our worship. The Letter to

THINK ABOUT IT!

Imagine that a friend who is not Catholic asks you what makes someone Catholic. What essential beliefs would you share with your friend? How would you describe Catholic worship? How can you explain the scriptural basis for our worship?

LiTURGY CONNECTION

Pentecost

The Jewish Harvest Festival, or Festival of Weeks, is also called Pentecost, a Greek word that means "fifty." Do you know why the Harvest Festival shares the name Pentecost with the Christian commemoration of the coming of the Holy Spirit? The Acts of the Apostles describes this event: "When the day of Pentecost came, all the believers were gathered together in one place. . . . They were all filled with the Holy Spirit" (2:1,4). Acts is referring to the Harvest Festival, which takes place fifty days after Passover in the Jewish calendar. Jesus was crucified near the end of Passover. Fifty days after the Resurrection, Jews gathered in Jerusalem to celebrate the Harvest Festival—and then the Holy Spirit descended on Christ's followers. That is why the Church commemorates Pentecost seven Sundays (or fifty days) after Easter Sunday. Pentecost also concludes the Easter season on the Church's liturgical calendar.

the Hebrews says: "God does away with all the old sacrifices and puts the sacrifice of Christ in their place. Because Jesus Christ did what God wanted him to do, we are all purified from sin by the offering that he made of his own body once and for all" (10:9–10).

You might recall that during the Mass the people also make an offering. We offer bread and wine to symbolize that we are offering our lives back to God. We also offer money to support Christ's mission as it is carried on by the Church.

Passover and the Temple

The most important festival in the Old Testament is the Passover. This commemorates the great event that finally freed the Israelites from slavery in Egypt. You probably remember the story from the Book of Exodus. The Egyptian pharaoh had enslaved the Israelites, so God called Moses to challenge Pharaoh and free the people. God sent nine plagues upon Egypt to convince Pharaoh to let the Israelites go, but Pharaoh refused. But the tenth plague was so terrible that Pharaoh finally agreed to free them. In the tenth plague, the angel of God killed the firstborn Egyptian males, both human and animal. Only the Israelites were spared. Read Exodus, chapter 12, to see how this happened.

The firstborn Israelite sons lived because their families sacrificed a lamb or a young goat and used its blood to mark the doors of their houses. This is how the angel of God knew to pass over the house. God also commanded the Israelites to bake and eat unleavened bread in the days leading up to this

Did You Know?

Synagogues and Churches

In the New Testament, we read a lot about synagogues. Jesus prayed in them (see Luke 4:16), and Saint Paul preached in them (see Acts 9:20). Synagogues are places where Jewish people meet to pray, read Scripture, and study the Law. We do not know when or why Jewish people began to use synagogues, but we do know that they were in common use by the first century AD. In Jesus' time many cities where Jews lived had at least one synagogue.

The early Christians learned two things from the Jewish experience of synagogues. First, they learned to form local churches where people could gather to worship and celebrate the liturgy. Second, they learned to include reading and learning about Sacred Scripture in their worship services.

event. Unleavened bread is a bread made without yeast that remains flat. God commanded the Israelites to repeat this ritual every year as a religious festival to recall how God's power freed them from slavery and oppression. Even today, the Passover festival includes special foods with symbolic meanings and the retelling of the story of the Exodus.

Centuries later, after King Solomon built the Temple in Jerusalem, religious festivals changed in some

LIVE IT!

Participate in the Liturgy

Have you ever felt bored at Mass? You are not alone. Many adults and children find Mass to be a little dry at times. But it is important to engage fully with the liturgy, because it is the work of the whole Christ: head and body. Here are some suggestions to help renew your interest in the liturgy:

- Say or sing the responses, like "Amen" and "Thanks be to God."
- Focus on each word of the Scripture readings and prayers. Really paying attention to the words can help you to pray the liturgy.
- Read and reflect on the Scripture readings before going to Mass. Many parish bulletins or websites post the readings in advance to encourage this practice.
- Become a liturgical minister, like an altar server, lector, or musician.
- Recognize the great gift the Eucharist offers to us: Jesus' self-sacrifice for our salvation.

Not every liturgy will be exciting or memorable. But every liturgy does offer us abundant grace and the Real Presence of Christ. That is an exciting truth!

ways. The Temple priests now led the people in the public celebration of various festivals. All Israelites were now expected to travel to Jerusalem once a year to celebrate Passover. The Temple priests sacrificed the Passover lambs. They burned some of the meat at the Temple altar as an offering to God, kept some meat for them-

© pushlama/iStockphoto.com

selves, and gave the rest back to each family to use in their own Passover meals. While the Israelites were in Jerusalem, they were also expected to pay a tax to support the Temple and its priests.

This Jewish father and son are reading from the *Haggadah*, a book explaining the significance of Passover and its customs. Notice the unleavened bread (bread made without yeast) and the cup of wine on the table.

The Mass has its roots in the festival of Passover. You may already see some connections. The blood of the Passover lamb saved the Israelites, but the blood of Jesus Christ saves all people. Israelite families ate unleavened bread at Passover, and the bread at Mass that becomes Jesus' sacred Body is also unleavened bread. The Israelites' celebration of Passover began at the Temple, and we celebrate the Mass in a church. You will read more about these connections in chapter 29, "The Eucharist: The Heart of All Liturgy."

The Last Supper

Jesus and his disciples were faithful Jews. The Gospels tell us that they regularly participated in Jewish worship and festivals. Mary, Joseph, and Jesus celebrated

Passover in Jerusalem every year (see Luke 2:41). Jesus honored the Sabbath by worshipping in the synagogue (see Luke 4:16–17). Jesus and his disciples also traveled to Jerusalem to celebrate the Passover just before his Passion and death (see Matthew 26:17–18).

But at his last Passover meal, now known as the Last Supper, Jesus did something new. He established the **Eucharist**. The Last Supper is the Christian celebration of Christ's saving work through his sacrificial death and Resurrection. In the First Letter to the Corinthians, Saint Paul describes the first Eucharist:

> For I received from the Lord the teaching that I passed on to you: that the Lord Jesus, on the night he was betrayed, took a piece of bread, gave thanks to God, broke it, and said, "This is my body, which is for you. Do this in memory of me." In the same way, after the supper he took the cup and said, "This cup is God's new covenant, sealed with my blood. Whenever you drink it, do so in memory of me." (11:23–25)

The Last Supper fulfills all the forms of worship found in the Old Testament. The Old Testament sacrifices for the forgiveness of sins are fulfilled by Jesus' sacrifice on the cross for the forgiveness of our sins. The offerings of bread and wine in thanksgiving for God's gifts are fulfilled by the offering of Jesus' Body and Blood for our sake. The saving power of the blood of the Passover lamb is fulfilled by Jesus' saving power.

You must celebrate this day as a religious festival
to remind you of what I, the LORD, have done.
Celebrate it for all time to come.

Exodus 12:14

Church History

Mass in Many Languages

Have you ever attended Mass in a language you don't understand? Could you follow what was going on? If not, how did that affect your ability to worship?

In the early Church, worship was conducted primarily in Greek. Then Latin gradually became the Church's official language, because Latin had been the "common tongue" of the Roman Empire. For many centuries afterward, the primary language of Catholic worship remained Latin, no matter what culture you lived in or what language you spoke. The Mass was said in Latin, and the Sacraments were celebrated in Latin. This was the case well into the first half of the twentieth century.

But ripples of change began as early as 1909. Pope Pius X held a liturgical conference where liturgists began to discuss whether liturgy in local languages (or the vernacular) would promote greater understanding and participation. People were beginning to realize that the liturgy requires everyone, not just the priest, to participate. Forty years later Pope Pius XII approved the use of local languages for celebrating the Sacraments. But perhaps the most sweeping change happened as a result of the Second Vatican Council. In 1963 the Council issued its *Constitution on the Sacred Liturgy (Sacrosanctum Concilium)*, which set forth many liturgical reforms and opened the door to celebrating the Mass itself in the local language. Latin remains the official language of the Church's worship, but many people today find they can participate most fully in the Eucharist when they celebrate Mass in their own language.

21 INTRODUCTION TO LITURGY

What activities are important for Catholics to participate in? Your list might include studying the Bible and going to religion classes. You might list feeding the poor. Treating everyone kindly and following the Ten Commandments are probably on your list too. Imagine if a parish did all these things but never got together to pray, especially for Mass and the other Sacraments. It would be hard to recognize such a parish as Catholic. Getting together for Mass and for the other

Participating at Mass involves all five of our senses. Can you name one example of how you use each sense in the Sacrament of the Eucharist?

© Bill Wittman/www.wpwittman.com

official prayers of the Church is an essential part of being Catholic.

Mass and the other official prayers of the Church are called liturgies. Liturgy is a communal, public, official prayer of the Church. *Communal* means we participate in liturgy together with one another, in communion with the Trinity—God the Father, God the Son, and God the Holy Spirit. *Public* means liturgy is not the private prayer of individuals by themselves. *Official* means liturgy is celebrated under the direction and guidelines of the Pope and the bishops. In the liturgy, above all we celebrate the Paschal Mystery—the Passion, death, Resurrection, and Ascension of Jesus Christ, through which he destroyed death and restored our life.

There are many different forms of liturgy. Some are Sacraments, like Baptism, Matrimony, and the Eucharist. The Eucharist is the Church's most important liturgy. Other liturgies are special prayers, like morning prayer or blessings. Not all prayer, however, is liturgy. Your nighttime prayers or saying the Rosary are good prayers. However they are not liturgies, because they are not communal, public, and official.

Important though liturgy is, you might struggle to find it interesting. You're not alone if you feel this way. According to a recent survey, 61 percent of Catholic teens find going to church boring at least some of

Pray It!

God of time and history, you walk with me unseen yet surround me with your presence. Fill me with your Spirit and open my eyes that I may recognize the extraordinary love of Christ in ordinary acts of faith. May I always praise you with the saints and angels every day of my life. I ask this through Christ, our Lord. Amen.

Fun Fact

Did you know that the date of Easter depends on the movements of the sun and the moon? Easter does not fall on the same date each year, as Christmas Day does. Rather, it changes each year. Easter is always the first Sunday after the first full moon after the first day of spring.

the time (Smith, *Soul Searching*, page 62). But the survey also reports that at least 40 percent would choose to go to Mass every week even if it were completely their decision (page 37). If you fall under this category, you are blessed. You have discovered one of the greatest treasures of the Catholic faith.

As with any treasure worth having, you need to do some work to find it. This section will give you a guide to the Church's liturgical treasures. It will also provide you with some of the tools to uncover and appreciate the liturgy's hidden richness.

Did You Know?

Liturgy Is Work

The word *liturgy* comes from the Greek word *leitourgia*, which is made up of the words for "work" and "people." In ancient Greece *leitourgia* meant any public work exercised on behalf of the people to serve the common good. This work could be religious, political, or practical. Caring for the poor, serving in the army, or even picking up trash would have been considered a liturgy. These were works of the people for the benefit of the community.

Over the centuries, liturgy became associated with only the religious part of community life. Eventually only the actions of the priests were considered to be the liturgy. Today, however, liturgy is understood as the work of the whole Christ. The whole Christ is the Head, which is Jesus Christ, and the members of the Body, which includes all the baptized and all those who have already died and entered the Kingdom.

Reading the Map of the Liturgy

When you start a journey, first you need to know where you are going, right? One of the tools to understanding the Church's liturgy is to realize that the liturgy is not a place we go. Rather, it's an event that involves action. In other words, we don't *go to* Mass so much as we *participate* in Mass. In a sense, *liturgy* is more a verb than it is a noun. In fact, liturgy is work. It is God's work, in which we participate.

In the Church's liturgy, we participate in the work of the Holy Trinity by giving thanks and adoration to God the Father. God the Father is the source of every blessing throughout history. The greatest of these blessings is the gift of his Divine Son, Jesus Christ. We become his brothers and sisters through the power of the Holy Spirit.

© Bill Wittman/www.wpwittman.com

Mass is not a spectator sport. Getting involved in liturgical ministries, like being a lector, can help you appreciate the richness of the Mass. What ministries interest you?

The Key to Unlocking Symbols

If the liturgy had a key, it would be the Holy Spirit. Without the Holy Spirit, we would not see what lies beyond the words, actions, and objects of the liturgy.

Every liturgy is made up of symbols. To understand them, we need to know the symbolic language of faith. In symbolic language, *symbol* doesn't mean "fake." It means exactly the opposite.

Liturgical symbols express a reality that is completely real and deeply meaningful. Yet our attempts to describe these symbols never fully express their meanings. It's like trying to describe your relationship with your best friend or the love you feel for your pet. Try as you might, it's hard to explain it fully. **Symbols** are things visible to us that help put us in touch with something that is real, but invisible, like love. Sounds confusing, right? But our lives are filled with symbols we already understand.

For example, a graduation ceremony uses many symbols: the cap and gown, the diploma, the march, the graduates themselves. Let's explore one of these symbols.

A diploma is a piece of paper with your name, your school's name and seal, the date, and the principal's signature. For someone unfamiliar with what a diploma is, it could be seen as nothing more than a piece of paper. However, you know that the diploma represents, or symbolizes, all the years you went to school, your tests, research papers, grades, and all you've learned. Add to that all the goals you have for your future, your school friends and teachers, and the ceremony itself. When you connect all these things with the diploma, it is no longer just a piece of paper. Instead, it is a symbol of your past experience, your present accomplishment, and the possibilities that lie ahead. A meaningful symbol helps us remember the past, appreciate the present, and see future possibilities.

© YinYang/iStockphoto.com

How would you respond to someone who says that a diploma is just a piece of paper, worth only a few pennies?

Sacrament and Symbol

Liturgical symbols work in a similar way but are even more powerful. This is because Christ is made real in those symbols and works through the Holy Spirit to transform the present. As we see in Sacred Scripture, whenever people encounter Christ, they are changed.

© Brooklyn Museum/Corbis

Jesus heals a blind man.
Sacraments help us
experience Christ even
though we cannot see
or touch him.

But we can't see Christ today, can we? The Risen Christ is unrecognizable to human eyes. This is because his Resurrection has transformed him and because he has ascended to Heaven. Even his closest friends couldn't recognize him at first after the Resurrection. But they did recognize him when he was made known through symbolic actions, gestures, and words.

> When [the blind man] came near, Jesus asked him, "What do you want me to do for you?" "Sir," he answered, "I want to see again." Jesus said to him, "Then see! Your faith has made you well." At once he was able to see.
>
> Luke 18:40–43

Think About It!

How many symbols can you find in your parish church? Pick one or two and discuss what they mean for Catholics. Which is your favorite symbol and why?

Today, the Holy Spirit works through our liturgical celebrations to help us see Christ present and active in our midst. We use the adjective *sacramental* to describe these celebrations. Something is sacramental if it makes Christ's presence known. The liturgy is sacramental, because Christ is present and his saving presence is made known to us through the work of the Holy Spirit. The Spirit prepares us to encounter Christ and gives us the eyes of faith to recognize him.

The **assembly**, the people God calls together to celebrate the liturgy—the Church—is also sacramental. It is something with visible characteristics that helps us see the reality of Christ's presence. Because of this the Church is sometimes referred to as a **sacrament**. Through the work of the Holy Spirit, the Church makes Christ, who is invisible, visible to the world.

Illustration by Elizabeth Wang, "Through the offering of Jesus our High Priest in the Mass, we are united with all the saints in their praise of God in Heaven," copyright © Radiant Light 2008, www.radiantlight.org.uk

One of the main effects of liturgy, especially when we celebrate Mass, is that all who participate become one. They are united to one another and to all the saints throughout time. This happens because in the liturgy, they are caught up in the love of the Trinity. Therefore, when we pray the liturgy, we participate in the reality taking place right now in Heaven and on earth, where all the saints and angels are united with us in praising God. When we pray the liturgy, we participate in the work of the Blessed Trinity—Father, Son, and Holy Spirit.

Can you see the saints in this artistic image of a Eucharistic liturgy? The picture illustrates the familiar words we hear at Mass: "Now we join the angels and the saints as they sing their unending hymn of praise: Holy, Holy, Holy . . ."

> [Jesus] sat down to eat with them, took the bread, and said the blessing; then he broke the bread and gave it to them. Then their eyes were opened and they recognized him.
>
> Luke 24:30–31

Unity in Diversity

The Church's official liturgies developed differently in various parts of the world. Many of the symbols, words, and actions were the same ones handed down over the centuries from the Apostles. However, the liturgies looked different depending on which part of the world you were in. A Mass in Greece, for example, was different from one in Rome.

Similarly, today as people from all over the world gather for liturgy, their celebrations may differ somewhat due to cultural differences. Yet the diverse liturgical rites or traditions faithful to Apostolic Tradition show how the Church is universal, or Catholic, because they all express the same mystery of Christ. Therefore, even in diversity, the Church remains one body. This is because we follow the teachings of Christ as we have received them from the Apostles and their successors, the bishops.

Time Is a Symbol Too

Time is also a symbol that holds deep meaning. Your birthday, for example, commemorates the day you were born. It's just a date on the calendar, yet it has meaning for you and your family. On that day, you remember the past, you celebrate the present, and you hope for the future.

The Church also has special days and seasons during the year when we celebrate particular aspects of the mystery of Christ. On set days of the Liturgical Year, we keep memorials of the saints—first of all Mary, the Mother of God, then the Apostles, martyrs, and other saints. By doing so, the Church shows that she is united with the liturgy of Heaven.

Sunday: The First Easter

The most important day in the Christian calendar is Sunday, because it is the day on which Jesus rose from the dead. It is also the first day of Creation and

Pray with the Liturgy of the Hours

One of the liturgies of the Church is called the Liturgy of the Hours. The two most important hours are morning and evening. This is because they represent Christ's Resurrection (seen in the sunrise) and his death (seen in the sunset).

One way you can participate in these liturgies at home is to recite a brief prayer in the morning and at night. When you wake up, make the Sign of the Cross and say, "O Lord, open my lips, and my mouth shall proclaim your praise." Just before you go to sleep, make the Sign of the Cross and say, "May the Lord Almighty grant us a peaceful night and a perfect end" (Johnson, *Benedictine Daily Prayers*, pages 903 and 932).

the day of Pentecost. It is called the eighth day, because it is the day beyond time when Christ will come again. Because of all this, we call Sunday the Lord's Day.

Liturgical Seasons

Our liturgies throughout the Liturgical Year unfold the whole mystery of Christ, from his Incarnation and Nativity through the Ascension and Pentecost. In Advent and Christmas, we commemorate how the Son of God became one of us, and we wait with joyful hope for his return. In Lent and Easter, we celebrate how Jesus saved us by going to the cross, being crucified, rising from the dead, ascending to Heaven, and sending us the Holy Spirit. Throughout the rest of the year, we experience the joy of living as God's children on earth until we are gathered together into the eternal joy of Heaven.

Sunrise, sunset. Prayer is the best way to start and end your day with God.

© ImagineGolf/iStockphoto.com

PEOPLE OF FAITH
Saint John XXIII (1881–1963; Pope 1958–1963)

© 2013 Saint Mary's Press/Illustration by Vicki Shuck

He was born Angelo Giuseppe Roncalli in Italy. Later he became known as "Good Pope John." During his lifetime, the world experienced two World Wars, communism, and the Holocaust. In the Church, there was fear of the modern world. Yet Saint John XXIII embraced the world and called it "his parish."

When he became Pope at almost seventy-seven years old, many thought he would be "transitional," having little impact. Yet this was not the case.

In 1962 Pope John XXIII gathered all the bishops of the world in Rome. He also invited religious leaders, scholars, women, and even the news media. This gathering began four sessions called the Second Vatican Council. He wanted the Church to read the signs of the times and work for unity and peace within herself and with the entire modern world. He died in June 1963, after the first session of the Council. Yet what he began changed the way the Church related to the modern world. John XXIII paved the way for John Paul II, the ultimate "media Pope," by being the first to welcome TV crews to the Vatican. He let the world see for the first time how the Church worked. Like John Paul II, he also had a sense of humor. When asked how many people worked in the Vatican, he answered, "About half."

John XXIII was canonized in 2014 (with John Paul II). We celebrate his feast day on October 11, the day the Second Vatican Council opened.

28 SACRAMENTS: CELEBRATING CHRIST'S PRESENCE

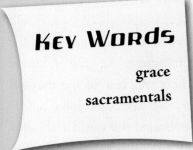

Key Words

grace

sacramentals

What have been some significant events in your life so far? Was it the birth of a baby sister or brother? Was it when you succeeded at something big? Maybe you lost a family member or friend because of a move, divorce, sickness, or death.

A new baby brother or sister brings big changes in a family's life. Sacraments celebrate big changes in our life with God.

© Galina Barskaya/Shutterstock.com

You may have felt different after such an event. You may have felt completely changed and had to live your life in a new way. For example, if you've experienced the birth of a younger sibling, some of the changes you might have experienced included a new place in the family order. You also may have had to take on new responsibilities.

As Catholics we have moments that also change us, whether we know it or not. But such changes are different from anything else in our lives, because it is God who changes us. These unique occasions are called Sacraments. Following are the Seven Sacraments: Baptism, Confirmation, the Eucharist, Penance and Reconciliation, Anointing of the Sick, Matrimony, and Holy Orders.

Baptism, Confirmation, and the Eucharist are Sacraments of Christian Initiation. This is because they are the foundation of Christian life. Baptism is always the first Sacrament celebrated because it is through this Sacrament that we become members of Christ and become part of the Church. Confirmation strengthens us and is necessary to complete baptismal grace. The Eucharist completes Christian initiation. It is the high point of Christian life, and all the Sacraments are oriented toward it. Anointing of the Sick and Penance and Reconciliation are Sacraments of Healing because through them the Church continues Christ's work of healing and forgiving sins. Holy Orders and Matrimony are Sacraments

PRAY IT!

Creator God, you have made everything—time and space, plants and animals, even me and everyone I love. You called all your creation good, and I know you are with me wherever I go. Bless this day, which you have made. Let me spend it in a way that glorifies you and brings your love into the world. Amen.

FUN FACT

Some people, places, or things the Church might bless include homes, engaged couples, pets, church bells, farm fields, boats, cars, rosaries, altars, organs, church doors, children, parents, pregnant couples, seeds, water, oil, statues, travelers, parks, cemeteries, schools, palm branches, and ashes.

Have you ever had a pet, your home, or a religious object blessed?

at the Service of Communion. This is because these Sacraments contribute to the Church's mission primarily through service to others.

Encounters with Christ

Sacraments are liturgies that use symbols. This means they use movement, gestures, and things like water and light, in addition to words, to communicate. Sacraments communicate that God is present in the midst of the community. Through Sacraments we encounter Jesus Christ and his saving power, called grace.

Material signs like water, oil, bread, and wine, which are used in the celebration of the Sacraments, are signs that something extraordinary is present. They are things we can see that help us recognize what we can't see. They help express the divine mystery of God's love. Sacraments are the fullest way we encounter God.

The birth of Jesus shows us that God became man, born as a baby—like each one of us.

© paul prescott/Shutterstock.com

God with Us

The first time we knew fully that God was with us was when God became man. Because of this, we say that Christ is the original sacrament. In Jesus' ordinary birth and life, people saw God doing something extraordinary. They saw it in the meals Jesus ate with people. They witnessed God's power when Jesus forgave sins. They knew it when Christ's touch healed the blind and the lame. When Jesus Christ rose from the dead and ascended into eternal life, people knew God truly is with us.

> With a loud cry Jesus died. . . . The army officer who was standing there in front of the cross saw how Jesus had died. "This man was really the Son of God!" he said.
>
> Mark 15:37,39

He is risen! This is the most important belief of Christians—that Jesus rose from the dead. During Mass we state this belief in the Nicene Creed: "[He] rose again on the third day in accordance with the Scriptures."

© sedmak/iStockphoto.com

Before Christ ascended to Heaven, he promised the gift of the Holy Spirit. The Spirit is the breath and presence of God. The Holy Spirit changed ordinary disciples into something extraordinary. They became Christ's Body and continued the work Jesus began. Today, through the Holy Spirit, the ordinary works of the Church become the extraordinary presence of God in the world. In this way the Church is like a sacrament.

© Lisa F. Young/Shutterstock.com

In the Church the Holy Spirit carries out the work of salvation. The Church is a sign of Christ's presence and the instrument through which the Holy Spirit still changes the world.

The Church continues to do the things Jesus did: gathering people, praying, forgiving, and healing. And through her liturgical actions, the Church participates in the liturgy of Heaven.

Have you ever thought of friendship as a mystery—something you can't quite explain but you know is real?

Go, then, to all peoples everywhere and make them my disciples: baptize them in the name of the Father, the Son, and the Holy Spirit, and teach them to obey everything I have commanded you.

Matthew 28:19–20

The Russian artist Andrei Rublev created this icon as a way to illustrate the mystery of the Trinity.

© Abramova Kseniya/Shutterstock.com

Sacred Mysteries

The Sacraments are sacred mysteries, instituted by Christ and entrusted to his Church. The meaning that is communicated in every Sacrament is that God loves us completely. We call this loving relationship with God **grace**. The visible rites through which the Sacraments are celebrated signify and make present the graces of each Sacrament. We encounter grace most fully in the Sacraments. Through grace, we become part of God's divine life—the life of the Trinity. It is pure love between the Father and the Son poured out to us by the Holy Spirit.

When we celebrate a Sacrament, we need to come to it with an attitude of openness to God's love and grace. This isn't as easy as it sounds. Sometimes God's love will challenge us. Sometimes it will make us realize we need to live our lives differently. Every time we encounter God's grace, something changes. Something new is created. Something weak is strengthened. Something dead is brought back to life. If we celebrate a Sacrament with

Liturgy Connection

The Memorial Acclamation

In the middle of every Mass, the priest says, "The mystery of faith." One of the responses we can make is "We proclaim your Death, O Lord, and profess your Resurrection until you come again" (*Roman Missal*). This is called the Memorial Acclamation. This response speaks of Christ's overwhelming love for us, even to death. This truly is a mystery, the mystery of unconditional love. But the mystery goes deeper, because Christ showed us a love stronger even than death. Further, his amazing love transcends time, because Christ promises to come again to gather all of us. This is why the mystery of Christ's love is the mystery of our faith.

THiNK About It!

Almost all blessings have the same structure. Once you learn this easy four-part structure, you can write your own blessings. Just remember: "you–who–do–through."

You: Begin by naming God. Think of a description of God, like "God, our Father" or "Creator God."

Who: Now remember something good God has done. For example, "You made all the creatures of the earth" or "You give me my family."

Do: This is where you ask God to do something good again, like, "Please bless my family."

Through: Finally, end the prayer by asking it through Jesus: "We ask this in the name of Jesus, the Lord. Amen."

Now what and whom will you bless?

the required disposition, or attitude, we will that God's grace will bear fruit in us.

Signs of Grace

In the Sacraments, we encounter God's grace in tangible ways. God calls us to participate in the Sacraments so we can encounter his loving grace in our lives in unique and powerful ways.

God calls us to encounter new life in Christ through Baptism and Confirmation. Christ's Body and Blood feed us in the Eucharist. God calls us back to him in the Sacrament of Penance and Reconciliation and heals us spiritually in the Sacrament of Anointing of the Sick. God calls us to lives of service and commitment in the Sacraments of Matrimony and Holy Orders.

Some of these Sacraments are celebrated many times over a lifetime. Others are celebrated only once.

Living a Changed Life Every Day

You don't have to wait for the celebration of a Sacrament to encounter God's grace. Over the centuries, the Church instituted and began using sacred signs called **sacramentals**. These signs prepare us to receive grace. Sacramentals prepare us to celebrate the Sacraments with the attitudes we need to let the Sacrament do what it's meant to do. They make us ready to cooperate with the grace we receive. Sacramentals also ask God to bless the different events and stages of our lives.

Sacramentals include things like making the Sign of the Cross on another person, signing yourself with holy water, having your forehead marked with ashes, or blessing your home, car, or pet. They also include

Did You Know?

Blessings

Among the many kinds of sacramentals, blessings hold an important place. God blesses creation with his grace, calling it good. In turn, people bless God by praising him and remembering all the good things he has done. They also bless other people, asking God to help them live the changed lives they have received or will receive in a Sacrament. We can also bless places and objects, asking God to help us use them wisely for the good of all people.

Anyone can do a blessing, even you or your parents. A deacon, priest, or bishop specifically leads particular blessings. These blessings are liturgies of the Church (that means they are public prayers) and often include some Scripture readings and spoken prayers.

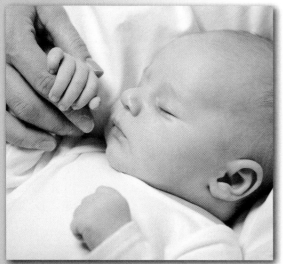

© Nina Vaclavova/Shutterstock.com

A parent can bless a child. You can bless your parents. Blessings are simple ways to communicate God's love.

sacred objects, such as holy water, statues of the Virgin Mary or the saints, rosaries, and blessed palms used at the Passion Sunday, or Palm Sunday, liturgy. You might use a sacramental each day. For example, maybe your parents make the Sign of the Cross on your forehead and say a prayer before you leave for school. You might pray a blessing at mealtime. You might also use holy water to bless yourself, or a rosary to pray.

LIVE IT!

Join Your Heart and Mind

At the Second Vatican Council, held from 1962 to 1965, the bishops said, "It is necessary that the faithful come to it [the liturgy] with proper dispositions, that their minds should be attuned to their voices" (*Constitution on the Sacred Liturgy* [*Sacrosanctum Concilium*], 11). To be attuned means to be "in sync or in harmony." The bishops ask that our minds be in tune with our voices when we celebrate the liturgy. This means we should pay attention to what we say and sing at Mass, rather than be present with a lack of attention. Next time you participate in a liturgy, listen to what you say and sing. Then find ways to sync your actions and thoughts during the week with what you pray on Sunday.

© Bill Wittman/www.wpwittman.com

Do you think most people realize that the Sacraments are encounters with God? If not, what might help them see this?

CHURCH HiSTORY

The Council of Trent

Today, we know Christ instituted the Seven Sacraments. But identifying them required long prayer and study by the early Church. From time to time, the Church has also needed to address mistaken teachings about the Sacraments. For example, in the early 1500s, the Protestant reformer Martin Luther argued that of the Seven Sacraments the Catholic Church recognized, only Baptism and the Eucharist are valid. In response the Council of Trent affirmed that Christ instituted all Seven Sacraments. The Council also explained teachings about specific Sacraments to address challenges raised by the Protestant reformers. Today our understanding of the Seven Sacraments owes much to the Council of Trent.

29 The Eucharist: The Heart of All Liturgy

Eucharisto is a Greek word meaning "to give thanks." This is what we do in our Eucharistic celebrations.

The **Eucharist** is the heart and high point of the Church's life. We gather in response to God's love. We try to bring our best selves and give heartfelt thanks to God. But our thanksgiving falls short of the extraordinary goodness of God. Because we are members of the Body of Christ, however, our thanks are joined to

At a Seder supper, the youngest child asks a series of questions that prompts the adults to tell the story of Passover.

© Leland Bobbé/Corbis

308

Christ's sacrifice of praise to the Father. Christ gave his fullest self in thanksgiving to the Father when he offered himself on the cross, once for all. Through his perfect offering, Christ pours out the grace of salvation on his Body, the Church.

> What can I offer the LORD for all his goodness to me? I will bring a wine offering to the LORD, to thank him for saving me.
>
> Psalm 116:12–13

Making the Past Present

Jews and Catholics do a special kind of remembering called **anamnesis**. Every year at Passover, Jewish people tell the story of how their ancestors escaped slavery in Egypt on the night the angel of death passed over the land (see Exodus, chapter 12). But the Jews don't tell the story as if it were only a past event. They believe that the same thing that happened in the past is happening again right now in the present. Just as he did their ancestors, God frees them.

In the Eucharist, we recall the past in a similar way. We remember Christ's Passover, when he passed over from suffering death to eternal life. His blood, which he poured out on the cross, is the blood that saves us,

PRAY IT!

Lord Jesus, sometimes it's hard to pray at Mass. I get so distracted, and sometimes I don't understand what is happening. Help me just to respond as best I can, to believe what I pray, and to live what I believe, so I can be your Body for all those who need you most. Amen.

LiTURGy CONNECTiON

The Eucharist Frees Us from Sin

Before Communion we sing, "Lamb of God, you take away the sins of the world, have mercy on us." The image of Jesus as the Lamb of God comes from the ancient Jewish Passover ritual. In the spring, the Jews killed an unblemished lamb and smeared its blood on the doorposts of a family's house. In the Exodus story (chapter 12), the sign of the blood saved the family from death and freed them from slavery.

The sacrifice of Jesus frees us from the slavery of sin. The Eucharist is a sacrifice that forgives our venial, or less serious, sins and helps us avoid committing mortal sins in the future. The Eucharist is offered in reparation for the sins of the living and the dead. This is why Masses are often celebrated in remembrance of someone who has died.

like the blood of the Passover lamb in Exodus. In the Eucharist we recall what he did in the past through his life, suffering, death, and Resurrection, but we also celebrate that his saving action is present today.

We call this kind of remembering anamnesis because it reminds us who we are: children of God. It reminds us to whom we belong: Christ. The meaning of *anamnesis* is easy to remember if we recognize that its opposite is *amnesia*. People with amnesia can't remember who they are or to whom they belong.

You Are What You Eat

What the Church says God does in a Sacrament really happens. What you see is what you get. In the Eucharist, when we eat and drink the consecrated bread and wine, we eat and drink the Body and Blood of Christ. This is called **Communion**. Communion transforms us, unites us more closely with Christ, and enables us to become more fully a part of the Body of Christ. This is because we are being intimately united in love with Christ. We actually become more like Christ. One reason this happens is because when we receive Communion, our venial, or less serious, sins are forgiven. Our union with Christ also strengthens us to resist more serious sins.

But this union goes even further. When we receive Communion, we're united in love not only with Christ but also with all of his Mystical Body, the Church.

> The bread we break: when we eat it, we are sharing in the body of Christ.
>
> 1 Corinthians 10:16

Call and Response

Communion is only one part of the Sacrament of the Eucharist. First, Christ gathers us into an assembly. We hear God's call to worship, and we respond by coming together on Sunday. Then we listen to the

© Bill Wittman/www.wpwittman.com

When you receive the Eucharist, you become the Body of Christ. What can you do to make Holy Communion all it is meant to be?

Illustration by Elizabeth Wang, "We join the Angels at Mass, who echo our worship, as if waving bright banners of gladness, as we celebrate Christ's glorious Resurrection," copyright © Radiant Light 2008, www.radiantlight.org.uk

The word *communion* means "union with." When we celebrate the Eucharist, we are in union with all the faithful who have gone before us, all who will come after us, and, of course, all who are with us now.

The Word of God, proclaimed by a priest or deacon, is an essential part of the Mass that is not to be missed.

Word of God proclaimed in Sacred Scripture. We listen especially to Christ, who speaks to us in the Gospels.

Next we respond by giving thanks to God the Father for everything he has done. Most of all, we thank God for sending us his only Son, Jesus Christ. In our thanksgiving we remember how Jesus took bread and wine and blessed them. We remember how he broke the bread and poured the wine and how he shared them with his disciples. We follow his command and do the same.

The priest, on our behalf, asks the Holy Spirit to change the bread and wine into the Body and Blood of Christ. Over the bread and wine, he says the words that Jesus said at the Last Supper: "This is my Body which will be given up for you. . . . This is the chalice of my Blood" (*Roman Missal*). Through the action of the Holy Spirit, the bread and wine become

© Bill Wittman/www.wpwittman.com

the Body and Blood of Christ. We are then called to share in the banquet prepared by Christ, who gives us his Body and Blood.

Even though there are a number of important parts to the liturgy, the celebration of the Eucharist is one single act of worship and praise of the Father through the Son, in the love of the Holy Spirit.

Who Celebrates the Eucharist?

Priests and bishops preside over the celebration of Mass. Only validly ordained men can preside at the Eucharist. They are the only ones who can consecrate the bread and wine so they become the Body and Blood of Christ. The role of the **presider** at Mass is

Live It!

Keep Sunday Holy

Sunday is the most important day of the week, because it's the day of Jesus' Resurrection. It is also the foundation of the whole Liturgical Year. For this reason Sunday is the most significant time to celebrate the Eucharist. For the Christian family, it's a day of joy and rest from work.

Following are some ways you can make Sunday a more significant part of your week: Be sure to participate in Mass. Rest from work that you can instead do on the other days of the week. Spend time with your family and do something nice for someone else. Look more closely for God's presence in everyone around you.

© Pascal Deloche /Godong/Corbis

When we celebrate the Eucharist, we fulfill Jesus' command to "do this in memory of me" (Luke 22:19).

unique and essential because he represents Christ and is acting in the person of Christ. The priest is so essential that without a priest we cannot celebrate the Eucharist.

Mass is not the action of the priest alone though. Who else is involved in the action of the Mass? Perhaps you are thinking of the choir or music director. Musicians contribute a lot to Mass. They sing and lead many of the responses, but Mass involves the action of others too. Perhaps now you are thinking of the readers, altar servers, Communion ministers, other liturgical ministers, or even the assembly. All these people assembled celebrate Mass, and each person is called to actively participate.

Did You Know?

Source and Summit

The Eucharist is "the source and summit" of the Church's life. When we remember Christ's sacrifice and share in it through the Eucharist, we become part of the Mystical Body of Christ in Heaven. We participate in the unity of the Church and witness a glimpse of our future already taking place in Heaven.

Liturgy is sometimes described as the work of the people. This is because no one is meant to be a spectator at Mass. But above all, Mass is God's work, which we participate in. When we celebrate Mass, we participate in the work of the Trinity. It's really Christ who is doing the work in communion with the Father and the Holy Spirit. Christ is the most perfect priest. He is the eternal high priest who offers the perfect sacrifice—his own self—to the Father. In the Mass, Christ acts through the priest to offer his Body and Blood in thanksgiving to the Father. All the members of his Body participate in the work of the Eucharist by joining with Christ through the priest.

The Role of the Assembly

If Christ is doing the work of the Eucharist, we can sit back and relax, right? Guess again. Saint Teresa of Ávila is believed to have written, "God has no body now on earth but yours; no hands but yours; no feet but yours." Christ leads, enables, and directs us. But we, the members of his body, must do work too. This is why the bishops at the Second Vatican Council said: "[The] Church earnestly desires that all the faithful should be led to that fully conscious, and active participation in liturgical celebrations which is called for by the very nature

THiNK ABouT IT!

How does participating in the Eucharist make you thankful? What are you thankful for? How does the Eucharist help you feel more united to Christ and the Church? What is your favorite part of Mass and why? How does this part of Mass help you live as Christ for others?

315

FUN FACT

The essential signs of the Eucharist are bread and wine. The bread must be made with only wheat flour and water. Nothing else can be added. The wine must be made from grapes only and must contain at least 5 percent alcohol. If it becomes vinegar, or if too much water is added so it is no longer wine, it cannot be used for Mass.

of the liturgy. Such participation by the Christian people . . . is their right and duty by reason of their baptism" (*Constitution on the Sacred Liturgy* [*Sacrosanctum Concilium*], 14).

The first way we participate is by coming to the Eucharist with an open and humble attitude. We need to be open to listening for God's voice. (This is the meaning of *obedience*, because *obey* is related to the Latin word *audire*, meaning "to hear.") This helps us be ready to receive the grace of God in the Sacrament.

If anything in our life seriously prevents us from listening to and obeying God, we must address it before we share in Communion. If we have committed a mortal sin, we must not share in Communion until we have received absolution in the Sacrament of Penance and

Altar serving is a liturgical ministry that many young people enjoy. Being involved in this way can make the Eucharist even more special.

© Bill Wittman/www.wpwittman.com

Reconciliation (see chapter 35, "The Sacraments of Healing," of this handbook).

We also participate in the Eucharist by joining in the responses, songs, silences, and gestures. This kind of participation is really not optional. It puts us in touch with the Christian spirit. Our participation in the liturgy helps us learn how to be Christian.

Finally, we participate by leaving the Eucharist with a promise to do in the world what we have done at Mass—live as Christ for others.

Church History

The Easter Duty

In the early Church, people shared in Communion every time they participated in the Eucharist. However, over the centuries, for various reasons, more and more people stopped receiving Communion, even though they might attend the Eucharist each week or even each day. By the sixteenth century, most people were receiving Communion only outside Mass or as they were dying.

In more recent times, the Church has been encouraging everyone who has celebrated First Communion and is free of mortal sin to share in Communion whenever they participate in a celebration of the Eucharist. At least once per year, during the Easter season, all Catholics who are able to receive Communion are obligated to do so. This is called the Easter duty. It is best to think of this as the bare minimum and to strive to participate in Communion every Sunday.

30 THE EUCHARIST: THE LITURGY OF THE WORD

Key Words

Liturgy of the Word
Logos
Lectionary
ambo

When you get together with your family or friends, do you tell or hear stories often? Like the one about when your grandparents met for the first time or your best stories about your favorite pet?

Do your family members have favorite stories to tell about one another—stories that everyone has heard over and over but are still worth telling?

© Alex Mares-Manton/Asia Images/Corbis

These stories help communicate who your family is. They are your shared history and identity. That's why they are retold at family gatherings. When newcomers join your family, they hear these stories too. Telling, listening, and retelling these stories helps tie families together.

© ImagineGolf/iStockphoto.com

This Bible looks old and well used. How used is your Bible?

In a similar way, every time the Church gathers to pray, events from her history are retold. In liturgical celebrations these events are shared during the **Liturgy of the Word**. The Liturgy of the Word is such an important part of the liturgy that we cannot have a liturgical celebration without it. The Liturgy of the Word consists of readings from the Bible; a homily by a bishop, priest, or deacon; the Creed; and prayers for the Church, the world, and people in need.

Jesus, the Word of God

The Book of Genesis tells the story of God's creating the world by speaking. "God commanded, 'Let there be light'—and light appeared" (1:3). The Word of God creates something new. God's Word brings order where there was only chaos. God's Word is life.

Pray It!

Jesus, Word Made Flesh, Even though you are God, you chose to become like me. Dwell in me and use my voice to speak your Word. Let me proclaim your Good News where there is hunger, and let me hear your voice where there is suffering. Help me be a part of your Word, spoken to bring new life. Amen.

LiTURGY CONNECTiON

The Lectionary: A Calendar for the Bible

Although all the readings we hear in the Liturgy of the Word come from the Bible, we don't read directly from the Bible itself. We read from the **Lectionary** (and the *Book of the Gospels*, which contains only the Gospel readings from the *Lectionary*). The *Lectionary* is a little bit like a calendar with readings. It shows the parts of the Bible we are to read on specific days of the year. Every day of the Liturgical Year and every Sacrament and special liturgy have assigned readings. These readings are the same for all Catholics throughout the entire world. Only on rare occasions, and usually only with the permission of the bishop or pastor, can the assigned readings be changed. The assigned readings can never be replaced with nonbiblical texts, even if they have a religious theme.

Jesus Christ is God's Word Made Flesh. God created something new when he raised Jesus from the dead. Jesus reordered the way we live. This is so we would live for God and not ourselves. God's Word, made flesh in Jesus Christ, gives us new life.

Jesus is called the **Logos**, a Greek word that translates as "word." Its meaning, however, is more like "thought," "logic," or "meaning." Jesus is the *Logos*, because when we see Jesus and listen to him, we can begin to see and understand God.

> In the beginning the Word already existed; the Word was with God, and the Word was God. . . . The Word became a human being and . . . lived among us.
>
> John 1:1,14

The Liturgy of the Word

In the Liturgy of the Word, we receive Christ through the words of Sacred Scripture. On Sundays the Liturgy of the Word comprises readings from the Old Testament, a psalm that is sung or recited, a reading from the letters of the New Testament, and a reading from one of the Gospels. This is followed by a homily in which a bishop, priest, or deacon explains the readings and applies their meaning to our

© Claudia Kunin/CORBIS

A Jewish youth reads from the Torah, which consists of the first five books of the Old Testament.

Illustration by Elizabeth Wang, "The Blessed Virgin Mary is the 'Holy House' who bore the Son of God in her womb and is forever to be honoured, copyright © Radiant Light, 2008, www.radiantlight.org.uk

How does this picture illustrate John 1:1,14?

lives today. The homily is followed by the recitation of the Nicene Creed. In the Creed, we express our core beliefs and renew our baptismal promises. The Liturgy of the Word concludes with the Prayer of the Faithful. In the Prayer of the Faithful, we pray for the needs of the Church, for the world, for those entrusted with leading Christ's Church on earth, for people in need, and for our community's particular needs.

> This passage of scripture has come true today, as you heard it being read.
>
> Luke 4:21

Did You Know?

Lectionary ABCs

The Sunday readings are arranged in a three-year cycle. In Year A, the Gospel reading is from Matthew. Year B is Mark, and Year C is Luke. John's Gospel is read throughout the year on certain Sundays. The Liturgical Year begins on the First Sunday of Advent, which falls in late November or early December.

The first reading usually comes from the Old Testament. It is related in theme to the Gospel. Next, a psalm summarizes the theme. The second reading comes from one of the New Testament letters. It doesn't always relate to the theme because it is read continuously. That means we start at the beginning of the letter and read a portion each Sunday until we come to the end. The last Scripture reading is always from one of the Gospels.

The Gospel Reading

When the Gospel is proclaimed at Mass, we give it special reverence by adding more festive elements to the proclamation.

Just before the proclamation of the Gospel, we stand and sing an acclamation to Christ, the Word. Usually the acclamation is "Alleluia!" During the acclamation, a deacon, priest, or bishop processes to the ambo with a book called the *Book of the Gospels,* which contains only the readings from the four Gospels. The **ambo** is a reading stand where Scripture is proclaimed. In some parishes, altar servers carrying candles and sometimes incense accompany the deacon, priest, or bishop.

Feeding on the Word

The Word of God is more than just stories handed down to us. Instead, it is the bread that sustains us. Both the Word of God and the Eucharist feed us in Mass. This is why the Liturgy of the Word and the Liturgy of the Eucharist are closely connected. In the Liturgy of the Word, Christ, the *Logos* of God, feeds us. This prepares us to be fed by Christ, the Lamb of God. Therefore we show reverence to both the Word and the Eucharist, because both give us life.

Think About It!

Do you have a favorite Scripture passage? Who are the main characters and events in that passage? Are you like any of the characters, or has a similar event happened to you in your own life? What can you learn from the people in the Scripture account that you can apply to your own life?

FUN FACT

Before the Second Vatican Council introduced changes to the Mass, people heard only a New Testament reading before the Gospel at Sunday Mass. The Old Testament was proclaimed only on weekdays. Back then, if you went to Mass every Sunday for a year, you would hear only 1 percent of the Old Testament and 17 percent of the New Testament. Today, if you go to Mass every Sunday for three years, you will hear 14 percent of the Old Testament and 71 percent of the New Testament (USCCB Committee on the Liturgy, *Newsletter*, page 27).

In addition to hearing the Word proclaimed in Sacred Scripture, we are fed by the Word through the homily. A bishop, priest, or deacon takes the readings we have just heard and helps us look at our lives through the lens of those readings. Then he shows us how the readings apply to our lives today. Therefore, the homilist's task is to interpret the meaning of Scripture for our lives.

> You must not depend on bread alone to sustain you, but on everything that the LORD says.
> Deuteronomy 8:3

During the homily the priest shows us how Scripture, even though it was written thousands of years ago, applies to our lives today.

© Bill Wittman/www.wpwittman.com

Having been fed by the Word, we publicly state our core beliefs. We do this by saying the Creed or by renewing our baptismal promises. We conclude the Liturgy of the Word with the Universal Prayer, or Prayer of the Faithful, which includes intercessions for the Church, for the world, for those entrusted with leading Christ's Church on earth, for people in need, and for our community's particular needs. We name those things in our world that are in need of God's life-giving Word. We ask God to help us be like Christ,

Live It!

Practice Holy Reading

To make the readings come alive on Sunday, try an adapted form of an ancient type of prayer called *lectio divina* (from the Latin for "holy reading").

First, choose one of the readings for the upcoming Sunday. Find it in a Bible and sit in a comfortable, quiet place to read it. Close your eyes and breathe deeply. Open your eyes. Slowly read your reading several times. Try reading it once out loud. Listen with your heart.

Second, ask yourself: What does this mean for me? What is God trying to say to me? Journal your thoughts if you like.

Third, respond with your heart. God has spoken to you with his heart. What would you like to say to God at this moment with yours?

Fourth, rest in silence with God. Breathe deeply and give thanks for your conversation with God.

the Living Word, so we can be a life-giving word to all those in need. When we pray the Prayer of the Faithful, we imitate Christ, who prayed to the Father for those he loved and for those who were suffering. Praying for others is one way we exercise the responsibilities of our Baptism when we were recreated to be like Christ.

The devil tempts Jesus to turn stones into bread, but Jesus replies that we need the Word of God as much as bread. Why?

PEOPLE OF FAITH
Saint Anthony of Padua

© 2013 Saint Mary's Press/Illustration by Vicki Shuck

Saint Anthony is revered as one of the Church's greatest preachers, who brought many lost people back into the faith. He had a beautiful voice and a captivating way of speaking. His homilies were well written and made people think. He was known as the "hammer of the heretics," because his sermons helped defend the Church against the false teachings that were being spread during his lifetime.

Saint Anthony's original reason for becoming a priest was to become a martyr. Martyrs were people who were killed because of their faith in Christ. Anthony was moved by the recent martyrdom of five Franciscans. Anthony left his comfortable life in Portugal to join the Franciscan order in Africa in hopes of dying for the faith. His poor health, however, changed his plans. Instead, he spent his short life with the Franciscans in Italy to become one of the greatest spiritual writers of the Church, venerated for his great teachings.

Less than a year after Saint Anthony's death, Pope Gregory IX canonized him. His feast day is June 13.

31 THE EUCHARiST: THE LiTURGY OF THE EUCHARiST

Key Words

Liturgy of the
Eucharist
Eucharistic Prayer
epiclesis
Transubstantiation

There is a Jewish saying that the person who eats without first thanking God is a thief. Sounds harsh, right? But it makes sense. You've probably been taught to say thank you whenever you receive a gift. Well, everything we have, including our food, is a gift from God. Therefore, it's only right to thank God before we share a meal. We do

Have you ever been asked to bring up the gifts at Mass? It is an honor to represent the faith community in this way.

© Bill Wittman/www.wpwittman.com

just that in the part of the Mass that follows the Liturgy of the Word. It is the **Liturgy of the Eucharist**. Let's take a closer look at each part of the Liturgy of the Eucharist.

> What shall I bring to the LORD, the God of heaven, when I come to worship him? . . . What he requires of us is this: to do what is just, to show constant love, and to live in humble fellowship with our God.
>
> Micah 6:6,8

Giving Back to God What God Has Given Us

The Liturgy of the Eucharist begins with the Preparation of the Gifts. Here, representatives from the assembly bring bread and wine to the altar, and money is collected from the people. This money will go toward helping people who are poor and toward supporting the work of the Church.

When we bring bread and wine to the altar and collect money, we show that it is God who has given us these gifts. It is God who cares for our every need.

PRAY IT!

Blessed are you, God of all creation. You gave me the gift of life and all that I have. I want to say thank you by offering you my life lived well. Use me and my talents and give me only what I need, so I can always be grateful to you and attentive to those who have so little. Amen.

FUN FACT

"The Lord be with you." "And with your spirit." This dialogue happens four times in the Eucharist: at the start of Mass, before the Gospel reading, at the Preface, and before the end of Mass. This dialogue reminds the priest and the people that God is present in our midst and that his Spirit is within us as we celebrate the Eucharist.

The Eucharistic Prayer

The next part of the Liturgy of the Eucharist is the core of the Mass. Here, the priest leads the assembly in the **Eucharistic Prayer**, which is the Church's great prayer of thanksgiving to the Father. Because the Eucharistic Prayer is so important, we will look more closely at its main parts.

Preface and Holy, Holy, Holy

"On your mark! Get set! Go!" When you hear these words at the start of a race, your ears perk up. Your eyes focus, and your entire body is alert. Something big is about to happen.

At the beginning of the Eucharistic Prayer is a special dialogue between the priest and the people, as follows.

Priest: The Lord be with you.

People: And with your spirit.

Priest: Lift up your hearts.

People: We lift them up to the Lord.

Priest: Let us give thanks to the Lord, our God.

People: It is right and just.

This dialogue is a little like a signal to us that something important is about to happen. So listen up. With these words, the priest invites us to pray with him. Even though he will do most of the speaking, the Eucharistic Prayer is the prayer of everyone gathered. The priest speaks on behalf of the community, and we pray with him. All of us, together with the priest, focus on God and join our prayers with those of the angels and saints in Heaven.

The next part of the Eucharistic Prayer is called the Preface. This is a summary of the good things the Father has done for us throughout history. It is called the Preface because it will lead us to the main reason we are so thankful—the gift of God's Son, Jesus.

Giving to people in need goes beyond the collection during Mass. Anytime we give to those in need, we are being Gospel people, loving one another as Christ has loved us.

© MachineHeadz/iStockphoto.com

FOOD BANK

LiTURGY CONNECTiON

Liturgical Colors

The color of the vestments sets a tone and indicates the nature of the liturgical feast or season.

- **White** symbolizes hope and purity. It is used during the Christmas and Easter seasons and at funeral masses.
- **Red** signifies the outpouring of Christ's blood and is used on Passion Sunday and Good Friday. It is also worn on the feast days of the Apostles and martyrs. Red also symbolizes the fire of the Holy Spirit, so it is worn on Pentecost and for the Sacrament of Confirmation.
- **Violet** is used during Advent to signify preparation and during Lent to signify penance.
- **Green** symbolizes hope and is used during Ordinary Time.

You'll hear many different prefaces throughout the year, but you'll always know it's the Preface because it begins right after the dialogue on page 330. Every Preface says why we are grateful to God. Listen to the Preface of the Eucharistic Prayer for Masses with Children (I), as follows. What are we thanking God for here?

We thank you for all that is beautiful in the world and for the happiness you have given us. We praise you for daylight and for your word which lights up our minds. We praise you for the earth, and all the people who live on it, and for our life which comes from you.

At the end of the Preface, we pray, "Holy, Holy, Holy Lord . . ." This acclamation is called the *Sanctus* and may be spoken if no one is available to lead the singing.

Holy, holy, holy! The LORD Almighty is holy! His glory fills the world.

Isaiah 6:3

The Work of the Holy Spirit

The next section of the Eucharistic Prayer is often brief, and if you tune out, you might miss it. It's called the **epiclesis**, a Greek word meaning "calling upon" or "invocation." Here the priest asks the Father to send down the Holy Spirit over the gifts of bread and wine. As the priest does this, he places his hands over the gifts, with his palms facing down.

The priest is asking the Father to send the Holy Spirit to change the bread and wine into the Body and Blood of Christ. Later in the prayer, there will be

The artist illustrates the connection between the community gathered for the Eucharist on earth and those in Purgatory and in Heaven. Can you see the image of the Trinity? Mary and the saints? the souls in Purgatory?

Illustration by Elizabeth Wang, "Through the one Sacrifice of Christ, re-presented at every Mass, we are united with the Heavenly Court and the souls of Purgatory," copyright © Radiant Light 2008, www.radiantlight.org.uk

another *epiclesis*. At that time the prayer will be for the Father to send his Spirit upon us. You see, in the Eucharistic Prayer, we get changed too. The Holy Spirit changes us from individual people into one body. The Holy Spirit changes those who eat the consecrated bread and wine—the Body and Blood of Christ—into the Body of Christ.

"On the Night Before He Died . . ."

The Institution narrative and Consecration are probably the most familiar part of the Eucharistic Prayer. It recalls Jesus' words at the Last Supper on the night before he died. Through the power of the Holy Spirit the bread and wine are changed into the Body and Blood of Christ.

Did You Know?

Using Our Gifts

If Jesus had taken up a collection at the Last Supper, what do you think he would have asked for? It probably wouldn't have been money. Instead, Jesus would have asked us to do what he did throughout his life. He cared for the poor, took care of the sick, and shared his life with strangers and friends. In other words, he used his gifts to help those in need. So we are called to do the same. We are called to take the gifts God has given us—the ability to work and the talents we have—and give them back to God to help those in need.

© Bill Wittman/www.wpwittman.com

The priest is at a moment of *epiclesis* during Mass. Find this key word and read why *epiclesis* is so important.

This change in the bread and wine is called **Transubstantiation**. This means that the essence or substance of the bread and wine changes into the Body and Blood of Christ. However, the appearance, smell, and taste of the elements do not change. Through the words and actions of a validly ordained priest, the Transubstantiation of the bread and wine into the Body and Blood of Christ takes place. Under the species of bread and wine, Christ himself becomes present in a true, real, and concrete way. He is fully present in Body, Blood, soul, and divinity.

The Eucharistic Prayer isn't over after the Institution narrative. We still

Think About It!

Contributing to the collection at Mass is about giving thanks to God for everything he has given us. All we have comes from God, who gives us all our gifts to bless us and those in need. When we give money at Mass, it is a way to participate in God's care for those in need by contributing to the work of the Church. You don't need to give much, just give something. If you receive an allowance, give a percentage of it each week. Also give of your talents and time.

need to be attentive to the entire prayer. The Institution narrative and Consecration are followed by the Mystery of Faith. This is also called the Memorial Acclamation. Here, in song or spoken word, we remember Christ's love for us on the cross. We remember that the Father raised him from the dead. We remember that Christ will come again to unite us all forever.

Although there were no photographers at the Last Supper, many artists have depicted the occasion when Jesus instituted the Eucharist. What do you think it would have been like to be at the table with Jesus at the Last Supper?

Giving, Receiving, and Interceding

We're not done yet. We remembered Christ's sacrifice on the cross so we might live. In this next part, called the oblation, we ask God to receive our own sacrifice.

© Historical Picture Archive/CORBIS

The sacrifice we offer to the Father in the Eucharist is the sacrifice of our praise. This sacrifice is represented by our thanksgiving to the Father, our remembrance of his Son, and the gifts we have placed on the altar, which the Holy Spirit changes. What we actually offer to God is our lives lived as his children.

The next part consists of intercessions through which we ask the Father to remember his Church. We pray that the Church on earth will be united with Mary and Joseph and all the Apostles and saints. We ask God to bless our Church's leaders. We also pray that God remember us. Finally, we pray for all the dead and ask God to unite us again in his Kingdom.

Live It!

Mean What You Pray

If we mean what we say, then the Eucharistic Prayer and our Amen will require us to sacrifice like Jesus. We will need to sacrifice our selfishness, give up our comforts and prejudices, and take up Christ's cross.

The best way to live this prayer is by giving our fullest attention to it during Mass. This is hard to do for such a long prayer, so at first try focusing as best you can at the beginning and end of the prayer. When the priest begins the Preface dialogue with "The Lord be with you," that's your signal to listen up. When you begin this dialogue, stand tall with your head held high. Then at the end of the prayer, sing or say the people's Amen attentively and with meaning.

© Brooklyn Museum/Corbis

Jesus offered his love and healing to those who were poor and those who were sick, caring for them and healing them. He asks us to do the same.

Saying Yes

When we come to the end of the Eucharistic Prayer, we summarize our thanksgiving into a doxology. A doxology is a statement of praise to the Trinity. We gather all we have said, sung, and hoped for in the Eucharistic Prayer and give all glory and honor to the Father. We do this through Christ, with Christ, and in Christ. And we do this all in the unity of the Holy Spirit.

The last part of the doxology is the people's Amen. Here we sing or say "Amen." When we say "Amen," we mean, "Yes, make it happen." We really want what we have prayed for—to be one with Christ and one another. When we are completely united with Christ and one another, we would love everyone as Christ loves us.

The tapestry called "The Communion of Saints" hangs in the Cathedral of Our Lady of the Angels, in Los Angeles. Notice the ordinary-looking people walking beside canonized saints. What do you think the artist is saying?

© Bill Wittman/www.wpwittman.com

Church History

Can the Celebration of the Eucharist Change?

In the deepest sense, the celebration of the Eucharist, since the evening of the Last Supper, has not changed at all. At every Mass, as Jesus instructed, through the words of the priest and the action of the Holy Spirit, ordinary bread and wine become the Body and Blood of Christ.

But, with the permission of the Church, the way we celebrate the Eucharist can change. In some parts of the world, in the earliest days of the Church, Mass was celebrated in Greek. ("The Lord Have Mercy" is an English translation of the Greek *Kyrie eleison*.) Gradually, as the Roman Empire expanded, the Latin language became the language of the people and the language of the Mass. At Vatican Council II, permission was given for the Mass to be said once again in the language of the people, or the vernacular. In the United States, we celebrate Mass in English, in Spanish, in Vietnamese, and sometimes in other languages too.

When the Mass was in Latin, the altar boys were primarily responsible to give the responses (such as "And with your spirit") in the name of the people. However, in the 1960s, "dialogue Masses" were encouraged, in which the people themselves spoke the Latin responses. However, with the Mass now being celebrated in the language of the people, we are given the opportunity to say or sing these responses for ourselves. This was the reason for this major change: to help the people participate in celebrating the Eucharist.

32 The Eucharist: Communion and Sending forth

If you were hosting Thanksgiving dinner, what would you need? Food, of course. Special, fancy food, probably, and dessert. What else? A dinner table with nice plates, utensils, and glasses. Anything else? Of course you would have family and friends gathered. Those gathered around the table would laugh, tell stories,

The word *Eucharist* means "giving thanks to God." When we celebrate Mass, it is something like sharing a great Thanksgiving feast.

© Larry Williams/Corbis

340

give thanks, and enjoy one another's company. This companionship would probably continue after dinner. Perhaps during such a gathering an old grudge or hurt would be forgiven or new friendships made. Whatever the people do, it's safe to say that to have a Thanksgiving dinner, you need more than just food.

It's a little bit the same when we talk about the Eucharist or Communion. Each of these words means more than the Body and Blood of Christ we eat and drink in the Sacrament.

Eucharist also means "giving thanks to God." The Eucharist is not only the consecrated bread and wine—the Body and Blood of Christ—that we eat and drink. It's the whole event. It's gathering and greeting one another at the doors of the church. It's sharing our Church family's history and all the good things God has done for us throughout time. It's blessing God and all the gifts he has given us, especially the bread and wine that become the Body and Blood of Christ. It's sharing our life together the way a family shares its life—by eating together.

In a similar way, the word *Communion* means more than the Body and Blood of Christ we receive at the moment we receive it. It also means our union with Christ and one another, especially when we gather to eat and drink his Body and Blood.

PRAY IT!

Jesus, Son of God, teach me to pray with open hands and an open heart.

Jesus, Lamb of God, nourish my body that I may do your will.

Jesus, Love of God, send me where you need me to go and help me give others the love and joy you give me.

This I pray in your holy name. Amen.

FUN FACT

What do children do when they want to be picked up? They reach their arms up above their heads and open their hands. We can do something similar, called the **orans** posture, when we pray to God our Father during the Lord's Prayer. We can raise our eyes and hands, also imitating the image of Christ on the cross. The posture looks like a cry to our Father. Early Christians used this posture too.

In this chapter we'll look at the high point of the Sacrament of the Eucharist—the Communion Rite.

Our Family Prayer

The Eucharistic Prayer asks God to change not only the bread and wine (see chapter 31, "The Eucharist: The Liturgy of the Eucharist," of this handbook). It also asks God to change us so we might become one body in Christ.

After the Eucharistic Prayer is finished, our next action is to pray out loud as one family to our one God, our Father. We use the words Jesus taught his own disciples— the **Lord's Prayer**.

A woman prays the Lord's Prayer in the *orans* position. Read the Fun Fact article on this page to find out more about this gesture.

One of the lines we pray is, "Forgive us our trespasses as we forgive those who trespass against us." Have you tried sharing a meal with someone who hurt you or someone you hurt? It's not easy, is it? But once we forgive the other person or receive forgiveness, eating together is much easier. Therefore, we ask the Father to forgive any wrongs we have committed. At the same time, we promise to forgive others. (For more about the Lord's Prayer, see chapter 49, "The Lord's Prayer: The Perfect Prayer," of this handbook.)

> Our Father in heaven: May your holy name be honored; may your Kingdom come; may your will be done on earth as it is in heaven.
>
> Matthew 6:9–10

A Sign of Peace

We put our promise into action with a sign of peace. At the **Sign of Peace**, the deacon or priest invites us to share a sign of Christ's peace with one another. This can be a handshake, kiss, hug, or some other gesture. Usually, we say "peace be with you" as we share the sign.

The Sign of Peace reminds us that the Eucharist is not just about God and me. Loving our neighbor is essential to loving God.

© Bill Wittman/www.wpwittman.com

Jesus, the Paschal Lamb

Next is the Fraction of the Bread, when the priest, with the help of a deacon or other priests, breaks the consecrated bread into smaller pieces so it can be shared with everyone. A fraction is a portion of a whole, a term that is also used in math.

During the Fraction of the Bread, we sing a litany to Jesus, the Lamb of God. A **litany** is a form of prayer, spoken or sung, in which a leader begins a dialogue, often using different phrases, such as various names for Christ. The people respond to each phrase by repeating the same words. In the Lamb of God, we recall that Jesus is our Paschal Lamb, whose blood frees us from the slavery of sin. (*Paschal* comes from a Greek term that means "Passover.") The cantor or choir addresses Jesus, the Lamb of God, who takes away our sins. We respond, "Have mercy on us." As the priest finishes breaking the consecrated bread, the Body of Christ, our response changes to, "Grant us peace." This reminds us of our hope for unity and peace with each other.

Communion: Becoming One Body

Now we come to Communion, the high point of our entire Eucharist. It's the main reason we come to Mass and the thing that gives us strength throughout the week. This is when we become what we have been praying for by the power of the Holy Spirit. It is when we become one with Christ.

Becoming one with a person means knowing that person will never leave you. The person will never reject you or make fun of you. The person will love you no matter what. In Communion, we become one with Christ, who will do all this and more for us. Communion is eating and drinking with the one who knows

LITURGY CONNECTION

Supper of the Lamb

After the Fraction of the Bread, the priest says: "Behold the Lamb of God, behold him who takes away the sins of the world. Blessed are those who are called to the supper of the Lamb."

Who are "those"? Of course, he means us and everyone else gathered for Mass. The priest is inviting all who are present who are Catholic to participate in Communion.

He also means those all over the world gathered for Mass and those who are in Heaven. These words remind us that the Church is bigger than just our own parish. The Church is universal and eternal.

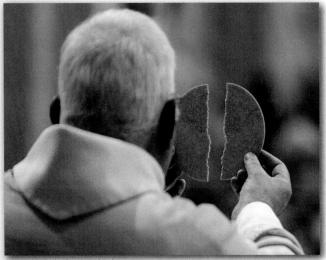

© Pascal Deloche/Godong/Corbis

Did you know that when the priest breaks the consecrated bread into smaller pieces, it is called the Fraction of the Bread?

THiNK ABOUT IT!

In Communion when we receive only one of the consecrated elements—the Body or Blood of Christ— we still fully receive Christ because he is present in each element. Why does the Church encourage us to receive from the cup as well?

everything about us and loves us no matter what. When we receive the Body and Blood of Christ, we receive Christ, real and present, and he will never leave us. When we receive Christ, our connection with the Church also grows stronger. This is why Saint Augustine called the Eucharist the "mystery of unity" (Sermon 272).

This is also why we sing as we share Communion. When we sing together, our individual voices become one voice. Singing together shows our union with one another through the Holy Spirit. Singing also expresses joy in a fuller way than speaking does.

The *Body of Christ* refers to both the consecrated bread and wine and to all the people who are part of the Church. In

© P Deliss/Godong/Corbis

When we say "Amen" at Communion, we are saying "Yes, this is the Body of Christ" and "Yes, we promise to be the Body of Christ."

Communion when we come forward and the extraordinary minister of Holy Communion says, "Body of Christ" and "Blood of Christ," we respond "Amen," that is, "Yes, let it be so."

In the gifts of Christ's Body and Blood, we see clearly his love for us. When we say "Amen" and eat his Body and drink his Blood, we become united completely with Christ and his mission. His mission is to show everyone the immense love of his Father. Christ himself did that by loving others, even to the point of dying on the cross.

Once everyone has shared in Communion, we pray together in silence or sing together a song of praise. In the silent prayer or song, we give thanks to God for giving us the gift of the Eucharist. Finally, we end the Communion Rite with a prayer asking that the Communion we have shared will indeed change our lives.

Sent to Announce the Gospel

How does the Eucharist change our lives? The Eucharist unites us with Christ and nourishes our soul. But will people recognize that we are members of the Body of Christ? Will we be different after we share in all these graces of the Eucharist?

> As the Father sent me, so I send you.
> John 20:21

Did You Know?

The Pilgrim Church

Sometimes the Church is called the Pilgrim People of God. You may have an image in your mind of the Pilgrims who settled part of the English colonies in North America hundreds of years ago. The key is to realize we call them Pilgrims because they were travelers rather than because they were settlers. In the same way, we are pilgrims because we are on a journey, not because we've arrived. This means that while we live on earth, we are making our way to Heaven.

The pilgrim image also refers to the Israelites wandering in the desert for forty years as they journeyed to the Promised Land (see Deuteronomy 2:7). It refers too to the disciples on the road to Emmaus. On the way, they met a stranger who turned out to be the Risen Christ (see Luke 24:13–35). We are disciples on the way to Heaven. Along the way, we meet Christ.

In one of his writings on the Eucharist, Pope Saint John Paul II described the Eucharist in many ways. He said it was a call for Catholics to tell others about Jesus. He said it is the way all people will begin to care for one another; it is the way Christians promise to make the world a better place. These are all actions we do outside of Mass.

Saint John Paul II also said that the Eucharist doesn't isolate Catholics from the world. Instead, the Communion we share and the unity we encounter with Christ and one another help us bring people together. The loving unity we share is like a magnet that draws others into the same loving relationship we have with Christ. That's why almost immediately after we share in Communion, the final part of the Eucharist sends us forth to spread the Good News of Jesus. This means that we are called to love and serve God not only at Mass but also in the world. We will find God in the world most clearly in people who are poor.

In fact, the "Eucharist commits us to the poor" (CCC, 1397). This means that when we say yes to Christ in the Eucharist, we say yes to people who are poor. We promise to think about others who are in need and to do what we can to help them. That's why we leave Mass to share with others the gifts we have received there.

The Mass sends us out to give the gifts of the Eucharist to others. These are love and friendship, attention to and compassion for others, forgiveness, hope, and joy. When you see a person who is lonely, you can give him or her the gifts of love. You can be kind to her or him, even if the person does not respond with kindness, because you have received forgiveness yourself in the Eucharist. You can do something to help that person feel happy, because you have received so much joy from Christ. The world will be changed because of God's love we encounter in the Eucharist.

> Whenever you did this for one of the least important of these brothers of mine, you did it for me!
>
> Matthew 25:40

Live It!

A Sign of Reconciliation

It's fun to greet friends during the Sign of Peace. But this ritual isn't about catching up. It's actually a serious gesture.

Remember that in the liturgy, Christ is acting and speaking. When we say "Peace be with you" and shake a person's hand or hug the person, it is really Christ's peace we are sharing. That's a powerful thing, because Christ's peace changes the world! It turns enemies into friends. It heals wounds and hurts. It ends war and injustice. Sharing Christ's peace is serious business.

It may be more important to share a sign of peace with people you aren't friends with or people with whom you need to reconcile. But this isn't always possible. Next time you share the Sign of Peace, also think about the person you need to reconcile with, and pray for him or her. Do something during the week to move closer toward reconciliation with the person.

People of Faith
Saint Augustine

"Be what you see, and receive what you are."

CITY OF GOD

The Confessions

The Blessed Trinity

© 2013 Saint Mary's Press/Illustration by Vicki Shuck

Saint Augustine might be the world's most reluctant saint. From the age of seventeen, Augustine lived a wild life. He also searched for the truth and meaning of life. His mother, Saint Monica, was a devout Christian who prayed each day for her son's conversion to Christianity.

After studying the writings of Saint Paul, Augustine realized that his lifelong search for meaning could be answered in Christ. He was still reluctant to be baptized, because then he would have to give up his undisciplined lifestyle. Eventually, he was baptized. He later became a priest, and then the Bishop of Hippo in North Africa.

Saint Augustine is known for his sermons to those preparing for Baptism (the catechumens) and those recently baptized (the neophytes). He gave one of his most famous instructions to the neophytes as they were standing near the altar to receive Communion for the first time. He pointed to the Eucharist and said, "Be what you see, and receive what you are" (Sermon 272). From this phrase of Saint Augustine, we get the saying, "You are what you eat." Saint Augustine's point is that we receive the Body of Christ, and we become the Body of Christ.

Saint Augustine is venerated as a Doctor of the Church and as one of the great Fathers of the Western Church. His feast day is August 28.

33 THE SACRAMENT OF BAPTISM

Key Words

Baptism

catechumenate

What do these symbols say about what it means to be Christian?

© Bill Wittman/www.wpwittman.com

It can be as light as air, yet as hard as rock. Two-thirds of your entire body and three-fourths of your brain are made up of it. A trillion tons of it disappear into the air each day. Yet 75 percent of the earth is covered with it. You can't go a week without it. But too much of it can kill you.

What is it? It's water. Water makes life possible. When scientists search for life on other planets, they look for signs of water. Water makes all things grow. We live and breathe in water before we're born. After that we enjoy it when we swim, surf, soak, or sail.

Water also kills. Hurricanes and floods have destroyed entire cities. Overwatering kills plants. Drinking too much water can be fatal. People die each day from drowning. Water gives life. It also destroys life.

The waters in the Sacrament of Baptism are like that. They give us new lives. And they end our old ones. Let's look at how Baptism does this.

> By our baptism, then, we were buried with him and shared his death, in order that, just as Christ was raised from death by the glorious power of the Father, so also we might live a new life.
>
> Romans 6:4

The Birth of a Catholic

In the Sacrament of Baptism, we are born into new lives in Christ. Baptism is the first Sacrament of the forgiveness of sins. It unites us to Christ, who died and rose, and gives us the Holy Spirit. Through Baptism we become like Christ, who died on the cross. Like Christ we are resurrected to a completely new and eternal life.

Life without Baptism may be thought of as a life lived sort of half awake. We're not equipped to see all the ways God is present in our lives. But in Baptism, we are awakened. We start new lives, and we are clothed with Christ. We see the world the way Christ saw it, as filled with the Father's goodness. We are able to live as Christ did by loving others. In Baptism we become sons and daughters of the Father and brothers and sisters of Christ. We

PRAY IT!

God of Heaven and earth, You made the waters and filled the seas with life Shower your mercy upon me and wash me clean of my faults. Refresh my spirit and fill my thirst that I might live each day as your child, dead to sin and alive for you alone. Amen.

become temples of the Holy Spirit. Through Baptism we become part of the Body of Christ, the Church, and we share in Christ's priesthood. That means we are people who, through Christ, know the Father and help others know him too.

Baptism enables us fully to become the people God created us to be. It frees us from sin and makes union with God, or salvation, possible for us. We need the Church for salvation, because it is the Church, through Christ, that baptizes.

> No one can enter the Kingdom of God
> without being born of water and the Spirit.
>
> John 3:5

The Waters of Baptism

Water also cleans. We bathe and shower in it. We wash dishes with it. Rain cleans the air and makes everything fresh.

Baptism also washes us clean. The waters of Baptism wash away sin. Baptism is the first Sacrament we receive and the first way our sins are forgiven. Most important, it washes away Original Sin, the sin every human being inherits from Adam and Eve. Humans are imperfect, because to be human is to not be God, who is perfect. Our first parents, Adam and Eve, proved that even when everything else is perfect, we humans can still make mistakes and bad choices. But Baptism removes the stain of Adam and Eve's sin from our human natures and gives us a second chance. The waters of Baptism change our natures so completely that we are left with a new kind of mark on our soul. It leaves a permanent spiritual sign on our human natures. This sign consecrates us. That means it makes us holy. It changes us forever into adopted children of God. It sets us apart to worship him. The mark that Baptism makes on us is permanent and can never be removed. This is why Baptism cannot be repeated.

Did You Know?

Infants and Baptism

From the earliest times, the Church has baptized infants in the faith of the Church with the hope that one day they will make the faith of the Church their own. God's love is a pure gift to us, which means we don't need to do anything to earn it. This is why we don't wait to baptize until people are older. Nothing we could do at any age makes us any more deserving of God's love than we already are at birth. By baptizing babies we show our trust in God's goodness even when we don't deserve it or ask for it. As members of God's family, they will learn to love and respond to God. God will love them as his own forever.

The Church can baptize someone immediately if the person is in danger of death. Any person can baptize someone in danger of dying if no priest or deacon is available as long as that person has the intention of doing so and pours water on the person's head, while saying, "I baptize you in the name of the Father, and of the Son, and of the Holy Spirit."

The Baptismal Font

Jesus was baptized in a river. Today, we use baptismal fonts. Some of the early fonts were round to imitate the shape of a womb. This showed that Baptism is like rebirth. Others were rectangular like a tomb or shaped as a cross to show our death to sin. Still others were octagonal. This is because the number 8 has important symbolic meaning for Christians. Our seven-day week reflects the Bible's account of seven days of Creation. Referring to an eighth day is a way of saying something is really new in creation. That new, wonderful thing is Christ's Resurrection. Fonts with eight sides symbolize this. How does your parish font look?

Rite of Baptism

Ever since her beginning, the Church has been celebrating Baptism. The way the Sacrament has been celebrated has changed throughout the centuries. But the primary action in the Rite of Baptism has stayed the same. We immerse a person in water or pour water over his or her head, while we call upon the name of the Trinity: the Father, the Son, and the Holy Spirit.

The process for initiating a person in the Catholic Church varies according to age. Infants and young children celebrate the Rite of Baptism for Children. They are baptized and anointed with Chrism. When they get older, they will celebrate the Sacraments of the Eucharist and Confirmation, typically in that order. Adults and older children go through a similar process, but the rite that is followed is called the Rite of Christian Initiation of Adults (RCIA). The candidates are baptized, confirmed, and given the Eucharist all at the same liturgy.

In both ways of initiation, **Baptism** is the first step to becoming united with Christ through the Church. It is the beginning of a Christian's life. Confirmation strengthens people for their new lives. The Eucharist unites them in Christ and nourishes them for their new lives in him with his Body and Blood. Christian initiation is accomplished through these three Sacraments, whether celebrated in one liturgy or several liturgies spread out over many years.

For adults, many rituals are celebrated over a long period of time leading up to their Baptisms. Their preparation is called the **catechumenate**. It is how an adult learns the Christian way of life.

© Bill Wittman/www.wpwittman.com

Styles of baptismal fonts vary. What type do you have at your parish?

After Baptism a child learns how to be a Christian from his or her parents, godparents, and other Christians. Infants don't go through a catechumenate like adults. But their parents and godparents do spend time preparing themselves so they can be good teachers for their children as they grow.

Let's look at some of the symbols from the Rite of Baptism for Children.

Meeting at the Threshold

Stand in a doorway. It's a bit uncomfortable because it's an in-between space. You're in neither one room nor the other. The time of your life that you're in right now might feel a little like a doorway. You're not really a child. You're not an adult either. Sometimes it might be hard to know where you fit in. Doorways are also powerful places, because they are how you move to a new space. They let you out when you feel confined. They bring you in when you feel left out.

An unbaptized person is spiritually outside the Church. But Jesus called himself the Door. Through him we enter his family and find where we belong (see John 10:7–9). This is why the Baptism ritual begins with the celebrant going to where the parents, godparents, and child are and greeting them. This may be at the Church entrance or in specially designated seats.

> It is no longer I who live, but it is Christ who lives in me.
>
> (Galatians 2:20)

THiNK AbOUT IT!

How many different ways can you name to show how water gives life? How do you think these life-giving uses for water are related to the Church's understanding of Baptism? Are there any ways that water kills or destroys? How do you think these deadly images for water are also related to Baptism?

Giving Your Name

After being welcomed by the celebrant, the baby's parents announce to the assembly their baby's name. They also ask the Church to baptize their baby. The priest or deacon asks the parents whether they understand the responsibility that comes with their request. Baptizing their baby means they promise to bring up their baby to love Christ. They will need to teach their child what it means to follow Christ.

The parents aren't the only ones with a big responsibility. All those gathered for the Baptism are asked whether they will help the parents bring up the child in the Christian faith. If you're at a Baptism, you also share in this responsibility.

Marked with the Cross

When we enter the Church, we make the Sign of the Cross on ourselves. We do the same for those who are about to be baptized. The priest or deacon and the baby's parents and godparents make the Sign of the Cross on the baby's forehead. This shows that the baby now belongs to Christ.

© Bill Wittman/www.wpwittman.com

The priest or deacon comes to greet a family seeking Baptism for their child. Baptism is like a door that opens to all other Sacraments of the Church.

Rejecting Satan and Accepting Christ

Part of belonging to Christ means rejecting anything that isn't Christ. Just before the baby is baptized, he or she has to publicly reject Satan and accept Christ. Of course, babies can't make this statement for themselves. That's why the priest or deacon asks the parents and godparents to renew their own baptismal promises or vows, when they first rejected Satan and accepted Christ. These are the promises they will teach their child. He asks them: "Do you reject Satan, all his works, and all his empty promises?" Then he asks: "Do you believe in God the Father? in Jesus Christ? in the Holy Spirit and the holy catholic Church?"

Many people do not realize that each time they make the Sign of the Cross, they are expressing their Christian identity.

© Bill Wittman/www.wpwittman.com

FUN FACT

The history of Baptism is a rich one. It begins with the many accounts involving water in the Old Testament. In Creation, God separated the waters from one another and from the land (see Genesis 1:9). Through God's intervention, Noah and his family were saved from the Flood (see Genesis, chapters 6–9.) God's saving power parted the Red Sea so the Israelites could cross to safety (see Exodus, chapter 14.) These are just some early examples of God's saving power, which will be fully revealed in Christ.

Baptized in the Name of the Trinity

The baby is baptized in the baptismal font. The infant may be immersed in the baptismal water three times, or the minister may pour water over the baby's head three times. As he does this, he says, "I baptize you in the name of the Father, and of the Son, and of the Holy Spirit." The words of this Trinitarian formula cannot be changed.

Anointed with Sacred Chrism

The title *Christ* means "anointed." Therefore, in the next part of the rite, the baby's head is anointed with Chrism. (For more about Chrism, see chapter 34, "The Sacrament of Confirmation," of this handbook.) This anointing shows that the baby is now a follower of Christ and a member of his Body, the Church.

Clothed in Christ

After the anointing, the baby is clothed in a white garment. This garment's color—white—symbolizes the purity of a new Christian life.

A Child of Christ's Light

The newly baptized baby is now a child of the light. He or she receives a candle lit from the Paschal candle. The baby can't hold the candle, of course. Instead, the candle is given to the baby's

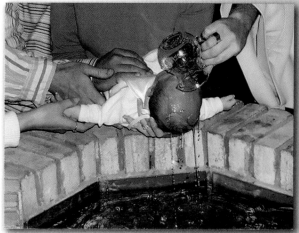
© Anne Kitzman/Shutterstock.com

parents or godparents. The priest or deacon asks them to keep the flame of faith alive for the baby until the baby meets Christ in Heaven.

If you were baptized when you were too young to remember, ask your family to share their memories of the celebration with you.

Salvation without Baptism

Baptism is essential for salvation, yet a person who has lived an extraordinary life of faith but didn't get to be baptized can still be saved. Unbaptized people who die for the faith, adults who have begun the process of preparation for Baptism, and those who seek God and strive to live out values consistent with the principles that Jesus taught can be saved if they sincerely desire to know God in their lives and try to live as God would have them live.

Flame from the Paschal candle is passed to the families of the newly baptized along with an exhortation: keep the flame of faith alive.

© Francisco Amaral Leitão/ Shutterstock.com

God wants all people to be saved. His love can find a way to save us even without Baptism. Therefore, when a baby dies before being baptized, or an older person dies without knowing Christ or the Gospel, we pray for the person's salvation and trust in God's mercy. We also trust that God's plan of salvation includes people from other religions.

Live It!

Readiness for the Christian Life

In the Rite of Christian Initiation of Adults, during the Rite of Election, the godparents are asked to attest to the candidates' readiness for Baptism by answering these questions:

- Has the candidate faithfully listened to God's Word proclaimed by the Church?
- Has the candidate responded to that Word and begun to walk in God's presence?
- Has the candidate shared in the company of our Christian brothers and sisters and joined with them in prayer?

Those of us who are already members of Christ's Church may find these questions valuable for us to reflect on as they relate to our own lives. Make a commitment to listen to God's Word, walk in his presence, and participate in the Church's liturgical prayer and devotions.

PEOPLE OF FAITH
Saint Elizabeth

© 2013 Saint Mary's Press/Illustration by Vicki Shuck

Almost everything we know about Saint Elizabeth comes from the beginning of Luke's Gospel. Elizabeth was married to Zechariah, a priest of the Temple in Jerusalem. She was also the mother of John the Baptist, and the cousin of Mary, the Mother of Jesus.

In the Gospel of Luke, we learn that although Elizabeth was thought too old to bear children, she became pregnant with a son. Her son would become known as John the Baptist, and he would prepare the way for Jesus' ministry.

Elizabeth was the first to recognize Jesus as the Messiah even before his birth. While she and Mary were both with child, Mary visited Elizabeth, and John leapt in Elizabeth's womb upon Mary's arrival. Elizabeth announced that Mary and her unborn child were blessed. She also called Mary blessed for having believed God's promise. Elizabeth's proclamation has become part of the Hail Mary.

Elizabeth's name means "God is faithful." We celebrate her feast day on November 5.

34 THE SACRAMENT OF CONFIRMATION

KEY WORDS

Sacred Chrism
age of reason

You might not realize it, but you use oil almost every day. How many ways can you think of? Many foods you eat are probably cooked with it. Soap has oil for cleaning. Oil in lip balm heals your lips. And ointment you put on a cut has oil.

Oil is everywhere. It's an essential ingredient for many food and everyday products. It's essential for the Church too.

Did you know that you must be baptized before you are confirmed? The water of Baptism is the gateway to Confirmation and all the other Sacraments.

© cworthy/iStockphoto.com

Water and Oil

In the Sacrament of Confirmation, a baptized person is anointed with a consecrated oil called **Sacred Chrism** and is strengthened with the Holy Spirit.

Confirmation is so closely tied to Baptism that it is almost impossible to speak about it without also talking about Baptism. This is because Confirmation adds to the gift of new life we received in Baptism. When we were baptized, we received the Holy Spirit. Confirmation is like getting an extra gift. It deepens and seals in the Gift of the Holy Spirit that we receive in Baptism. The oil used in Confirmation symbolizes the power of the Holy Spirit. The Spirit keeps us close to the Father and his Son, Jesus Christ. It also gives us a stronger tie to the Church. It sends us out strengthened to carry on the Church's mission. Confirmation helps us put our faith into words and actions.

> Set me as a seal on your heart, as a seal on your arm.
>
> Song of Songs 8:6, NRSV

Sealed for Life

Like Baptism, the Sacrament of Confirmation places a permanent mark on our soul that can never be taken away. (For this reason Confirmation is celebrated only once in a lifetime.) It's the mark of God's chosen ones. This mark

PRAY IT!

Spirit of God, you anoint me with your gifts and empower me to use them. Set your seal upon me and bless my words and deeds that all may know I am your child and your witness to the world. Amen.

protects us from the power of evil. It also brings out our unique talents and gifts. It does this by blessing us with the Gifts of the Holy Spirit. We are called to use our unique talents to serve the Church as full, maturing members of the Body of Christ. Just as its name implies, Confirmation confirms in us the faith that God planted there when he first called us before Baptism.

THiNK About It!

The title *Christ* means "anointed one." Jesus Christ is the anointed king chosen by the Father to save his people. When you were baptized, you took on a new identity as a Christian. The anointing with Sacred Chrism that you received strengthened you to do the work of Christ. What do you think you have been anointed to do? How do Baptism and Confirmation give you the strength to serve others?

East and West

In the earliest centuries of the Church, the anointing with oil of the newly baptized was done by the bishop immediately following Baptism. But as the Church grew larger, and as more people were being initiated, bishops couldn't be everywhere to baptize and anoint all the new Christians. Two different practices emerged as a result.

The Church in the West (that is, the former western part of the Roman Empire) still wanted the bishop to confirm the newly baptized. This was because the West focused on the connection the bishops had to the Apostles of Jesus. Jesus commissioned the Apostles. They themselves commissioned new bishops. Those bishops ordained new bishops. Therefore, every bishop is directly connected in a long line to Jesus. Because of this connection,

Western Churches delayed the Confirmation until a point in time when the bishop could do the anointing. This practice eventually led to the separation of Confirmation from Baptism by many years.

> The Spirit of the Lord is upon me, because he has chosen me to bring good news to the poor.
> Luke 4:18

The Churches in the East (that is the former eastern part of the Roman Empire) also valued the connection to the Apostles. But for them the connection was less in the presence of the bishop and more in the oil he blessed. Therefore, whether or not the bishop was present, Eastern Churches continued to confirm immediately after Baptism as long as they had oil blessed by the bishop. Confirmation was then followed by the Eucharist, when the newly baptized person received Communion for the first time. This

How do you use your God-given talents to serve the Church and other people?

© iPandastudio/iStockphoto.com

practice clearly shows the close connection and unity among the three Sacraments of Christian Initiation— Baptism, Confirmation, and the Eucharist.

Age and Confirmation

In the Eastern Churches today, anyone who is baptized is immediately confirmed and given the Eucharist. It doesn't matter if the person is a baby or an adult.

Today, most dioceses in the West (this includes the United States) continue to separate the celebrations of Baptism and Confirmation by many years.

Live It!

Choosing a Confirmation Sponsor

Choosing a Confirmation sponsor is important, and the Church spells out some basic requirements. A sponsor needs to be mature, a member of the Catholic Church, and already fully initiated through the Sacraments of Baptism, Confirmation, and the Eucharist. When a baptismal godparent also serves as the Confirmation sponsor, it clearly shows the connection between Baptism and Confirmation and strengthens an existing relationship.

But these are minimal requirements. A well-chosen sponsor can help you grow in faith. Don't pick a sponsor because he is fun or she hasn't had a turn yet. Pick a sponsor who actively practices his or her faith and who will assist you as you prepare for Confirmation. A good sponsor is also one who will support you as you continue to grow in faith beyond your Confirmation.

If you were baptized as a baby, this is probably your experience too. In fact, most Catholics in the United States today do not celebrate Confirmation until they are in their teens. U.S. bishops determine the age for their own dioceses.

If you were baptized after you reached what we refer to as the age of reason, however, your experience probably reflects the typical practice in the Eastern Churches. That is, when you were initiated, you likely celebrated Baptism, Confirmation, and the Eucharist in that order in the same liturgy. The **age of reason**, usually considered age seven, is when a person is old enough to understand what she or he is doing. The person is capable of knowing the difference between right and wrong. Adults who are baptized are also confirmed and given the Eucharist at the same liturgy, typically the Easter Vigil.

The ages of Confirmation candidates vary. How old are most candidates in your parish?

© Bill Wittman/www.wpwittman.com

Rite of Confirmation

Because most people in the United States today are confirmed many years after their Baptism, let's look at that way of practicing Confirmation.

Before you can be confirmed, you need to have reached the age of reason. This is because in the rite, you must also profess your faith. If you have committed any serious, or mortal, sins, you must first confess them in the Sacrament of Penance and Reconciliation (see chapter 35, "The Sacraments of Healing," of this handbook). Next, you have to ask for the Sacrament freely. That means no one can force you to celebrate it. Last, you need to be ready to live your life as a disciple of Christ. Confirmation calls you to speak about your faith both in the Church and in your daily life.

Read about these three sacred oils in the Liturgy Connection article in this chapter. How many of these oils have you been anointed with in your lifetime?

© Ezz Mika Elya/Shutterstock.com

The essential parts of the Sacrament of Confirmation are the anointing of the forehead with Chrism (in the East, other parts of the body are also anointed) along with the laying on of hands and the following words: "Be sealed with the Gift of the Holy Spirit."

Renewal of Baptismal Promises

Because Baptism is closely connected to Confirmation, the Confirmation Rite includes some reminders for us. Let's imagine now that you're about to be confirmed. One of the things in the Confirmation Rite that

Did You Know?

The Awesome Gifts of the Spirit

Seven Gifts of the Holy Spirit are given to the newly confirmed: Wisdom, Understanding, Right Judgment (Counsel), Courage (Fortitude), Knowledge, Reverence (Piety), and Wonder and Awe (Fear of the Lord). (For descriptions of all the gifts, see chapter 18, "Grace and the Gifts of the Holy Spirit," of this handbook.)

This last gift, Wonder and Awe, is closely tied to fear, as in "Fear of the Lord." But this doesn't mean that we should be afraid of God. It means we realize how awesome God is. God is much greater than anything we can think of. In fact, a definition of God by Saint Anselm was "that than which greater cannot be thought" (*St. Anselm's Proslogion*). Think of the greatest thing ever. Then try to imagine what is beyond that—that's God. Magnificent and powerful though God is, he still cares for each one of us. Now that's an awesome God.

LITURGY CONNECTION

Holy Oils

The Church uses three different types of holy oils in her liturgies, as follows:

+ **Sacred Chrism**, consecrated olive oil with perfume, represents the sweet fragrance of Christ and the good works of his Body, the Church. Sacred Chrism is used in the Sacraments of Baptism, Confirmation, and Holy Orders and to consecrate objects for sacred work.

+ **The Oil of Catechumens** is blessed olive oil used to anoint those preparing for Baptism.

+ **The Oil of the Sick** is blessed olive oil used in the Sacrament of Anointing of the Sick to anoint the forehead and hands of people who are seriously ill or near death. The anointing strengthens the sick and prepares those who are dying.

These holy oils are kept in a box called an ambry. A church's ambry is often found near the baptismal font or in a wall niche within the worship space.

would remind you of your Baptism is the renewal of baptismal promises. Here, the bishop asks you the same questions your parents were asked back when you were a baby about to be baptized: "Do you reject Satan? Do you believe in God the Father? Do you believe in Jesus, his Son? Do you believe in the Holy Spirit? Do you believe in the catholic Church?" Because you couldn't even talk yet at your Baptism, your parents responded to these questions for you. At your Confirmation, you speak for yourself and publicly renew your baptismal promises.

Laying On of Hands

In the laying on of hands, the bishop extends his hands over you and all the candidates. In this action the bishop is asking the Holy Spirit to come upon you and be with you. As the bishop does

© Bill Wittman/www.wpwittman.com

Which Gift of the Holy Spirit do you most need?

this, he leads a prayer asking God the Father to send the Holy Spirit upon you. He also asks the Spirit to help and guide you with the spiritual gifts you will need to live your faith fully.

What are some things these spiritual gifts help you do? They help you feel more confident and courageous about your faith. This lets you talk about your faith more easily with your friends and with those who ask you about your Catholic beliefs. The gifts help you know how to use your talents to serve the Church and others in need. They help you be able to make better decisions between right and wrong.

Anointing with Sacred Chrism

Finally, the bishop anoints you, making the Sign of the Cross on your forehead with Sacred Chrism. As he does this, he calls you by your name, saying, "Be sealed with the Gift of the Holy Spirit." You respond "Amen." Then you and the bishop share a sign of peace. All the Gifts of the Holy Spirit are yours. Are you ready to use them?

Who's Who at Confirmation

Read the Fun Fact in this chapter to find out what kind of tree this is and how it is like Jesus.

The ordinary minister of the Sacrament of Confirmation is the bishop. However, he can give priests permission to confirm. Priests do not need permission to

© Noam Armonn/Shutterstock.com

confirm someone if they are also baptizing that person, as is the case at the Easter Vigil with catechumens.

Each confirmation candidate has a sponsor. This person is usually the person's godparent from Baptism. During the rite, the sponsor stands with the candidate as a sign of support and a reminder of their Baptism.

> When the Holy Spirit comes upon you, you will be filled with power, and you will be witnesses for me.
>
> Acts 1:8

Church History

Baptism and Confirmation in the Early Church

In the early ages of the Church, adult candidates for Baptism renounced their old way of life and their old allegiances to Satan and to sin. As a sign of conversion, the candidates faced west (associated with darkness and the devil) to renounce sin, and then faced east (associated with the rising sun and the light of the Risen Christ) to affirm their Christian beliefs.

It was also the custom to perform a "double anointing" after Baptism. The priest who baptized also anointed the neophyte—a Greek word meaning "beginner"—upon coming out of the baptismal pool; this anointing was followed by a second anointing from the bishop. The first anointing with Sacred Chrism, by the priest, is still part of the Rite of Baptism for Children. This anointing is the sign of the participation of the newly baptized in the priestly, prophetic, and kingly office of Christ. Today when an adult is baptized and confirmed, the first anointing is omitted and only the postbaptismal anointing, that of Confirmation, is performed (see CCC, 1291).

35 THE SACRAMENTS OF HEALING

KEY WORDS

venial sins
mortal sins
Penance
contrition
absolution
laying on of hands

Have you ever been so sick you had to stay in bed all day, unable to go to school or see your friends? Perhaps you felt so awful you just wanted to curl up under the covers and sleep.

Have you ever felt guilty? You know, the kind of guilt where you felt like you didn't even want to show your face to anyone?

Everyone has days like these. But this is not what God wants for us. God wants us to live every day as fully and joyfully as possible. Yet sometimes, because of sickness, we can't fully enjoy the gift of life God gives us. At other times, the joy we can experience is dimished or lost because of sins we have committed that have hurt our relationship with God and with others.

At times like these, the Church offers us two Sacraments of Healing. These are the Sacrament of Penance and Reconciliation and the Sacrament of Anointing of the Sick.

Have Mercy on Me, a Sinner

When we have sinned, our sins can be forgiven and our relationship with God and others healed and strengthened through several Sacraments. The first is Baptism. It washes away Original Sin and our personal sins. It unites us to Christ and gives us the Holy Spirit. In the Sacrament of the Eucharist, we can ask for and receive forgiveness for **venial sins**. For **mortal sins** that we commit deliberately after Baptism, God provides the Sacrament of Penance and Reconciliation. This Sacrament is also called conversion, confession, **Penance**, or Reconciliation.

Jesus willed that the Church be able to forgive sins through the ministry of priests and bishops. When we celebrate the Sacrament of Penance, God forgives our sins and wipes away the damage that sin causes in our relationships with him, ourselves, and others. Through the Sacrament, God strengthens us to live as he wants us to live.

The Sacrament of Penance is about conversion or change. But conversion doesn't just happen, like turning on a light switch. It is a process, a change of heart that turns us away from sin and toward God. It's like a journey in which a person

Pray It!

Jesus, Healer and Savior, only you know what is in my heart and what I need to be whole again. Open my eyes so I can see myself as you see me—forgivable and blessed. Touch my heart and bless all who suffer in mind, body, or spirit, that together we might praise you with all your people for your great and immense love. Amen.

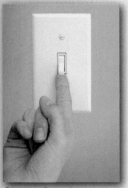

© LawrenceSawyer/
iStockphoto.com

Conversion is not as easy as turning on a light switch, but it does involve seeing our relationship with God in a new light.

THINK ABOUT IT!

Some people think of God's grace as they think of the electric company. If they don't pay their bills, their electricity gets turned off. In other words, if they don't do the right things, God stops loving them. What would you say to someone who thinks about God's love in this way?

suddenly realizes he is walking down the wrong path. The person can choose to keep going or to stop, turn around, and go a different way.

Through the process of conversion, we change our points of view and return to God. With the help of the Holy Spirit, we can begin to undo the harm our sins cause. Hopefully, we start to feel sorrow for what we have done. Once we decide to avoid sinning again and make up for what we have done, we are ready to turn around. We are ready to celebrate the Sacrament of Penance and Reconciliation.

A change of heart leads to repentance, or **contrition**. This means we feel sorrow or remorse. Sometimes we feel or express sorrow for something wrong we did because we're afraid of being punished. For example, you might apologize to your sibling for something you did, only because your parents will ground you if you don't. This is called imperfect contrition, because we are sorry because of a consequence we might suffer for the harm we caused. Then there are other times when we feel so bad about something we did that hurt others or offended God that we sincerely seek forgiveness. This kind of contrition comes from our love of God and our trust in his mercy. When our repentance arises from our love of God, it is called perfect contrition.

Reconciliation in Four Movements

Reconciliation is a process with several steps or actions. In the Sacrament of Penance and Reconciliation, there are four basic actions. Three are actions of the penitent (the person who wants to confess). The fourth is the action of the priest (or confessor). All these movements, with a reading from Scripture and possibly a song, make up the Sacrament of Penance and Reconciliation.

> "Turn away from your sins and believe the Good News!"
>
> Mark 1:15

Step One: Being Sorry

You have to be sorry before you can be forgiven. The penitent, with the help and encouragement of the priest, expresses sorrow. This is called an act of contrition. You can do an act of contrition by saying a prayer, like the *Confiteor* ("I confess to Almighty God . . .") (see appendix A, "Catholic Prayers," of this handbook). Or you might just say in your own words how sorry you are. Then the priest helps you remember that in Penance, as in Baptism, you get to wipe the slate clean and start over again.

The Spanish painter Goya painted *Saint Peter Repentant.* Even great saints like Peter were sinners. We all need God's mercy.

© Francis G. Mayer/Corbis

FUN FACT

The priest who hears your confession is bound by Church law never to say anything to anyone else about what you confessed in the Sacrament of Penance and Reconciliation. No exceptions. This is often called the sacramental seal, because whatever a priest heats in confession is kept private, under all circumstances.

That is, you die to sin and rise to new life. The priest might also help you do an examination of conscience. By doing so, the priest helps you look at your life and the areas where you haven't lived the way God wants you to live.

> Above everything, love one another earnestly, because love covers over many sins.
>
> 1 Peter 4:8

Step Two: Confessing Sin

You can't just be sorry. You have to say what you're sorry for. In the Sacrament of Penance and Reconciliation, we say out loud what we are sorry for because we believe in God's mercy. In this second step, we confess to the priest all the grave sins we can remember. Although it isn't necessary to confess venial sins, the Church strongly encourages us to do so.

Confessing our sins to a priest is something like having a conversation with Jesus.

© Bill Wittman/www.wpwittman.com

Step Three: Working to Repair the Damage

If we are disrespectful to our parents or to a classmate, confessing that to a priest is good. But we also need to do something to heal the pain we have caused. In this third step, the priest helps us think of things we can do to make up for, or repair, the damage that was done because of our sin. This is called reparation, satisfaction, or Penance. For example, we might go to the person we hurt and say we're sorry. We could do something nice for him or her. We could also pray more, be nicer to others, or give up something we like for a while. The more serious the sin, the more we need to do to fix the damage. Although it might be hard or even impossible to fix things completely, trying to make up for what we did helps us live the lives God wants for us.

LITURGY CONNECTION

Extraordinary Ministers of Holy Communion

Have you seen people being dismissed from Mass after Communion, each carrying a small round container (called a pyx) in which the priest has placed the Eucharist?

These are extraordinary ministers of Holy Communion who visit parishioners who can't attend Mass due to sickness. These ministers share with the homebound some of the readings and songs from the Mass. Then they administer the Body of Christ to them.

These extraordinary ministers go anywhere people too elderly or ill to travel to their local parish for Mass may be. Along with bringing the greatest gift—the Eucharist—to the sick or homebound, they share the gift of their companionship and compassion.

Step Four: Being Forgiven

When we've done something wrong, there's nothing like hearing "I forgive you." This final part is the gift of the Rite of Penance. Here our sins are pardoned or forgiven. This is called **absolution.** *Absolution* means "freeing from guilt." God forgives us through the words of the priest. As the priest prays the prayer of absolution, he places his hands over our heads in a gesture of forgiveness.

We are reconciled with God and the Church when we honestly confess all our grave sins to a priest and receive absolution. Only priests whom the Church has given authority to forgive sins in the name of Christ can do so. However, a priest can forgive sins even without this permission when someone is in danger of death.

> The one thing I do . . . is to forget what is behind me and do my best to reach what is ahead.
>
> Philippians 3:13

Reconciling with others when we have hurt or been hurt is essential to healthy relationships.

© Nicolesa/Shutterstock.com

Did You Know?

The Effects of the Sacraments of Healing

The Sacrament of Penance and Reconciliation has a number of wonderful effects on us, such as the following:

+ It turns us away from sin and toward God, reuniting us and strengthening our relationship.
+ It restores our relationship with the Church.
+ If we are in a state of mortal sin, it saves us from eternal separation from God (Hell).
+ It frees us from some of the consequences of our sin, such as a weakened ability to resist temptation and unhealthy attachments to things and other people.
+ It gives us peace of mind and spiritual comfort.
+ It give us strength to resist sin in the future.

When we are sick, the special grace of Anointing of the Sick helps us in the following ways:

+ It helps us see that Christ knows what we are going through, because he also suffered.
+ It joins our suffering to Christ's suffering.
+ It strengthens us and gives us peace and courage to bear suffering with faith in Christ.
+ It forgives our sins.
+ It brings us back to health if that is God's will.
+ It prepares us for the day when we will die and pass to eternal life with God.

© Bill Wittman/www.wpwittman.com

Receiving absolution is a sign of God's love and forgiveness.

Reconciliation in Three Forms

Penance and Reconciliation happens in three ways. The first way is individually with a priest. Usually, the priest and the person sit face-to-face. Many parishes have a special room designated for this called a reconciliation room. Sometimes, the priest and the person sit or kneel in a confessional. They can't see each other, but they speak through a small opening in the wall.

Did you celebrate your first Reconciliation in a liturgy with other people? In this second form, a group prays, sings, and listens to Scripture readings. Then, each goes to a priest for individual confession. Even though it's a group liturgy, the confessions remain private.

The third way is one you have probably never seen because it is used only in extreme circumstances, which are identified in the Church's law. It involves general absolution. This means that the priest absolves the penitents together. The people then celebrate individual confession at a later time.

Brought Back to Life in the Community

Sin is a spiritual sickness, and it separates us from the community. Physical sickness in our bodies also keeps

us away from the communi-
ty—literally. In Jesus' society,
those who were sick were in
some way separated from
the community too. These included people with leprosy,
people who were blind or
deaf, those possessed, and

© Brooklyn Museum/Corbis

those whose bodies were paralyzed. They were reunited to the community's daily life of prayer and work
by the healing love of Christ. Jesus' healing cured
them. But it did more than that. It brought them back
to life in the community. Jesus healed them to restore
their relationships with God and the community.

Jesus heals people with
leprosy. Every time
Jesus miraculously
cured people, he
healed them spiritually
as well as physically.

When the Church prays for people who are sick
and celebrates the Sacrament of Anointing of the Sick
with them, we are asking God to strengthen and heal

Did You Know?

The Role of People Who Are Sick

Even in their weaknesses, people who are sick have an important role
to play in the Church. When we see them suffering, we are reminded
of how precious and fragile life is. They also show us how strong
God's love can be even in the middle of so much pain. They help us
think of what is really important in life—not material things, but
the love we can share with one another. Their sickness also reminds
us that we depend on God for life and that we are given that life
through Christ's death and Resurrection. The Church is enriched by
the powerful witness of those who are sick.

© Bill Wittman/www.wpwittman.com

The Sacrament of Anointing of the Sick is not just for people who are dying. A person may receive the Sacrament before surgery, when seriously ill, or because of old age.

the person who is sick and to reunite him or her with the community.

Anointing of the Sick

The Sacrament of Anointing of the Sick is for Catholics who are seriously ill or in danger of death because of either sickness or old age. In the Sacrament, God gives those who are suffering sacramental grace to help them through their sickness or old age. The Sacrament can be repeated if the person's condition gets worse.

The Sacrament can take place in a church, a hospital, or even a home. It is important that members of the person's family and other members of the Church are present to pray with and for them. But only bishops and priests can administer the Sacrament.

Parishes sometimes celebrate a communal Anointing of the Sick in conjunction with Mass. During this liturgy, those who are sick are invited to come forward for anointing.

The essential parts of Anointing of the Sick are the anointing and the prayer of the bishop or priest over the person who is sick. This prayer asks God for the special grace of the Sacrament.

The Celebration of the Sacrament

The Sacrament of Anointing of the Sick begins with the Prayer of the Faithful. This is followed by the laying on of hands, the anointing, and the prayer after anointing.

Prayer of the Faithful

Trusting in God's mercy, the people who are gathered pray a short litany for the person who is sick. The entire Church is present in this community, and the people who are sick, even in their illness, are united in prayer with them.

> When one of [the lepers] saw that he was healed, he came back, praising God in a loud voice.
>
> Luke 17:15

A bishop performs the laying on of hands during the Sacrament of Anointing of the Sick. Jesus often touched the people he healed.

Laying On of Hands

Then the minister lays his hands on the head of the person who is sick. This gesture, called the **laying on of hands**, shows that the sick person is the focus of the prayer. It is a sign of the healing power of God and a silent calling of the Holy Spirit upon the person. It is the way Jesus healed many of those in his own community.

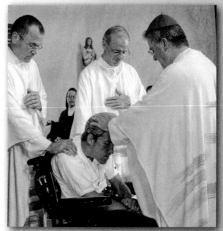

© Bill Wittman/www.wpwittman.com

Anointing

Next, the minister anoints the forehead and hands of the person who is sick. (In the Eastern Church, other parts of the body are also anointed, especially those parts that are in pain or need healing.) The oil used for the anointing is olive oil, usually blessed by the bishop at the Chrism Mass. If the bishop has not blessed the oil, the minister of the Sacrament may bless the oil himself. The prayer said during the anointing asks God to help the person with his love and mercy and to save and raise up those who are sick.

Live It!

Living a Penitential Lifestyle

Catholics are called not only to celebrate the Sacrament of Penance and Reconciliation but also to live a penitential lifestyle. To live a penitential lifestyle means to remember every day that we are not perfect. It also means remembering that the goal of our lives is not to be perfect but rather to praise God for his love. In other words, God does not expect us to be perfect. He wants us to be faithful. Following are some ways you can live a penitential lifestyle:

- reconcile with friends or family
- care for others
- pray to the saints
- accept suffering
- defend the poor
- admit when you're wrong
- gently correct others and accept correction yourself
- give and ask for forgiveness
- live your Christian faith

Prayer after Anointing

Finally, the bishop or priest prays a special prayer over the person who is sick. The prayer expresses the Church's hope for the person and her trust that God will strengthen the person in his or her sickness.

Church History

Penance in the Early Church

Early Christians believed Christ would return soon and the world would end. They believed the baptized had to live upright lives for only a short time. After a while it was clear that Christ was not returning right away. Rituals and regulations emerged to guide the celebration of the Sacrament of Penance and Reconciliation as more and more Christians who had sinned sought to restore their relationships with God and the Church through the Sacrament of Penance.

By the fourth century, Penance was public and often severe. Sinners had to endure long and harsh penances before they could be forgiven. These penitents often wore ashes (which we still do on Ash Wednesday), rough sackcloth, and even chains. They did not have wine or meat. Sometimes as a sign of their sorrow, they didn't even bathe or cut their hair. Because Penance was so hard, many waited until they were near death to confess their sins.

36 THE SACRAMENTS OF MATRIMONY AND HOLY ORDERS

Key Words

vocation

ministerial priesthood

common priesthood of the faithful

Have you ever made a really big promise, one that would cause you or others pain if you broke it? Has someone ever made an important promise to you? Promises help us know how to live, and they help us in our relationships.

The first promises we make as Catholics are in Baptism, when we promise to believe in the Father, Son, and Holy Spirit. All the other

A couple spends a lifetime living out the vows they made in marriage.

© Blend Images/Shutterstock.com

promises we make as Catholics are based on these baptismal vows (see chapter 33, "The Sacrament of Baptism," of this handbook).

Let's look at two Sacraments adult Catholics can celebrate that help them live out their baptismal promises—the Sacrament of Matrimony and the Sacrament of Holy Orders. Matrimony and Holy Orders are the two Sacraments at the Service of Communion. As this name indicates, these Sacraments are directed toward service for and the salvation of others.

The Sacrament of Matrimony

Special relationships in our lives help us know God's love. Of course our relationships aren't always perfect, because we're not perfect. Married people know this well. Despite truly loving each other, a married couple may still have days when they feel like their love is tested or even absent. When a baptized man and a baptized woman celebrate the Sacrament of Matrimony, however, Christ takes their imperfect love and joins it to his perfect love. Imagine trying to twist two pieces of thread together, and they just keep unraveling. But add a third piece of thread and braid them. The threads won't come apart. In a marriage, Christ's love is like that third thread. His

PRAY IT!

Father God, you promise me light and life, and each day you fulfill your word. Help me keep my own promises and let my word always be true. Strengthen all who have promises to keep and bless them with your Spirit so they may serve you faithfully. Amen.

Fun Fact

Have you seen a bride walk down the aisle with her father to meet her groom? This practice comes from a time when daughters were considered family "property." The father was giving away his property to the groom's family. The Catholic Marriage Rite emphasizes the couple's freedom and equality. It suggests that both the bride and the groom walk down the aisle. They can be escorted by both sets of parents.

divine promise to love us strengthens our human promises to love each other. Christ's promise to the Church—his Bride—is stronger than any promise we can make.

When you see a man and woman celebrate the Sacrament of Matrimony, you are actually seeing a sign of Christ's love for the Church. The Sacrament strengthens them to love each other with the love Jesus Christ has given to the Church. Through their promises, Christ blesses them to love deeply and live faithfully until they live eternally with the Trinity.

> For this reason a man will leave his father and mother and unite with his wife, and the two will become one.
>
> Ephesians 5:31

In Good Times and in Bad, in Sickness and in Health

Christ's promise to his Church—and the spouses' promise in marriage—is a covenant. A covenant is stronger than a contract. In a covenant each party keeps the promise, no matter what the other party does. In the Bible, God made a covenant with his people to always love them as his own. Even when they ignored God and rejected him, he continued to love them.

God never forces anyone to love him. It's the same in a marriage. To be a real covenant, the man and woman must enter marriage willingly. They need to give their lives freely and totally to each other, in order to live a covenant of faithful and fruitful love.

In their covenant, the husband and wife give everything they have to each other in a personal way. They share everything, not just what they own but also who they are—the good and the bad. They promise to love each other, no matter what.

God created marriage for the good of the married couple, and for the good of his Church. Christ took our need to be close to another person and made it into a symbol of his love for us. In the marriage covenant between a husband and wife, we see the true love of God. God's love blesses and brings new life. The marriage enables the husband and wife to share life and love with any children they are blessed with. A child is the supreme gift of married life, and being open to children is essential to marriage, but those who are not blessed with children have the opportunity to share their love in other ways.

> Happy are those who have been invited to the wedding feast of the Lamb.
>
> Revelation 19:9

I Will Love You and Honor You All the Days of My Life

Marriage is a vocation. A **vocation** is a way of life people choose in response to God's call to live out their faith. Pope Benedict XVI called vocation "God's task for each one of us" (papal greeting, March 25, 2007). Some people's vocation calls them to join a religious group of brothers or sisters and serve the Church as a member of a religious community. Some men are called to become deacons, priests, or bishops. Other people are called to serve the Church through the Sacrament of Marriage. Some remain single, living their faith through deep friendships. All these, except being single, are vocations for life.

Because marriage is a lifelong vocation, it is permanent by its very nature. Divorce attempts to separate what God has joined together through marriage. Those who get divorced and marry other spouses go against God's law or plan. Their actions contradict our faith. This is why the Church asks those who have been divorced not to receive Holy Communion. Yet the Church still loves them and still calls them to share in her liturgical worship. Those who are divorced are called to live out their faith by attending Sunday Mass and continuing to educate their children in the Catholic faith.

Those who are divorced can marry and remain in communion with the Church if they receive an annulment. This involves having the previous marriage declared null by the Church. Such a declaration means that when the wedding took place, the standards for a sacramental marriage did not exist. This doesn't mean that a civil marriage didn't exist. It also doesn't mean the husband and wife didn't love each other or that their children are illegitimate.

© elan/Shutterstock.com

Couples exchange rings at their wedding as a sign of their love and faithfulness to each other.

Did You Know?

Who Ministers at a Marriage

In Matrimony the ministers are the two people in the couple because they—not the priest or deacon—give their vows to each other. Of course, it is Christ who is doing the promise-making. But the two being married, through Christ, make their promises to each other.

In the Sacrament the priest or deacon is the Church's witness and leads the blessing over the couple. The couple selects their own witnesses (usually the best man and maid of honor) who fulfill the required legal roles. The witnesses support the couple throughout their married life. Finally, the assembly is a community of faith witnessing to the marriage and ready to support the couple in their vocation.

© Bill Wittman/www.wpwittman.com

A nuptial blessing asks God to send his Spirit upon the couple. What a sacred way to begin married life!

The Rite of Marriage

Marriage is a public vocation. So the marriage vows are made publicly in a liturgy called the Rite of Marriage.

Have you ever been to a Catholic marriage liturgy? What symbols and actions do you remember most? Let's look at some of them.

Intentions and Consent

The most important action is the consent (or vows). These are the promises the man and woman who are getting married make to each other. First, the priest or deacon has to be sure the man and woman are not being forced into the marriage. So he asks them the following:

1. Do you really want to give your lives to each other?
2. Will you be faithful to each other until death?
3. Will you accept children and raise them in the Church?

If the couple says yes, they make their vows. They declare that they are making a covenant to love and be faithful to each other.

Blessing and Exchange of Rings

You can't see a promise. We use the symbol of rings to represent the promise of marriage. The Church blesses the rings, and the bride and bridegroom place them on each other's fingers.

Nuptial Blessing

The last part of the rite is the nuptial blessing. In this prayer the priest or deacon asks God to send his Spirit upon the married couple. He prays that they may be faithful to each other.

The Sacrament of Holy Orders

Married persons enter into a covenant to serve the Church by serving their families. Men who are ordained to be bishops, priests, or deacons also enter into a covenant to serve. They promise to serve the People of God in a more public role.

Some baptized men are called to share in Christ's mission of service as priests. They are ordained into **ministerial priesthood**. They serve in the name of Christ and represent him in the community. Although everyone is called to a vocation, only bishops have the

© Bill Wittman/www.wpwittman.com

In this picture, who belongs to the common priesthood of the faithful and who belongs to the ministerial priesthood?

responsibility and right to call someone to the Sacrament of Holy Orders.

The work of ordained ministers is different from that of the laity. Ordained ministers receive a sacramental grace. This gift is a sacred power that enables them to serve the Church in a unique way. Men who receive the Sacrament of Holy Orders serve the Church by teaching the faithful, leading divine worship, and governing the Church.

> You are the chosen race, the King's priests, the holy nation, God's own people, chosen to proclaim the wonderful acts of God, who called you out of darkness into his own marvelous light.
>
> 1 Peter 2:9

?

Did You Know?

The Common Priesthood of the Faithful

Did you know that all of us, by Baptism, share in the priesthood of Christ? We call this the **common priesthood of the faithful**. Christ is called priest, prophet, and king. To share in his priesthood means we participate in his mission. In his name, we are sent into the world to worship, witness, and serve.

Rite of Ordination

There is an Ordination Rite for each of the three types of ministerial service—deacon, priest, and bishop. Let's look at some of their symbols and actions.

Examination and Promise

At every ordination, the ordaining minister is a bishop. He asks the candidate to promise to serve the Church. After making the promise, the candidate admits he can keep it only with God's help.

Litany of the Saints

In the Litany of the Saints, we ask all the saints to pray for the man being ordained and for the Church. As we do this, he lies facedown on the floor. This shows his obedience to the Church. It symbolizes his weakness and need for God. It shows his humility.

Laying On of Hands and Prayer of Consecration

Next, the bishop lays his hands on the candidate's head. This action transmits the power and blessing of the Holy Spirit. The Holy Spirit gives the candidate the grace he will need to do his ministry.

As in the laying on of hands in Confirmation, the Holy Spirit leaves a permanent, invisible mark on the candidate. This mark identifies him as a minister dedicated to

© Alessandra Benedetti/Corbis

Why are these men facedown on the floor? Find out by reading about the Rite of Ordination.

serve God's people. By the laying on of hands and the special prayer that follows it, he is ordained. Because the mark is permanent, he can never be ordained again for that order.

Fraternal Kiss

The rite ends with the fraternal kiss. Fraternal means "brotherly." The newly ordained share this sign of peace with the brothers in their order. This embrace shows their permanent bond to the Church and each other.

Three Degrees of Holy Orders

Since the beginning of the Church, there have been three types of ordained ministers: bishops, priests, and deacons. We can't be the Church without all three. While there are three degrees of ordained ministry, it is only the bishop and the priest that are part of the ministerial priesthood. It is the deacon's role to help and serve them.

THINK ABOUT IT!

At an ordination the men being ordained lie facedown on the floor during the Litany of the Saints. What does this unusual posture mean?

Bishops

The bishop receives the fullness of Holy Orders. This means he gets his mission directly from Christ handed down through the line of bishops. If you trace the bishops backward, looking at who ordained whom, you'll end up at the Apostles—whom Jesus personally sent to continue his work. This makes a bishop a successor to the Apostles. Each bishop is a member of the community of bishops. They are the visible leaders of the Church. Each bishop is obedient to the Pope, who is the successor to the first Pope, Peter.

Priests

At their ordination, the priests' hands are anointed with Chrism. This gives them the authority to lead Mass. Into their hands, the bishop places the bread and wine that will be consecrated for Communion.

Priests are the bishop's coworkers. With him they form a community that takes responsibility for caring for a diocese. The bishop puts each priest in charge of a parish or gives him another function in the diocese. The priests rely on the bishop for their authority as they carry out their ministry.

LITURGY CONNECTION

The Garments of Ordination

Ordained men receive special garments to signify their roles in the Church.

Deacons wear a stole (a long, thin cloth) over one shoulder and a dalmatic, a tunic with large sleeves.

Priests also wear a stole, but it drapes over both shoulders like a yoke. They also wear a chasuble, which is a round, sleeveless garment.

Bishops wear the dalmatic and the priest's stole and chasuble. They also wear a ring symbolizing their promise and a miter (a liturgical headdress) showing their governing office, and they carry a staff, or crozier, because they are shepherds of the Church.

© Bill Wittman/www.wpwittman.com

When deacons are ordained, they are given a *Book of the Gospels.*

Deacons

Deacons take on tasks of service to the Church and the world that demonstrate their commitment to the Gospel. Deacons do not receive the ministerial priesthood; however, through their ordination they share in Christ's mission in a special way. They serve the Church as ministers of the Word by proclaiming the Gospel and preaching. They assist with liturgies by distributing Communion, presiding over funerals, and assisting at and blessing marriages. They dedicate themselves to numerous other ministries of service. All of the deacon's tasks are carried out under the authority of his bishop.

Live It!

Family Prayer

The home of a Christian family is called the domestic church. This is because Christians first hear about Christ and learn their faith at home. The home is meant to be a community of grace and prayer and a school of human virtues and Christian love.

Make your home a reflection of what it means to be the domestic church. As a family, designate one place in your home as the family prayer center. Place in it a candle, a Bible, and a cloth matching the color of the liturgical season. Include pictures of people you want to pray for and a bowl of holy water. Use the water to bless yourself and one another. Gather there with your family daily or on special days, like birthdays, to pray a blessing.

PEOPLE OF FAITH
Saint John Baptist de La Salle
(1651–1719)

© 2013 Saint Mary's Press/Illustration by Vicki Shuck

"Let us remember that we are in the holy presence of God." Saint John Baptist de La Salle spoke this prayerful reminder often in his work as a priest and advocate for schoolteachers and the children they serve.

John Baptist was born in France to a wealthy family. After ordination, he gave up his comfortable life and devoted his energy to schools for those who were poor. He gave his wealth away and devoted his life to training teachers. He developed new ways of teaching that we still use today. For example, he created the grade system, grouping students of similar abilities together. He also directed his teachers to teach only in the language of the people instead of in Latin.

He began the Institute of the Brothers of the Christian Schools (Christian Brothers). They are dedicated to teaching people who are poor. He knew what kind of commitment was required to be a teacher. John Baptist worked hard to support them in their commitment to educating children.

His feast day is April 7. He is the patron saint of teachers.

PART 3

CHRISTIAN MORALITY AND JUSTICE

1. I am the LORD your God: you shall not have strange gods before me.
2. You shall not take the name of the LORD your God in vain.
3. Remember to keep holy the LORD's Day.
4. Honor your father and your mother.
5. You shall not kill.
6. You shall not commit adultery.
7. You shall not steal.
8. You shall not bear false witness against your neighbor.
9. You shall not covet your neighbor's wife.
10. You shall not covet your neighbor's goods.

31 THE BIBLE: THE OLD LAW AND THE NEW LAW

KEY WORDS

Old Law

New Law

Beatitudes

Have you ever heard the Bible described as a compass for our lives? This symbolism means that the Bible points us in the right direction to have good relationships with God and with other people. One way the Bible acts as a compass is by providing laws to guide our moral choices.

The Ten Commandments give us the rules for living good, moral lives, according to God's Law.

© jsp/Shutterstock.com

Happy are those whose greatest desire is to do
what God requires; God will satisfy them fully!
Happy are those who are merciful to others;
God will be merciful to them!

Matthew 5:6–7

The Bible has many moral laws and guidelines. One book, the Book of Leviticus, is almost all laws. But the most important laws we find in the Old Testament to guide our behavior are the Ten Commandments. The *Catechism of the Catholic Church* uses the Ten Commandments as the outline for its teaching on Christian morality. The next chapters in this handbook do the same thing. But the Ten Commandments are incomplete without Jesus' New Law of Love. This chapter looks at the moral laws in the Bible and explains how the New Law completes and fulfills the Old Law.

The Old Law

The **Old Law** is part of the Sinai Covenant, the covenant God made with the Chosen People at Mount Sinai during the Exodus. The Ten Commandments summarize the Old Law. As a prophet of God, Moses delivered the Old Law to the Chosen People. Read the account in Exodus, chapters 19–20. You can also find another version of the Ten Commandments in Deuteronomy, chapter 5.

PRAY IT!

Lord Jesus, sometimes I know exactly what you want me to do, but I don't have the courage to do it. Help me have the strength, courage, and confidence to always act as your true and faithful disciple. Amen.

A better name for the Old Law might be the Original Law. The Old Law is not outdated or expired. Jesus said: "Do not think that I have come to do away with the Law of Moses and the teachings of the prophets. I have not come to do away with them, but to make their teachings come true" (Matthew 5:17). This is why the Ten Commandments are still important moral laws for us today.

The Jewish word for the Old Law is Torah. But Torah can also mean "teaching." God gave his Chosen People the Ten Commandments to teach them how to live in right relationship with him and with one another. The first three Commandments teach us how to love and honor God. They are summed up in Deuteronomy: "Love the LORD your God with all your heart, with all your soul, and with all your strength" (6:5). The other seven Commandments teach us how to love and respect one another. They are summarized in Leviticus: "Love your neighbors as you love yourself" (19:18). Do these summaries sound familiar? In the New Testament, we read that Jesus quoted these verses to summarize the Old Law (see Mark 12:30–31).

THiNK AbouT IT!

Jesus did not abolish the Old Law, or the Original Law. He still wants us to keep the Ten Commandments. But to that Law he added the Beatitudes, the "new attitudes" of the New Law. (You can find them listed in appendix B , "Catholic Beliefs and Practices," of this handbook.) Read the Beatitudes carefully, and choose one that appeals to you in some way. How is this beatitude a "new attitude" for you? How would you live out this new attitude in your everyday life?

The Ten Commandments are general laws, not specific laws. They teach us important moral principles and values to guide our life. The Old Testament also contains many specific laws that guided the people who lived when it was written. For example, a law in the Book of Exodus says, "If a bull gores someone to death, it is to be stoned, and its flesh shall not be eaten; but its owner is not to be punished" (21:28). Many of these laws and punishments do not apply to us today because we live in a very different culture. We must look to the Church to help us apply the Ten Commandments to our time and culture.

> Ask God to bless those who persecute you—
> yes, ask him to bless, not to curse. Be happy
> with those who are happy, weep with those who
> weep. Have the same concern for everyone. Do
> not be proud, but accept humble duties.
>
> Romans 12:14–16

The New Law

Jesus said he came not to do away with the Old Law but instead to fulfill it. The Chosen People failed again and again to keep their covenant with God and to follow the Law he gave them. But through Jesus' suffering, death, Resurrection, and Ascension, he established a New Covenant with all people.

© Zvonimir Atletic/Shutterstock.com

This stained-glass image depicts Jesus during the Sermon on the Mount.

He also taught us a **New Law**, which fulfills and completes the Old Law. And he sent the Holy Spirit to give us the gifts and the strength we need to live out his New Law.

Although Jesus' New Law is found in many places throughout the Gospels, we find its clearest expression in the Sermon on the Mount (see Matthew 5:1—7:29). Take a few minutes to read this famous sermon. What values did Jesus teach that are very different from the common values in his time and in our time?

In the Sermon on the Mount, Jesus starts with a series of blessing statements called the **Beatitudes**, such as "Happy are those who mourn" (Matthew 5:4). Some people might think: "What? How can I be happy if I am mourning?" But Jesus is teaching us that people mourn because they are compassionate. They care about other people deeply. They are moved when they see other people sad or in pain. God wants us to be compassionate—it is a sign of our love for others. The Beatitudes teach us the values that we need in order to live the New Law.

Then Jesus delivers this surprising interpretation of one of the Ten Commandments: "You have heard that people were told in the past, 'Do not commit murder; anyone who does will be brought to trial.' But now I tell you: if you are angry with your brother you will be brought to trial. . . . And if you call your brother a worthless fool you will be in danger of going to the fire of hell" (Matthew 5:21–22). Is Jesus saying that being angry at someone or calling someone names is as bad as murdering someone? Not exactly. Jesus is teaching that the New Law is a Law of Love. Every sin we commit represents a lack of love for God and for our neighbor. In the Sermon on the Mount, Jesus gives many more examples of how the Ten Commandments are about more than what we should or should not do. The Ten Commandments are meant to teach us how to love.

Did You Know?

The Beatitudes

A state of beatitude is true happiness, the happiness that comes from being in perfect union with God. This is the goal of our life—of our existence. The eight Beatitudes that Jesus teaches in the Sermon on the Mount (see Matthew 5:3–10) are the key to knowing this happiness. We will experience this happiness only partially in our life here on earth, but we will experience it perfectly in Heaven.

FUN FACT

In the Gospel of Matthew, Jesus teaches about the New Law from a hillside (see Matthew 5:1). But in Luke he does it from a "level place" (6:17). By setting Jesus' teaching on "the Mount," a hillside, Matthew probably wanted to emphasize that Jesus was like Moses, who brought the Old Law from a mountain.

Jesus' New Law teaches us that we must love all people, even those who mistreat us (see Matthew 5:38–48). You can follow the Old Law and still hold feelings like anger, lust, jealousy, or revenge in your heart. But if we hold on to those feelings, we will not be in right relationship with God or one another. That is why the New Law, the Law of Love, teaches us that we must let go of those feelings and let the Holy Spirit fill our hearts with love for all people. How can we do this? We cannot do it on our own—it is only possible with the grace God provides (for more about grace, see chapter 18, "Grace and the Gifts of the Holy Spirit," of this handbook).

Practical Moral Advice

Many other passages in the Bible give us guidelines for making good moral choices. The Book of Proverbs in the Old Testament is a great place to find guidelines. Here are some examples:

- "Anyone who hides hatred is a liar. Anyone who spreads gossip is a fool" (10:18).
- "Hard work will give you power; being lazy will make you a slave" (12:24).
- "If you want to be happy, be kind to the poor; it is a sin to despise anyone" (14:21).

Many of the letters in the New Testament also contain practical moral advice. Saint Paul and other writers of the Epistles wanted to help the early Christians understand the Law of Love and how to live it out. In the First Letter to the Corinthians, Saint Paul describes what true love looks like. Here is a sample passage from the chapter:

> Love is patient and kind; it is not jealous or conceited or proud; love is not ill-mannered or selfish or irritable; love does not keep a record of wrongs; love is not happy with evil, but is happy with the truth. Love never gives up; and its faith, hope, and patience never fail. (13:4–7)

The Letter to the Ephesians has a long section describing what it means to live according to the New Law. Here is a sample:

> If you become angry, do not let your anger lead you into sin, and do not stay angry all day. Don't give the Devil a chance. If you used to rob, you must stop robbing and start working, in order to earn an honest living for yourself and to be able to help the poor. Do not use harmful words, but only helpful words, the kind that build up and provide what is needed, so that what you say will do good to those who hear you. (4:26–29)

Check out Ephesians 4:17—5:20 to see the whole passage. Remember, these are just examples of the moral teaching you can find in the Bible to guide your moral decision making. Let God's Word in Scripture be the compass guiding you to a happy and holy life.

Live It!

Living by Scripture

This chapter quotes several passages from Scripture that could help you to live your life in a better way. The quotation from Ephesians, chapter 4, warning against the use of harmful words, may merit extra attention. How can you "live by" this Scripture in your life? How can you avoid harmful words and increase the helpful words you say each day? Here are some tips:

+ Remember that words matter. Words have power to hurt, and words have power to heal.

+ Those who hurt others, in words or in actions, are demonstrating their own lack of self-worth and self-confidence. If you build yourself up at the expense of others, you may feel good momentarily, but that feeling will not last. It is better to build yourself up—and let God's life shine in you—by exploring and expressing your own gifts and talents. No one can take these away from you.

+ What would Jesus say? If we share the life of Jesus through Baptism, we are called to live like Jesus. We are called to speak like Jesus—face-to-face, in texts, and in all other means of communication. Jesus is the Word we speak to one another in our human words of help and compassion.

PEOPLE OF FAITH
Saint Paul

© 2013 Saint Mary's Press/Illustration by Vicki Shuck

If there ever was a fervent follower of the Old Law, it was Saint Paul the Apostle. Paul was so zealous for his Jewish faith that he persecuted the followers of Jesus. He saw them as heretics because they were not following the Old Law as strictly as he thought they should be! In fact, when the first deacon, Stephen, was stoned to death, Paul held some of the coats of the attackers.

While on the road to Damascus, where he was going to find some of these heretics, called Christians, and bring them before the chief priests in Jerusalem, Paul was struck down by a bright light. Paul (known in the Jewish world as Saul) saw and heard the Risen Jesus, who said to him: "Saul, Saul! Why do you persecute me?" (Acts 9:4).

This encounter changed Paul forever. He now realized that what the Christians believed was true. Jesus, the teacher and preacher who had been crucified, was truly risen, and was truly the Messiah. The Old Law had brought Paul to this moment; from now on, he would follow the New Law. Because Paul had been blinded by the light, his companions had to lead him by the hand into Damascus. A holy Christian man, Ananias, had been instructed by the Lord to heal Paul of his blindness and to baptize him. Following his conversion, Paul became an important leader of the early Church and one of the Church's greatest missionaries. Through his writings and travels, countless people throughout the Roman Empire became followers of Christ.

38 LIVING THE MORAL LIFE

KEY WORDS

free will

natural law

virtues

"Where are you going?" Sometimes the answer is simple—"to school" or "to my friend's house," for example. At other times the question will be hard to answer, such as when you're making important life decisions, like whether to go to college or to get a job.

To help us follow the right path for our lives, God gives us guidance that can lead us closer to him. God wants us to draw nearer to him in this life and to live with him in happiness forever in Heaven.

Maps can help us get where we want to go. Morality can get us where God wants us to go.

© iofoto/Shutterstock.com

The virtues, along with God's Laws found in Sacred Scripture and taught to us by the Church, help get us there.

In this chapter, we'll explore what it means to live the life of morality and justice that God intends for us.

> I chose you before I gave you life, and before you were born I selected you to be a prophet to the nations.
>
> Jeremiah 1:4

Off to a Great Start

God has a plan for us even before we are born. God forms us in our mother's womb with a spiritual soul, an active mind, and a free will. These gifts draw us toward God. They allow us to respond with love to his love and seek true, never-ending joy in his presence in Heaven.

Free will, the gift from God that allows us to choose what we do, is the basis for our moral responsibility. This doesn't mean we can do whatever we want. God's law obligates us to do good and avoid evil. This moral law is the inner voice, or conscience, that we hear when we have to choose between right and wrong. Original Sin, the wound that all humans have that makes us open to choosing wrong and evil options, makes this choice harder.

Pray It!

Loving God, let me never forget that you made me wonderfully, loved me from the start, and gave me great and countless gifts. When temptations and hard times come, as I know they will, help me turn to you for your help and guidance. Give me the strength to make good choices that lead to a virtuous life, today and always. Amen.

417

Despite this hurdle, God has always promised us salvation. Think back to Abraham, who pleased God and was promised countless descendants. Ever since that time, God has made and kept promises. Ultimately, God's promises lead to the Beatitudes, promises Jesus makes in the Gospels of Matthew and Luke. He promises true happiness, or beatitude, in the Kingdom of Heaven—a desire God has put in our hearts.

Jesus shares the Beatitudes to help us connect the desires in our hearts with where we're going. Our final destination is the Kingdom of Heaven, where we will see God and live forever as his children. The Holy Spirit will give us the grace to help us make better moral choices and lead us to the glory of Heaven.

"Happy are those who know they are spiritually poor; the Kingdom of heaven belongs to them!"

Matthew 5:3

People gather around Jesus, listening to him teach. One of the most important teachings Jesus shared with his followers was the Beatitudes, rules for living that will bring true happiness.

© Brooklyn Museum/Corbis

Walking the Talk

The Old Law, the first rules God gave for living a moral life, is summed up in the Ten Commandments. To live according to God's Law, we can look to Sacred Scripture as a light for our path. We must learn God's Word through faithful prayer and study, and put it into practice in our lives. This is how we develop a well-formed conscience.

Ultimately, Jesus makes the law simple to understand: "Do for others what you want them to do for you" (Matthew 7:12). We have the freedom to choose whether to follow Jesus. This freedom makes us responsible for what we choose to do.

Live It!

Take Control of Bad Habits

We talk a lot in this chapter about good habits. You know there are plenty of bad habits too. Some even become addictions, and addicts often join support groups to try to break bad habits.

Doesn't it make sense to form a support group with friends who will help you avoid bad habits or even practice good ones? Maybe you and your best friend can help each other give up soda—even if it's just during Lent—by agreeing to drink only water at lunch. Maybe you and a friend can help each other avoid gossiping if that's a habit you struggle with. Whatever bad habits you might have, make a commitment to take control of them and to grow in virtue.

FUN FACT

Certain orders of religious sisters wear clothing called a habit. Just as virtues are behavioral habits we practice until they become a way of life, a sister's habit symbolizes her choice of a holy lifestyle. She chooses each day to wear a habit, just as she chooses virtuous habits such as prayer and simple living.

© Richard Ransier/Corbis

That's a powerful responsibility, and Saint Paul encourages us to take it seriously. Sacred Scripture tells us that God guides us with fatherly laws that call us to follow the path to eternal happiness and avoid evil ways.

Keep on working with fear and trembling to complete your salvation, because God is always at work in you to make you willing and able to obey his own purpose.

Philippians 2:12–13

You're Born with It

From birth everyone is equipped with an understanding of what is good. We call this the **natural law**, because it's part of our human nature. God made us in his image, and natural law lets us take part in God's wisdom and goodness. It's the basis of our human dignity and rights, as well as the duties that come with our rights. We can know natural law by using God's gift of reason.

Because natural law expresses God's moral vision, it never changes. The rules that support natural law are always correct throughout all time. Do you treat people the way you want to be treated? That's a common example of natural law that doesn't change, no matter your circumstances. Natural law brings people together and should form the basis for society's laws.

Of course, with all the sin that exists in the world, it's clear that some people are ignoring natural law. In fact, God's Chosen People, the Israelites, wandering the desert with Moses, chose to ignore moral rules that should have come naturally. Amid that chaos, God gave Moses the Ten Commandments. God wanted to give his Chosen People all the help possible in knowing the rules that already are part of our human nature but that sin often obscures.

The Ten Commandments cover serious matters and obligations. However, obeying the Commandments also governs less serious matters and actions. For example, the Fifth Commandment, "Thou shall not kill," does not forbid only murder. It also tells us that we must treat one another with compassion and kindness.

Higher Love

God uses the teachings and prophecies of the Old Law to prepare us for the Good News of Jesus in the Gospels. About thirteen hundred years after Moses went up Mount Sinai and received the Ten Commandments, people were continuing to search for God's guidance. They found it in Jesus Christ. They had the Commandments but needed the grace of the Holy Spirit, which comes from faith in Jesus, to

THINK ABOUT IT!

Temptation is all around us. Some of our favorite activities can become bad habits that lead us to sin if we don't control our use of them.

Discuss with your friends or family how bad practices can hurt your relationships with them and with God.

Then talk about best practices that you and others use to avoid temptation. If you can't overcome a problem on your own, maybe someone you love will have a solution. You may not know until you discuss it.

live lives of selfless love. This is the New Law, God's moral law made perfect.

The Sermon on the Mount is the ultimate expression of the New Law. In it Jesus teaches us to love our enemies, avoid greed and the desire for revenge, and live humbly. Through the Sacraments the New Law communicates grace to us.

Virtues

Virtues are habits we develop to help us consistently do the right thing. They allow us to use our minds and our free wills in a more perfect way. Because these virtues come with being human, they can be acquired by human efforts.

Virtues may not seem easy at first, but over time, with practice, they come more naturally. It's similar to the way, as a young child, you learned to do simple addition, but gradually built on that to master more difficult math.

Human virtues grow as we learn more about life, do good acts, and remain obedient to the Commandments even when things get tough. With God's grace, virtues become holy habits that make it easier to be good.

Chief among the human virtues are four cardinal virtues, on which the other virtues depend. *Cardinal* comes from the Latin word for "hinge," because cardinal virtues are pivotal to our moral lives. Like hinges, these habits are stable and guide our behavior to swing in the paths of faith and reason.

The four cardinal virtues are prudence, justice, temperance, and fortitude.

- Prudence is good judgment, exercised with caution. It sets the pace for the other virtues. Instead of just rushing into a choice, prudent people think before they act.

© George P. Choma/Shutterstock.com

- Justice is all about giving both God and our neighbors what is due to them. It goes beyond just giving our fair share and stretches us to put the needs of others before our own.

- Temperance means balance and self-control. We like to eat and play, but we can hurt our bodies with too much of either. People may find work to be rewarding or they may enjoy alcohol, but temperance helps us avoid addictions to them.

- Fortitude gives us the strength to overcome temptations to do wrong, no matter how intense they are. It helps us overcome fears and make sacrifices.

Cardinal virtues are like hinges: they help open the door to a good life. Read about them in the Did You Know? sidebar in this chapter.

We have to work to develop virtues and work to keep them. Remember, though, that God is with us in our quest to live a holy life.

Always Closer

"Come near to God, and he will come near to you" (James 4:8). This call captures the magnetic energy of God's love. Faith, hope, and love—called the theological virtues—help us come near to God to live in relationship with the Holy Trinity. The wonderful thing is that God himself is the source of these virtues. We know God by faith, we hope in his promises, and we can't help but love him, for God is love.

Faith, hope, and love guide and energize the human virtues. They make our relationships with God and our neighbors more perfect.

Living a moral life is one way we worship God. We become a living sacrifice, along with other members of the Body of Christ. Our celebration of Mass and the nourishment of the Eucharist strengthen us to live Christian lives.

Did You Know?

The Theological Virtues

The theological virtues are faith, hope, and charity. Faith is belief in God. It's not only God's invitation to believe in him but also our response. We're not programmed like robots to love God. He wants us to love him freely. If we respond by believing in God, we are called to spread our faith by sharing it and living it.

Hope keeps us focused on the happiness of Heaven, even when life gets hard. We learn to trust Christ's promises, not relying on our own strength but on the grace of the Holy Spirit.

About love Saint Paul writes, "These three remain: faith, hope, and love; and the greatest of these is love" (1 Corinthians 13:13). Saint Paul also said, "I may have all the faith needed to move mountains—but if I have no love, I am nothing" (1 Corinthians 13:2).

PEOPLE OF FAITH
Saint Joseph

© 2013 Saint Mary's Press/Illustration by Vicki Shuck

God called Saint Joseph to be the husband of Mary and the earthly father of Jesus. Joseph heroically did what God wanted even when it caused him to suffer. He married Mary, although she was mysteriously pregnant. He left his relatives, friends, job, and home to lead his family into Egypt so Jesus would be safe from King Herod's massacre of the innocent children.

Joseph showed the same steady faith and obedience to God's will during his quiet years in Nazareth. He fulfilled the ordinary duties of a husband, parent, worker, and citizen. Like any good father, Joseph taught Jesus many things, including his own trade of carpentry. In her autobiography, Saint Teresa of Ávila encourages praying to Saint Joseph. Jesus, she says, who obeyed him on earth, honors Joseph in Heaven by always doing what he asks.

It's easy to imagine Joseph as a reliable, upright person who does what needs to be done without a lot of talk. His commitment to doing the right thing in the Gospels inspires us to do what God wants without whining or complaining. He teaches us to look at and listen to Jesus in silent prayer. The Church celebrates the feast of Saint Joseph the Husband of Mary on March 19 and Saint Joseph the Worker on May 1.

39 MORAL DECISION MAKING

KEY WORDS

justification
Magisterium
doctrine

Have you ever felt tangled in temptation or tied up in a knot of lies? You may at times find yourself cornered by conformity or choosing something convenient instead of what you know is right in God's eyes. The good news is that God offers us all kinds of help to be good—to be what he knows we can be.

How is your conscience like a knife? Find out by reading this page.

© Difydave/iStockphoto.com

426

Wouldn't it be nice to have a tool to cut through the tension and challenge of making good, moral decisions? Well, you do. It's your conscience. That's the God-given voice inside you that helps you use reason to judge whether an act is right or wrong.

As with any good tool, you must not let your conscience get dull or rusty. Your conscience must be kept sharp to cut through life's challenges. A well-formed conscience is truthful and solid. It doesn't conform to peer pressure or popular trends but rather to the true good for which God made us. Conscience makes its judgments based on reason in a world that's not always reasonable. It's important to do all you can to form your conscience.

> The peace that Christ gives is to guide you in the decisions you make.
>
> Colossians 3:15

The Sources of Moral Actions

We consider three things when we judge the morality of an act: the object, the intention, and the circumstances. Some actions are always wrong. For other actions the degree of right or wrong can depend on the intention and circumstances. Let's use an actual tool—a hammer—and an action it can

PRAY IT!

Lord, sometimes it's hard to do the right thing. Help me be stronger, so when I have a tough decision to make, my choice will please you. When I mess up and sin, give me the strength to say I'm sorry. Your love will restore me, Lord. Bring me back to you. Amen.

be used for as an example to explore the morality of human acts. A doctor can whap your knee with a rubber hammer to test your reflexes. Your little brother can whap the same knee, causing you pain while giving him a twisted sense of satisfaction.

The object, or what's happening in both examples, is the use of a hammer to whap your knee. The intention differs. Your doctor cares about your health, whereas your brother has an entirely different goal in mind! Circumstances also are important. They can change the degree of goodness or evil in an act. For example, if your brother is only three years old, the pain he causes you may be great, but he's not as guilty.

All three sources must be considered to make a judgment about the moral goodness of an act. Let's consider the following examples.

Object

Some choices are always wrong, no matter what good might come of them. Moral evil isn't justified even if some good results. For example, scientists might cure diseases by research done on stem cells taken from human embryos (unborn babies), but human life is lost in the process. The good intention (healing) doesn't make an evil object (destroying a human embryo) good. People sometimes make this point by saying, "The end doesn't justify the means."

Intention

As noted earlier, the intention is an important factor in determining whether an act is good or bad. It's wrong to pull a fire alarm at school to avoid taking a test, because your intention is bad. But pulling the fire alarm is a good act if there really is a fire and your intention is to warn people.

Circumstances

There are times when responsibility for our actions is lessened or wiped out due to circumstances like ignorance, fear, or threats. For example, what if a school bully threatens to hurt your best friend if you refuse to share test answers? If you help the bully cheat, the threatening circumstance (the threat of harm to your friend) lessens your responsibility for your actions.

Freedom and Conscience

We always have the right to exercise freedom, especially in moral and religious matters. But freedom doesn't give us the right to do or say anything we want.

The ability to make good moral decisions depends on having a conscience that is well formed. Our conscience can help us make the right choices by following God's Law and human reason, or it can stray from reason and law and do wrong. We

FUN FACT

In 2005 the U.S. Supreme Court ruled that the Ten Commandments could not be displayed in public buildings if the main purpose was to promote religion. Things were different in 1956. To publicize his classic movie *The Ten Commandments*, director Cecil B. DeMille had public displays of the Ten Commandments erected around the country. Most were placed in or near government buildings.

must always obey the certain judgment of our conscience. Our conscience is like a moral muscle. The stronger the muscle is, the more we can trust it. We exercise our conscience by thinking about the good and bad of every situation we encounter. But we're not on our own to figure things out. Sacred Scripture, the Church's teachings, prayer, and the guidance of holy people and the Holy Spirit all help us form our consciences and live the "good life." That's what God wants for us.

If we ignore our consciences and fail to develop them, we don't escape responsibility for our actions. We are still responsible for our choices and any wrong we do. It is said that ignorance of the law is not an excuse for breaking it. A poorly formed conscience is no excuse for sinning either.

Sins Both Great and Small

Venial sins are offenses against God's will that weaken our relationships with God and others, as well as hurting our personal character. Sin is rooted in our free will, which is found in our hearts. Charity, or love, also lives in our hearts. Venial sin wounds charity but does not destroy it. In fact, with God's grace, charity can repair damage that venial sin does.

Ultimately, a person might commit a mortal sin, choosing on purpose to do something that goes seriously against God's Law. A mortal sin requires that you know you are committing a serious sin and that you freely choose to do it. You cannot commit a mortal sin by accident or if someone is forcing you to do it. Mortal sin causes eternal death. If we don't seek forgiveness, mortal sin can mean eternal separation from God. It also destroys charity, which helps us love God. Without charity, we can't experience eternal happiness with God.

Aiming for God

If your life were an arrow, what would your target be? The Greek word we translate as *sin* was originally an archery term. It meant how far you missed the mark, or bull's-eye. If eternal happiness with God is our target, sin is a sign we've gone astray.

Sin is anything we say or do that goes against God's Law. As followers of Christ, sin is a step off our path of following Jesus, who always

LITURGY CONNECTION

The *Confiteor*

At the start of Mass, we pray for forgiveness, admitting that we are sinners in need of God's love and mercy. One prayer we sometimes say is the *Confiteor*, Latin for "I confess" (see appendix A, "Catholic Prayers," of this handbook). In this prayer we admit to poor moral choices we've made or good things we've failed to do. It's important to think about the words of this prayer, because they help us remember that our poor choices hurt our relationships not only with God but also with the whole community.

Though this penitential rite seems routine, the act of publicly admitting our wrongs is a good spiritual exercise. It gears us up for the examination of conscience that we do before the Sacrament of Penance and Reconciliation.

If your target is to be the kind of person God created you to be, how close are you to being "on target" in your everyday decisions?

© Joe Gough/Shutterstock.com

obeyed God. Sin is a failure to love not only God but also our neighbors. This hurts our human nature and our relationships with others.

Jesus shows us that our relationships with God, others, and ourselves should be the focus of our lives. He teaches us that we must love God with all our being and love our neighbors as we love ourselves. Christian morality aims for this target—that is, choosing to be the people God made us to be.

> If you want to, you can keep the Lord's commands. You can decide whether you will be faithful to him or not.
>
> Sirach 15:15

Sin often starts in small ways. Focusing too much on money and the things we want, for example, can come between us and God, as well as between us and other people. Things, or the money needed to get them, become too important. Possible consequences can include wanting more or better things than our friends have. Or our things may start to make us feel superior to some people and envious of others.

Is it wrong to feel this way? For an answer, look to the Tenth Commandment, which tells us not to covet our neighbor's goods. Repeating sins may seem harmless, but doing so leads us to form bad habits called vices. Just the opposite of virtues, vices make it easier to commit sin. They can become deadly sins called capital sins that distance us from God and others.

Whenever our sin separates us from God and from others, God wants to bring us back together. Through a process called **justification**, God restores our broken relationships after we have sinned. *Justification* is a word that refers to God's act of making us worthy of being united with him. God forgives our sins, makes us holy, and renews our spiritual lives. God gives us love, which helps us turn toward him and away from sin.

THinK About It!

Saint Paul shared advice in his Letter to the Colossians that's still important to us today. Read Colossians 3:1–17, and think about the things Saint Paul says we need to get rid of and the traits we need to clothe ourselves with.

Saint Paul tells us to "teach and instruct one another with all wisdom" (Colossians 3:16). What wisdom can you share with others that will help them live in a way that's pleasing to God? What is one thing that's worked for you as you seek Christ's peace?

Through God's love we are freed from sin, and we enter new lives made possible through Jesus' Passion, when he suffered and died for our sins. Our lives, now on earth and forever with God, are gifts given to us out of immense love. It is this love that supports and sustains us as we strive to make good moral decisions—decisions that keep us turned toward God, as well as those that get us turned back around after we do something wrong.

The Seven Deadly Sins

The Church warns us about seven very harmful sins. We call them capital, or deadly, sins because they lead us toward other sins and away from God. For example, the drive to have more and better stuff might lead us to steal, disrespect our parents, or value things over God. Following is a quick look at these sins:

- **pride:** the belief that you're better than others
- **greed:** an unhealthy desire for money and things
- **envy:** resentment against people who have more things, privileges, or success than you
- **wrath:** intense anger that leads us to get even instead of making things right
- **lust:** the out-of-control desire to enjoy yourself, especially in sexual ways
- **gluttony:** the practice of eating or drinking too much
- **sloth:** laziness, or slacking when action is needed

Rock-Solid Guidance

Making good decisions is not always easy, but God and the Church offer us support. Natural law, the Ten Commandments, and, of course, God's grace help us. Something else the Church offers is a set of guidelines that helps us grow in our love of God and neighbor. These guidelines are called the Precepts of the Church (see appendix B, "Catholic Beliefs and Practices," of this handbook). The Precepts encourage us to do the things that help us live the right way, such as participating in the Church's liturgy and seeking forgiveness for our sins in the Sacrament of Penance and Reconciliation. When we participate in the life of the Church and make friends with people who are also trying to live the good life God wants for us, our decision making can be much easier than if we try to go it alone.

The teachings of the Pope and the bishops are a huge help to us too. In fact, their teachings are essential if we are to live as God wants us to live. They help us understand Christ's teachings and how they apply to the situations we encounter today. The Pope and the bishops in union with him form the

© Brian Singer-Towns/Saint Mary's Press

"Peter: you are a rock, and on this rock foundation I will build my church" (Matthew 16:18). With these words Jesus made Peter and all the popes that have followed him the spiritual and moral leaders of the Church.

Magisterium, the official teaching authority of the Church. We can rely on the Magisterium's explanation of **doctrine**—teachings based on God's Revelation by and through Jesus Christ—because the Magisterium is infallible. This means the Magisterium is without error when it speaks about doctrine, including the teachings related to moral living. The Pope and the bishops uphold and explain the Church's moral teachings, helping us all to understand and live out these teachings.

Live It!

Be a Critical Consumer

Moral decision making affects every part of our lives. Our consciences, and therefore our decisions too, can get clouded by advertising messages. We can't escape it, but we can control it.

Consider some of the following common things and the messages we get about them. How could you respond?

Clothing. Do fashion designers care about what clothing says about you, or do they just want you to buy their brand? Be sure the clothing you wear makes a positive moral statement about you.

Food. Companies may package and market their food to look tasty, but is it good for you? Read labels and choose healthy options.

Technology. Does technology make you cooler, or does it actually distance you from your friends? Set down the cell phone or iPod and just enjoy being with people.

PEOPLE OF FAITH
Saint Peter Claver

© 2013 Saint Mary's Press/Illustration by Vicki Shuck

Imagine being captured and thrown into a dark, dirty ship for a two-month voyage, leaving behind forever your family and everyone and everything you know. That was reality for some slaves brought to the New World in the 1600s. Many of these slaves ended up in Cartagena, a major city in Colombia, in South America.

Moved with compassion for these men, Fr. Peter Claver (1581–1654) began to minister to the slaves coming off the ships in Cartagena. The slaves had been forced to travel in inhuman conditions, spending much of their time in shackles. They got little food or water, and many became ill or died. Father Peter rushed to the arriving ships to care for the newly arrived slaves. With his helpers, he cared for the sick, buried the dead, and provided food and comfort for the living. Through their words and actions, they showed love to the enslaved men and gave them hope.

Saint Peter Claver's example was so powerful that more than 300,000 slaves were baptized and converted to Christianity—the faith of their captors.

Peter was born in Spain. He was just fourteen years old when he began studying in Barcelona to be a priest. He felt a call to become a missionary. He became known as the "saint of slaves" in Cartagena. Father Peter knew slaves would never have freedom, but he worked tirelessly to give them hope. He led them to Jesus, who suffered like them and for them, and he prepared them for joy in Heaven.

40 Honoring God

Key Words

idolatry
atheism
venerate
Sabbath

Praising and respecting God are important. There are countless ways to praise God and show your love for him. Maybe you and your family can make an extra effort on vacation to find a Mass on Sunday. Or perhaps you can set aside your ego and take the risk of singing in your parish's choir, despite what your friends might think. Actions like this are a way to show your love for God and the important place he has in your life.

The First Commandment: Honor God

In these next few chapters, we'll explore ways to live out the Ten Commandments, starting here with those that focus on our love of God.

"Love the Lord your God with all your heart,
with all your soul, with all your strength, and
with all your mind"; and "Love your neighbor as
you love yourself."

Luke 10:27

The First Commandment, "I am the Lord your God. You shall not have strange gods before me," calls us to love, believe in, and hope in God.

When we pray to God, worship him as he deserves, and keep the promises we make to him, we're obeying the First Commandment.

Whenever we pray, whether at church or in a private place, it's important to give our full attention and try to block out distractions that might get in the way of our focus on God. Those distractions could include our cell phones or thoughts about our plans with friends later in the day.

The First Commandment is first for a reason. Our happiness in life is based on it. Our relationship with God brings us great joy.

God makes it clear that he will "tolerate no rivals" (Exodus 20:5). That was the case when the Israelites broke the First Commandment by worshipping a golden calf. This Scripture account presents God as being so angry with his people that he threatened to destroy them.

Pray It!

God, give me, I pray, the
eyes to see the false gods
that I put before you,
the strength to avoid
the things that turn my
attention from you, and
the courage to pursue
the true greatness that
comes from putting
you first in my life and
putting others' needs
ahead of my own. Amen.

The Bible warns us against the dangers of false gods. Things like money, possessions, and popularity can become our golden calves—our idols. Making these things more important than God is **idolatry** and violates the First Commandment. Another form of idolatry is superstition, which is the belief that a person or object has powers that actually belong only to God. A lucky rabbit's foot isn't lucky and won't do you any good. Likewise, a chain letter that foretells a particular outcome—good or bad—based on whether you forward the letter to others has

?

Did You Know?

Do the Math: The Eighth Day

Both Christians and Jews see Sunday as the first day of the week. It is the day of the Sun, the light that broke through the darkness on the first day of Creation.

Jews observe their Sabbath on Saturday, because God made it holy by resting on the seventh day from all the work he'd done. The Gospels tell us that Jesus rose the day after the Sabbath.

Saint Justin, who wrote the earliest description we have of the Lord's Day, noted that Christians gather on Sunday instead of the Sabbath not simply because it recalls the light of God's first Creation but also because we celebrate the Resurrection of Jesus, the Light of the World.

Though Sunday is the first day of the week in the calendar, the Church considers the Lord's Day to be the eighth day. Because the Bible speaks of seven days of Creation, the "eighth day" is a way of referring to the first day of a new creation.

no connection to future events that do or do not happen. Some people go much further, trying to foretell the future or placing their trust in some type of magic. All these practices deny the power of God and his plan for each of us.

© Bill Wittman/www.wpwittman.com

It's wrong to disrespect or abuse religious practices. You may hear comedians ridicule the Catholic faith, or you may see artists do disgusting or violent things with crucifixes or holy statues. This is sacrilege, and it violates the First Commandment. Buying and selling spiritual favors also is a sin against the First Commandment. For example, a preacher should not promise to cure someone's illness in exchange for a donation, and material donations to religious organizations or causes cannot be promoted or used as a way to ensure eternal salvation. Salvation and miracles come only from God, and it's wrong for humans to believe they can buy or control God's will.

Atheism, which is the denial of God's existence, is the most extreme way to break this Commandment. Any person or political system that rejects God takes a tragic turn from God's love and other gifts.

Catholics make an important distinction between idolatry and veneration. Some Christians do not keep holy art or statues in their churches because they

We might think it strange that the Israelites worshipped a golden calf. But how can money, power, possessions, and popularity be the "golden calves" of today?

441

FUN FACT

Catholics do a great job of keeping Ash Wednesday holy, even though it isn't a Sunday or a holy day of obligation. Catholic churches are usually packed that day. It's a great way to begin Lent. We are encouraged to attend Mass that day and receive the mark of the cross in ashes on our foreheads.

consider them close to idolatry. But look around most Catholic churches and you'll see a crucifix, statues of Mary and other saints, and other sacred images. Do we worship these things, as the Israelites bowed to the golden cow? No, we **venerate**, or meditate on, these images as we pray. We believe that doing this is a way of honoring the presence of God in the world. Christians have rejoiced for nearly two thousand years that the Word of God became flesh when Jesus was born. Our belief in God's loving presence is strengthened by the ability to see God among us. We adore only God, but we respect God's presence in the life of Mary and the saints by praying with sacred images—this is not idolatry.

The Second Commandment: Keep God's Name Holy

What's in a name? We like it when our friends call us by our names or by favorite nicknames. It can hurt when someone abuses our names, maybe by putting a mean adjective in front of them. We want people to respect our names and use them with love.

The Second Commandment, "You shall not take the name of the Lord, your God, in vain," is a clear call to respect God's name. God's name is so sacred that even today, some Jews will not speak or write

God's name. It is holy for us too, as Jesus teaches in the Lord's Prayer: "Hallowed [holy] be thy name."

Listen to some everyday conversations, and you can hear that certain people struggle with the Second Commandment. Jesus invites us to call God by name but only in ways that respect and please God. Keeping this in mind helps us avoid abusing God's holy name.

There are random and trivial uses of God's name, sometimes to get a laugh or sound cool. It's not cool to use God's name improperly, or in vain, which

Live It!

Honor God through Your Language

Loving God requires us to control our tongues and avoid words that disrespect his name and offend him. Here are some ideas you can try to get into the habit of, using only good language that honors God and does not offend him:

- Find new ways to express frustration. Some people substitute similar words, like "gosh," "darn," and "snap," but these make it too easy to slip back to actual bad words. Try "Heavens!" instead. It sounds corny and may inspire you to say nothing at all.
- Hold yourself accountable. Ask your family members or friends to join you in cleaning up your language. Make a "slip-up jar" and put a quarter in it whenever you slip and use God's name in vain or in a disrespectful way. Give the money to a charity.
- Remember that God loves you. When Jesus faced his worst stress (see Mark 14:32–36), he called out to his Father, "Abba." You are a child of God. Call God's name with love when you need his help.

means for no real value. It's even worse to use the name of God, Jesus, Mary, or the saints in ways that are intentionally offensive. That's called blasphemy, and you'll hear it on concert stages, from coaches in stadiums, and sometimes popping up in conversations among folks you hang out with. It's important to avoid the abuse of God's name and encourage others to do the same.

> And so, in honor of the name of Jesus all beings in heaven, on earth, and in the world below will fall on their knees, and all will openly proclaim that Jesus Christ is Lord, to the glory of God the Father.
>
> Philippians 2:10–11

THiNK About It!

The Church requires that we observe the Lord's Day by attending Mass every Sunday or Saturday night. Unfortunately, not all Catholics attend Mass regularly. What are some reasons you could give someone to encourage him or her to attend Mass every Sunday?

Sometimes a person will blurt out "I swear on the Bible" to try to convince you something is true. What's true is that there are only two times to take such oaths: either when you are testifying in court or when you are promising to uphold a law. Oaths like these are sacred promises, because they call on God to make sure that the witness tells the truth or that the leader lives up to a commitment. If they don't, it's a false oath, calling God to be a witness to a lie. Lying under oath, which is called perjury, is a serious sin. It disrespects God, who is always faithful to his promises.

The Third Commandment: Keep Sunday Sacred

Sunday is supposed to be a day of rest, right? It may not seem that way when your parents wake you up for church on Sunday morning. But rest is more than just sleeping. Sunday is a day to celebrate our love of God and re-create ourselves by refreshing our minds, bodies, and spirits, all for God's glory.

God rested on the seventh day, after the hard work of the first Creation. He established the **Sabbath** as "a day of rest dedicated to me" (Exodus 20:10). In the Jewish tradition, the Sabbath is from sundown Friday to sundown Saturday. Jews still observe the Sabbath through prayer, fasting, and worshipping together on Saturday. How did we Christians wind up with our holy day on Sunday?

The Third Commandment, "Remember to keep holy the Lord's Day," has a fresh ring to it, because what we're observing reflects the Christian practice of the Jewish Sabbath tradi-tion. We celebrate the day on which Jesus rose from the dead to new life. It's a day on which we recall the new creation that started with Jesus' Resurrection.

No 24/7 for my people! When God gave us the Sabbath, he gave us a break. A Jewish family lights the Sabbath candle at sundown on Friday.

© Andrew Aitchison/In Pictures/Corbis

© Ocean/Corbis

Make it a practice to be on time for Mass. Just as you wouldn't be late for an important event or gathering, be on time for the celebration of the liturgy.

The main way we keep the Lord's Day holy is by participating in the celebration of the Eucharist. Sunday is the Church's most important holy day, and going to Mass on Sundays and other holy days of obligation is a serious obligation for Catholics. Attending Mass on Sunday and holy days of obligation is one of the Precepts of the Church, and to miss Mass without a serious reason is a sin (see appendix B, "Catholic Beliefs and Practices," of this handbook). There's a reason behind this rule. You can stay in your room and pray for an hour every Sunday, but your Catholic faith is bigger than just your personal relationship with God. As the Body of Christ, it is essential for the Church to come together to worship God. The Sunday Eucharist is the opportunity to praise God through song, prayer, and Scripture, and to receive the Body and Blood of Christ with the whole community on the day that God set aside for rest and for worshipping him. It is pleasing to God when his people come together with one heart, join their voices in song and prayer, hear God's Word proclaimed, and share the Body and Blood of Christ. It's important for the family of God to come together regularly, just as many families try to gather for meals as often as they can. God insists we make a date—Sunday or Saturday evening—to get together with one another and with him.

Along with avoiding activities on Sundays that keep us from attending Mass, we also should make time to relax our minds and bodies. We can do this by avoiding chores and activities that can be done on another day. We should also make a point of spending time with family and friends. Keeping Sunday holy in these ways brings us closer to becoming the people God made us to be.

Church History

The Sale of Indulgences

Granting an indulgence is one way the Church can reduce someone's punishment in Purgatory. You can receive an indulgence for performing certain devotions, like making a pilgrimage. A book called the Manual of Indulgences lists the devotions for which the Church grants indulgences.

In the early 1500s, some Church officials sold indulgences, a sin against the First Commandment. They encouraged people to think of indulgences as a magic way to avoid the consequences of sin—not as a sign of Christian piety. Johann Tetzel, a Dominican friar, was infamous for selling indulgences to raise money for papal building projects. Many criticized this sinful practice. Pope Leo X (1513–1521) issued a document to teach Christians the real purpose of indulgences, and the practice of selling them stopped.

41 Honoring Family

Key Words

honor
discipline
society

Although teens may not admit this publicly, in surveys, most say that one of their parents is their hero. They also rate family unity as their number one value. The need for a strong, loving family is so great because God created us that way.

Eating together is healthy for both parents and children: physically, emotionally, and spiritually.

© Monkey Business Images/Shutterstock.com

448

Of course, family life doesn't always seem so wonderful. For example, when a parent tells you, "I'm doing this for your own good," it usually doesn't feel that way. Some families have serious problems.

Most parents try hard to give their children all they need, especially love. Sometimes their love means the children won't get what they want. It's obvious that if a six-year-old wants to play with matches, a loving parent would not allow it. But it might be less obvious to you that a parent not allowing a thirteen-year-old to stay out without a curfew is also showing loving care. We often take for granted the good things parents do and focus too much on the times they don't let us do what we want to do. At such times, it helps to remember a few of the following things:

- **Only God is perfect, and God is love.** But sometimes even God says no out of love for us.

- **Parents are older and wiser in many ways.** It also helps to remember that they got some of their wisdom by learning from their mistakes, which they do not want you to repeat.

- **Parents must answer to God.** Ultimately, your parents must answer to God, who put them in charge of you.

PRAY IT!

Heavenly Father, you give us life through our parents. You call our parents to guide us. Please strengthen our parents to be strong for us, especially when we need them most. Help us appreciate their patience and sacrifices. Help us be patient and learn from their strengths and their mistakes so we might someday be good parents too. Amen.

The Fourth Commandment: Honor Your Parents

Through the Fourth Commandment, God calls us to honor our parents. Along with respecting our parents, we must also respect other adults whom God has given authority over us for our benefit.

Honor means "to show great respect or courtesy." It's what we try to do on Mother's Day and Father's Day, but it should happen every day. You can honor your parents by doing chores the first time you are asked. Better yet, help your parents without being asked, or do more than they expect. If they ask about your day at school, share something interesting. They really do care. God put them in your life to care for you.

When a man and a woman marry and have children, they take on a sacred responsibility. Every new life they bring into the world is a miraculous gift from God. Your parents have the duty to provide for your physical needs, like food, clothing, and shelter. They also are supposed to meet your spiritual needs. This includes teaching you about faith, prayer, and the virtues.

Think About It!

Mary and Joseph both experienced worry and even fear when they learned that Mary was pregnant with Jesus. However, an angel told each of them, "Do not be afraid" (Matthew 1:20, Luke 1:30), and they trusted in God.

Being a parent is an awesome responsibility. What are some responsibilities your parents have in caring for you that might cause them worry? How does God help them? How can you be a source of reassurance and support for them in carrying out these responsibilities?

© Bill Wittman/www.wpwittman.com

In fact, the Church wants each family to be a school of virtues. Your parents teach virtues through their words and actions. Simple words such as "I love you" or "I forgive you" teach powerful lessons. So does discipline.

> Teach children how they should live, and they will remember it all their life.
>
> Proverbs 22:6

You may see discipline as punishment, but think of it as a way of learning. In fact, the word *discipline* comes from the same root as *disciple*, which means "learner." **Discipline** simply means learning self-control by accepting the authority of your family. Even

Catholic parishes and schools can help parents fulfill the promise made at their child's Baptism: to raise their child in the faith.

FUN FACT

It may seem odd that the Fourth Commandment relates to both our parents and our country. But people often use family terms such as *fatherland* when talking about their countries or *mother tongue* about their native languages. George Washington was the "father of our country." Even the word *patriot* comes from the Latin word for "father."

when you don't understand your parents' decisions or when their decisions go against your preference, you owe your parents respect, gratitude, and obedience. You also have to do your part to help them according to your ability.

Your respect for your parents makes family life go more smoothly.

"Respect your father and mother" is the first commandment that has a promise added: "so that all may go well with you, and you may live a long time in the land."

Ephesians 6:2–3

Celebrating milestones, like graduation, are opportunities for a parent to say, "You are my beloved child, with whom I am well pleased."

© Rob Lewine/Tetra Images/Corbis

Being Family Is Hard Work

Of course, respect between children and parents is a two-way street, as Paul writes to the Colossians: "Children, it is your Christian duty to obey your parents always, for that is what pleases God. Parents, do not irritate your children, or they will become discouraged" (3:20–21).

Your parents try to meet your basic needs, and that includes guiding you and giving you encouragement. They should support you in your studies, your activities, and your plans for a vocation. They should teach and remind you that your first calling is to follow Jesus.

On Earth as It Is in Heaven

Jesus taught his disciples that God's Kingdom is not only in Heaven but also in our daily lives on earth. God wants us to help build a society that values truth, justice,

LITURGY CONNECTION

A Blessing for Parents

Listen closely the next time you're at a Baptism. The rite includes blessings for the child's parents. Your parents may have heard the following or similar words when you were baptized:

> May almighty God, who gives life on earth and in heaven, bless the parents of these children. They thank him now for the gift he has given them. May they always show that gratitude in action by loving and caring for their children. (70)

Families are to be schools of virtue, teaching us those good habits that help us make good choices. Your parents' efforts to nurture your faith are their way of living up to a call they received at your Baptism.

freedom, and solidarity. **Society** is a community of people who depend on one another. We support our society by sharing with charities our talents, time, and money. We also need to support the government in its efforts to improve society.

Governments, for their part, are required to respect human rights and protect our ability to live in freedom. We are blessed with many rights, such as the right to gather with other people, the right to express our opinions, and the right to worship God. When governments take away people's basic rights, they are not following God's Law.

?

Did You Know?

Your Family: The People of God

Our Church draws some clear connections between herself and the families that come together to worship and serve.

The Church is the family of God. The core of the Church, from her earliest days, has been families. In the Acts of the Apostles, we see entire families who become Christian at the same time (see Acts 18:8).

Our Church also looks at families as the domestic church, to be modeled after the Holy Family. Our families are called to learn together by word and example.

Parents are called to teach their children about the Catholic faith and encourage them to consider how they might serve the Church. Parents also should introduce children to daily prayer and daily reading of Scripture.

When leaders take away our freedom, we can learn from the example of Jesus' first disciples. Things were going pretty well for them until the authorities felt threatened and ordered them to stop preaching about Jesus. Peter and the Apostles had the courage to say, "We must obey God, not men" (Acts 5:29), even though standing up like this might cost them their lives. When society's laws disrespect God's Laws, we must resist, even to the point of disobeying the human-made laws.

We can hope it never comes to that, but it's up to us to make sure our leaders' decisions and actions help lead us to our destiny. Do they lead us closer to or further away from the love and justice Jesus described when he taught about God's Kingdom? We

> When governments work well, they help us take care of one another. When our leaders fail to make good decisions, we are called to challenge them.

© Paul Colangelo/CORBIS

need to speak out and make our values heard, so that what the Gospels teach inspires our leaders as they make rules that govern us. If we don't, our leaders might abuse their powers and may even become dictators.

A good example of the need to resist immoral laws is slavery, or treating people like property that can be bought and sold. For centuries many nations, including the United States, had laws allowing slavery. Committed people called abolitionists, often led by Christians, fought to make slavery illegal.

We'd like to think that people have learned from the mistakes of the past.

Are the days gone forever when society allowed people to abuse other people? No, we still see bullying and discrimination in our society, and we know that slavery still exists in some parts of the world.

Live It!

The Wisdom of Parents

You can learn a lot from your parents. Just pay attention. How do they spend their time? How much time do they devote to your activities or to helping you with homework? What are their priorities? Do they discipline with love and respect? Do they provide good advice? Do they guide you in your faith? Ask them about their prayer lives, or better yet, be part of them. Take time to pray with, and for, your parents.

Again, we must lift up the moral law that forbids slavery. We shouldn't allow power or money to distort the way we look at people. Bad things surely happen if we do.

When we broaden our vision and see all people as part of our human family, good things happen. When both neighbors and strangers value and respect each other as children of God, we get a glimpse of the joy that Jesus told us is possible.

Church History

Catholics in the American Colonies

During the reign of Queen Elizabeth I in England, Catholics experienced persecution. They could only practice their faith in private. Catholics were viewed with suspicion, because people feared they were loyal only to the Pope. Some Catholics were executed for treason because of these fears.

Then Lord Baltimore, a Catholic, was granted land for an American settlement. He founded the colony of Maryland and extended freedom of worship to all. Many Catholics fled England to take refuge in Maryland. However, non-Catholics began to outnumber Catholics in the colony and once again passed laws discriminating against Catholics. But after the American Revolution, the Bill of Rights extended freedom of religion to all citizens.

Catholics in America had worked hard for acceptance in this country and did not want a foreign bishop. The American priests asked Pope Pius VI to allow them to nominate the first American bishop—an unusual request, because only the Pope can appoint bishops. Pope Pius VI agreed to this request and approved their choice of John Carroll, who became the first bishop of Baltimore, in the first diocese of the United States.

42 RESPECTING LIFE

KEY WORDS

abortion
legitimate defense
suicide
euthanasia
scandal

It's a recipe for chaos. Take five-pound sacks of flour and add high school students. Stir up everyone's imagination by pretending the sacks are babies and the students are their parents. Then let things bake for a week.

What this recipe yields depends on the human ingredients. If teens are not responsible, the "baby" rolls off the car roof as "Mom" drives home from school. Poof! The more caring "parents" guard every teaspoon of their

The "seamless garment" approach to life includes opposition to the death penalty as well as to abortion.

© Reuters/CORBIS

458

precious bundle. Either way, in this common high school assignment, young people learn that taking care of babies requires a lot of time and effort. Hopefully they also learn that life is a gift to be respected and protected.

Unlike flour "babies," we humans are sacred, from the moment we are conceived until the moment we die. That's because God makes us in his image. Because of this we have a special relationship with the living God. He is the sole reason for our being. No one can take away this dignity.

Our rights and dignity as human beings begin before we are born. We are human at the moment of our conception, when our mother's egg and father's sperm unite to create life. Unborn children have the rights of any person, starting with the right to life itself. **Abortion** is a procedure that intentionally ends an unborn child's development. Choosing to have an abortion or performing abortion is a grave sin. Abortions became legal in the United States in 1973. Other nations allow it also. But as we have learned, something may be legal but not moral. Abortion is a serious violation of moral law. Catholics and other Christians lead the fight against abortion, but the moral truth about the rights and dignity of the unborn should be obvious to people regardless of religious belief.

PRAY IT!

Dear Lord, you created us in your image. You made us good. Help us do good by respecting and protecting all life. Let us be life-giving in our words and actions. Let us speak out for those who can't speak for themselves and make our world a better, safer place for all people to live. Amen.

FUN FACT

Hearing is one of the last senses to develop in unborn babies. But they can hear us in there! Experts say babies recognize their mother's voice immediately after birth. Newborn babies also respond to stories and songs they heard in the womb. In studies of great musicians, scholars have often found that exposure to good music began in the womb.

Because our rights exist before we are born, an unborn baby needs protection and care like any human. This includes caring for the health of the baby and its mother. Health care can be as simple as supporting an expectant mother's need to eat properly and get enough rest. In extreme cases, doctors can perform procedures to protect or heal an unborn child. The Church supports this medical care.

From Womb to Tomb

We learn a lot about the dignity of life early in the Bible. God created Adam and Eve, and he was proud of his work. He called them good. After all, they were like him, made in his image. Adam and Eve had two children, Cain and Abel. Cain grew up to be a farmer, and Abel grew up to be a shepherd. When God was more pleased with Abel's offering of firstborn lambs than he was with Cain's offering from his fields, Cain attacked and killed Abel. God protested Cain's actions and made it clear that killing for any reason is wrong. God even protected Cain himself from being killed by someone else in revenge (see Genesis 4:1–15).

Every human life is sacred from the moment a person is conceived until his or her natural death. The key word here is *natural*. Murder, the act of killing someone on purpose, is a sin against the sacredness of life. Murder rejects not only the dignity of the victim but also the holiness of God, who makes each of us good.

> Then God said, "And now we will make human beings; they will be like us and resemble us."
>
> Genesis 1:26

The path that leads to the extreme action of murder is made up of simple steps. For example, our respect for life can be eroded by violent video games, movies, TV shows, and music. We need to be careful not to let outside influences lead us to believe that violence is okay.

What if there is truly no other way to stop someone from hurting us or someone else? If someone is in a kill-or-be-killed situation, then the principle of

Pictures from inside the womb help us realize how beautifully made babies are— long before birth.

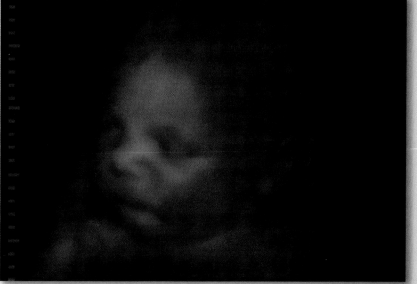

© Valentina Razumova/Shutterstock.com

legitimate defense makes it necessary to protect oneself or others. Of course, we must do everything possible to avoid taking the life of someone who threatens us. For example, if a thief threatens to hurt you and demands your MP3 player, just let the thief have it instead of fighting for it. Your music and your player are less valuable than your life or the thief's life.

Liturgy Connection

Honoring God as Creator

At Mass listen closely for the many names we use to refer to God's creative power, such as the following:

+ "Maker of Heaven and Earth"
+ "The Giver of Life"
+ "Lord, God of All Creation"

These titles recognize God as our Creator.

Reflect on how each of these titles can inform our understanding of the Fifth Commandment and of the value of human life.

The Fifth Commandment: Living and Dying with Dignity

The Fifth Commandment, "You shall not kill," deals with many more situations than you'll see on a TV crime show.

God made life good, but the paradise he created for us seems to wither with every bad choice people make. Sometimes life can seem out of control, too hard to live. But **suicide**, the taking of your own life, is not the answer. It rejects God's great love, his gift of hope, and his call to respect our lives and the lives of others. It takes over a decision that only God can make: the decision of when life should end. That is why "You shall not kill" includes not taking our own life through suicide. The ef-

© Monkey Business Images/Shutterstock.com

Suicide is a permanent solution to temporary problems. Telling a trusted adult about someone (including yourself) who is in great emotional pain can save a life!

fects of suicide go well beyond the person who commits it. It hurts God and our neighbors. It tears up the victim's family and friends. It deprives the world of the victim's many gifts.

Sometimes people with fatal diseases or those who are suffering great pain seek the wrong kind of help. They may feel they have the right to die. In other cases a patient may be incapable of making decisions, but family members want to alleviate the person's suffering by ending his or her life. Ending the life of someone because she or he is suffering is called **euthanasia**. Regardless of how or why it is done, euthanasia is murder. Remember that for an action to be moral, the act itself, not just the intention, must be good (see chapter 39, "Moral Decision Making," of this handbook). Euthanasia is a sin against the Fifth Commandment. Choosing to end life, for any reason, denies the dignity of the person and the respect due to God, who created each of us. Prayer, hospice programs, and pain medicines make it possible to avoid the temptation of euthanasia. Most communities have hospice programs that allow very ill people to die with dignity, in God's time.

Sometimes a decision is made to not use extraordinary means (which might be very painful, expensive, or burdensome, or of doubtful benefit) to keep a person alive. This decision is not the same as euthanasia. Discontinuing certain medical treatments can be moral when the intention is not to cause death, even if such a decision means that the person will die sooner than he or she would with treatment.

Think About It!

Maybe you've never taken care of a baby, but we all know what it feels like to be vulnerable and to depend on others to meet our needs. What are some of a baby's greatest needs? Food? Protection? Love? What gifts does God provide us to take care of babies, elderly people, or people with special needs?

The World We Live In

Wedged between the Bible's first stories of life and death is a story of the first scandal.

The story of a woman and a man eating an apple may not seem scandalous compared to today's tabloid news. But the Church defines *scandal* differently. **Scandal** is simply an action or an attitude—or the failure to act—that leads someone to sin. It's a serious offense, and perhaps no story captures this better than the story of Adam and Eve, called the Fall.

The Scripture account of the Fall is where we first witness the sinful nature of humans. Adam and Eve represent all of us. In the account of the Fall, we see temptation harm Adam and Eve's relationship with God.

> If anyone should cause one of these little ones to lose his faith in me, it would be better for that person to have a large millstone tied around his neck and be drowned in the deep sea.
>
> Matthew 18:6

Live It!

Your Choice for Life

Do you wonder what you can do personally to help prevent abortion? You and your friends can start by promoting chastity. For an unmarried person, chastity means not having sex outside marriage. Next, you might go public with your beliefs by joining a Life Chain event or writing a letter to your legislators.

What can you do if a girl you know—maybe a classmate—becomes pregnant? How might you respond if she believes abortion is her only option?

First, listen. Don't judge. Offer your friendship. Strongly encourage her to tell her parents, a pastor, or a school counselor. Contact an organization like Birthright. Help her learn more about adoption. Many loving families are eager to adopt.

Consider donating to an agency that supports expectant mothers who need help. You could organize a baby shower to collect items to donate.

Above all, pray that expectant mothers always choose life.

Nothing is more harmful to the human spirit than war. Earlier you read that sometimes a person or even a nation must defend itself from someone who threatens it. These situations must be avoided by any means necessary. "War is not always inevitable," Pope Saint John Paul II said in 2003. "It is always a defeat for humanity" ("Address of His Holiness Pope John Paul II to the Diplomatic Corps"). Because of the many evils and injustices that are part of war, we must avoid warfare if at all possible.

But even if nations can't—or won't—avoid war, they must follow the requirements of moral law as they fight a war. This means they must follow universally accepted principles that arise from natural law as well as the teachings of the Church. These principles include giving respect and humane treatment to wounded soldiers, to prisoners, and especially to people who aren't fighting. Such laws protect the innocent and prevent forces from wiping out entire nations or ethnic minorities, which is called genocide. No matter the risk to themselves, soldiers must resist orders calling for such brutal use of force.

As military superpowers in the 1960s built entire stockpiles of weapons that could wipe out huge cities and their residents, the Church spoke out. "The arms race is one of the greatest curses on the human race and the harm it inflicts on the poor is more than can be endured" (CCC, 2329). Decades later, people still lack food, shelter, medicine, education, and other necessities while their leaders invest in weapons and warfare. This is sinful. The Church is well known for protecting unborn babies. We also want to improve the world into which they're born.

Church History

The Encyclical *Of Human Life*

On July 25, 1968, Pope Paul VI issued an encyclical titled *Of Human Life* (*Humanae Vitae*, in Latin). In this encyclical, the Pope, after reviewing recommendations and opinions from scientists, married couples, and bishops, affirmed that human life is so precious that it cannot be regulated by artificial means (that is, by birth control pills or devices).

The reasons given by the encyclical are based on what married life is all about. Marriage is all about unity, faithfulness, and openness to children (see CCC, 1643; and *Humanae Vitae*, 9). If you give someone the gift of yourself but hold part of the gift back, are you giving your whole self? Artificial regulation of birth is "holding back" part of the gift.

However, married people can regulate the size of their families through natural family planning—that is, without using artificial means of regulation. Natural family planning helps couples to cooperate with each other in planning their families in a natural way. The bottom line is that children are to be welcomed as gifts of married life!

43 RESPECTING TRUTH AND PROPERTY

Key Words

restitution

reparation

envy

Have you ever worried about forgetting your school locker combination? That's normal, but nothing to lose sleep over. But imagine if you arrived at your locker tomorrow and all your stuff was gone. Or what if someone wrote something nasty about you on your

How would you feel if someone trashed your locker and stole your things? Why is the Seventh Commandment, "You shall not steal," so important?

© Jeffrey Coolidge/Corbis

locker door? In both cases you'd feel violated, because you were robbed of something.

The Seventh Commandment: Take It to the Limit

The Seventh Commandment, "You shall not steal," forbids theft, or taking someone's belongings against that person's will. Stealing can take many forms, beyond the taking of an object that belongs to another person. Let's explore how far this Commandment reaches.

Stealing can include the taking of something intangible—that is, something that isn't physical or that you can't hold or touch. This includes things like music and movies that can be illegally downloaded online. Whether the band or movie producer knows it is happening or not, illegally downloading music and movies is a form of theft, because you are taking for free something that other people created and produced at a cost as a means of livelihood for themselves and others.

Similarly, if you studied hard for a test, anyone who might copy your answers is not only cheating but also stealing from

Pray It!

Lord, it can be easy to find words to tear people down, cheap words that find flaws in others or hurt the people I envy. Forgive me when I use words to harm others. Help me find words to heal and to forgive when I've been hurt. Help me find words to lift up the good gifts in others and to praise you for all you've done for me. Amen.

you. It's your work. Others have no right to take it from you.

Every way you can imagine of taking and using someone's property without her or his consent is a sin against the Seventh Commandment. No matter what was stolen or how it was taken, the one who stole it needs to make the situation right. This requires making **restitution**, which means returning what was stolen. In a similar way, someone who has damaged another person's property must make **reparation**. This requires somehow fixing or replacing the damaged property.

Another form of stealing that doesn't involve taking an object that explicitly belongs to another person is the unjust use of the earth's resources. Americans make up only 5 percent of the world's population but

Illegally downloading music is a form of stealing. "Everybody's doing it" arguments make it more tempting, but that doesn't make it right.

© Anna Peisl/zefa/Corbis

consume 30 percent of its resources. This unjust distribution of resources, such as water, food, and sources of energy, is a violation of the Seventh Commandment.

The Seventh Commandment calls us to be fair and charitable in the way we share earthly goods and the fruits of human labor. God created the world's resources for everyone to share. The need to share the world's resources is more important than our right to own as much property as we can get. Saint Basil, a great leader of the Church in the fourth century, made this connection long ago:

> When someone steals another's clothes, we call that person a thief. Should we not give the same name to one who could clothe the naked and

Imagine that one person in this group of twenty gets one-third of the pizza. The other nineteen have to split the rest. The world's resources are divided in a similar way. How fair is that?

© Shutterstock

FUN FACT

You can't take your possessions to Heaven, but you can take your team loyalty to the grave. Casket makers now produce models featuring the logos and colors of your favorite football or baseball teams. For a few hundred dollars more than a plain casket would cost, you can customize your casket and make a statement among everybody buried at your cemetery!

does not? The bread in your cupboard belongs to the hungry; the coat unused in your closet belongs to the one who needs it; the shoes rotting in your closet belong to the one who has no shoes; the money you hoard up belongs to the poor.

The Tenth Commandment: The Danger of Envy

Despite how much you might have, it's likely that someone else has more or better stuff than you. Just as it's wrong to steal what belongs to others, it's also wrong to be envious of what belongs to others. The Tenth Commandment,

How often do you contribute your own money to the collection at Mass?

© CEFutcher/iStockphoto.com

472

"You shall not covet your neighbor's goods," forbids an unhealthy desire for wealth and the power that comes with it.

Envy, one of the capital sins (see chapter 39, "Moral Decision Making," of this handbook), is being jealous about the things other people have to a point of wanting their stuff for yourself. As Christians, we can humbly accept the reality that we all have different gifts and material things. We can even thank God for another person's good fortune. Although those attitudes may be hard to reach, we start by trusting that God will provide all we need.

> Much is required from the person to whom much is given.
>
> Luke 12:48

Jesus told his disciples to travel lightly (see Matthew 10:9). That's good advice for us as we head for Heaven. In order to attain eternal life in Heaven, we must detach ourselves from earthly riches. To emphasize this point, Jesus said, "It is much harder

LITURGY CONNECTION

The Washing of Hands

Have you ever wondered why the priest washes his hands at Mass? A lot of people think it has something to do with Pontius Pilate, but that is not correct.

In the early Church, people sometimes offered gifts such as live chickens. These were brought up with the bread and wine at the offertory. So it was necessary for the priest to wash up after this. Now the priest washes his hands to symbolize his desire for purity of heart.

It's still important that we share what we have with the Church. Consider how your gifts can help make the Church stronger. Bring cash or checks, but please, no chickens!

for a rich person to enter the Kingdom of God than for a camel to go through the eye of a needle" (Luke 18:25).

The Eighth Commandment: What's in a Name?

Words can damage a person. Let's say someone stole everything you own. If you have a good reputation, you can still hold your head high. But imagine if someone damages your reputation by spreading false gossip about you. That can hurt worse than losing all your material possessions. Damaging the reputation of another person, especially with false or mean words, is sinful. Even if the gossip is true, spreading it injures the person's honor and reputation, which we must respect.

The Eighth Commandment, "You shall not bear false witness against your neighbor," also means practicing the virtue of truthfulness. Keeping the Eighth Commandment means we must always be truthful in what we say and do. We must avoid saying things we know are not true. We must also avoid saying things we don't mean, just to win the approval of others, and we must avoid misleading others by hiding

THiNK AbouT IT!

What's the one item you own that would hurt the most to have taken by a thief? Why is that? Is it because of its material value or its sentimental worth?

What would hurt more—to lose that item to a thief or to have your reputation damaged by gossip or rumors?

the truth. Lying, or saying something we know to be untrue in order to deceive others, is a violation of the Eighth Commandment. When we deceive another person, we are required to make reparation for the harm our lie caused to others.

> So do not start worrying "Where will my food
> come from? or my drink? or my clothes?" . . .
> Your Father in heaven knows that you need
> all these things. Instead, be concerned above
> everything else with the Kingdom of God and
> with what [God] requires of you, and he will
> provide you with all these other things.
> Matthew 6:31–33

The Sacrament of Penance and Reconciliation always restores our relationship with God. The Sacrament can also help in the hard work of making things right with people we've hurt. A priest can help you figure out the best way of making reparation to others.

Telling the truth does not mean sharing private information that could hurt another person. For example, if a friend shared something confidential with you and asked you not to share what he or she told you with others, you must not break the confidence. This is especially important if revealing your friend's private information could embarrass him or her. The same applies to private information that you know about someone that you may have discovered indirectly, not through the person. It is important not to make that information public, especially if doing so could damage the person in some way. Of course, when another person's well-being or safety are at risk because of a secret they are keeping, then it would be appropriate to seek out a caring and responsible adult and enlist his or her assistance in helping the other person through a tough or dangerous situation. Keeping confidence is a matter of utmost importance to a priest hearing confession. A priest is obligated to always keep secret everything we confide to him when we make our confession.

Live It!

Practice Truthfulness Online

"Don't believe everything you read in the newspaper" used to be a common warning. It's still good advice, but with the growth of the Internet, blogs, online encyclopedias, and other information sources, we should be more careful than ever.

Society has a right to information based on truth and rooted in justice. Whichever side of the media you're on—providing information or using it—you should be cautious and fair.

For example, the Internet gives everyone the opportunity to be a reporter or to be news. Be truthful if you use websites that allow you to post personal pages. Don't give too much information or make yourself out to be someone you're not. Be cautious about believing or responding to what others say.

People of Faith
Archbishop Oscar Romero

© 2013 Saint Mary's Press/Illustration by Vicki Shuck

Imagine being a poor farmer in a land ruled by the rich. They could force you off your farm. If you protested, you might be kidnapped, tortured, or killed. This was El Salvador in the 1970s.

In 1977 Oscar Romero became archbishop of San Salvador, the capital city of El Salvador. Not long after that, his friend Fr. Rutilio Grande was killed. Father Grande had spoken boldly on behalf of the poor. Archbishop Romero realized that Jesus was executed for the same reason.

Every Sunday, poor El Salvadorans found hope as they listened to Archbishop Romero preach on the radio.

"How beautiful will be the day when a new society, instead of selfishly hoarding and keeping, apportions, shares, divides up, and all rejoice because we all feel we are children of the same God!" he said. "Anyone committed to the poor must suffer the same fate as the poor. And in El Salvador, we know the fate of the poor: to be taken away, to be tortured, to be jailed, to be found dead."

Thousands of El Salvadorans, including many priests and catechists, died in the struggle for rights and dignity.

On March 24, 1980, Romero was killed while celebrating Mass. Though those responsible for his murder may have hoped to silence him, his spirit lives on and continues to inspire the El Salvadoran people and all those who work for justice.

44 Respecting Sexuality

Key Words

sexuality

chastity

adultery

fornication

masturbation

pornography

homosexuality

concupiscence

temperance

You don't have to look far to see sexuality on display. Ads use it to sell burgers and blue jeans. TV shows treat sexual relations as a competition. Music stars wear outfits that leave little to the imagination. It's all out there.

Sexuality is about more than sexual relationships. **Sexuality** is about our identity as male or female, which includes our interest in and desire for sexual activity. Sexuality is one of life's greatest gifts. As your body

People today are constantly bombarded with sexual messages. Read this chapter to learn about sexual integrity in a sex-saturated society.

478

grows and changes, this gift becomes a stronger influence in your life. You'll find it challenging to respond to outside temptations and inner urges in a way that respects the gift and its giver—God.

Our bodies are evidence of God's great love. This is because we are able to love God and others through our bodies. Jesus tells us that the way we love others shows our love for God. He also tells us to love others as we love ourselves.

How do you want to be loved? Do you think your desire pleases God?

> The body is not to be used for sexual immorality, but to serve the Lord.
>
> 1 Corinthians 6:13

The Sixth Commandment: Sexuality Is a Gift

God was pleased by the way he made us: "God created human beings, making them to be like himself. He created them male and female" (Genesis 1:27). Your sex—that is, whether God created you as male or as female—is a gift. Both males and females reflect God's image in ways that are unique to each. By embracing and living our roles as males or females, we give glory to God. We reach the full potential God wants for us.

PRAY IT!

Lord Jesus, in times of sexual temptation, keep me strong. Give me temperance and patience, with myself and others, to save the gift of my body, so I may someday share it with my spouse and celebrate love in a way that honors you. Amen.

God also gives us personal dignity by creating us as either male or female. Each of us should realize and accept our identity as male or female.

Like many gifts, the gift of our sexuality can be misused. Jesus came to free people from the true death, the separation from God, that sin causes. The Bible has many accounts of how sexual sins damage our relationship with God, with others, and with ourselves. Jesus restored proper relationships simply because he was a model of sexual wholeness and purity, or **chastity**. He calls us to be honest and healthy by respecting his gift: our own sexuality and that of others.

?

Did You Know?

The Sacrament of Marriage

The Sacrament of Matrimony, or Marriage, is important in God's plan. Marriage is one man and one woman sharing a love that is total, unique, and exclusive. Married people have a responsibility to protect their relationship from all things that might hurt or destroy it. Obviously adultery is a big threat to marriage. Having more than one spouse (called polygamy), also goes against God's plan for true marriage. So does any attempt by two people of the same sex to marry each other. Living together in a sexual relationship without being sacramentally married is another offense to marriage.

Sometimes married couples aren't able to resolve conflicts, and they separate or divorce. Divorce, however, is not part of God's plan. It attempts to separate what God has joined together, and it creates upheaval that can harm families and even society (see CCC, 2400).

The Sixth Commandment challenges us to "not commit adultery." **Adultery** is sexual relations between two people, at least one of whom is married to another. But every person is called to be sexually pure, married or not.

It's important not to let our body's urges overwhelm our minds and spirits. Our bodies, minds, and spirits weave together into our personal integrity. Chastity holds us together when temptations threaten to unravel our integrity. Discipline, prayer, and an awareness of God's Commandments and virtues help us live a chaste life. We also need patience and persistence. Remember that mastering our desires is a lifelong process.

A rope unravels a little bit at a time. So can someone's sexual integrity. What are some of the consequences of giving in to sexual temptations?

Sexual Integrity

Before we explore ways people struggle with self-control, let's see why the Church cares so much about whether sexual raltionships take place only in marriage. God created sexual relationships for two purposes: to make new life and to express a loving union between a husband and wife and give them joy. These purposes must be woven into the minds, bodies, and spirits of a couple.

© teeeejay/iStockphoto.com

When one of these purposes is missing, sex fails to reflect our love for God. Sometimes young people get lost in lust and then engage in sex. Lust, the intense and uncontrolled desire for sexual pleasure, is different from love. Unfortunately, people who are interested in sex only for the pleasure have little commitment to their partners. They also don't think about the baby that could result or the people who would share the challenge of raising that baby.

For these reasons, sexuality shouldn't be treated as a plaything. Having sexual relations outside marriage, which the Bible calls **fornication**, dissolves our sexual wholeness. It may seem like everybody's doing it, but studies show that most young people your age are not. The false perception that "everyone is doing it" is wrong, and so is using this perception as an excuse to sin.

> God wants you to be holy and completely free
> from sexual immorality.
>
> 1 Thessalonians 4:3

Another challenge to chastity is **masturbation**. This is genital activity alone or with another person that stops short of sexual intercourse. It's a selfish pleasure that can easily become addictive. There's no possiblity of creating life, so masturbation just means using—or abusing—oneself. It's also no way to prove love to another person. Oral sex, for example, is a type of masturbation that exploits another person. It can also cause sexually transmitted infections. But the greatest cost of quick pleasure today is the damage it causes to the bond with your spouse in the future.

Pornography—explicit images or written descriptions meant to stimulate sexual feelings—cheapens our sexuality and damages human dignity. Pornography is more widespread than ever. The exploitation that once was limited to magazines or videos now floods the Internet. Some young people, perhaps trying to be cool, even post sexual photos of themselves online or send them in text messages. Pornography is dangerous because it's so addictive and it warps a person's respect for the dignity of others and the true goodness of sexuality.

Homosexuality

When we discuss sexuality, the subject of **homosexuality** requires special focus and care. Some people have strong sexual attractions to people of the same sex. This is sometimes called "having a homosexual inclination." Our Church affirms that people with homosexual inclinations are children of God. They must be treated with respect and compassion.

LITURGY CONNECTION

The Sign of Peace

When the priest says, "Let us offer each other the Sign of Peace," most folks shake hands casually. The Sign of Peace goes back to the early Church, when Christians exchanged a kiss of peace before Communion. Paul encouraged this practice: "Greet one another with the kiss of peace" (Romans 16:16).

This simple embrace, also called a holy kiss, reflected the caring love of God, not romantic, human love. Then and now, it's how we show we are at peace with one another before we receive Jesus, the Prince of Peace. Jesus tells us to resolve conflicts before we come to the altar: "Go at once and make peace with your brother, and then come back and offer your gift to God" (Matthew 5:24). Remember this as you share the Sign of Peace.

FUN FACT

One way to describe the Church's relationship with Christ is by using the image of the loving bond between a man and a woman in marriage. Jesus calls himself the bridegroom (see Mark 2:20). His love is so strong that he gave up his life for the Church. That's why you may hear people refer to the Church as the Bride of Christ.

Although the Church welcomes people with homosexual inclinations, homosexual acts are sinful because they are contrary to natural law and because they cannot result in new life. All people are called to be sexually pure, according to their states in life. People with a homosexual inclination face a lifelong challenge of self-control. The Church encourages them to go regularly to Mass and receive the Sacrament of Penance and Reconciliation. The Church also encourages those with a homosexual inclination to seek strength and support in wholesome friendships. God's grace and their own prayers, along with the prayers and encouragement of all in the Church community, will help them on their journey.

Before You Say "I Do"

No other commitment we can make to one person compares to marriage. God knows this. He created sexual intercourse to be an expression of love between married partners only.

Before a couple takes marriage vows, the priest asks them, "Have you come here freely and without reservation to give yourselves to each other in marriage?" They must make a free choice to enter into a faithful love, and for the rest of their lives they must uphold this covenant to be faithful in their marriage. Right after the vows, the priest says, "What God has

Why is it more special to wait until your birthday or Christmas to open your gifts? Imagine the joy of a bride and groom who wait until their wedding day to give each other the gift of sex.

© kozmabelatibor/iStockphoto.com

joined, men must not divide." This reminder applies to all who hear it, including the couple.

A married couple faces many challenges, including keeping the vow to "accept children lovingly from God."

The two spouses share in God's creative power, and that gives them a powerful responsibility. They may wish to space the births of their children, but they must do this through natural methods. They may have good reasons to avoid pregnancy, but these reasons are not excuses to use morally wrong methods. Immoral methods include being surgically sterilized; using chemical contraceptives; or using barrier methods, such as a condom or diaphragm.

Think About It!

Some young people always feel like they need to be going out with somebody. Some classmates may say that experimenting sexually is a sign that you're cool, or that not going out on dates shows that you're not. Ads and media can pressure you to rush into relationships before you are ready.

How do you ignore the outside pressures and be yourself? How can you be sure your comfort level with relationships also pleases God?

485

The Ninth Commandment: Keeping Your Heart Clean

There's more to the Sixth Commandment than meets the eye. We find even more guidance in the Ninth Commandment: "You shall not covet your neighbor's wife." This Commandment goes beyond wanting someone's wife or husband. It acknowledges the tendency to sin that we all experience as a result of Original Sin. This is called **concupiscence**. Intense

?

Did You Know?

The Wise Choice

A little knowledge can be risky. Consider the story of Adam and Eve, after they ate from the tree of knowledge. The Book of Genesis says, "They realized they were naked; so they sewed fig leaves together and covered themselves" (3:7).

You're wise enough to know that lust arises when people dress or act immodestly. You also know what can happen if you have sex.

The only sure way you can avoid pregnancy and please God in matters of sexuality is by not having sex. Sexual abstinence—not having sex until you are married—is your wisest choice. Most important, it is the chaste choice.

Also, abstinence is 100 percent safe and moral. When you are older and ready to wed, the Church can teach you about natural family planning. For now, rest assured that abstinence is the right choice.

desire for sexual pleasure is called lust. This desire can overwhelm us, as the body rebels against the spirit. Lust makes us less able to make good moral decisions. It becomes a daily struggle.

> My friends, fill your minds with those things that are good and that deserve praise: things that are true, noble, right, pure, lovely, and honorable.
>
> Philippians 4:8

We are not alone in facing such struggles. The Holy Spirit gives us **temperance**, a virtue that helps us overcome our passions (see chapter 38, "Living the Moral Life," of this handbook). Temperance is a wonderful example of how God has provided us with a virtue to help us fight a sin. With sexual temptation all around us, avoiding it is not always so simple. Chastity must be our lifestyle. Chastity begins as we purify our hearts by focusing our desires on God's plan for sexuality.

What you wear sends a message about who you are. Choosing clothes that are attractive yet modest can help protect your sexual integrity.

Our moral personalities are centered in our hearts. Jesus teaches us: "From your heart come the evil ideas which lead you to kill, commit adultery, and do other immoral things" (Matthew 15:19). On a more positive note, he also tells us, "Happy are the pure in heart; / they will see God!" (5:8).

© Hurst Photo/Shutterstock.com

Purity of heart helps us see things from God's perspective. We see the body—ours and our neighbor's—as a dwelling of the Holy Spirit and as evidence of God's beauty. Don't you hope other people see you the same way? Trendy clothes, cosmetics, perfumes, or body sprays can't change your heart. Wouldn't you rather that people be attracted to who you are and what's inside you?

The virtue of modesty protects our intimate centers. We send signals to others by the clothes we

Live It!

The Heart–Body Connection

Keeping our hearts pure means we must keep the rest of our bodies clean too. Here are some clean thoughts:

- **Your eyes.** Watch what you watch. Avoid TV shows and movies that trivialize or cheapen the gift of love.
- **Your ears.** Now hear this! Tune out songs with sexually tempting or abusive lyrics.
- **Your mouth.** Don't tell jokes or use obscene language that cheapens sex or makes fun of people's bodies.
- **Your hands.** Keep them to yourself. While you're at it, fold them as you pray for strength against temptation.

Jesus says that if our eyes or hands make us lose our faith, we should get rid of them (see Matthew 5:29–30). He is exaggerating to make a point. Jesus wants us to take seriously our call to keep our hearts and bodies pure.

wear, the words we say, and the way we act sexually. When your shirt doesn't say or show too much, when your pants don't sag too low or your skirt isn't too short, or when you avoid using curse words, you have chosen modesty. Modesty is a choice not to follow the crowd or rush toward a false sense of maturity. Patience and self-discipline are keys to modesty, which leads to purity of heart. That puts us on the two-way road to sexual respect.

Church History

In Defense of Marriage and the Church

England's King Henry VIII (1491–1547) wanted to end his marriage to Catherine of Aragon so he could marry Anne Boleyn. But Pope Clement VII denied his request for a divorce. So Henry asked the English Parliament to make him supreme head of the Church of England. In 1533 Parliament passed an act that required all English subjects to take oaths recognizing Henry's supremacy over the Church.

Bishop John Fisher and Sir Thomas More disagreed with Henry's desire to dissolve his marriage, and they felt he was committing adultery by marrying Anne Boleyn. They also could not swear an oath that placed the king above the spiritual authority of the Pope. Because they followed their conscience, they were convicted of treason and beheaded in 1535. More's last words on the scaffold are well known: "I die the King's good servant, but God's first." Both men were canonized in 1935. Today, we celebrate their joint feast day on June 22.

45 WORKING FOR JUSTICE

KEY WORDS

social justice
charity
common good
solidarity

Hopeful voices often rise up on dark days. People hear about human tragedies or natural disasters and respond generously. "I just want to do my part," they say. Then they roll up their sleeves or open their wallets to help strangers. But are folks always so willing to help others?

Imagine if we were. When we learn to love as God loves, we see strangers as neighbors. Our sacrificial actions can break down

In the aftermath of Hurricane Sandy, millions of people wanted to help. Are people always so willing to help others?

© MIKE SEGAR/Reuters/Corbis

walls of hate and replace them with bridges of hope. Incredibly, every one of us can help prevent future tragedies from happening. Yes, that means you!

That All May Be One

To love as God loves, it helps to understand what God is like. The Bible reveals that God is three Divine Persons—Father, Son, and Holy Spirit—in one God. These three Divine Persons are a communion of perfect love and peace. We must follow the example of the Holy Trinity by being a community that loves and cares for all people.

> I pray that they may all be one. Father! May they be in us, just as you are in me and I am in you. May they be one, so that the world will believe that you sent me.
>
> John 17:21

The Church works to transform our world into a loving community where people respect one another, share the earth's goods, and settle conflicts peacefully. Our goal is **social justice**—a respect for all creation and for human rights that allows people to get what they need to live in dignity.

PRAY IT!

Lord, when do I see you hungry or thirsty? When do I see you as a stranger or an outcast? Open my eyes, Lord, to help me see you in the eyes of my sisters and brothers in need. Let my eyes shine with welcome for the strangers I see. Let my eyes run with tears of compassion for the hurting. Let my eyes focus more sharply on the path that leads to justice, so that someday I'll gaze forever into your eyes. Amen.

What do people need? We need more than just things—food, shelter, clothing, and health care, although these are important. We need respect. We need the freedom to shape our own destinies. We also need life-giving relationships with other people. Sound complicated?

Suppose some bullies took your friend's lunch money. Would you offer her half your sandwich? Or would you give her just the crumbs left after you eat it? If you split the sandwich, how would you feel later in the day about being hungry? What can you do

?

Did You Know?

Charity and Justice

Imagine being hungry every day of your life. You need to have food. You also need to change whatever is causing your hunger. The Church takes on both needs through works of charity and justice.

We begin with **charity**, which means working to meet people's immediate physical needs. But we also work for justice, which means challenging society to eliminate the things that cause people to be hungry, homeless, jobless, and so on.

Feeding someone is a work of charity. But you don't have enough food to share with every hungry person in the world. That's where justice comes in. Working for justice starts by asking, "Why are people hungry?" Then you must listen to the answer. For example, some hungry people are suffering because of drought or famine. Other hungry people might need jobs to earn the money for food. If we bring people together to support the right needs, we help make the Good News happen.

to stop the bullies tomorrow? Can you form a group to prevent bullying, so your friend isn't victimized every day?

© Will & Deni McIntyre/CORBIS

Saint Paul tells us we are Christ's body. Each of us is a unique and necessary part of the body. "If one part of the body suffers, all the other parts suffer with it" (1 Corinthians 12:26). As a Christian you respond to other people's pain or suffering with compassion. We should see ourselves in other people, whether they're friends or strangers, and give them the same dignity and rights we hope they'll give us.

> Love your neighbor as you love yourself.
> Matthew 22:39

What does sharing a lunch have to do with bullying? Read the story on the previous page. Then read the Did You Know? sidebar to find out how the story relates to charity and justice.

Together for Good

If you decided to take action to stop bullying that happens in your school, you would be working for the **common good**. Working for the common good means all people, as either individuals or groups, are given the opportunity to fulfill all their needs and the needs of their family. Every group—from your parish, to your school student council to the U.S. Congress—

FUN FACT

Saint Vincent de Paul was a French priest in the 1600s who helped poor people. A group named for him continues his great work today. It's a wonder he ever had a chance to do any good. Pirates captured Vincent soon after he was ordained, and he was sold into slavery for seven years. But after this rough start, he still had plenty of time to do God's work of charity and justice.

must work to pursue the common good and create and support institutions that improve the condition of human life. Catholic social teaching tells us we all have a duty to work together for the common good.

Our society should make it easier, not harder, to live in freedom and to practice virtues—the good habits that help us accomplish good things and make good choices. A country's laws should reflect God's Law. And human laws must never require people to do anything against God's Law. People in authority must "work and care for the good of all"[1] (*CCC*, 1897). Saint Paul says that authorities are established by God and must serve him: "They are God's servants working for your own good" (Romans 13:4).

The laws of every nation must be in keeping with God's Law. What if they are not?

It doesn't always seem that way. We often witness political leaders behaving in greedy, power hungry, or self-serving ways. They're not alone. All the way back to Adam, we see humans, including ourselves, making self-centered choices. The challenge for leaders is to be truly committed to the common good. Political leaders must work for the good of all people, and they must do so by respecting his Commandments—God's moral law.

Helping poor people is everyone's responsibility, but Jesus tells us to be humble about it: "When you give something to a needy person, do not make a big show of it" (Matthew 6:2). We should give people what they need without taking away their pride and without trying to show off. Giving money, goods, and respect to people in need is pleasing to God.

Each person has God-given dignity because each person is created in God's image. To maintain that dignity, we all must work for the common good. We must create and support institutions that improve human conditions. Society works for the common good and helps bring about social justice when it provides what people need to live out their God-given dignity.

LITURGY CONNECTION

Do You Have Ears to Hear?

Be an intense listener at Mass. When you hear a reading from a prophet like Isaiah, think about his words of hope and to whom he was giving hope. Close your eyes when you listen to the Gospel and think about the people in the stories. What kind of fear or despair did they feel? What did victims, outcasts, and sinners hope that Jesus would do or say?

At its root, the word *compassion* means "to suffer with." Listen with compassion, feel the pain, and experience the joy Jesus brings.

© Rick D'Elia/Corbis

Give people fish, and they eat for a day. Teach them to fish, and they eat for a lifetime. How does the photo illustrate this saying?

Today, in many countries around the world, people continue to struggle for justice. Their problems are complex and far bigger than any one person—or even the people of one country—can overcome alone. Athough local, state, and national governments must work for the common good, we also need to organize society to work for justice on a global level. International federations such as the United Nations (UN), as well as charitable organizations like Catholic Relief Services (CRS), offer hope that injustice can be overcome when people come together.

The Secret Is Out

Catholic social teaching has been called our Church's best-kept secret, but its wisdom comes alive when we learn and live it.

Our moral vision of society begins with respect for human life and dignity. We are made in God's image, gifted with a soul, and redeemed by Jesus. So we all share an equal dignity, and we are all entitled to all the rights God intended humans to have. That goes for unborn babies, people dying in hospitals, and criminals in jail.

Catholic social teaching is concerned with making sure all people have what they need—food, clothing, shelter, health care, respect, education, work,

© Shepard Sherbell/CORBIS SABA

Helping people in Haiti is an example of charity. Why is it important to also work for justice for the people of this poor country?

community, freedom, and all the fundamental rights that flow from human dignity—to live out the vocation God calls us to.

A good test for our society is to see how our poorest and weakest, or most vulnerable, members are doing. It is a social sin when the gap between the rich and the poor is so great that some people live in extreme luxury while others go without food, jobs, homes, or health care. The gap between those who are rich and those who are poor in our world grows bigger every day, so we must work hard to bridge that sinful gap. We say the Church has an "option for the poor and vulnerable." This means the Church, like Jesus, who loved and helped so many people in need, must get involved when people's rights or well-being are being threatened. Jesus tells us he was sent "to bring good news to the poor" (Luke 4:18).

THiNk About It!

In the Creation account in the Book of Genesis, God gave dominion, or authority, over creation. What choices have humans made that help preserve the environment? What choices have hurt the environment? What choices can you make to help care for God's creation?

Happy are you poor; the Kingdom of God is
yours! . . . But how terrible for you who are
rich now; you have had your easy life!

Luke 6:20,24

It's great news when good jobs and wages bring
people out of poverty. Work should be more than something people do for a paycheck. Our work is how we
join God in his ongoing work of creation. This brings
dignity to work. That means workers should never be
taken for granted. They should have fair wages, the
right to join unions, and the ability to start their own
businesses.

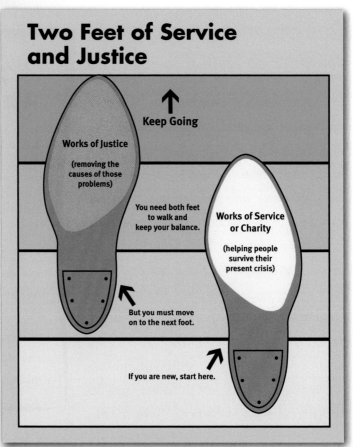

Two Feet of Service and Justice

Keep Going

Works of Justice

(removing the causes of those problems)

You need both feet to walk and keep your balance.

Works of Service or Charity

(helping people survive their present crisis)

But you must move on to the next foot.

If you are new, start here.

Adapted from USCCB, *Poverty and Faith Justice*, page 20

Everyone is our brother and sister: from a child stitching soccer balls in China to an unborn baby in a womb to an old woman suffering from hunger in Africa. Their needs are ours. Living in **solidarity** means not only that we share our material goods though charity but also that we share our friendship and prayers with other people. Pope Paul VI taught us, "If you want Peace, work for Justice" ("Message of His Holiness Pope Paul VI for the Celebration of the Day of Peace"). Our efforts for justice can prevent wars and bring unity to a divided world.

Live It!

Make a Difference

So many people have so many needs in the world. How can our efforts make a lasting difference? Remember these tips:

+ **Don't go it alone.** Work with friends who care about the problems you do.
+ **Ask why.** For example, don't just organize a food drive every year. Ask why people are hungry. Ask your elected leaders what they're doing to help.
+ **Dig deeper.** Before you volunteer somewhere or do a service project, read about the issue you're addressing (for example, hunger) on the Internet or in newspapers or magazines. See what the Bible and Church teachings say about that issue. Then when you serve, you'll be more aware.
+ **Smile.** Even though the work may be hard or seem hopeless, your smiles offer the gift of hope to the people you serve. You're making a difference.

© kirin_photo/iStockphoto.com

Recycling is one way to care for God's creation. Can you name other ways you can be a good steward?

We also need to be one with the earth itself. In the Book of Genesis, God tells us to care for all creation. It's time for all of us to be good stewards of the land, water, plants, and animals. Keep in mind the wisdom of the Iroquois, a league of American Indian nations. They advocate for making decisions based on how our choices will affect the next seven generations. The changes we make now to conserve energy, water, and other resources will have a lasting effect on generations of people to come after us.

Remember the brave Apostles who would not let society's laws keep them from preaching. They would have been killed if not for Gamaliel, a Pharisee, who told his fellow leaders: "Leave them alone! If what they have planned and done is of human origin, it will disappear, but if it comes from God, you cannot possibly defeat them" (Acts 5:38–39). What the Apostles planned did come from God. Now it's your turn to be part of God's plan.

PEOPLE OF FAITH
Dorothy Day

© 2013 Saint Mary's Press/Illustration by Vicki Shuck

If changing the world seems to be impossible, get to know Dorothy Day.

Dorothy lived many of her childhood years in Chicago's slums. Although she overcame poverty, she never forgot the pain it causes. She wanted to help others in need.

Dorothy was a great writer and journalist with a strong sense of compassion and vocation. She prayed to find ways to use these gifts.

During the Great Depression in the 1930s, Dorothy met Peter Maurin, a man with a mind for social change. He wanted to start a newspaper, so together they launched the *Catholic Worker*. Each edition applied the Gospel to modern problems.

Writing was not enough, so Dorothy led the way in taking direct action. She established Catholic Worker houses, which opened their doors to hungry, homeless people. Catholic Workers marched with striking workers and went to jail for war protests.

Today, more than 185 Catholic Worker communities promote nonviolence, voluntary poverty, prayer, and hospitality for people in need. Dorothy's desire became a revolution.

"The greatest challenge of the day is how to bring about a revolution of the heart," she said, "a revolution which has to start with each one of us."

502

PART 4

PRAYER

Our Father, who art in heaven,
hallowed be thy name;
Thy kingdom come.
Thy will be done on earth as it is in heaven.
Give us this day our daily bread,
and forgive us our trespasses,
*   as we forgive those who trespass against us,*
and lead us not into temptation,
but deliver us from evil.
Amen.

46 The Bible: Models of Prayer

Key Words

praise
petition
Magnificat

What new skill have you learned in the last two years? Maybe you learned a new sport, a new game, or the features on a new phone. How did you learn your new skill? Did you read instructions, have someone show you, or just learn it all on your own? One great way to learn or improve a skill is by watching a person who already has that skill. This person can be

Our parents, godparents, and other family members can be great models of prayer. Perhaps they taught you your first prayers, or shared their favorite way to pray.

© CEFutcher/iStockphoto.com

a role model or mentor to show you the skill you want to learn or improve.

Can you think of some religious skills that we can learn and improve on? One is how to pray. You will learn more about praying and the different types of prayer in the next few chapters. But you can best learn how to pray by having good role models to imitate. You might already know a good role model for prayer: perhaps a parent or grandparent, a sibling, or a priest or nun. You can also find good role models for prayer in the Bible. This chapter looks at three of them: King David, the Virgin Mary, and Jesus Christ himself, who taught us how to pray.

King David

King David had great faith in, and great love for, the Lord. We see the great trust he placed in God when he fought the giant named Goliath: "The LORD has saved me from lions and bears; he will save me from this Philistine" (1 Samuel 17:37). We also see David's faith when he prayed for guidance before going into battle (see 23:2). And we see his great joy in the presence of the Lord, when the Ark of the Covenant was brought to Jerusalem: "David, wearing

PRAY IT!

Let us praise the Lord, the God of Israel!
    He has come to the help
        of his people and has
        set them free.
He has provided for us a
        mighty Savior,
    a descendant of his
        servant David. . . .
Our God is merciful and
        tender.
He will cause the bright dawn
        of salvation to rise on
        us
    and to shine from heaven
        on all those who live
        in the dark shadow of
        death,
to guide our steps into
        the path of peace.

(Based on the Canticle of Zechariah, Luke 1:68–69,78–79)

only a linen cloth around his waist, danced with all his might to honor the LORD" (2 Samuel 6:14).

We can read some of David's prayers in the historical books and in the Psalms. He modeled several different forms of prayer for us. One of those forms is **praise**. David has a wonderful prayer of praise in 2 Samuel 7:18–29. Here are a couple of verses:

How great you are, Sovereign LORD! There is none like you; we have always known that you alone are God. There is no other nation on earth like Israel, whom you rescued from slavery to make them your own people. The great and wonderful things you did for them have spread your fame throughout the world. (Verses 22–23)

Another form of prayer is **petition**, asking God for something. David needed God's help with plenty of things: political enemies, foreign invaders, ruling a kingdom. Psalm 28, which David may have written or inspired, is this type of prayer.

O LORD, my defender, I call to you.
    Listen to my cry! . . .
Hear me when I cry to you for help,
    when I lift my hands toward
        your holy Temple.
                        (Verses 1–2)

THiNk AbouT IT!

King David, the Virgin Mary, and Jesus are models of prayer. Look over the prayers of King David presented in this chapter. Choose one from each of these three models. Write each one in large letters on a sheet of art paper. Decorate the borders. Place the prayers in your room at home, and use them for your morning or night prayers. (Hint: You can find more of David's prayers in the Book of Psalms.) What can you learn from praying the prayers of these great models of prayer?

This painting, *King David Before the Ark of the Covenant*, is by Giambattista Pittoni. It illustrates David's sorrow as he begs God's forgiveness. Why might it take courage to ask for forgiveness?

© Arte & Immagini srl/CORBIS

Perhaps David's best-known prayer is his prayer asking God for forgiveness. David was guilty of both adultery and murder, two very serious sins. In Psalm 51 he asks for God's forgiveness with very moving words. You should read the whole Psalm, but here is a portion:

> Be merciful to me, O God,
>> because of your constant love.
>
> . . . .
>
> Wash away all my evil
>> and make me clean from my sin!
>
> I recognize my faults;
>> I am always conscious of my sins.
>>> (Verses 1–3)

> Create a pure heart in me, O God,
>> and put a new and loyal spirit in me.
>
> Do not banish me from your presence;
>> do not take your holy spirit away from me.
>>> Psalm 51:10–11

FUN FACT

Cousins are relatives that are often about the same age and often share important milestones at a similar time. Although Elizabeth was older than Mary, both of them were pregnant at the same time. Both were going to be mothers. Their sons, Jesus and John the Baptist, would be cousins too! Ask God to bless your own cousins!

David's example shows us how to ask for God's help and forgiveness.

The Virgin Mary

The Virgin Mary, the Mother of God, is another wonderful prayer role model. Her heart was completely committed to God's will, even before the birth of Jesus. When the angel Gabriel appeared to her to tell her that she would give birth to the Son of God, she must have been filled with questions (see Luke 1:26–38). But without hesitation she answered, "I am the Lord's servant . . . may it happen to me as you have said" (1:38). Mary is our best model for saying yes to God in our prayers.

> You are the most blessed of all women,
> and blessed is the child you will bear!
> Luke 1:42

When Mary visited her cousin Elizabeth, she spoke words that have become one of the most treasured prayers in the Bible. It is called the Canticle of Mary, or the **Magnificat**. You can read it in Luke 1:46–55. Mary started the prayer by praising God for his faithfulness to her:

> My heart praises the Lord;
> my soul is glad because of God my Savior,
> for he has remembered me, his lowly
> servant!
>
> (Verses 46–48)

Then she praised God for his justice:

> He has filled the hungry
> with good things,
> and sent the rich away
> with empty hands.
>
> (Verse 53)

In the *Magnificat,* Mary models confidence in God's loving goodness. She shows her awareness of his saving work in the world. We should follow Mary's example and also look for signs of God's presence in our lives.

Jesus Christ

It was Jesus Christ, the Son of God made man, who taught us how to pray. Some people might think they could never be like Jesus. We need to remember that Jesus has a human nature, just like us. Because of his human nature, he needed to maintain his relationship with his Father through prayer, just as we do.

LITURGY CONNECTION

The Washing of the Feet

Once a year, during the Liturgy of Holy Thursday, we experience the ritual of the washing of the feet. In this ritual, the priest, like Jesus, takes a towel, a pitcher, and a bowl of water, and washes the feet of twelve parishioners. Why does he do this? And what does this have to do with prayer?

When Jesus washed the feet of his disciples, he was sending them a message. The message was the exact same message he sent when he changed bread and wine into his Body and Blood: Do this (see John 13:14–15). Jesus was again being a teacher, asking his disciples to follow him not only with their minds and hearts but also with their actions.

In the washing of the feet, Jesus taught us that service to others is prayer in action. Prayer changes us into people who can love and serve. And when we serve others, we are truly blessed (see John 13:17).

Here are some of the many ways we find Jesus praying in the Gospels. Learn from Jesus and make these your ways of praying too.

- **Jesus prayed alone.** We read in the Gospel of Luke, "But he [Jesus] would go away to lonely places, where he prayed" (5:16). Jesus knew it was important to spend time alone with God.

- **Jesus prayed with others.** We know that Jesus prayed with others in synagogues, on the Sabbath. He also prayed with his disciples: "Jesus took Peter, John, and James with him and went up a hill to pray" (Luke 9:28).

- **Jesus prayed for others.** At the Last Supper, Jesus prayed for his disciples: "I have made you known to those whom you gave me. . . . I pray for them" (John 17:6,9). He also prayed for us! "I pray not only for them, but also for those who believe in me because of their message" (verse 20).

- **Jesus prayed both short prayers and long prayers.** Sometimes Jesus was moved by the moment to pray a spontaneous short prayer, like this one: "Father, Lord of heaven and earth! I thank you because you have shown to the unlearned what you have hidden from the wise and learned" (Luke 10:21). But at other times he prayed all night long (see Luke 6:12).

You might recognize the memorable account of when Jesus prayed in the garden on the Mount of Olives after the Last Supper. He knew he was about to suffer and die. The Gospel of Matthew tells us what he did: "He went a little farther on, threw himself face downward on the ground, and prayed, 'My Father, if it is possible, take this cup of suffering from me! Yet

Live It!

Live Your Prayer

As followers of Jesus, we are called to live our prayer. What does this mean? It means that our prayer is not just words alone but actions as well. The models of prayer we studied in this chapter can help us to connect our prayers to action.

+ King David admitted his faults. This is hard for anyone to do, whether one is a king or a student in middle school. But admitting what we have done wrong is the first step in putting things right! Asking forgiveness and confessing our sins in the Sacrament of Penance and Reconciliation are the best things we can do to help ourselves grow into mature Christians.

+ The Virgin Mary praised God and prayed for others. At the beginning of Jesus' public ministry, we see Mary ask him for a favor: She asked a favor for a newly married couple who had run out of wine at their wedding. Mary reminds us that it is always good to ask God to bless others.

+ Jesus trusted in God's will. Jesus spoke with his Father often, and was obedient to his will. We see this especially the night before his Passion. Although Jesus feared the suffering that was to come, he followed his prayer with action and fulfilled the Father's will.

not what I want, but what you want'" (26:39). This prayer shows us Jesus' human nature. He did not want to suffer—none of us wants to suffer. But doing his Father's will was his life's purpose and mission. This is a beautiful example of what our prayer can be: We can pour our hearts out to God, but in the end we commit ourselves to doing God's will.

> I pray not only for them, but also for those who believe in me because of their message. I pray that they may all be one. Father! May they be in us, just as you are in me and I am in you. May they be one, so that the world will believe that you sent me.
>
> John 17:20–21

Did You Know?

Why Do We Pray to Mary?

Mary is not only the Mother of God. We also call her the Mother of the Church, which means she is the mother of all Christians. This is why many Catholics also pray to Mary. This does not mean that we think Mary is God or that she grants people special favors. But by praying to her, we acknowledge her special role in God's plan. And we know that she loves us very much and will also pray for the needs we bring to her.

Church History

The Upper Room

Before Jesus' Ascension he instructed his disciples to go back to Jerusalem and wait for the coming of the Holy Spirit. Mary and the Apostles gathered in the "upper room," which, for that reason, became an important symbol of prayer to the early Christians. Because the Last Supper also took place in an "upper room," these two rooms were often considered to be the same place. Sometimes the upper room is called the cenacle, from a Latin word meaning "meal." The actual "upper room" no longer exists in Jerusalem. However, a replica, which was built by the Crusaders in the twelfth century, can be found there. It is located above the Tomb of David and near the Benedictine Abbey of the Dormition on Mount Zion.

The floor of this twelfth-century building goes back to the second century, and may have been the site of a church existing in the year AD 130. In the early years of the Church, churches were built over or near significant holy places, so the actual upper room may have been nearby. During his papacy, on March 23, 2000, Saint John Paul II visited the upper room on this site and celebrated Mass there.

In 1826, in France, Saint Therese Couderc and Fr. Stephen Terme founded the Sisters of the Cenacle. This congregation, which is now established around the world, devotes itself to the ministry of prayer, helping people deepen their relationship with God through retreats, spiritual direction, adult faith formation, and other spiritual ministries.

41 PRAYER: CONVERSATION with God

Messages to God

Do you ever wish you could send a text message to God? In today's world of cell phones and instant messaging, we are used to communicating with other people quickly. No matter where you go, you can reach friends and family by using technology. Technology has brought us

Talking to God is as simple as having a conversation with a best friend. If you could send a text message to God, what would you say?

God — 7:55 AM

I am here for you. Talk to me.
7:30 AM

Hey God . . .
7:49 AM

My life is confusing. Help me get thru today.
7:51 AM

I love you!
7:52 AM

closer together by giving us the tools to be in constant touch with one another.

Prayer is our way of staying in touch with God at all times. When you pray, you strengthen your relationship with God as you would with your friend.

What Is Prayer?

When you were a young child, your parents probably chose your friends for you. You played together, sharing toys and doing fun things. Now that you are older, friendships mean something different. You can choose your own friends, and the conversations go beyond the sandbox or playground to deeper subjects. The more time you spend with a person, the more you have to talk about: movies, sports, school, people you know. You share good times, as well as problems you have. Good friends never run out of things to say to each other.

Likewise, when you were a young child, your parents introduced you to God. Since then you have been learning more about God the Father, Jesus Christ, and the Holy Spirit, through the Church. For thousands of years, the Holy Spirit has been teaching the children of God to pray. The

PRAY IT!

Jesus, send us your Spirit so we can know God's will for us too. Teach us to pray constantly so we may grow as close to the Father as you are. Give us faith to always pray, even when it seems like our prayers are not being heard. Help us to know that our loving Father in Heaven always hears us and responds with love. Amen.

Holy Spirit teaches us through Sacred Tradition, the living transmission of God's truth to us. The Holy Spirit in the Church keeps the lines of divine communication open between us and God. God is always inviting us to be on his wavelength through prayer. Any time you take a moment to raise your heart and mind to God, you are praying. When you take the time to tell God about your day, share your worries, ask for advice, or

?

Did You Know?

The Psalms:
Great Prayers for All Ages

Sacred Scripture tells us that people have been talking to God since he breathed life into Adam and Eve. In every book of the Bible, you will find both holy people and sinners who call out to God for help. You can hear their voices praising God, giving thanks for all he has done for them. Check out the Psalms for some of the greatest prayers of all time. Like different types of music, they help us express some of the same emotions and concerns people had three thousand years ago. The following are a few psalms and their subjects:

+ Psalm 3: Morning Prayer for Help
+ Psalm 10: A Prayer for Justice
+ Psalm 59: A Prayer for Safety
+ Psalm 85: A Prayer for the Nation's Welfare
+ Psalm 95: A Song of Praise
+ Psalm 102: The Prayer of a Troubled Youth
+ Psalm 141: An Evening Prayer

request good things from him, God is listening. Like any good relationship, the more time you spend with God in prayer, the easier the conversation. You never run out of things to say to each other.

Tuning In to God

The key to a growing relationship is spending time together, talking, and listening to each other. God never gets tired of wanting to be with us. Starting with Genesis, the first book of the Bible, we hear the stories of God calling and humans responding. Abraham and God made a sacred agreement, or covenant, with each other. Moses argued with God because he did not like the assignment to lead God's people out of Egypt. The prophets complained to

When friends spend a lot of time together, they get to know each other pretty well. Likewise, spending time with God can make your relationship stronger.

© Corbis

FUN FACT

Humans breathe more than twenty-three thousand times each day. Without that air coming into and leaving our bodies, we cannot live. Just being aware of our breathing can be an act of prayer. Imagine inhaling God's life twenty-three thousand times a day!

God too but responded to his call. We know Jesus and his Father talked with each other throughout Jesus' life on this earth. The history of God's people shows us that prayer is always a back-and-forth exchange. God reaches out to get our attention, and we respond.

Today, God might use other ways to get our attention. Remember that God's love is like sound waves broadcasting during every nano-second of our lives. Prayer is something like the radio that helps us tune in so we can experience this love. Like our favorite stations, God is always available to us, but unless we take the time to tune in, we fail to recognize the power of grace—God's presence in our lives.

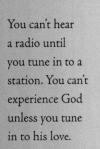

You can't hear a radio until you tune in to a station. You can't experience God unless you tune in to his love.

© ben bryant/Shutterstock.com

Tuning in to God may take just a few moments, or we might spend a longer time, as we would when we listen to our favorite songs or artists. When we pray, we can take a few seconds to check out how God is playing in our lives. We may want to linger longer, listening and experiencing the divine music that plays constantly in our soul.

When we take time to give thanks to God for a new day, we are praying. When we stop to admire something in nature, we praise God, our Creator. Any time we acknowledge that God is the source of blessings in our lives, we raise our minds and hearts to God. We are tuning in and paying attention to God, who is trying to get our attention. Because God blesses us, we bless him in return.

> Be joyful always, pray at all times, be thankful in all circumstances. This is what God wants from you.
>
> 1 Thessalonians 5:16

LITURGY CONNECTION

Praying the Mass

Have you ever considered that Mass is a prayer? In fact, it is the *ultimate* prayer of the Church. Just as you get together with your friends to share stories, music, and a meal, so we gather as the People of God. From the opening Sign of the Cross, we are talking with God, who is present with us in a real way. God is with us when we hear the proclamation of Scripture and when we share the Body and Blood of Jesus. Because Jesus Christ is really present with us, Communion is the perfect communication between God and us.

© ruigsantos/Shutterstock.com

Check out the Jugular Prayer in the Live It! article on the next page. God dwells within you. You can feel it!

Check out the Jugular Prayer in the Live It! article on the next page.

When to Pray

Because God is always communicating with us, are we supposed to pray nonstop? That is exactly what Paul tells us. We are to pray constantly. Prayer is as essential to our soul as air is to our bodies. Because nothing can separate us from the love of God, it is always possible to pray.

If you are always praying, when would you go to school, spend time with other friends, or get your homework done? How about sports or other activities or just having fun? How can you pray when you are sleeping? Isn't it impossible to tune in to God at every moment of every day?

Because God is always communicating with us, just being open to his presence is an act of prayer. We grow in our faith and our spirituality by being aware that God is loving us throughout our day. The more often we tune in, the more we experience the benefits of an active prayer life. Just as your mind and heart are always working even when you are not thinking about it, your soul is always at work too.

THiNk ABoUT IT!

Who taught you to pray? What was your favorite prayer as a young child? What is your favorite prayer today? What times of day do you pray it?

When Prayer Is Difficult

Sometimes it's difficult to pray. Life can be hectic, and we may feel overloaded at times. With TV, computers, magazines, and radio, we are often bombarded with too much information. So many distractions can keep us from tuning in to God as often as we should. At other times we may feel as though we experience a dropped call when we pray. Do you ever wonder if God is listening? Do you sometimes just feel like not talking to God?

LIVE IT!

The Jugular Prayer

Praying constantly may seem impossible, but prayer can be as close as your fingertips. You can easily raise your mind and heart to God by actually feeling the connection between your brain and your heart. Do this by praying the Jugular Prayer.

First, place your first and second fingers on the side of your neck until you locate the pulse of your jugular vein. Feel the blood flowing from your brain to your heart. Be aware of God's life within you.

Just practicing this act of touch can remind you of God's presence. Use it to slow yourself down during the day. Try it in the middle of an argument or to ask God's inspiration during a stressful moment. It is an "anytime, anywhere prayer" (Hays, *Prayer Notes to a Friend*, page 33).

Some of the greatest friends of God—the saints—have described similar difficulties with prayer. Even before the kind of technology we have in our lives today, some people throughout the ages have felt distracted. Others have described feeling separated from God. They talk about a kind of dryness in their relationship.

Like any friendship, our relationship with God will have ups and downs. But God is amazingly patient. He wants us to keep calling, just as he keeps calling us. Our desire to be faithful through these difficult periods is all he asks of us. When we keep turning back to God even when we seem to get a busy signal, we experience **conversion**, a change of heart that keeps us in touch with the one who loves us beyond all our understanding.

> LORD, you have examined me and you know me.
> You know everything I do; from far away you
> understand all my thoughts. You see me, whether
> I am working or resting; you know all my
> actions. . . . Your knowledge of me is too deep;
> it is beyond my understanding.
>
> Psalm 139:1–3,6

PEOPLE OF FAITH
Saint Teresa of Ávila

© 2013 Saint Mary's Press/Illustration by Vicki Shuck

Saint Teresa of Ávila used the image of a castle to describe her prayer life. She was born in 1515 in Ávila, Spain, where some of the great castles of Europe still remain. In her book *The Interior Castle*, Saint Teresa pictured the soul as a beautiful castle where God lives in the innermost chamber. Some of the rooms are up above, others down below, others to the sides. But in the center and middle is the main dwellingplace where the secret exchanges between God and the soul happen. Only through prayer can a person enter this secret place.

Although she lived a life of holiness, Saint Teresa did not always find it easy to pray, to explore her interior castle. She compared prayer to physical exercise. At first, it is hard and does not seem to produce immediate results. But those who practice prayer often experience feelings of excitement, joy, and peace. Life seems to come alive for them. God invites you to visit him in your interior castle. Will you go on this adventure?

48 Tuning In to God

Do you have a favorite radio station? Do you listen to some singers or bands more than others? Does a particular kind of music appeal to you more than others? Perhaps you like rock or rap, country or classical. Whatever your taste, music can touch your soul. Remember that prayer is the way we get in touch with the divine music in our soul. God is always broadcasting his love to us and asking us to tune in. God invites us to be in relationship with him every nanosecond of our lives. Prayer is our response to that invitation.

What kind of music is on your playlist? Try putting different kinds of prayer on your "pray list."

© Ivan Strba/iStockphoto.com

> I urge you, friends, by our Lord Jesus Christ
> and by the love that the Spirit gives: join me in
> praying fervently to God for me.
>
> Romans 15:30

Forms of Prayer

God is open to all kinds of prayer, but there are a few tried-and-true ways of listening and talking to God. The Holy Spirit makes sure the Church is true to the message of Jesus and teaches her how to pray using the five different basic forms of prayer. In your life as a Christian, you have probably been using all of these five basic forms of prayer without even realizing it: petition, blessing, intercession, praise, and thanksgiving. Let's take a look at the different types of prayer the Church recommends as ways to talk with and listen to God.

Prayers of Petition

How many times a day do you ask God for something you want? Perhaps you have prayed for the answer to a test question or the ability to do well when you compete. Such prayers are good. They remind us of God's presence in our lives. Have you considered making deeper requests of God—for things you truly need? Consider praying for help with an important decision, comfort during tough times, or forgiveness when you have hurt someone. Whenever we ask God for

PRAY IT!

Loving God, the gift of your presence is like divine music that I can hear every moment of my life. Through the Holy Spirit, teach me the ways to recognize your divine presence. Help me tune out the background noise of my life so I can tune in to your constant love for me. Help me share with others the music of your love. Amen.

525

FUN FACT

Ever wonder why we say "God bless you" when someone sneezes? In the sixth century, when Gregory the Great was Pope, he asked people to pray as a way to combat the bubonic plague. Because a sneeze could signal the start of the disease, the people would say "God bless you," hoping that the person who sneezed would not get sick.

Saying grace before meals is a type of prayer called a blessing. What other kinds of prayer can families do together?

© glenda/Shutterstock.com

something, we use a form of prayer called petition. Asking is the most common kind of prayer, but there are different ways to ask.

Prayers of Blessing

When we pray for God's loving care for a particular person, place, or activity, we are using a type of prayer called a **blessing**. We are able to pray blessings because God has first blessed us. We pray blessings before meals ("Bless us, O Lord, and these thy gifts . . .") or when someone sneezes ("God bless you"). During Mass we bless God ("Blessed be God forever"), and God blesses us ("Bow down for the blessing").

Prayers of Intercession

When people ask you to pray for them, they are asking you to put in a good word for them. They must think pretty highly of your relationship with God. Any time you pray on behalf of someone else, it is a prayer of **intercession**.

Every Mass includes prayers of intercession. When we "pray to the Lord" for the intentions of the world, the Church, people in need, or members of our community, we are asking for God's help for others.

Prayers of Praise

Prayer is not just about petitions, or asking God to take care of our needs and wants. We also need to tell God how much we appreciate who he is and what he does for us. These are prayers of praise.

Prayers of praise can be as simple as noticing the beauty of creation or as powerful as the prayers of Mass. Do the following prayers sound familiar to you?

> We praise you, we bless you, we adore you, we glorify you, we give you thanks for your great glory, Lord God, heavenly King, O God, almighty Father.

> May the Lord accept the sacrifice at your hands for the praise and glory of his name, for our good, and the good of all his holy Church.

Did You Know?

Schools of Spirituality

The Church has different schools of spirituality that share the living tradition of prayer. Many of these have developed from the lives of the saints. Franciscans—those inspired by the life of Saint Francis of Assisi—are especially aware of nature as a place to encounter God. Ignatian spirituality encourages followers of Saint Ignatius of Loyola to use their imagination when praying. As you grow in your prayer life, different spiritual practices can be precious guides along the way.

You are indeed holy, O Lord, and all you have created rightly gives you praise.

(From Eucharistic Prayer III)

We hear these and many more prayers of praise at Mass.

Prayers of Thanksgiving

It is right for all creation to give God praise. It is also right to tell God how thankful we are. We do not have to wait for a special day of the year for **thanksgiving**. We are called to be grateful throughout every day. During Mass we pray in union with the priest when he says, "It is truly right and just, our duty and our salvation, always and everywhere to give you thanks." As Catholics we gather to give thanks in a special way through the Eucharist. In fact, the word *Eucharist* comes from a Greek word that means "thanksgiving."

Just like any sport, learning to pray takes practice. The more you do it, the better you get at it.

© Nice One Productions/Corbis

528

Learning to Pray

Do you remember how you learned to pray? Like learning to talk, you may not have a specific memory. You just started picking up the words and the gestures from others. A simple prayer before meals or before bedtime became daily prayer. Through these daily prayers and the Sunday Eucharist, you grew in your prayer life. Year after year, through liturgical feasts and seasons, you learn more and more the language and practice of prayer.

Prayer does take practice. But like anything else in our lives, the more we practice, the easier prayer becomes. Participating in the liturgy of the Church helps us develop good habits of prayer. Reading the Bible and hearing the Word of God proclaimed at Mass are also big helps to our prayer life.

> Hope does not disappoint us, for God has poured out his love into our hearts by means of the Holy Spirit, who is God's gift to us.
>
> Romans 5:5

The virtues of faith, hope, and love also help us pray. Without the gift of faith, prayer would not make much sense. The virtue of hope keeps us from being disappointed when God may not

LITURGY CONNECTION

The Liturgy of the Hours

The Church has official prayers for different times of the day, including morning and evening prayer, called the Liturgy of the Hours. Bishops, priests, monks, and religious sisters and brothers have practiced this form of prayer since the earliest centuries of the Church. More recently, laypeople have rediscovered this ancient cycle of prayers. The Liturgy of the Hours is another way the Holy Spirit helps us hear the Good News.

© Bill Wittman/www.wpwittman.com

Who first taught you to make the Sign of the Cross or say the Hail Mary? Prayers you learn by heart will stay with you for a lifetime.

THiNK ABouT IT!

Web browsers let you set favorites for links you visit often. Which memorized prayers would you list as your favorite links to God? Art, music, and drama can help us tune in to God. Think of specific examples of art, music, or drama (including movies and TV shows) that might help your prayer life. How might some art, music, or drama be an obstacle to prayer?

seem to answer our prayers exactly the way we expect. Paul teaches us that love is the greatest virtue of all. Love is the motivation of all prayer. God loves us; we love God in return.

We first learn about God's love through the love of others. Even before babies can speak, they experience God through the love of their families. Often one of the first sentences a child learns is "I love you." These simple words become the basis for all relationships. They also become the starting point for prayer. Parents, grandparents, siblings, and other members of a Christian family teach children that God loves them and listens to them. The Christian family is the first place for a child's education in prayer.

By living and teaching about love, families nurture the seeds of prayer that God implanted in the human heart. Eventually, children begin to learn prayers "by heart." From watching and listening to others, you probably learned how to make the Sign of the Cross and say grace before meals. Later came longer prayers that are part of the treasury of our faith: the Hail Mary, the Lord's Prayer, the Act of Contrition. Memorized prayers are the family traditions that are passed on from generation to generation. They help us remember who we are and to whom we belong.

© Philippe Lissac/Godong/Corbis

Personal Prayer

Christians have practiced three major expressions of Christian prayer through the ages: vocal prayer, meditation, and contemplation.

Vocal prayer uses words to speak to God. The words can be spoken aloud or silently, and we can pray them alone or in a group. Memorized prayers are one kind of vocal prayer. So are prayers you make up yourself. This kind of prayer is also sometimes called spontaneous prayer. You can always use your own words to tell God what you are feeling or thinking.

There are other kinds of personal prayer. For example, instrumental music, meditation, and contemplation are powerful ways to pray. Meditation uses our thoughts, imagination, and emotions to get in

The Rosary is a popular prayer. What other devotions in the Live It! sidebar on the next page have you tried?

531

touch with God. Using Scripture, the Rosary, pictures, or creation, meditation is a way to focus our minds and hearts on what God is trying to tell us.

Contemplation, sometimes defined as "resting in God," is a wordless prayer. It is another way of listening for God's movement in our lives. By being silent long enough to hear the divine music, we enter into union with God—Father, Son, and Holy Spirit. All these expressions of prayer—vocal prayer, meditation, and contemplation—are ways to remember that we live in the heart of God, and that God lives in our hearts.

LiVe It!

Learning about Devotions

In addition to liturgy, other forms of piety, or special expressions of devotion to God, can help us in our prayer lives. Different cultures have various devotions that have received the Church's seal of approval. They all help spread the Good News of Jesus Christ.

How many of these are familiar to you? Pick one of the following and try it as a new form of prayer:

- Eucharistic Adoration
- Rosary
- *Posadas*
- *Angelus*
- *novenas*
- Stations of the Cross
- devotions honoring Our Lady of Guadalupe
- scapulars
- Miraculous Medal
- devotion to the Sacred Heart of Jesus

PEOPLE OF FAITH
Jean Vanier

© 2013 Saint Mary's Press/Illustration by Vicki Shuck

Jean Vanier's great respect for life has opened doors. Many people with mental disabilities who might have been admitted to institutions now live in loving homes because of what Jean Vanier called "a yearning for love." Jean's respect for life has grown with him from youth into old age, as he changes the world one heart at a time.

Jean, born in 1928, was a young Canadian naval officer, focused on war and discipline, when he first felt the yearning for something deeper. He described the yearning this way: "It was probably a desire to come back into myself and to find what was most important inside of myself, which was my heart."

Jean met a priest who made him aware of the thousands of people with disabilities who were living in institutions. In 1964 Jean felt God call him to invite two men, Raphael and Philippe, to leave their institutions and live with him in a house in France.

Their home was named L'Arche, after Noah's ark. L'Arche has grown to more than 130 communities worldwide. In these communities caregivers and people with mental challenges live in loving, faith-based homes.

Jean's ministry honors God, but it also has helped him grow: "To be human is that capacity to love which is the phenomenal reality that we can give life to people," he once said. "We can transform people by our attentiveness, by our love, and they can transform us."

49 THE LORD'S PRAYER: THE PERFECT PRAYER

KEY WORDS

quintessential
communion
synagogue

Imagine being one of Jesus' best friends. You have traveled with him, watched him perform miracles, and heard him teach crowds of people. You have been in his inner circle, so you have shared meals with him, spoken with him, and been part of his daily life. You have noticed that Jesus often goes off to pray.

Jesus' friends figured that he knew the best way to pray. When they asked him to teach them how, he gave them the Lord's Prayer.

© Brooklyn Museum/Corbis

Because of who he is, you figure he must be a master at praying. You want him to teach you how to pray.

In Luke's Gospel this scenario is just what happens with Jesus' friends. They recognize how important prayer is in Jesus' life, and they want to know the best way to pray. In response to their request, Jesus gives them a prayer that expresses everything they need to live as one of his followers. Two thousand years after Jesus first taught it to his disciples, Christians all over the world still pray the Lord's Prayer, also called the Our Father.

Throughout the history of the Church, the Lord's Prayer has been handed on from generation to generation. The *Catechism of the Catholic Church* calls it the "quintessential prayer of the Church" (2776). That means it is the perfect example of our ongoing conversation with our God, who created us.

> One day Jesus was praying in a certain place. When he had finished, one of his disciples said to him, "Lord, teach us to pray, just as John taught his disciples."
>
> Luke 11:1

What makes the Our Father—the Lord's Prayer—the perfect way for God's people to pray? Let's take a look at ten reasons.

PRAY IT!

Our Father, who art in
  heaven,
hallowed be thy name.
Thy kingdom come.
Thy will be done
on earth as it is in heaven.
Give us this day our daily
  bread,
and forgive us our trespasses,
as we forgive those who
  trespass against us,
and lead us not into
  temptation,
but deliver us from evil.
Amen.

1. Jesus Himself Gave Us the Lord's Prayer

Who would know better how to pray than Jesus? He gives us the words the Father gave him. Because Jesus is both fully divine and fully human, he also knows in his human heart our needs, the needs of all of his human brothers and sisters. He is the best model for our prayer.

Live It!

Pray Always

If there are at least ten reasons why the Lord's Prayer is the perfect prayer, there are at least ten different times daily when you could say this prayer. Consider the following times when you might stop and pray the Lord's Prayer:

1. first thing in the morning when you wake up
2. when you go outside and notice the beauty of God's creation
3. when you are hungry
4. when you see someone else who may be hungry
5. when someone says something to hurt you
6. when you say something that hurts someone else
7. when you are tempted to do something you know is wrong
8. when you are scared, upset, or worried
9. when something bad happens to you
10. before you go to bed

2. The Lord's Prayer Teaches Us How to Pray

When Jesus taught his disciples to pray, he did not give them some kind of secret formula to repeat without thinking. He taught them a way of praying. Remember the terms *praise* and *petition*? Jesus began by addressing God and praising his name and then petitioning, or asking, for what we need in life. Although the exact words of the Lord's Prayer have been translated in different ways through many generations, the way of praying that Jesus gave us has not changed.

3. The Lord's Prayer Is Addressed to the Father

Praying to God as Father may seem obvious to us, but to the people of Jesus' time, calling upon God as our Father must have sounded a bit strange. They were not used to thinking of God in such a personal way.

© AlexMotrenko/iStockphoto.com

Do you ever wonder what to say when you pray? The Lord's Prayer is the perfect prayer for any circumstance.

FUN FACT

Quintessential. This impressive word comes from two Latin words: *quint* ("five") and *essential* ("essence"). Ancient philosophers thought that nature contained four essences, or elements: earth, fire, water, and air. Something perfect had a fifth element from the heavens. What an impressive word to describe the prayer that came from God.

4. The Lord's Prayer Helps Us Know Who God Is

We can call on God as Father because Jesus revealed to us who God is. Jesus wants us to know that God is not some distant being who hurls thunderbolts from on high. Instead, God is a personal, loving God. Jesus shows us how to relate to God—as an approachable, loving Father. That must have been an amazing concept for Jesus' disciples. If we stop to think about it, it is still an amazing thought—that God wants to be as close to each of us as is an ideal and loving father.

When you pray the Lord's Prayer at Mass, do you pray with confidence because you know these are the words our Savior gave us?

© Bill Wittman/www.wpwittman.com

538

5. The Lord's Prayer Helps Us Know Who We Are

When Jesus instructs us to say "Our Father," he invites all of us into relationship with his Father. When we pray to the Father, we are in communion with him and with his Son, Jesus Christ. To be in **communion** with someone means we share the closest kind of relationship possible. The Lord's Prayer clearly tells us we are sons and daughters of God. How awesome is that?

> So Jesus called a child to come and stand in front of them, and said, "I assure you that unless you change and become like children, you will never enter the Kingdom of heaven."
>
> Matthew 18:2–3

6. The Lord's Prayer Helps Us Be More like God Our Father

Have you ever watched young children try to act like their parents? When they play, they often try to speak and act like their mothers and fathers. It is natural for children to want to grow up to be "just like Mom or Dad." When we pray to our Father, we should develop the will to become like God, our Father.

LITURGY CONNECTION

The Perfect Prayer

Right after the Eucharistic Prayer and before Communion, the priest invites us to stand and pray the Lord's Prayer. When we stand to pray, we are saying the prayer of the whole Church. Because we are the Church, the Our Father is most meaningful and effective when we pray it together. The Lord's Prayer sums up everything we have asked for in the Eucharistic Prayer and gets us ready to receive the Body and Blood of Christ in Communion. Mass is the perfect place for the perfect prayer.

7. The Lord's Prayer Helps Us Have Humble and Trusting Hearts

Have you ever been told, "Stop acting like a little child"? It might seem strange that when Jesus wanted to make a point with his adult followers, he told them to be like little children. Jesus recognized that children are humbler and more trusting than adults. Their hearts are more open to the love God offers them. The Our Father reminds us that we are children of God, and we ought to act like it.

THiNK About It!

Conversion and conversation come from the same word, one that means "to change." How do conversations with other people change you? Are those changes always good? How can the Lord's Prayer, a heart-to-heart conversation with God, change you?

8. The Lord's Prayer Is about "We," Not "Me"

When Jesus taught us to pray to *our* Father, not *my* father, he was reminding us that being in relationship with God means we are also in relationship with one another. If God is our Father, we must be concerned with all members of the human family. God's love has no limits, and neither should our prayers. When we pray, our focus should extend to all people.

9. The Lord's Prayer Is *the* Prayer of the Church

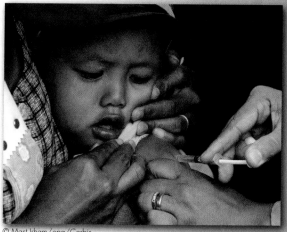

© Mast Irham/epa/Corbis

In the early days of the Church, Jesus' disciples prayed the Lord's Prayer three times a day. Ever since then the People of God have prayed the Our Father as part of their liturgical lives. It is an essential part of the Liturgy of the Hours (see the Liturgy Connection in chapter 48, "Tuning In to God," of this handbook). Of course we pray the Lord's Prayer at every Mass. Next time you stand and pray as Jesus taught us, remember that you are continuing the two-thousand-year-old prayer of the Church.

Read the Did You Know? sidebar below to find out how health care is part of our "daily bread."

?

Did You Know?

More than Food

When we pray for our daily bread, we are not asking God just for food. We are asking also for everything we need to live. That includes things we might take for granted, like education, books, technology, health care, the comforts of home, and so forth. As you pray for "daily bread," thank God for all the good things he gives you and ask him for the good things you need to live, not just for yourself and the people you know, but for all people, especially those most in need.

10. The Lord's Prayer Is Truly a Summary of the Whole Gospel

Could you summarize in 30 seconds or less everything Jesus came to teach us about living the Christian life? In the middle of his Sermon on the Mount, Jesus does just that when he stops to teach us the Our Father (see Matthew 6:9–15).

When Jesus began teaching his friends to pray, he told them to say, "Our Father." He wanted to tell them that God loves all people. And we should too.

Almost four hundred years later, Saint Augustine, one of the most important saints of the Church, said, "Run through all the words of the holy prayers [in Scripture] and I do not think that you will find anything in them that is not contained and included in the Lord's Prayer"[1] (CCC, 2762).

© David Turnley/Corbis

Church History

Church Architecture

Have you noticed the differences in architecture between one parish church, or cathedral, and another? The aim of all church architecture is to help us lift our minds and hearts to God through the visual beauty of space. Let's take a tour of some common church architecture.

- **Basilicas.** In the Roman Empire, basilicas were official buildings built by the Romans for civic needs. After Christianity became legal under the Emperor Constantine, many of these civic buildings were given to the Christians as churches. Their architecture is called Romanesque, after the Romans, and many of them had large, round domes. Many of our large parish churches built in the United States were modeled after these Roman basilicas.

- **Byzantine.** Many Eastern churches are built in the Byzantine style. From the outside, these churches are notable for their twisted-looking domes, called "onion" domes. Inside, elaborate decoration and the use of icons (painted pictures of Jesus, Mary, and the saints) are common.

- **Gothic.** This style of architecture features pointed arches over windows and doors, tall, thin towers, and sometimes "flying buttresses," which are long arms of stone that hold up the walls from the outside. It originated in the cathedrals of the Middle Ages, and many churches we see today are based on this very popular style of church architecture that seems to point to Heaven.

- **Modern church architecture.** Modern churches are often characterized by the use of materials like plate glass, steel, and concrete. Compared to earlier ages, their interior decoration is minimal. Plain glass, rather than stained glass, is often used for the windows. Sometimes, to emphasize the communal aspect of worship, the church is built in a rounded or arc-like shape.

50 THE LORD'S PRAYER: A PRAYER FOR ALL TIME

KEY WORDS

trespass

temptation

Many people think of the number 7 as a lucky number. There are seven days of the week and seven seas. The ancient world considered it the perfect number because it was the sum of two perfect shapes: a triangle with three sides and a square with four sides.

The number 7 is significant in the Bible too. There, it represents completeness. God created the world in seven days (see Genesis 1:1—2:3). Jesus

In this chapter you will discover how the number 7 and the Lord's Prayer are related.

© Georgios Kollidas/Shutterstock.com

tells us to forgive seventy times seven (see Matthew 18:22). He expels seven demons from Mary Magdalene (see Luke 8:2). The Gospel of Matthew tells us that when Jesus stops in the middle of his Sermon on the Mount to teach the crowd how to pray, he gives them a prayer with seven petitions (see Matthew 6:9–13). Seven is the perfect number for the perfect prayer. In this chapter we will explore the seven petitions, or requests, in the Lord's Prayer.

Seven Petitions

Like the Ten Commandments, the Lord's Prayer consists of two parts. In the Ten Commandments, the first three Commandments are directed toward our relationship with God. The last seven are about our relationships with others. Similarly, the Lord's Prayer contains three petitions that focus on the glory of God the Father. Then there are four requests that name our human needs and desires.

Before we begin the seven petitions, we address God as Father. This name reminds us of the close, personal relationship we enjoy as children of God. By saying *our* Father, Jesus tells us that God's love extends to all people. When we say the words "who art in heaven," we are not naming a physical, faraway place.

PRAY IT!

God, our Father, when we pray for ourselves and our needs, we know you listen to us. Today we pray for the needs of those who do not know how to pray or have no one to pray for them. We ask that you grant our brothers and sisters in every corner of the world all they need to be well fed, to be safe, and to have the opportunity to know you and love you as your Son, Jesus, has taught us to do. Amen.

Our prayer is not a long-distance call. Heaven is a way of life or state of being. When we address our Father in Heaven, we recognize his nearness to us, and we pray for even greater closeness with God. We are something like the child who stretches out her arms and cries out because she wants to be picked up and held.

1. "Hallowed Be Thy Name"

The word *hallowed* is not commonly heard today. It means "holy." The first of the seven petitions sounds more like praise of God's name than a petition to ask for something. But "*hallowed* be thy name" is actually a request for help in keeping God's name holy. When we show deep reverence for God's name, we draw

God, our Father, reaches out to tenderly comfort one of his children. The phrase "hallowed be thy name" reminds us how close God wants to be to each of us.

Illustration by Elizabeth Wang, "Our littlest prayers are welcomed, heard, and rewarded by God, who is like a father stroking his beloved child," copyright © Radiant Light 2008, www.radiantlight.org.uk

closer to him. When we use God's name lightly or abuse it, we are saying he is not important in our lives. "Hallowed be thy name" is a request to be in awe of our awesome God.

2. "Thy Kingdom Come"

You'll notice when you read the Gospels that the term *Kingdom of God* keeps coming up. It is the central theme of Jesus' mission on earth. It is the Good News, because God's Kingdom, or God's Reign, is a time of justice, peace, and love. In this second petition, Jesus

Did You Know?

The Hail Mary

Have you ever heard of a "Hail Mary" pass in football? In 1975 Roger Staubach, a devout Catholic playing quarterback for the Dallas Cowboys football team, threw a desperation pass, then closed his eyes and said a Hail Mary. His receiver caught the ball and ran into the end zone for the game-winning touchdown. Although Mary, the Mother of God, is not partial to any sports team, this play shows how popular the Hail Mary is among Catholics.

The Hail Mary begins with the announcement of Jesus' birth (see Luke 1:28) and ends with a prayer for the "hour of our death." When we pray to Mary, we ask her to ask Jesus for whatever we need—from touchdowns to matters much more serious. Both the Hail Mary and the Our Father are part of the playbook of Catholic prayers.

FUN FACT

Jesus taught his friends to pray in Aramaic, the common language of his time and culture. Today, the Our Father is prayed in more than fourteen hundred languages. The Convent of the Pater Noster in the Holy Land keeps track of all these languages. The walls of this church contain 140 large tiles, each inscribed with the Lord's Prayer in a different language.

teaches us to ask God for the final coming of his Kingdom. But we don't have to wait for the end of the world. We can also be part of the Kingdom of God right here, even if the world is not perfect yet. When we pray this petition in the Lord's Prayer, we ask God to help us put our priorities in order. The world often tells us happiness can be found primarily in material things. Jesus' message is just the opposite.

> Your Father in heaven knows that you need all these things. . . . Be concerned above everything else with the Kingdom of God and with what he requires of you, and he will provide you with all these other things.
>
> Matthew 6:32–33

3. "Thy Will Be Done on Earth as It Is in Heaven"

Whenever a parent, teacher, or coach gives you a task, it helps to be clear about what they want you to do. You have to know their will, or what they want and how they want it done. If you don't know, you might not finish the job properly. On the night before he died, Jesus was clear in his instructions to us. He did not make a suggestion. He gave us a command: "As I have loved you, so you must love one another" (John

13:34). When we pray the third petition, we ask God to help us understand how to do his will by loving the way Jesus showed us and taught us. The experience of giving and receiving love is a taste of Heaven on earth.

4. "Give Us This Day Our Daily Bread"

The words "Give us this day our daily bread" make an excellent grace before meals. In every culture on earth, people eat some form of bread. We ask for our daily bread for ourselves, our families and friends, and everyone in the world. We are reminded that there are millions of people who do not have enough to eat. We also remember millions who are hungry for God.

This photo was taken in the Convent of the Pater Noster (which is Latin for "Our Father"). Read the Fun Fact in this chapter to discover how many translations of the Lord's Prayer there are.

© Sandro Vannini/CORBIS

5. "Forgive Us Our Trespasses, as We Forgive Those Who Trespass against Us"

Just as each of us needs daily nourishment, we all need forgiveness. Jesus encourages us to recognize our sins and ask for mercy. A **trespass** is another name for a sin. In this fifth petition, there is a big condition. We must first forgive those who have hurt us. This can be a tall order. However, if we seek

Live It!

Online Temptation

When you pray the words "lead us not into temptation," do you ever consider how many temptations you face daily? Often temptations exist side by side with good things in your life. For example, on the Internet you can find both treasures and trouble. Social networking sites are a fun way to communicate with friends, but they can lead to destructive gossip that ruins reputations. Online video sharing can be entertaining, but can also present harmful images and occasions for sin.

Internet policies at school and at home can help you make good choices every time you log on to your computer. Prayer can help you make good judgments in following those policies. Pray the Our Father and ask God to help you avoid temptation online and in all settings.

revenge rather than reconciliation, the cycle of sin or hurt becomes more difficult to stop. If we are unwilling to forgive others, our hearts remain closed to God's love and forgiveness.

> As I have loved you, so you must love one another.
>
> John 13:34

6. "Lead Us Not into Temptation"

This may sound like an odd request for God—not to lead us into temptation. But the sixth petition helps us recognize that although we are good, made in the image and likeness of God, we also possess the tendency to do wrong. We coexist with millions of people who also have this tendency; together we are often misguided about God's will for us. A **temptation** is an invitation to do something wrong. Too often the invitation is hard to resist. This petition asks God to help us avoid saying yes to people and situations that could ultimately lead to sin or tragedy.

Think About It!

Adam and Eve wanted to taste the forbidden fruit. Calling something "forbidden fruit" is a way of referring to temptation. It is something that looks good but goes against God's will. What are some of the most common temptations young people face today?

7. "But Deliver Us from Evil"

Listening to almost any news report can remind us of how much evil exists in this world. It is easy to become discouraged and to believe that the forces of evil will overcome all that is good. However, the concluding words of the Lord's Prayer are a petition that God will deliver us from those things that would harm us because they attempt to turn us away from God. We pray this last petition in the same way we pray all of the Lord's Prayer: in communion with the whole Church for the needs of the whole human family. We pray with confidence that good will ultimately triumph over evil.

We end the Lord's Prayer with "Amen," meaning "so be it" or "it is true." Jesus uses this term frequently throughout the Gospels. The last book of the Bible refers to him as the Amen (see Revelation 3:14).

How can the Internet lead us into temptation?

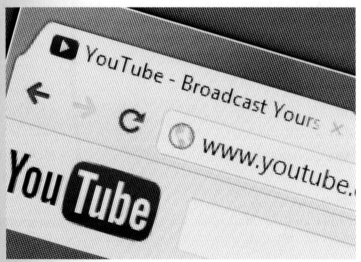

© bloomua/Shutterstock.com

PEOPLE OF FAITH
Pope Francis

© 2013 Saint Mary's Press/Illustration by Vicki Shuck

In March 2013, the former Archbishop of Buenos Aires, Cardinal Jorge Bergoglio, was elected Pope and took the name Francis, after the saint of the poor, Saint Francis of Assisi. In the following days, Pope Francis explained that his choice of a name was significant. He chose the name Francis to signal to the Church and to the world that he would endeavor to bring an attitude of simplicity into his life as Pope and into the life of the Church. In his first homily as Pope, he reminded the Church and the world to care for and protect those who are poor.

As Archbishop of Buenos Aires, Pope Francis had already been living a simple life in everyday ways. Rather than living in an elaborate mansion, he chose to live in a small apartment. Rather than employing a cook, he prepared his own meals. Rather than being chauffeured in a sleek limousine, he rode the city bus to his office. As Pope, he continued this attitude of simplicity by choosing to stay in a smaller apartment at the Vatican Guest House rather than moving into the more elaborate Papal Apartment. (He will use the Papal Apartment to greet guests at receptions and other formal occasions.)

In choosing the name Francis, Pope Francis is following the path Jesus chose, as recorded in Scripture. In beginning his papacy by praying the Our Father and the Hail Mary with the crowds gathered in Saint Peter's Square in Rome, Pope Francis turned to these traditional and well-known scriptural prayers to unify the hearts of all believers.

Appendix

A Catholic Prayers

Act of Contrition

My God, I am sorry for my sins with all my heart.
In choosing to do wrong
and failing to do good,
I have sinned against you
whom I should love above all things.
I firmly intend, with your help,
to do penance,
to sin no more,
and to avoid whatever leads me to sin.
Our Savior Jesus Christ
suffered and died for us.
In his name, my God, have mercy. Amen.

Act of Faith

My God, I firmly believe you are one God in three Divine Persons, Father, Son, and Holy Spirit.
I believe in Jesus Christ, your Son, who became man and died for our sins, and who will come to judge the living and the dead.
I believe these and all the truths which the Holy Catholic Church teaches, because you have revealed them, who can neither deceive nor be deceived.
Amen.

Act of Hope

O my God, trusting in your infinite goodness and promises, I hope to obtain pardon of my sins, the help of your grace, and life everlasting, through the merits of Jesus Christ, my Lord and redeemer. Amen.

Act of Love

My God, I love you above all things, with my whole heart and soul, because you are all-good and worthy of all my love. I love my neighbor as myself for love of you. I forgive all who have injured me, and I ask pardon of all whom I have injured. Amen.

Angelus

V. The angel of the Lord declared unto Mary,

R. And she conceived of the Holy Spirit.

Hail Mary . . .

V. Behold the handmaid of the Lord,

R. Be it done unto me according to your word.

Hail Mary . . .

V. And the Word was made flesh,

R. And dwelt among us.

Hail Mary . . .

V. Pray for us, O Holy Mother of God,

R. That we may be made worthy of the promises of Christ.

Let us pray: Pour forth, we beseech thee, O Lord, thy grace into our hearts; that we to whom the Incarnation of Christ, thy Son, was made known by the message of an angel, may, by his Passion and Cross, be brought to the glory of his Resurrection, through Christ our Lord. Amen.

Apostles' Creed

I believe in God, the Father almighty, Creator of heaven and earth, and in Jesus Christ, his only Son, our Lord, who was conceived by the Holy Spirit, born of the Virgin Mary, suffered under Pontius Pilate, was crucified, died and was buried; he descended into hell; on the third day he rose again from the dead; he ascended into heaven, and is seated at the right hand of God the Father almighty; from there he will come to judge the living and the dead. I believe in the Holy Spirit, the holy catholic Church, the communion of saints, the forgiveness of sins, the resurrection of the body, and life everlasting. Amen.

Confiteor ("I Confess")

I confess to almighty God and to you, my brothers and sisters, that I have greatly sinned in my thoughts and in my words, in what I have done and in what I have failed to do, through my fault, through my fault, through my most grievous fault; therefore I ask blessed Mary ever-Virgin, all the Angels and Saints, and you, my brothers and sisters, to pray for me to the Lord our God.

Glory Be

Glory be to the Father, and to the Son, and to the Holy Spirit, as it was in the beginning, is now, and will be forever. Amen.

Grace Before Meals

Bless us, O Lord, and these your gifts,
which we are about to receive
from your bounty,
through Christ our Lord. Amen.

Grace After Meals

We give you thanks, almighty God,
for these and all your gifts
which we have received
through Christ our Lord. Amen.

Hail Mary

Hail Mary, full of grace,
the Lord is with you;
blessed are you among women,
and blessed is the fruit of your womb, Jesus.

Holy Mary, Mother of God,
pray for us sinners
now and at the hour of our death.
Amen.

The Lord's Prayer
(also called the Our Father)

Our Father, who art in heaven,
hallowed be thy name.
Thy kingdom come.
Thy will be done
on earth as it is in heaven.
Give us this day our daily bread,
and forgive us our trespasses,
as we forgive those who trespass against us,
and lead us not into temptation,
but deliver us from evil. Amen.

Magnificat (Mary's Song)
(see Luke 1:46–55)

My being proclaims the greatness of the Lord,
my spirit rejoices in God my Savior,
for he has looked with favor on his lowly servant.
From this day all generations will call me blessed.
The Almighty has done great things for me,
and holy is his Name.
He has mercy on those who fear him
in every generation.
He has shown the strength of his arm;
he has scattered the proud in their conceit.
He has cast down the mighty from their thrones,
and has lifted up the lowly.
He has filled the hungry with good things,
and the rich he has sent away empty.
He has come to the help of his servant Israel
for he has remembered his promise of mercy,
the promise he made to our fathers,
to Abraham and his children forever.

Memorare

Remember, O most gracious Virgin Mary, that never was it known that anyone who fled to your protection, implored your help, or sought your intercession was left unaided. Inspired by this confidence, we fly unto you, O virgin of virgins, our mother. To you do we come, before you we stand, sinful and sorrowful. O mother of the Word Incarnate, despise not our petitions, but in your mercy, hear and answer us. Amen.

Morning Prayer

Almighty God, I thank you for your past blessings. Today I offer myself—whatever I do, say, or think—to your loving care. Continue to bless me, Lord. I make this morning offering in union with the divine intentions of Jesus Christ who offers himself daily in the holy sacrifice of the Mass, and in union with Mary, his Virgin Mother and our Mother, who was always the faithful handmaid of the Lord. Amen.

The Nicene Creed

I believe in one God, the Father almighty, maker of heaven and earth, of all things visible and invisible.

I believe in one Lord Jesus Christ, the Only Begotten Son of God, born of the Father before all ages. God from God, Light from Light, true God from true God, begotten, not made, consubstantial with the Father; through him all things were made. For us men and for our salvation he came down from heaven, and by the Holy Spirit was incarnate of the Virgin Mary, and became man.

For our sake he was crucified under Pontius Pilate, he suffered death and was buried, and rose again on the third day in accordance with the Scriptures. He ascended into heaven and is seated at the right hand of the Father. He will come again in glory to judge the living and the dead and his kingdom will have no end.

I believe in the Holy Spirit, the Lord, the giver of life, who proceeds from the Father and the Son, who with the Father and the Son is adored and glorified, who has spoken through the prophets. I believe in one, holy, catholic and apostolic Church. I confess one baptism for the forgiveness of sins and I look forward to the resurrection of the dead and the life of the world to come. Amen.

Prayer of Saint Francis

Lord, make me an instrument of your peace:
>   where there is hatred, let me sow love;
>   where there is injury, pardon;
>   where there is doubt, faith;
>   where there is despair, hope;
>   where there is darkness, light;
>   where there is sadness, joy.

Divine Master,
>   grant that I may not so much seek
>   to be consoled as to console,
>   to be understood as to understand,
>   to be loved as to love.

For it is in giving that we receive,
>   it is in pardoning that we are pardoned,
>   it is in dying that we are born to eternal life.

Prayer to the Holy Spirit

V. Come, Holy Spirit, fill the hearts of your faithful.

R. And kindle in them the fire of your love.

V. Send forth your Spirit, and they shall be created.

R. And you will renew the face of the earth.

> Let us pray:

> Lord, by the light of the Holy Spirit, you have taught the hearts of your faithful. In the same Spirit, help us to relish what is right and always rejoice in your consolation. We ask this through Christ our Lord. Amen.

The Rosary

The Rosary is perhaps the most popular devotion to Mary, the Mother of God. The central part of the Rosary consists of the recitation of five sets of ten Hail Marys (each set is called a decade). Each new decade begins by saying an Our Father, and each decade concludes with a Glory Be. Individuals keep track of the prayers said by moving from one bead to the next in order.

The recitation of the Rosary begins with a series of prayers, said in the following order while using as a guide a small chain of beads and a crucifix.

1. the Sign of the Cross
2. the Apostles' Creed
3. one Our Father
4. three Hail Marys
5. one Glory Be

After these introductory prayers, the recitation of the decades, as described above, begins.

The praying of a five-decade Rosary is connected with meditation on what are called the mysteries of the life of Jesus. These mysteries too are collected into series of five—five Joyful, five Luminous, five Sorrowful, and five Glorious Mysteries. The mysteries of the Rosary are listed on page 562. Individuals who are praying devote one recitation of the Rosary to each set of mysteries. She or he chooses which set of mysteries to meditate on while saying the decades of Hail Marys. Therefore, the complete Rosary consists of twenty decades.

With a little practice, the regular praying of the Rosary can become a source of great inspiration and consolation for the Christian.

Joyful Mysteries

- The Annunciation
- The Visitation
- The Birth of Our Lord
- The Presentation of Jesus in the Temple
- The Finding of Jesus in the Temple

Luminous Mysteries

- The Baptism of Jesus
- Jesus Reveals Himself in the Miracle at Cana
- Jesus Proclaims the Good News of the Kingdom of God
- The Transfiguration of Jesus
- The Institution of the Eucharist

Sorrowful Mysteries

- The Agony of Jesus in the Garden
- The Scourging at the Pillar
- The Crowning with Thorns
- The Carrying of the Cross
- The Crucifixion

Glorious Mysteries

- The Resurrection of Jesus
- The Ascension of Jesus into Heaven
- The Descent of the Holy Spirit on the Apostles
  (Pentecost)
- The Assumption of Mary into Heaven
- The Crowning of Mary as Queen of Heaven

Sign of the Cross

In the name of the Father
and of the Son
and of the Holy Spirit. Amen.

Stations of the Cross

1. Jesus is condemned to death.
2. Jesus takes up his cross.
3. Jesus falls the first time.
4. Jesus meets his mother.
5. Simon helps Jesus carry the cross.
6. Veronica wipes the face of Jesus.
7. Jesus falls the second time.
8. Jesus meets the women of Jerusalem.
9. Jesus falls the third time.
10. Jesus is stripped of his garments.
11. Jesus is nailed to the cross.
12. Jesus dies on the cross.
13. Jesus is taken down from the cross.
14. Jesus is laid in the tomb.

 # Catholic Beliefs and Practices

This section provides brief summaries of major Catholic beliefs and practices. Many items that are only listed here are explored in more depth in the main part of this book. If you would like more information about these beliefs and practices, consult the index at the end of the book.

Two Great Commandments
(see chapter 13)

- You shall love the Lord your God with all your heart, with all your soul, with all your mind, and with all your strength.
- You shall love your neighbor as yourself.

(See Matthew 22:37–40, Mark 12:29–31, Luke 10:27.)

Ten Commandments (see chapters 40–44)

1. I am the Lord your God, you shall not have other gods before me.
2. You shall not take the name of the Lord, your God, in vain.
3. Remember to keep holy the Lord's Day.
4. Honor your father and your mother.
5. You shall not kill.
6. You shall not commit adultery.
7. You shall not steal.
8. You shall not bear false witness against your neighbor.
9. You shall not covet your neighbor's wife.
10. You shall not covet your neighbor's possessions.

Beatitudes (see chapter 37)

- Blessed are the poor in spirit, for theirs is the kingdom of heaven.
- Blessed are they who mourn, for they will be comforted.
- Blessed are the meek, for they will inherit the earth.
- Blessed are they who hunger and thirst for righteousness, for they will be satisfied.
- Blessed are the merciful, for they will be shown mercy.
- Blessed are the clean of heart, for they will see God.
- Blessed are the peacemakers, for they will be called children of God.
- Blessed are they who are persecuted for the sake of righteousness, for theirs is the kingdom of heaven.

Corporal Works of Mercy
(see chapter 14)

- Feed the hungry.
- Give drink to the thirsty.
- Shelter the homeless.
- Clothe the naked.
- Care for the sick.
- Help the imprisoned.
- Bury the dead.

Spiritual Works of Mercy
(see chapter 14)

- Share knowledge.
- Give advice to those who need it.
- Comfort those who suffer.
- Be patient with others.
- Forgive those who hurt you.
- Give correction to those who need it.
- Pray for the living and the dead.

Theological Virtues (see chapter 38)

- Faith
- Hope
- Love

Cardinal Virtues (see chapter 38)

- Prudence
- Justice
- Fortitude
- Temperance

Seven Gifts of the Holy Spirit

(see chapter 34)

- **Wisdom.** A wise person recognizes where the Holy Spirit is at work in the world.

- **Understanding.** Understanding helps us recognize how God wants us to live.

- **Right Judgment (Counsel).** This gift helps us make choices that will lead us closer to God rather than away from God. The gift of right judgment, sometimes called counsel, helps us figure out what God wants.

- **Courage (Fortitude).** The gift of courage, also called fortitude, is the special help we need when faced with challenges or struggles.

- **Knowledge.** This gift helps us understand the meaning of what God has revealed, particularly the Good News of Jesus Christ.

- **Reverence (Piety).** This gift, sometimes called piety, gives us a deep sense of respect for God and the Church. A reverent person honors God and approaches him with humility, trust, and love.

- **Wonder and Awe (Fear of the Lord).** The gift of wonder and awe makes us aware of God's greatness and power.

Fruits of the Holy Spirit
(see chapter 17)

- Charity
- Joy
- Peace
- Patience
- Kindness
- Goodness
- Generosity (or Long-suffering)
- Gentleness (or Humility)
- Faithfulness
- Modesty
- Self-control (or Continence)
- Chastity

Four Marks of the Catholic Church (see chapter 22)

- One
- Holy
- Catholic
- Apostolic

Liturgical Year (see chapter 25)

- Advent
- Christmas
- Ordinary Time
- Lent
- Easter Triduum
- Easter
- Pentecost
- Ordinary Time

Seven Sacraments (see chapters 27–36)

- Baptism
- Confirmation
- Eucharist
- Penance and Reconciliation
- Anointing of the Sick
- Matrimony
- Holy Orders

Precepts of the Church

- Attend Mass on Sundays and holy days of obligation and rest from unnecessary labor on these days.
- Confess your sins in the Sacrament of Penance and Reconciliation at least once a year.
- Receive the Eucharist at least during the Easter season.
- Observe the days of fasting and abstinence established by the Church.
- Help to provide for the material needs of the Church according to your ability.

Holy Days of Obligation

- Christmas Day (December 25)
- Solemnity of the Blessed Virgin Mary, the Mother of God (January 1)
- Ascension of the Lord (the Thursday that falls on the fortieth day after Easter, though in some places the celebration is moved to the following Sunday)
- Assumption of the Blessed Virgin Mary (August 15)
- All Saints' Day (November 1)
- Immaculate Conception of the Blessed Virgin Mary (December 8)

Parts of Mass (see chapters 29–32)

Introductory Rites

- Entrance Chant
- Greeting
- Penitential Act
- Kyrie
- Gloria
- Collect

Liturgy of the Word

- First Reading
- Responsorial Psalm
- Second Reading
- Gospel Acclamation
- Dialogue at the Gospel (or Gospel Dialogue)
- Gospel
- Homily
- Profession of Faith (or Creed or Nicene Creed [or Apostles' Creed])
- Universal Prayer (or Prayer of the Faithful)

Liturgy of the Eucharist

- Presentation and Preparation of the Gifts
- Invitation to Prayer
- Prayer over the Offerings
- Eucharistic Prayer
  - Preface Dialogue
  - Preface
  - Preface Acclamation (or Holy, Holy, Holy)
  - The Mystery of Faith (or Memorial Acclamation)
  - Concluding Doxology
  - Amen

- Communion Rite
  - The Lord's Prayer
  - Sign of Peace
  - Lamb of God (or Fraction of the Bread)
  - Invitation to Communion
  - Communion
  - Prayer after Communion

Concluding Rites

- Solemn Blessing or Prayer over the People
- Final Blessing
- Dismissal

C GLOSSARY OF KEY WORDS

A

Abba The Aramaic word for "father" that Jesus uses to address the Father.

abortion The intentional ending of an unborn child's life. Choosing abortion and performing abortions are serious sins.

absolution Freeing from guilt. Absolution takes place during the Sacrament of Penance and Reconciliation, when the priest pardons sins in the name of God and the Church.

adultery Sexual activity between two persons, at least one of whom is married to another. Prohibited by the Sixth Commandment.

Advocate One who helps and supports another person. In the Gospel of John, Jesus refers to the Holy Spirit as the disciples' Advocate. *See also* Holy Spirit.

age of reason The age when a young person is old enough to understand the difference between right and wrong. This is generally regarded to be the age of seven.

alb A white liturgical garment.

ambo The reading stand where Scripture is proclaimed during the liturgy.

anamnesis A special kind of remembering. When we recall a past event, it happens again in the present. In the Eucharist we recall what Jesus did in his life, death, and Resurrection, and we celebrate that his saving action is present today.

angel A servant or messenger of God. Angels glorify God without ceasing and watch over each us every moment of our lives.

Annunciation The angel Gabriel's announcement to Mary that she was to be the mother of Jesus Christ.

Apostolic One of the four Marks of the Church, along with One, Holy, and Catholic. The Church is Apostolic because she was founded on Jesus' Twelve Apostles. *See also* Marks of the Church.

Ascension The event forty days after the Resurrection of Jesus Christ, when he was taken up to Heaven.

assembly The people that come together to celebrate the liturgy.

Assumption The belief that God took Mary directly into Heaven at the end of her life on earth.

atheism The denial of God's existence.

B

Baal and Asherah Two Canaanite gods of earth and fertility that the Israelites worshipped when they fell away from the one true God.

Baptism The first of the Seven Sacraments of the Church. Through Baptism, people become united to Christ and to the Church. *See also* Sacrament.

Beatitudes The teachings of Jesus during the Sermon on the Mount in which he describes the actions and attitudes that should characterize Christians and by which one can discover genuine meaning and happiness.

belief Something considered to be true.

bishop One who has received the fullness of the Sacrament of Holy Orders. A bishop takes care of the Church in a particular geographical area called a diocese. He is a sign of unity in his diocese and a member of the College of Bishops.

blessing A form of prayer in which we ask for God's loving care for someone.

C

catechumenate The process through which unbaptized adults and children who have reached the age of reason are initiated into the Church.

Catholic Along with One, Holy, and Apostolic, Catholic is one of the four Marks of the Church. *Catholic* means "universal." The Church reaches throughout the world to all people. *See also* Marks of the Church.

charity Working to meet people's needs out of love for God and neighbor. Charity, or love, is a theological virtue. *See also* virtue.

chastity The virtue of living your sexuality in a pure and healthy way, particularly by obeying the Sixth and Ninth Commandments.

Chosen People The Israelites. The people with whom God made the Old Testament covenant.

Sacred Chrism Perfumed olive oil that has been consecrated. It is used for anointing in the Sacraments of Baptism, Confirmation, and Holy Orders.

Chrism Mass The annual celebration during which bishops bless the oils to be used in their dioceses during the coming year. This Mass usually takes place on Holy Thursday.

Christians The name for the followers of Jesus Christ.

common good A social condition that enables all people to fulfill their human and spiritual needs.

common priesthood of the faithful The name for the priesthood shared by all who are baptized. The baptized share in the priesthood of Jesus Christ by participating in his mission.

Communion The sharing of Christ's Body and Blood in the liturgy.

communion The closest type of relationship shared among people and between people and God.

Communion of Saints The whole community of now-living faithful people united with all those who have died but are alive with God.

concupiscence The tendency of all human beings toward sin, as a result of Original Sin.

consubstantial Regarded as the same in substance or essence (as of the Three Persons of the Trinity).

contrition Sorrow for one's sins.

conversion A change of heart that turns us away from sin and toward God.

covenant A sacred agreement among people, or between God and a human being, where everyone vows to keep a promise forever.

creation God's actions though which all that exists has come into being.

creed A statement of what one believes. The Nicene and Apostles' Creeds are the Church's most important creeds.

D

discipline Self-control.

doctrine Official teaching of the Church based on God's Revelation by and through Jesus Christ.

E

ecumenism The work of Catholics and other Christians aimed at restoring unity among Christians.

envy Jealousy or sadness because someone else has more possessions, success, or popularity.

epiclesis A Greek word that means "invocation" or "calling upon." The *epiclesis* during the liturgy occurs when the priest calls upon the Holy Spirit.

Eucharist Mass or the Lord's Supper. *Eucharist* is based on a Greek term for "thanksgiving."

Eucharistic Prayer The Church's great prayer of thanksgiving to the Father. It includes the consecration of the bread and wine.

euthanasia Ending the life of a sick, handicapped, or dying person. Though some may view this as mercy, it is murder.

evangelize To actively work to spread the Good News of Jesus Christ.

Exile, the The period of the Israelite captivity in Babylon after the destruction of Jerusalem in 587 BC.

Exodus The book of the Bible that tells of the Israelites escape from Egypt to the Promised Land. Also, the Israelites journey out of Egypt.

F

faith Believing and accepting that God made himself known to us through his words and actions, especially through Jesus Christ. It is accepting God's truth with our minds and allowing it to guide our entire lives.

fornication Sexual intercourse between a man and a woman who are not married. It is morally wrong to engage in intercourse before marriage, and it is a sin against the Sixth Commandment.

free will The gift from God that allows us to choose what we do. It is the basis for our moral responsibility.

G

Gentiles A non-Jewish person. In Scripture the Gentiles were the uncircumcised, those who did not honor the God of the Torah. In the New Testament, Saint Paul and other evangelists reached out to the Gentiles, baptizing them into the family of God.

Gifts of the Holy Spirit Special gifts or graces we receive from God that help us live the way God wants us to live. The Seven Gifts of the Holy Spirit are Wisdom, Understanding, Counsel (or Right Judgment), Fortitude (or Courage), Knowledge, Piety (or Reverence), and Fear of the Lord (or Wonder and Awe).

God the Father The First Divine Person of the Holy Trinity.

Gospels The Good News of God's Revelation. The four Gospels—Matthew, Mark, Luke, and John—tell us about the person, life, teachings, death, and Resurrection of Jesus Christ.

grace The gift of God's loving presence in our lives that enables us to share in God's own divine life and love.

H

Heaven The state of being in perfect friendship and unity with God for eternity.

Heaven and earth A phrase that refers to everything that exists, the entire universe.

Hell The state of being separated from God forever.

Holy Spirit The Third Divine Person of the Trinity. *See also* Advocate.

homosexuality Sexual attraction to people of one's own gender.

honor To show great respect or courtesy.

human person A living being made up of both a physical body and an immortal, spiritual soul. All human persons are created in God's image.

I

idolatry The worship of such things as money, possessions, or popularity as if they were God.

Immaculate Conception The Catholic dogma that Mary was free of Original Sin from the moment of her conception.

Incarnation The truth that Jesus Christ, the Son of God and the Second Divine Person of the Trinity, is both fully God and fully man.

indulgence A way for the Church to reduce or even take away the purification that we would need in Purgatory.

intercession A form of petition in which we ask for God's help for others.

J

Jesus Christ Jesus is a Hebrew name that means "God saves." Christ comes from a Greek word used for "messiah" or "anointed one." The Son of God was named Jesus, signifying his role as Savior of the world. He was also called the Messiah or the Christ, signifying that he was the fulfillment of God's promises in the Old Testament. Jesus the Christ is true God and true man, the Second Divine Person of the Trinity.

Judges The eleven men and one woman who served the Hebrew people as tribal leaders, military commanders, arbiters of disputes, and enliveners of faith.

judgment An assessment of how we've lived our lives.

justification A process through which God restores our broken relationships after we have sinned.

K

Kingdom of God The Reign of God, which Jesus announced. It is characterized as a time of justice, peace, and love. The seed or the beginning of the Kingdom is present on earth right now. When the Kingdom is fully realized in the future, God will rule over the hearts of all people.

L

Last Supper A supper during the Jewish celebration of Passover that was the last meal Jesus shared with his disciples before being handed over for crucifixion, during which he instituted the Eucharist. It is commemorated on Holy Thursday.

laying on of hands A gesture used in the liturgy that signifies that the priest is calling upon the Holy Spirit.

Lectionary The book that contains the readings that have been selected for proclamation during the Church's liturgies throughout the year. All the readings are from the Bible.

legitimate defense The teaching that it is permissible to take action that causes harm to another person if it is necessary to protect yourself or others.

litany A litany is a form of prayer, spoken or sung, involving a dialogue between a leader and the people assembled. The people respond to each phrase said or sung by the leader with a constant refrain or acclamation.

liturgy The Church's official, public, communal prayer. It is God's work, in which the People of God participate. The Church's most important liturgy is the Eucharist, or Mass.

Liturgy of the Eucharist One of two major parts of Mass. It includes the Presentation and Preparation of the Gifts, the Eucharistic Prayer, and the Communion Rite.

Liturgy of the Word The first major part of Mass. It includes Scripture readings from the Old and New Testaments, including a Gospel reading; a Responsorial Psalm; a homily; the Creed; and the Prayer of the Faithful.

Logos A Greek word that is translated as "word." It means "thought," "logic," or "meaning." Jesus is the *Logos*, because when we see Jesus and listen to him, we can begin to see the mind of God and understand God's logic.

Lord's Prayer Another name for the Our Father, the prayer Jesus taught his disciples.

M

Magi The wise men who, upon discovering a strange star in the sky, traveled to Bethlehem to greet the newborn Jesus.

Magisterium The official teaching authority of the Church, whose task is to interpret and preserve the truths God wants us to know for our salvation, as revealed in Sacred Scripture and Sacred Tradition.

Magnificat Mary's prayer of praise when she visited her cousin Elizabeth. It is recorded in Luke 1:46–55. The name of the prayer is the first word of the prayer in Latin, which means "magnify."

Marks of the Church The four essential features or characteristics of the Church: One, Holy, Catholic (Universal), and Apostolic. *See also* Apostolic; Catholic.

masturbation Self-manipulation of one's sexual organs for the purpose of erotic pleasure or to achieve orgasm. Masturbation is a sin because the act cannot result in the creation of a new life. It is also wrong because it is self-serving, and God created sex not for self-gratification but to unify a husband and wife in marriage.

mediator A person in a middle position who facilitates communication and relationship between two people or groups. Because Jesus Christ is both God and man, he is the one and perfect mediator between us and God.

Messiah Hebrew word for "anointed one." The equivalent Greek term is *christos*. Jesus is the Christ and the Messiah because he is the Anointed One.

ministerial priesthood Received in the Sacrament of Holy Orders by bishops and priests, the ministerial priesthood is a means by which Jesus Christ builds up and guides the Church.

miracles A special sign beyond our understanding of the normal laws of human and physical behavior that make God's power and presence known in human history.

monotheistic Describing the belief that there is only one God.

mortal sin *See* sin, mortal.

mysteries A term used by early Christians to refer to the Sacraments.

mystery A truth that is so big and profound that no human being can completely know or understand it. We encounter mystery and enter into it.

N

natural law The God-given moral sense and voice of reason, which leads us to seek out what is good. It is called natural because reason is part of human nature.

New Covenant The covenant God established forever through his Son, Jesus Christ (see Luke 22:19–20). It is the fulfillment of the covenant God made with Noah, Abraham, Moses, and David.

New Law The Law of the Gospel of Jesus Christ, it is a Law of love, grace, and freedom. It is distinguished from the Old Law, or the Law of Moses.

O

Old Law The Law of Moses, the Ten Commandments. It contrasts with the New Law of the Gospel.

orans A prayer posture that involves raising one's eyes and extending both hands upward. It resembles the stance of a young child wanting to be picked up.

Original Sin The sin that Adam and Eve committed and the sinful condition that all human beings have from birth.

P

parables Types of stories Jesus often used that draw on situations known to the listeners and surprise elements to teach about the Kingdom of God.

particular judgment The judgment by God each person will face at the time of death.

Paschal Mystery The entire process of God's plan of salvation by which Christ saves us from sin and death through his Passion, death, Resurrection, and Ascension. We enter the Paschal Mystery by participating in the liturgy and being faithful followers of Christ.

Passion Jesus' suffering and death.

Passover The Jewish feast that commemorates the release of the Jewish people from captivity in Egypt.

Penance A reference to the Sacrament of Penance and Reconciliation, one of the Seven Sacraments of the Church. Through this Sacrament sinners are reconciled with God and the Church.

Pentecost The biblical event after Jesus rose from the dead and ascended to Heaven, when the Holy Spirit came on the disciples as Jesus had promised. The Church celebrates the Feast of Pentecost fifty days after Easter every year.

Pentateuch The first five books of the Old Testament.

People of God An image of the Church from the Bible.

petition A prayer form in which we ask God for forgiveness or for help with something.

Pope The name for the leader of the Church. *Pope* comes from a word meaning "father." Sometimes the Pope is called the Holy Father. He is the successor of Saint Peter, the first Pope and Bishop of Rome.

pornography Visual images or writings that describe sexual activity, created with the intent to arouse sexual feelings.

praise A form of prayer in which we tell God how much we appreciate all he does for us.

presider The priest or bishop who leads liturgical activity, such as Mass. Only ordained priests and bishops can preside at Mass.

prophet A person God chooses to speak his message of salvation. In the Bible, primarily a communicator of a divine message of repentance and hope to the Chosen People.

Q

quintessential An adjective that means "the best example of something." The Lord's Prayer is the quintessential prayer of the Church, because it is the perfect example of Christian prayer.

R

reconciles Restores relationships among ourselves and with God.

reparation Making up for the damage to property or the harm to another person as a result of one's sin.

restitution Returning property that was taken from someone unfairly.

Resurrection The passage of Jesus through death to new life after he had been crucified.

resurrection The conviction that not only our soul but also our transformed bodies will live on after death ("I believe in the resurrection of the body"). *See also* Resurrection.

Revelation God's communication about himself and his plan for humanity. Throughout history God's Revelation has been made known through creation, events, and people, but most fully through Jesus Christ.

S

Sabbath In the Jewish tradition, the Sabbath is from sundown Friday to sundown Saturday. Jews observe the Sabbath through prayer, fasting, and worshipping together on Saturday. Catholics fulfill the Commandment to "keep holy the Sabbath" on Sunday, because that is the day Jesus rose from the dead.

Sacrament An efficacious and visible sign of God's grace, instituted by Christ and entrusted to the Church, by which divine life is dispensed to us. The Seven Sacraments are Baptism, the Eucharist, Confirmation, Penance and Reconciliation, Anointing of the Sick, Matrimony, and Holy Orders.

sacramentals Sacred signs (such as the Sign of the Cross, holy water) instituted by the Church. They do not confer grace as Sacraments do, but they make us ready to cooperate with the grace we receive in a Sacrament.

Sacred Chrism Perfumed oil, consecrated by the bishop, which is used for special anointings in the Sacraments of Baptism, Confirmation, and Holy Orders. It signifies the Gifts of the Holy Spirit.

Sacred Scripture The Word of God, written under the inspiration of the Holy Spirit.

Sacred Tradition From the Latin *tradere*, meaning "to hand on." Refers to the process of passing on the Gospel message. It began with the oral communication of the Gospel by the Apostles, was written down in Scripture, and is interpreted by the Magisterium under the guidance of the Holy Spirit.

salvation history The pattern of events in human history through which God makes his presence and saving actions known to us.

sanctifying grace A free gift we receive from God. It heals us from sin, makes us holy, and restores our friendship with him.

Satan The fallen angel or spirit of evil who is the enemy of God and a continuing instigator of temptation and sin in the world.

scandal An action or attitude—or failure to act—that causes someone to sin.

Sacred Scripture A term for sacred writings. For Christians, Scripture is the books in the Old and New Testaments that make up the Bible. Scripture is the Word of God.

sexuality Our identities as males and females.

Sign of Peace The part of Mass when the people are invited to share a sign of Christ's peace with one another.

sin, mortal An action or offense so seriously against God's will that it completely separates a person from God. It is called "mortal" because it leads to eternal death. *See also* sin, venial.

sin, venial An action or offense against God's will that weakens our relationship with God and others and that hurts our personal characters; venial sins are not so serious that they cause complete separation between us and God.

social justice The respect for all creation and human rights that allows people to get what they need to live and to realize their God-given dignity.

society A community of people who depend on one another.

solidarity A close relationship or unity with others. Living in solidarity means we share with people who are poor or powerless not only our material goods but also our friendship and prayers.

Son of God A title frequently given to Jesus Christ, the Second Divine Person of the Trinity.

soul The spiritual element that gives humans life and survives after death. The soul is created by God at the moment of our conception.

Stations of the Cross Images of Jesus' Passion found on display in most Catholic churches.

suicide Taking one's own life.

symbols Objects, actions, gestures, or words that point beyond themselves to a deeper, more meaningful reality.

synagogue The place where Jews meet to pray and study.

synoptic "Seen together." Matthew, Mark, and Luke are called the synoptic Gospels because of their similarities.

T

temperance The cardinal virtue by which one moderates her or his appetites and passions to achieve balance in the use of created goods.

temptation Something that makes sinful things seem fun, exciting, or even good to do.

Ten Commandments The laws God gave Moses that guide human action. Jesus' command to love God and to love our neighbors is a summary of the Ten Commandments.

thanksgiving A form of prayer in which we express thanks and gratitude for the gifts God has given us.

Theotokos A Greek term that means "God-bearer." The Church uses this name for Mary, because she is the Mother of Jesus Christ, the Second Divine Person of the Trinity.

Sacred Tradition The living transmission of God's truth to us. It means both the central content of the Catholic faith and the way in which that content has been handed down through the centuries under the guidance of the Holy Spirit.

Transfiguration A mysterious event in which Peter, James, and John see Jesus speaking to Moses and Elijah, two important people from the Old Testament. The event is so called because Jesus' appearance was transformed and revealed his divinity.

Transubstantiation The change that takes place when the bread and wine become the Body and Blood of Jesus Christ during Mass.

trespass Sin (noun); to sin (verb).

Trinity The central Christian belief that there is one God in three Divine Persons: Father, Son, and Holy Spirit.

V

venerate To show deep reverence for something sacred.

venial sin *See* sin, venial.

virtues Good habits that develop and help us consistently do the right thing.The four cardinal virtues are prudence, justice, temperance, and fortitude. The three theological virtues are faith, hope, and love (or charity).

vocation The call from God to live a life of holiness. Some live out God's call as ordained priests, while others are called to marriage, to lives as members of religious communities, or to lives as single people.

W

Works of Mercy Acts of charity by which we help others meet their physical and spiritual needs.

worship Adoration of God, usually expressed publicly in the Church's official liturgy, as well as through other prayers and devotions.

Y

Yahweh The Old Testament name for God that he revealed to Moses. It is frequently translated as "I AM" or "I am who I am."

Index

A

F

I

J

Acknowledgments

The scriptural quotations marked NRSV are from the New Revised Standard Version of the Bible, Catholic Edition. Copyright © 1993 and 1989 by the Division of Christian Education of the National Council of the Churches of Christ in the United States of America. All rights reserved.

All other scriptural quotations are from the Good News Translation® (Today's English Version, Second Edition). Copyright © 1992 by the American Bible Society. All rights reserved. Bible text from the Good News Translation (GNT) is not to be reproduced in copies or otherwise by any means except as permitted in writing by the American Bible Society, 1865 Broadway, New York, NY 10023 (www.americanbible.org).

The prayers, devotions, beliefs, and practices contained herein have been verified against authoritative sources.

The quotations in this book labeled *Catechism of the Catholic Church* and *CCC* are from the English translation of the *Catechism of the Catholic Church* for use in the United States of America, second edition. Copyright © 1994 by the United States Catholic Conference, Inc.—Libreria Editrice Vaticana (LEV). English translation of the *Catechism of the Catholic Church: Modifications from the Editio Typica* copyright © 1997 by the United States Catholic Conference, Inc.—LEV.

The quotations on pages 26 and 97 are from *Dogmatic Constitution on the Church* (*Lumen Gentium*, 1964), numbers 16 and 53, at www.vatican.va/archive/hist_councils/ ii_vatican_council/documents/vat-ii_const_19641121_lumen-gentium_en.html. Copyright © LEV.

The quotation by Mother Teresa on page 106 is from *Faith and Compassion: The Life and Work of Mother Teresa*, by Raghu Rai and Navin Chawla (Rockport, ME: Element Books, 1996), page 158. Copyright © 1996 by Element Books Limited.

The words and prayers from the Mass on pages 157, 168, 176, 187, 249, 261, 303, 310, 312, 330, 332, 337, 345, 347, 526, 527–528, and 528 are from the English translation of *The Roman Missal* © 2010, International Commission on English in the Liturgy Corporation (ICEL) (Washington, DC: United States Conference of Catholic Bishops [USCCB], 2011), pages 669, 528, 655, 527, 646, 648, 649, 640, 667, 639, 531, 514, 667, 669, 669, 529, 674, 522, 530, 650, and 645 respectively. All rights reserved. Used with permission of the ICEL. Published with approval of the Committee on Divine Worship, USCCB.

The statistics on pages 184, 238, and 246 are from the *2012 Catholic Almanac*, Matthew Bunson, general editor (Huntington, IN: Our Sunday Visitor, 2012), pages 438, 335, and 335, respectively. Copyright © 2012 by Our Sunday Visitor.

The prayers on pages 198 and 223 from the English translation of *Rite of Confirmation (Second Edition)*, © 1975, ICEL, numbers 25 and 30; the prayer on page 453 from the English translation of *Rite of Baptism for Children* © 1969, ICEL, number 70; and the quotations on pages 484–485 from the English translation of *Rite of Marriage* © 1969, ICEL, numbers 24 and 26; are found in *The Rites of the Catholic Church*, volume 1, prepared by the ICEL, a Joint Commission of Catholic Bishops' Conferences (Collegeville, MN: Liturgical Press, 1990). Copyright © 1990 by The Order of Saint Benedict, Collegeville, MN. All rights reserved. Used with permission of the ICEL. Published with the approval of the Committee on Divine Worship, USCCB.

The statistics on pages 287 and 288 are from *Soul Searching: The Religious and Spiritual Lives of American Teenagers*, by Christian Smith (New York: Oxford University Press, 2005), pages 62 and 37. Copyright © 2005 by Oxford University Press.

The prayers on page 295 are from *Benedictine Daily Prayers: A Short Breviary*, compiled and edited by Maxwell E. Johnson (Collegeville, MN: The Liturgical Press, and the Monks of Saint John's Abbey, 2005), pages 903 and 932. Copyright © 2005 by The Order of Saint Benedict, Collegeville, MN. All rights reserved.

The quotations on pages 306 and 315–316 are from *Constitution on the Sacred Liturgy* (*Sacrosanctum Concilium*, 1963), numbers 11 and 14, at www.vatican.va/archive/hist_councils/ii_vatican_council/documents/vat-ii_const_19631204_sacrosanctum-concilium_en.html. Copyright © LEV.

The statistics on page 324 are from the United States Conference of Catholic Bishops' Committee on the Liturgy, *Newsletter*, volume 43, May–June 2007, page 27.

The prayer from the Mass on page 332 is from the English translation of *The Roman Missal* © 1973, ICEL (New York: Catholic Book Publishing, 1985), page 1102. Illustrations and arrangement © 1985–1974 Catholic Book Publishing Company. Used with permission of the ICEL. Published with the approval of the Committee on Divine Worship, USCCB.

The quotation on page 371 is from *St. Anselm's Proslogion, with A Reply on Behalf of the Fool*, by Gaunilo, and *The Author's Reply to Gaunilo*, translated by M. J. Charlesworth (London: Oxford University Press, 1965), page 117. Copyright © 1965 by Oxford University Press.

The quotation on page 394 is from "Greeting of His Holiness Benedict XVI to the Members of the Pastoral Council," at www.vatican.va/holy_father/benedict_xvi/speeches/2007/march/documents/hf_ben-xvi_spe_20070325_consiglio-pastorale_en.html. Copyright © 2007 LEV.

The quotation on page 466 is from "Address of His Holiness Pope John Paul II to the Diplomatic Corps," at www.vatican.va/holy_father/john_paul_ii/speeches/2003/january/documents/hf_jp-ii_spe_20030113_diplomatic-corps_en.html. Copyright © 2003 LEV.

The quotations by Oscar Romero on page 477 are from *The Violence of Love: Oscar Romero*, compiled and translated by James R. Brockman (Farmington, PA: The Plough Publishing House, 1998), pages 186 and 192. Text copyright © 1988 by the Chicago Province of the Society of Jesus.

The quotation on page 499 is from "Message of His Holiness Pope Paul VI for the Celebration of the Day of Peace," at www.vatican.va/holy_father/paul_vi/messages/peace/documents/hf_p-vi_mes_19711208_v-world-day-for-peace_en.html. Copyright © LEV.

The quotation by Dorothy Day on page 501 is from *Dorothy Day and the Permanent Revolution*, by Eileen Egan (Erie, PA: Pax Christi, 1983), page 22. Copyright © 1983 by Eileen Egan.

The Jugular Prayer on page 521 is adapted from *Prayer Notes to a Friend*, by Edward Hays (Leavenworth, KS: Forest of Peace Publishing, 2002), page 33. Copyright © 2002 by Edward M. Hays.

The quotations by Jean Vanier on page 533 are from an interview found at www.csec.org/index.php/archives/23-member-archives/332-jean-vanier-program-4321.

To view copyright terms and conditions for Internet materials cited here, log on to the home pages for the referenced websites.

During this book's preparation, all citations, facts, figures, names, addresses, telephone numbers, Internet URLs, and other pieces of information cited within were verified for accuracy. The authors and Saint Mary's Press staff have made every attempt to reference current and valid sources, but we cannot guarantee the content of any source, and we are not responsible for any changes that may have occurred since our verification. If you find an error in, or have a question or concern about, any of the information or sources listed within, please contact Saint Mary's Press.

Endnotes Cited in Quotations from the *Catechism of the Catholic Church, Second Edition*

Chapter 5
1. Cf. St. Augustine, *Quaest. in Hept.* 2, 73: J. P. Migne, ed., *Patrologia Latina* (Paris: 1841–1855) 34, 623; cf. *Dei Verbum* 16.

Chapter 11
1. *Gaudium et spes* 22 § 2.
2. St. Thomas Aquinas, *Opusc.* 57: 1–4.

Chapter 45
1. John XXIII, *Pacem in terris*, 46.

Chapter 49
1. St. Augustine, *Ep.* 130, 12, 22: J. P. Migne, ed., *Patrologia Latina* (Paris: 1841–1855) 33, 503.